W9-BRT-244

THE PROFESSIONAL CHEF'S®
Techniques *of* Healthy Cooking

THE PROFESSIONAL CHEF'S®
Techniques *of* Healthy Cooking

WITH FORWORDS BY

Craig Claiborne

AND

L. Timothy Ryan, C.M.C.
Senior Vice President, The Culinary Institute of America

Mary Deirdre Donovan
Editor

WITHDRAWN

641.57 P9645-1 1997

NOV 21 1997

VNR

Van Nostrand Reinhold

I(T)P® A Division of International Thomson Publishing Inc.

New York • Albany • Bonn • Boston • Detroit • London • Madrid • Melbourne
Mexico City • Paris • San Francisco • Singapore • Tokyo • Toronto

Copyright © 1993, 1997 by The Culinary Institute of America

I(T)P® an International Thomson Publishing Company
The ITP logo is a registered trademark used herein under license

Printed in the United States of America

For more information, contact:

Van Nostrand Reinhold
115 Fifth Avenue
New York, NY 10003

Chapman & Hall GmbH
Pappelallee 3
69469 Weinheim
Germany

Chapman & Hall
2-6 Boundary Row
London
SE1 8HN
United Kingdom

International Thomson Publishing Asia
221 Henderson Road #05-10
Henderson Building
Singapore 0315

Thomas Nelson Australia
102 Dodds Street
South Melbourne, 3205
Victoria, Australia

International Thomson Publishing Japan
Hirakawacho Kyowa Building, 3F
2-2-1 Hirakawacho
Chiyoda-ku, 102 Tokyo
Japan

Nelson Canada
1120 Birchmount Road
Scarborough, Ontario
Canada M1K 5G4

International Thomson Editores
Seneca 53
Col. Polanco
11560 Mexico D.F. Mexico

All rights reserved. No part of this work covered by the copyright hereon may be reproduced or used in any form or by any means—graphic, electronic, or mechanical, including photocopying, recording, taping, or information storage and retrieval systems—without the written permission of the publisher.

1 2 3 4 5 6 7 8 9 10 RRD - WL   02 01 00 99 98 97

Library of Congress Cataloging-in-Publication Data

The Professional chef's techniques of healthy cooking/the Culinary Institute of America
p.   cm.
Includes bibliographical references.
ISBN: 0-442-01126-1
1. Quantity cookery. 2. Nutrition. I. Title: Techniques of healthy cooking
TX820.P75
641.5'7—dc20   92-19495

Hardcover edition: 0-442-01126-1
Paperback editon: 0-442-02555-6

http://www.vnr.com
product discounts • free email newsletters
software demos • online resources

email: info@vnr.com

A service of I(T)P®

Contents

CONTENTS

PART II
The Guidelines at Work   89

PART III
Recipes   175

Recipes

Appetizers and Salads

Soups

Grilling, Broiling, and Sautéing

Roasting and Baking

Steaming, Poaching, and Simmering

Stewing and Braising

Pasta and Pizza

Desserts

Breakfast

Presentation and Service of Beverages

Foreword

There are times when the word "scholarly" has an odious quality, when it smacks of a "holier than thou" attitude. It is an unfortunate fact of life that the word "nutrition," when spoken aloud or written about, has some of the same unpleasant associations. It immediately signals a dissertation on something obscure, pedantic, erudite, and all those other things you used to hate in high school. It seems to say to the reader, "O.K., reach for the dictionary and let's get down to work."

This book is different and should have enormous appeal to the professional and non-professional cook alike. It educates and enlightens without being dogmatic. It spells out the basics of nutrition, and yet it proves that the preparation of food can be a miracle whether it is done simply for yourself, as your daily work, or as a way to please and indulge those you care for. It describes all the golden facts you need to know about cooking techniques from sautéing, grilling, roasting and baking, steaming, poaching and boiling, stewing and braising, to cooking in a microwave.

The first chapters in the book are dedicated to the definitions and fundamentals of nutrition. As outlined they are simply stated and easily understood. It starts out with what are termed "The Seven Guidelines." These are stubborn, hard-to-learn but clearly spelled out facts embracing the need to, and means to, moderate calories, fats and cholesterol, salt and sodium, and processed foods. It also elaborates on the importance of increasing

the variety of fresh, seasonal foods in our diets. Finally, there is a wise suggestion of nonalcoholic beverages, with the obvious recommendation that alcoholic beverages be used and served responsibly.

This book speaks in plain, comprehensive language and offers plenty of level-headed guidance to the cook. For example, it recognizes the fact that "it isn't feasible to cook with a calorie handbook in one hand and sauté pan in the other." It offers a brief explanation of the "exchange system" so that calorie control becomes an easier part of shopping, cooking, and dining.

It advises, further, that the human body needs more than mere calories to maintain health. Unlike most books on nutrition, this manual offers interesting menu ideas and recipes that do not often appear in the standard "diet" regime. The discussion of the various nutrition guidelines is anchored to a menu plan that includes a lunch of grilled chicken burritos, a rice pilaf, and steamed yellow squash with fresh herbs and jalapeños. Many of the recipes in the book are international in scope.

The book takes a marvelously sane approach to cooking, blending the joys of cooking, with a well-informed approach to new thinking about food ingredients, many of which were all-but-unheard of items only a few years ago, but with which we have become widely familiar. These foods are generally available in specialty food shops, grocery stores and supermarkets, reflecting such changes in the American diet as the recent accep-tance or craving for the foods of the American Southwest, and the borrowings from the Italian including pastas and pizzas. "Dishes," it points out, "inspired by Southwestern American cooking get most of their excite-ment from chilies and spices, not cheese and sour cream." "Pasta dishes," it continues, "combined with such flavor-ful ingredients as sun-dried tomatoes, fresh herbs, and a delicate splash of extra- virgin oil are a vast improvement over meat or cream sauces." And it is suggested that "Even pizzas can be prepared with such bold tastes and colors as grilled peppers, reduced-fat mozzarella or goat cheese, and wild mushrooms to replace high-fat pepper-oni and sausage toppings."

The cook can find several "tricks-of-the-trade" intended to trim calories and fats and still produce excel-lent results. "To reduce the calories of an oil and vinegar mixture, replace most of the oil with a thickened stock, or fruit or vegetable juice....Or, use a low- or non-fat dairy product such as yogurt, ricotta cheese or buttermilk to prepare a creamy dressing."

It is wisely noted that customers or guests at our tables who have refrained from ordering or eating a high-calorie main course may feel inclined to overcompensate and reward themselves at the end of a meal with one or more rich desserts. The careful cook should, in this case, encourage the person by offering low-calorie desserts that won't leave anyone feeling cheated, whether or not he or she is "watching the scales." Suggestions and

recipes abound for desserts that include carefully mea-sured amounts of chocolate, nuts, or even a small rosette of genuine whipped cream.

A similarly sensible approach is taken with such topics as the use of salt and oils in a balanced diet. We are advised that when we take moderation as the key, and take the few moments necessary to evaluate the effects we want to achieve, we can get maximum benefits out of the least amounts.

There is a highly worthwhile dissertation on the uses of herbs and spices in the kitchen. "To enhance foods that seem lackluster," the authors note, "one can add...basil, dill, oregano, thyme, bay leaf, lemon balm, savory, epazote, or coriander. Fresh herbs can give a new, different accent to familiar foods...."

The nearly 300 recipes included in the third sec-tion of the book were created specifically by the chef-instructors of the notable St. Andrew's Cafe at The Culinary Institute of America, with attention towards creating effective tools to train students, as well as with an eye toward good nutrition for the patron. They are soundly presented, and provide additional notes which allow the cook to modify recipes, substitute ingredients, and even create original recipes by using the techniques as a model.

The many pages that describe cooking techniques in this book are exceptional. There is, in fact, almost no subject relating to the kitchen and food preparation that is not covered in admirable depth in this work.

Craig Claiborne

Foreword and Acknowledgments

The influence of nutrition and nutritional cooking on the overall course of study at The Culinary Institute of America is no longer a simple thing for us to measure. As we pause to review the past few decades however, it becomes clear that the seeds of our current program have been growing steadily since The Culinary Institute of America enrolled its first students in 1946.

One of the three full-time faculty members on staff at that time was a dietitian. Theoretical nutrition has always been part of the educational program. But, in 1980, a significant step forward was undertaken.

Under the direction of Ferdinand Metz, C.M.C., the Institute began to develop a new restaurant, The American Bounty, that heralded a significant change in the way chefs and home cooks would prepare and serve foods. Mr. Metz's vision encompassed some startling innovations, especially in view of the prevailing wisdom that haute cuisine meant classical French cuisine, and that "home cooking" was hardly a term considered synonymous with fine dining.

The American Bounty restaurant opened to the public in 1982, and its menu was written as a celebration of the best that American regional cooking has to offer. It showcased not only the fine meats, fish, poultry, and game available in this land, but also the seasonal fruits and vegetables, grains, and legumes that make the cooking styles of each region special. What were once thought of as "side dishes" were brought into the overall balance of the dish, instead of being treated as an afterthought.

The immediate acceptance by the public of The American Bounty, has obscured the fact that such a restaurant concept was once so revolutionary. The signs that the time was ripe for the introduction of an American restaurant were there, but it is never an easy matter to read the difference between a major trend and a passing fad. A re-emergence of national pride and a consciousness of ourselves as having a "cuisine" was one factor that was correctly interpreted.

Another equally important change was the increased awareness of health, fitness, and nutrition. "Eating well" no longer meant a hearty breakfast of two or three eggs, bacon or sausage, and a heaping portion of homefries. Forgotten treasures from family tables around our nation fueled a growing appetite for foods that were fresh, appealing, and new, without giving us a "rich food hangover" the next day. And the growing pool of talented chefs trained in the United States, including those from The Culinary Institute of America, accepted the challenge of exploring these inspiring ingredients and healthful cooking techniques.

As a consequence of this new direction, producers and purveyors of foods have been encouraged to provide items that had all but disappeared from our collective national table: vine-ripened fruits and vegetables, whole grains, more varieties of fish and shellfish, free-range poultry, organically-raised meats, and more. The effect of putting this wholesome and exciting bounty into our shopping carts and kitchens has been to spur interest in cooking foods in a way that reflects their natural freshness, savor, and healthfulness.

As nutrition and nutritional cooking gained wider acceptance, it became clear that time had come for The Culinary Institute of America to provide an even more focused approach to teaching these subjects, in order to prepare our graduates to meet the growing public demand for healthful food. Accordingly, St. Andrew's Cafe, staffed by students and run in conjunction with a course devoted to the principles of nutritional cooking, was inaugurated in the spring of 1985.

Like any new venture, the path we followed was not always perfectly smooth. The lessons from those early efforts have been valuable. We served our share of tofu and sprout salads and printed an analysis of each item right on the menu. We soon learned that nutritional cooking can, and must, fit all the requirements of fine dining if it is to be successful. Today, the menus at St. Andrew's feature food that would be at home in any of the Institute's other restaurants.

When we outgrew our small facilities and were ready to give nutritional cooking a home of its own, we were fortunate to receive a $1 million grant from General Foods. This support, along with that of other organizations and individuals, made the General Foods Nutrition Center a reality. In addition to housing the refurbished St. Andrew's Cafe, the center boasts a state-of-the-art kitchen, a computer laboratory, classrooms, and offices. Working with the New York Medical College, we developed a set of nutritional guidelines, set forth in the first part of this book.

Along the way we have been fortunate to work with some special individuals. Catharine Powers, R.D., came to the Institute in 1985. One of the greatest talents she brought to the school was her ability to take a technical subject and talk about it with chefs in such a way that it was no longer threatening. Her work made the whole subject not only comprehensible, but compelling enough to inspire noticeable changes in kitchens throughout the school. Her constant work to upgrade the level of nutritional instruction has resulted in the current full-scale course that requires students to work with computers to create and analyze an original menu designed according to specific guidelines.

Mark Erickson, C.M.C., was another key player in making nutritional cuisine a valuable and valid part of our curriculum. Mark was trained according to classic French culinary principles. As both a master chef and a member of the United States Culinary Olympic team, his orientation was not necessarily toward "health food." His ability to embrace a completely new style of cooking was an inspiration to everyone. His work as an instructor, and later as an administrator at the Institute, made indelible impressions. Many of the recipes he developed for the St. Andrew's menu are featured in this book.

The Institute has continued to be exceptionally fortunate in the caliber of both instructors and students who have contributed to the success of the "St. Andrew's Concept." For their assistance in the development of the manuscript, creation of recipes, recipe testing, photography, food styling, and review of the book, we wish to recognize the following individuals and groups:

Staff Members: Gary Allen; Carol Caldwell; Mary Deirdre Donovan; John Grubell; Steven Kolpan; Lorna Smith; and Henry Woods.

Instructors: Viktor Bauman; Bob Briggs; Morey Canner; Monica Coulter; John DeShelter; Greg Fatigati; Vince Fatigati; John Jensen; John Nihoff; Philip Papineau; Tim Rodgers; Jerry Thompson; Marianne Turow; Rich Vergili; and Jonathan Zearfoss.

Students: Brant Cherney; Todd Constantine; Wendy Lusky; Adam Perry; Carol Ruginski; and Patricia Ruggles.

To the Institute's mail room and storeroom staffs.

Van Nostrand Reinhold Staff: Judith R. Joseph; Pamela Scott Chirls; Monika Keano; Michael Suh; Lilly Kaufman; Geraldine Albert; Louise Kurtz; Julie Markoff; Constance Quan; and Lisa Tippett.

To all of them, and to all of those within the Institute's family and beyond, we offer our grateful acknowledgment and appreciation.

L. Timothy Ryan, C.M.C.
Senior Vice President
The Culinary Institute of America

Preface

Good nutrition is nothing more than good food, properly selected and carefully prepared. And nothing less.

In order to produce "good food," today's chefs must know far more than simply how to cook it. The true professional must understand how food, cooking techniques, and nutrition are intertwined. The purpose of this book is to introduce and explore seven basic nutritional guidelines for cooking. These seven "rules" are intended to make nutrition a natural part of cooking in general.

There is a growing awareness, both by food professionals and the dining public, that we as a nation need to do something about our typical eating patterns. We eat too much fat and sodium and too many sweets. At the same time, we are taking in too little of the unrefined complex carbohydrates we need, shortchanging ourselves on a variety of nutrients and dietary fiber. The United States Department of Agriculture (USDA) has proposed changes in the dietary goals for Americans. These recommendations are drastic enough so that many people will need some help in making a smooth transition from their old eating patterns to new ones.

These "new" dietary goals, established in 1991, have their foundations in the recommendations of William Atwater, who worked for the USDA it. 1894. He suggested that men who worked at what we would call a "moderate activity level" divide their daily calories as follows: 52% from carbohydrates, 33% from fat, and 15%

from protein. This is remarkably similar to the 1991 USDA recommendations.

The chef has a special role to play in revising the typical diet. Unfortunately, nutritionally prepared foods have a reputation for lacking taste, color, and excitement. The training most chefs received has ingrained certain practices that need to be modified. This book approaches that challenge in three separate ways.

First, the seven guidelines for nutritional cooking are introduced and explained. Although *The Professional Chef's Techniques for Healthy Cooking* is not meant as a personal nutrition book, there is good, practical information about topics such as fat and cholesterol, salt and sodium, and the importance of fiber. For each guideline the information is presented so that it is useful from the chef's perspective. Even though this represents the most theoretical portion of the book, a clear emphasis is maintained on applying theory to real cooking situations.

The second part of the book takes a close look at the basic tools of any restaurant: the ingredients that are selected, the techniques that are applied to foods, and the recipes and menus created from the food and the techniques. One point became quite clear as the techniques section was being written: with surprisingly few exceptions, the techniques used in professional and home kitchens are already well suited to a nutritional style of cooking. As a result, the chef need not acquire an entirely new repertoire of special cooking techniques. Instead, he or she must simply learn to extract the greatest possible flavor by pairing the best and freshest foods with the most perfectly executed cooking technique. Concentrating on the positive aspects of nutritional cooking—clean, intense flavors, bold colors, and tempting contrasts of texture and temperature—keeps it from becoming a chore or a punishment.

The section that deals with menu and recipe development continues to guide the chef through the process of getting nutrition out of a textbook and onto a plate. Each restaurant type has a particular menu style, clientele, and staff. These factors must be taken into consideration, and nutritional offerings tailored to fit individual needs. Three methods for accumulating nutritional recipes are explained: evaluation to identify those already acceptable, modification to adapt successful recipes to fit the guidelines, and finally, the creation of new dishes.

The last section contains nearly 300 recipes, each formulated according to the guidelines established in the first section. Most of them were developed for St. Andrew's Cafe, the nutrition restaurant at The Culinary Institute of America. The ingredients are given in both U.S. and metric measurements, and many recipes include notes that suggest alternate ingredients, flavorings, or serving styles. An accompanying nutrient analysis provides the number of calories in a serving; protein, carbohydrate, and fat, expressed in grams; and milligrams of sodium and cholesterol. The values have been rounded.

There is a growing understanding of the importance of nutrition in our daily lives. Old habits die hard, however, and just knowing that we should make certain changes isn't enough to assure success. Add to that the fact that there are several issues that are still the subject of lively debate, and it is easy to see that anyone could find themselves confused and frustrated. No one can presume to have the final word on the ways in which sodium, cholesterol, caffeine, or alcohol can affect the development of diseases such as hypertension, cancer, or cardiovascular disease. And by the same token, there are no guarantees that eating broccoli or oat bran is a sure-fire "prescription" to prevent a disease or cure an existing condition.

What we do know is that certain modifications in our diets make good sense. Reducing sodium intake to less than 3000 milligrams, for example, won't hurt anyone and might help someone who is sodium-sensitive avoid the onset of high blood pressure. And another valuable lesson that we have learned is that a healthier cooking style can be delicious and appealing. Food that is "good for you" really ought to be just plain good.

The Food Guide Pyramids

According to the National Restaurant Association, Americans are spending an average of 44% of their food dollar outside of the home. Business people and frequent travelers are especially at the mercy of the nutrition they get from a steady diet of restaurant, hotel, and airline food. The type of food people expect to find on a menu today is fundamentally different than it was even a few years ago. Surveys and studies of customer preferences show that individuals are more and more likely to seek out simple, good-tasting, fresh foods that meet established nutrition criteria, if they are given an appealing option.

WHAT ARE THE NUTRITION CRITERIA TODAY?

Six of the ten leading causes of death in the United States have been linked to our diets. Industrialized countries often shortchange foods rich in unrefined carbohydrates and dietary fiber, foods that were once the mainstay of the average diet. Today, a typical diet will often overemphasize foods that have high levels of saturated fats, especially animal foods such as meats and cheese, as well as processed and refined foods pumped full of sweeteners, hydrogenated shortenings, and extra calories.

Americans have been urged to adopt a whole new approach to achieving a wide range of health-driven objectives. The message that the foods we eat, the way we live our lives, and the way we feel are interconnected is being broadcast through many channels. Dietary recommendations and suggested eating plans are available from organizations such as the American Diabetes Association, the American Cancer Society, and the American Heart Association, schools, including the University of California at Berkeley, Tufts University, and the New York Medical College; and not least important, the food pyramids prepared by private organizations and authors, as well as that prepared and distributed by the United States Department of Agriculture. Taken collectively, the following common recommendations emerge from these specific guides and diet plans:

- maintain a healthy body weight through a combination of healthful diet and exercise

- think of a balanced diet as something to be achieved over the course of a day or week, rather than each dish, recipe, or meal

- reduce total calories

- keep total fat intake at or below about 30% of daily calories

- replace saturated fats with monounsaturated fats

- drink sufficient water throughout the day

- eat a greater variety of fruits, vegetables, and starchy foods to assure adequate levels of vitamins, minerals, and fiber

- reduce portion sizes for meats, poultry, eggs, and whole milk cheeses, and cut back on the frequency of their occurrence in a daily or weekly diet

- avoid highly processed or refined foods

- keep sodium consumption below approximately 3000 milligrams per day

- reduce the amount of dietary cholesterol in the diet

- keep alcohol consumption at moderate levels (one to two glasses of wine a day for men, one per day for women)

THE PYRAMIDS

When the first food guide pyramid was introduced in 1991 by the United States Department of Agriculture (USDA), it marked a whole new way of understanding the importance of various foods within the diet. The "four food groups" and "square meals" taught to school children since the 1950s didn't make it obvious that we might be better off eating significantly more foods from one category and significantly less from others. Other pyramids have followed to meet the specific requirements of vegetarians and ethnic cuisines including those of the Mediterranean and Asian cultures.

USDA FOOD GUIDE PYRAMID

The USDA Food Guide Pyramid replaces the "four food groups." It is based on information outlined in

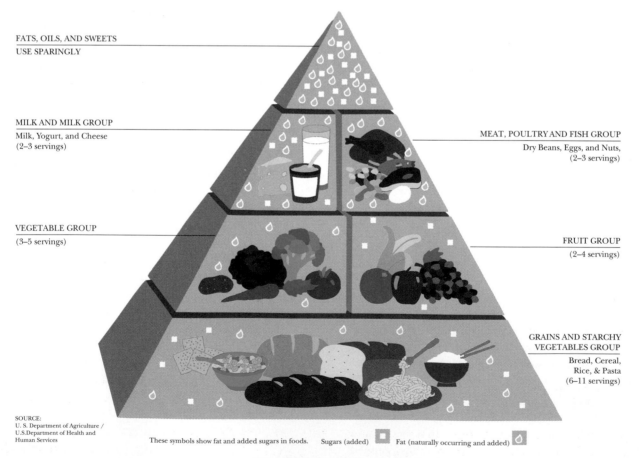

FATS, OILS, AND SWEETS
USE SPARINGLY

MILK AND MILK GROUP
Milk, Yogurt, and Cheese
(2–3 servings)

MEAT, POULTRY AND FISH GROUP
Dry Beans, Eggs, and Nuts,
(2–3 servings)

VEGETABLE GROUP
(3–5 servings)

FRUIT GROUP
(2–4 servings)

GRAINS AND STARCHY
VEGETABLES GROUP
Bread, Cereal,
Rice, & Pasta
(6–11 servings)

SOURCE:
U. S. Department of Agriculture /
U.S.Department of Health and
Human Services

These symbols show fat and added sugars in foods.   Sugars (added) ■   Fat (naturally occurring and added) ⬖

The USDA Food Guide Pyramid

the USDA dietary guidelines. The purpose of the changes suggested by these guidelines is to help people make better food choices in order to prevent or reduce their chances of succumbing to cancer, adult diabetes, atherosclerosis, stroke, heart disease, and cirrhosis of the liver—all leading causes of death in this country. What these guidelines and the pyramid are *not* is a treatment program for those individuals already afflicted with these particular conditions. Diet is just one part of the puzzle.

In order to use this pyramid, as well as the others discussed here, it is important to establish your own personal calorie needs. Refer to the worksheet on pages 16 and 17 to calculate your optimal daily caloric intake. If you are using the pyramids to devise menu offerings, it is a good idea to use a 2000-calorie limit as a starting point.

The broad base of the USDA Food Guide Pyramid shows representations of a variety of grain-based foods—pasta, rice, cereals, breads, and other grains. Whole or minimally processed grains are preferable, since they include an array of nutrients typically lost during milling, refining, or processing. In addition to stripping out nutrients, processing can also add refined sugars or fats. Six to eleven servings of these foods (depending upon your individual calorie needs) is optimal.

Fruits and vegetables make up the second largest component of the diet. Again, the closer to their natural state, the better. Cooking, juicing, freezing, and canning can affect the nutritional benefit of a food. Meeting this dietary requirement is not especially difficult, once we learn to expand our repertoire of vegetable dishes. Another key is to rethink the role of fruits and vegetables within a meal. They can be more than just "side dishes," and are often used appropriately in a number of other menu categories. For instance, sauces can be based on vegetable purées or juices. Stuffings and garnishes can be made from fruits and vegetables just as well as from meats or cheeses. Vegetable stews and other dishes can form, along with a grain, the entrée for a meatless option at one or more meals throughout the day or week. The recommendation for an individual (again, linked to that person's overall calorie requirement) is to eat three to five servings of vegetables and two to four servings of fruits.

Dairy products should be part of each day's diet. This is one area where it is quite easy to overconsume fats. Whole milk and whole milk foods such as yogurt or cheeses do not contain more calcium or protein than skim or low fat versions. It does take some time to get used to the mouthfeel of skim milk as a beverage. If you currently use milk or cream to make desserts, sauces, or as an ingredient in vegetable or grain dishes, it is easy to simply substitute a lower-fat version of some dairy ingredients. For those who simply can't adjust to skim milk, this may be the easiest way to incorporate the correct number of servings in a lower-fat form. Two to three servings a day are optimal.

Meats, poultry, fish, and eggs—the centerpiece of many American meals—are still included, but the serving size is reduced to 3-ounce portions (or larger portions but fewer servings). Beans and nuts are also included in this food group. Be aware that all of these foods contain varying amounts of naturally occurring fats. It is best to look for leaner cuts of meat and to use cooking techniques that do not introduce more fat. Two to three servings (totaling no more than 5 to 7 ounces) are recommended each day.

The very top of the USDA Food Guide Pyramid is fats, oils, and sweets. There are no actual numbers of servings recommended. In fact, the suggestion is to "use sparingly." What does that mean? For many individuals, it is difficult to keep track of these foods, since they are "hidden" in other foods. If you know what your daily calorie needs are, and if you eat the appropriate number of servings of foods from each group represented on the pyramid, any calories "left over" can be expended on these types of foods—ice cream, candies, whole milk cheeses, jams, and spareribs or bacon.

MEDITERRANEAN PYRAMID

The Mediterranean Pyramid represents a diet based on the traditional diet of Greece and Southern Italy. Researchers noticed that men from Crete had virtually no incidence of heart disease, hypertension (high blood pressure), and many forms of cancer that afflicted other countries. The traditional diet appeared to be the key to this statistic. And in fact, as Western dietary and life style habits have made greater inroads on these ethnic lifestyles, once-rare diseases are now cropping up in increasing numbers.

The Mediterranean Pyramid is the first in a series of pyramids built around healthy traditional food and

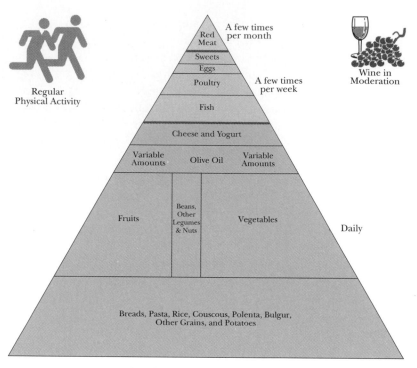

Mediterranean Food Pyramid

dietary patterns from regions throughout the world. A conference series, "Public Health Implications of Traditional Diets," has been undertaken by Harvard School of Public Health, Oldways Preservation & Exchange Trust, and the World Health Organization (WHO).

Instead of considering a single day's food intake strictly in terms of how much a food weighs and/or how many calories it contains, foods are evaluated and prioritized in the diet to account for more than that individual food's calorie count or primary nutrient. They are positioned on the pyramid in accordance with our current understanding of the ways in which these food choices can provide certain health benefits within the framework of that particular ethnic diet.

Since this pyramid evolved from the traditional diets of the Mediterranean, food choices are centered on foods served in a typical home prior to the 1960s. This was done to ensure that Western influences have not obliterated what is quintessentially Mediterranean. Some foods are recommended for daily consumption. Others may be recommended for inclusion only a few times a week or month.

Each day, foods such as polenta, rice, couscous, potatoes, breads, pasta, and other grains should constitute the "center of the plate." Fruits, vegetables, beans, and nuts are also an important part of the daily diet.

Olive oil, high in monounsaturated fat, is specified as the Mediterranean diet's principle source of fat. Olive oil should replace other fats, not be used in addition to fats such as butter, of course. Cheeses and yogurt are also part of a typical day's diet. Olive oil, cheese, and yogurt may contain significant amounts of fat, but they are important to include in appropriate amounts because they are rich sources of nutrients, including vitamins, anti-oxidants, and minerals.

Fish, poultry, eggs, and sweets can be consumed a few times each week in the Mediterranean model. Red meats are limited to a few times per month, or possibly included more often, but only if they are prepared and served in small quantities. This means that foods that a typical Western diet might feature in large quantities at two or more meals a day are now used essentially as condiments, meant to add flavor to the grains, legumes, and vegetables that make up the bulk of the day's food.

Researchers are continuing to delve into what it is was about the Mediterranean culture that confers such a significant health advantage. In so doing, they are uncovering solid evidence that diet alone is not the only answer. Certain lifestyle behaviors—family and friends gathering together as a group to dine and a slower, less stressful pace of life—are also likely factors. Regular daily physical activity is also part of the Mediterranean Pyramid. This feature, along with the option to include wine in moderation further distinguish this pyramid from the USDA Food Guide Pyramid.

ASIAN PYRAMID

The traditional diets of Asia, including China, Japan, Korea, India, Thailand, Vietnam, Cambodia, Indonesia, and other Pacific Rim countries, may be responsible for equally low rates of disease, such as those associated with traditional Mediterranean diets. This pyramid, like the Mediterranean Pyramid, has been established through a group effort, including Oldways Preservation & Exchange Trust, WHO, and Harvard School of Public Health.

The foods included in this pyramid differ slightly from those in the other pyramids, insofar as they are the typical food choices from those ethnic cuisines. However, much of what is true of the Mediterranean pyramid in terms of daily, weekly, and monthly recommendations remains the same.

Most of the day's calories should be derived from foods such as rice, noodles, millet, corn, and other grains. These foods should be minimally processed, in order to retain their nutrients. Also included daily, and in amounts only slightly less than those recommended for grains, are fruits, vegetables, and legumes, nuts, and seeds. Vegetable oil, rather than olive oil, is the preferred source of cooking fats. Fish and shellfish are an optional part of the daily diet, or they may be served less frequently. Although dairy foods are generally not part of the traditional healthy diets of Asia (with the exception of India), low-fat dairy foods may be included daily in small amounts, if desired.

Eggs, poultry, and sweets are not included in a typical daily menu, although they may be included once or twice a week, or more frequently but in smaller serv-ings. Red meat occupies the very top of the pyramid here as it does in the Mediterranean Pyramid. This indicates that it should be served either as a condiment in very small amounts or in slightly larger portions, but only as an infrequent treat, consumed monthly and still only in small portions.

VEGETARIAN PYRAMID

Nearly 12.5 million people refer to themselves as vegetarians today. While there are many types of "vegetarians," the growing numbers of vegetarians of all sorts have focused special attention on how to structure a healthy diet when animal foods are eliminated or greatly reduced in the diet. To read more about the different types of vegetarian diets, turn to page 56, "Themes and Variations in Vegetarianism."

The New York Medical College's Vegetarian Pyramid incorporates many of the same elements as the USDA Food Guide Pyramid. Foods are grouped into categories and appropriate numbers of servings are suggested from within each category.

The main differences between the USDA Food Guide Pyramid and the Vegetarian Pyramid can be found only as you near the top of the pyramid. Dry beans, nuts, seeds, peanut butter, tofu, and eggs (for those who are lacto-ovo vegetarians) are suggested to replace the meats, fish, and poultry suggested in the USDA Food Guide Pyramid.

The top layer of the USDA Food Guide Pyramid depicts foods to be used sparingly. For the vegetarian, this top layer indicates food deemed necessary, on a daily basis, in order to be sure that various nutrients are included in the diet. Blackstrap molasses and brewer's yeast contain certain B vitamins that might otherwise be missing in a strict vegan diet. For those who follow mainly vegetarian diets that still include animal foods such as cheese, eggs, or fish, these foods are probably not as critical.

Food choices are intensely personal. Preferences and expectations can vary widely from one group to another. The role of the chef, as the person most responsible for developing menu items to meet customer demand, is similar to that of the commander-in-chief of an army. The tools and tactics that worked in a previous campaign may not apply from one "campaign" to the next.

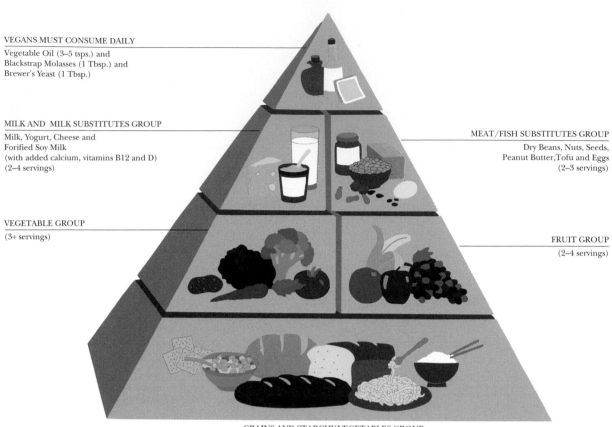

VEGANS MUST CONSUME DAILY
Vegetable Oil (3–5 tsps.) and
Blackstrap Molasses (1 Tbsp.) and
Brewer's Yeast (1 Tbsp.)

MILK AND MILK SUBSTITUTES GROUP
Milk, Yogurt, Cheese and
Forified Soy Milk
(with added calcium, vitamins B12 and D)
(2–4 servings)

MEAT/FISH SUBSTITUTES GROUP
Dry Beans, Nuts, Seeds,
Peanut Butter, Tofu and Eggs
(2–3 servings)

VEGETABLE GROUP
(3+ servings)

FRUIT GROUP
(2–4 servings)

GRAINS AND STARCHY VEGETABLES GROUP
Bread, Cereal, Rice, Pasta, Potatoes, Corn, and Green Peas (6–11 servings)

The Vegetarian Pyramid

The food guide pyramids, though not developed *and deployed when The Professional Chef's Techniques of Healthy Cooking* was first published in 1992, have changed the way people look at their diets. This brief overview of the pyramids and the ways that they have changed food selection options is intended as a valuable tool. Use this tool to build better menu options for your ever-evolving, nutritionally conscious customers.

I

The Seven Guidelines

These seven guidelines are based upon the findings of a number of organizations, including the U.S. Department of Agriculture, the U.S. Department of Health and Human Services, the Senate Select Committee on Health, and the American Heart Association. These guidelines can help the chef incorporate healthful techniques into menu planning, recipe development, and cooking procedures.

Each guideline is discussed from the chef's perspective. Reasons behind each guideline, as well as practical steps toward applying the guideline, are provided. There is no requirement to eliminate any food from the kitchen. Instead, the chef is encouraged to moderate the use of certain categories of food (especially those high in fats, cholesterol, protein, and sodium) and to increase the use of others (especially whole grains and meals, fruits, and vegetables). In brief, the guidelines are:

1. Moderate calories.

One of the major health problems facing Americans today is obesity. Being overweight is linked with serious health problems such as eating disorders, high blood pressure, heart disease, and stroke. The basis for the most effective weight management programs is balancing the energy (calories) one consumes with the energy (calories) one expends in the day. One of the chef's goals in providing nutritious meals, therefore, is offering dishes that are appealing and satisfying, while controlling their caloric content.

2. Moderate the use of fat and control cholesterol.

In some studies, high levels of fat and cholesterol in the diet have been linked with heart disease, obesity, and certain types of cancer. The average American obtains 42% of his or her daily calories from fat. This is about 12% higher than is considered healthful. Some people may not know which foods contain a lot of fat and cholesterol. Others may be too tempted by fat- and cholesterol-laden dishes to refrain from selecting them. By limiting the use of fats and cholesterol during preparation of enticing menu options, the chef can help patrons eat healthfully.

3. Increase the use of carbohydrate-rich foods and moderate the use of added sugars.

Carbohydrates are found in foods such as fruits, vegetables, milk, grains, meals, and legumes. Including a generous quantity and variety of these foods in the diet can be beneficial for two reasons. One is that carbohydrates, particularly complex carbohydrates, are linked with good health. The other reason is that a greater consumption of carbohydrate-rich food may help one reduce the consumption of protein-, fat-, and cholesterol-rich food. It is recommended that 50–60% of one's daily calories come from a variety of foods rich in carbohydrates.

4. Moderate the use of protein.

Proteins are provided by foods such as milk, eggs, cheese, meat, vegetables, grains, meals, and legumes. Protein is an important nutrient; however, it is often consumed in far greater amounts than people require. One of the major disadvantages of most diets that are high in animal protein is that they also tend to be high in fat and cholesterol. When portions of fruits, vegetables, grains, meals, and legumes make a plate look bountiful, smaller portions of higher-fat and higher-cholesterol meats and fish protein items may be more acceptable to patrons. Only 15–20% of one's daily calories should come from protein.

5. Moderate the use of salt and sodium.

There is still some disagreement about the effects of large quantities of salt and sodium in the diet. One possible health hazard may be the development of hypertension. The presence of salt in processed food is not always apparent to the taste buds but may be revealed on a product's label. When preparing foods from scratch, the chef does not have to rely on salt alone to season food to taste. Instead, he or she can use other flavorful ingredients such as herbs, spices, fruits, and vegetables.

6. Increase the variety of fresh foods served and moderate the use of processed foods.

As a general rule, the less processed a food is, the higher its nutritive value. Refined and processed foods should be used sparingly because they may have lost a significant amount of their original vitamins and minerals. Fresh fruits and vegetables, raw meats and fish, and whole meals and grains are ideal ingredients for nutritional cooking. Proper storage and handling are important to retain the nutrients these foods offer. Canned, frozen, and convenience forms of foods do have a valuable place in the kitchen, however. They should be selected for their nutritive qualities as well as for their availability and quality.

7. Offer a wide selection of water and nonalcoholic beverages, and serve alcoholic beverages responsibly.

A cocktail before a meal or a glass of wine with a meal may be considered by many patrons as an enhancement to their dining experience. Among the strategies that can facilitate responsible service of alcohol is offering a diverse selection of bottled waters, fresh juices, and "virgin" cocktails.

It is important to remember that none of the guidelines for nutritional cooking exists in a vacuum. Addressing the concerns of one guideline will almost automatically introduce a positive change in some other part of the meal. The decision to reduce a protein portion to meet the fourth guideline will mean that the chef must look to other foods such as grains and vegetables to "fill" the plate. In so doing, both calories and fats are reduced (the first and second guidelines) and complex carbohydrate servings are increased (the third guideline), as are the variety of vitamin- and mineral-rich fresh foods (the sixth guideline). Good nutrition should be a well-struck balance of all the essential nutrients in our diets in accordance with the goals and standards we have adopted, both personally and professionally.

Calories

Nearly everyone is familiar with the term "calories." Some people, in fact, can readily cite the caloric content of many different foods and beverages. Calories are a tool used in planning nutritional menus and recipes, but there is no need to memorize exact calorie counts of specific foods. In this chapter, *calorie* is defined and where calories are found is examined. Next, a worksheet for determining an individual's daily needs is explained. This figure can be used to help devise a personal eating plan to achieve one of three goals: maintain, lose, or gain weight.

The chef needs to be aware of calories in the kitchen, but it isn't feasible to cook with a calorie handbook in one hand and a sauté pan in the other. The exchange system, explained in this chapter, is one way to make counting calories unnecessary, while still keeping their numbers within appropriate ranges.

WHAT ARE CALORIES, AND WHERE ARE THEY FOUND?

Foods provide human beings with the energy needed to perform all the functions vital to life. This energy is measured in units known as kilocalories. A kilocalorie is the amount of energy or heat required to raise the temperature of 1 kilogram of water 1 degree Celsius. In general usage, the term "calorie" is normally substituted for kilocalorie, as it will be throughout this book. Calories are found in four basic food components: carbohydrates, proteins, fats, and alcohol.

The calorie content of a food is calculated by determining how many grams of the various calorie-providing components it contains and multiplying that number by the proper number of calories per gram. Carbohydrate and protein grams are multiplied by four, fat grams are multiplied by nine, and alcohol by seven. Calorie counts and information regarding other nutrients are available in publications such as *The Handbook of Nutritional Values of Foods in Common Units*. A person with access to a computer can make use of a variety of software programs designed to provide a caloric check and nutritional analysis of foods and recipes. For additional resources, refer to the Appendix.

Caloric values from any source are merely averages. They cannot possibly reflect all of the factors that might affect the nutritive value of a particular food. The figures found in handbooks or software programs are sufficiently accurate to provide valuable information for either personal use or for use in a foodservice establishment.

CALORIES IN FOOD GROUPS

It is not always important to calculate the calories in foods to know how much food should be consumed daily. Foods may be categorized into six "exchange" groups. Then, using the number of daily calories one needs, a specific number of exchanges from each category may be counted instead. This procedure is explained in greater detail in Focus 1-1: The Exchange System.

FOCUS 1-1   THE EXCHANGE SYSTEM

The exchange system was first developed as a diet plan for diabetics to help them control their disease by eating properly. This same plan is used by many people as an effective system for controlling their weight and meeting dietary goals for proteins, carbohydrates, and fats. Tedious calorie counting and strict adherence to a prescribed menu is avoided. Instead, selections are made according to the particular person's own food preferences from six food groups: grains, rice, and cereals; fruits; meat and meat alternatives; vegetables; milk and dairy products; and fats, sweets, and alcohol.

The number of exchanges selected from each group is determined by the number of calories a person needs each day to maintain, lose, or gain weight. The sample menu shown here is based on 2,000 calories. There are ten grain, five fruit, six meat, four vegetable, two milk, and seven fat exchanges. Some of the fat exchanges are "hidden" in other foods. The biscuit contains an exchange of fat, as well as a grain exchange. Each exchange of pork tenderloin is counted as one meat and one-half fat exchange. There is also a variety of foods and seasonings that are considered "free," which means that they are quite low in calories and contain virtually no fat. Items such as stock or broth, lemon juice, herbs, and coffee fit into this group.

Our sample menu shows the breakdown of exchanges to meet the requirements of a varied, balanced, and interesting menu plan.

BREAKFAST

Orange juice (1 fruit)
Toasted English muffin with peach or apple butter (2 grain + 1 fat)
Oatmeal with raisins and cinnamon (1 grain + 1 fruit)
Coffee with milk

continued ►

LUNCH

Grilled chicken burrito in a flour tortilla with sour cream (chicken, 2 meat;
tortilla, 1 grain; sour cream, 1 fat)
Brown rice pilaf (1 grain)
Steamed yellow squash with fresh herbs and jalapeños (1 vegetable)
Skim milk (1 milk)

SNACK

Whole-wheat crackers (1 grain)
Low-fat yogurt (1 milk) with fresh peach slices (1 fruit)

DINNER

Cuban black bean soup (1 grain)
Tossed green salad with tomatoes (2 vegetable) and vinaigrette (1 fat)
Pan-seared pork on a bed of pumpkin pasta with a warm apple compote
(4 meat + 2 fat, 1 grain, 1 fruit)
Broccoli with lemon glaze (1 vegetable)
Strawberry shortcake (berries, 1 fruit; biscuit, 1 grain + 1 fat;
dollop of heavy cream, 1 fat)
Dinner roll (1 grain)

FOODS RICH IN CARBOHYDRATES

Four exchange groups are devoted to carbohydrate-rich foods. These include starches and starchy vegetables, vegetables, fruits, and dairy products. Table 1–1 lists the nutrient and caloric contents of standard portions of some common foods in these groups.

Pasta, bread, rice, potatoes, beans, and squashes are examples of starches and starchy vegetables. An average exchange of them provides 80 calories, which includes 15 grams of carbohydrate and 3 grams of protein.

Vegetables, such as broccoli, carrots, cauliflower, asparagus, peas, and green beans, provide 25 calories in a typical exchange. This portion provides 5 grams of carbohydrate and 2 grams of protein. The size of an exchange may vary, depending on the vegetable. An exchange of most raw vegetables is usually 1 cup. An average exchange of a cooked vegetable is ½ cup.

Fruits such as apples, melons, bananas, peaches, and berries generally contain 60 calories in an exchange. The predominant nutrient in fruits is about

TABLE 1-1.
SERVING SIZE, CALORIES, AND COMPOSITION OF
CARBOHYDRATE-RICH FOODS

CATEGORY/ AVERAGE SERVING	CALORIES	CARBO- HYDRATE (G)	PROTEIN (G)	FAT (G)
Starch/Bread/Pasta				
(½ c. or 1 slice)	80	15	3	trace
Vegetable				
(½ c. cooked,				
1 c. raw)	25	5	2	—
Fruit				
(½ c. fresh or juice,				
¼ c. dried)	60	15	—	—
Milk (1 c.)				
Skim	90	12	8	trace
Low-fat	120	12	8	5
Whole	150	12	8	8

1-1. *Four types of foods supply a good amount of carbohydrates: breads, cereals, and starchy vegetables; fruits; vegetables; and milk.*

15 grams of carbohydrate. There is no protein or fat found in most fruits. A normal serving (or exchange) would be a small piece of a whole fruit equal to ½ cup, ½ cup of juice, or ¼ cup of dried fruit.

Milk and milk-based products, with the exception of butter and most cheeses, contain more carbohydrates than they do either protein or fat. The carbohydrate known as lactose is found only in milk and milk-based products. Lactose is difficult for some people to digest. This condition is explained in Focus 1-2.

FOCUS 1-2   LACTOSE INTOLERANCE

Enzymes help the body to digest foods. One enzyme, lactase, is required to digest lactose, the simple carbohydrate supplied in milk. The inability to produce enough, or any, of this enzyme in order to metabolize lactose properly is a condition known as lactose intolerance. The condition appears to occur in early childhood and is most often found in Asians, Greeks, and Africans.

What happens to the person who has lost the ability to produce enough, or any, lactase? If a food or beverage containing lactose is consumed, it is "eaten" by intestinal bacteria rather than absorbed by the body. Gas and other irritating agents are produced when the bacteria digest lactose. These by-products are essentially trapped in the intestines, and can cause nausea, pain, cramping, diarrhea, and excessive gas.

By itself, the condition is not especially harmful. The obvious solution is to avoid milk and milk products. The catch is that milk is one of the best sources of calcium available to humans. It is important to find ways to get a sufficient supply of calcium without causing the pain and discomfort that afflicts people with lactose intolerance when they drink milk. Certain dairy foods, such as yogurt and cheese, may be acceptable to some sufferers. These foods have been inoculated with a bacterial culture that breaks down some of the lactose. As a result, they have a lower level of lactose and cause less irritation to one's digestive tract. Milk treated with lactase is available through a number of different dairies. Individuals may also try taking a lactase supplement to help them digest lactose in dairy foods.

A separate condition, an allergic reaction to the protein in milk, can also cause unpleasant and uncomfortable reactions when any dairy-based product is consumed. In this case, one must get calcium from calcium-fortified foods such as soy milk or from non-dairy products. Numerous calcium sources can supply daily needs. Included among these are oysters, sardines, shrimp, tinned salmon (with the bones), and stocks and broths made from the bones of fish and poultry. Other examples are broccoli, beet greens, kale, nori, tofu, canned tomatoes, sesame seeds, stone-ground flour, and cornmeal.

Skim milk and skim-milk products, such as yogurt, ricotta cheese, and buttermilk, provide 90 calories in a 1-cup exchange, with 6 grams of carbohydrate, 4 grams of protein, and a trace of fat. Low-fat milk, labeled 1% or 2%, and low-fat milk products have 120 calories per cup, the same amount of carbohydrate and protein as skim milk, along with 2 grams of fat. Whole milk has 180 calories per cup, the same amount of carbohydrate and protein, and 10 grams of fat.

FOODS RICH IN PROTEIN

Meats, fish, and poultry are usually the first foods to come to mind as a good source of protein, which they are. Many vegetables and grains can be good sources as alternatives to meat, whether the intention is to reduce the meat in a diet plan or to prepare vegetarian dishes.

Foods composed primarily of protein usually contain some fat. The amount of fat in a food determines how many calories it contains per 1-ounce exchange. This information is useful when one is determining portion sizes or the amount of a particular ingredient that might be acceptable in a recipe.

1-2. PROTEIN-RICH FOODS

a *All protein-rich foods contain some fat. Lean and medium-fat foods such as beans, (from top left, navy beans, turtle beans, tofu, and lentils), fish such as salmon and shrimp, and well-trimmed meats such as USDA Choice beef, skinless chicken breast, pork loin, and lamb rib chops are all good choices that can help keep fats within desirable amounts.*

b *Some meats are naturally high in fat due to the amount of marbling or intramuscular fat they contain. The steak cut from the strip loin of beef shown here is USDA Prime, a grade that is based in part on the degree of marbling present. Untrimmed pork and lamb chops, chicken with the skin on, and egg yolks are also high in fat. The fat should be trimmed away if possible, or (in the case of egg yolks) the amount served should be carefully controlled.*

An exchange of a lean, protein-rich food contains about 55 calories, 7 grams of protein, and fewer than 3 grams of fat. (Remember that a gram of protein has 4 calories per gram and fat has 9 calories per gram.) Some lean, protein-rich foods are white-fleshed fish such as flounder, skinless breast meat from poultry, and shellfish.

Medium-fat, protein-rich foods contain about 75 calories in a single exchange. The breakdown here is 7 grams of protein and 5 grams of fat. Examples of medium-fat, protein-rich foods are eggs; "lean" cuts of USDA Choice meat such as the leg or tenderloin; and some fish, including salmon, bluefish, tuna, and swordfish. High-fat, protein-rich foods contain from 80 to slightly more than 100 calories per ounce, which are provided by 7 grams of protein and 7–9 grams of fat. Examples of high-fat proteins are duck with the skin left on, hot dogs, and cheddar cheese.

Based on these caloric values for an exchange of protein-rich foods, the calories in a standard serving can be calculated. The recommended serving size for a protein-rich food is 3½ ounces or 100 grams; this is often a far smaller portion than Americans are accustomed to eating. A lean, protein-rich food has fewer than 165 calories per serving. A medium-fat, protein-rich food has about 200–225 calories. A high-fat, protein-rich food has from 240 calories to more than 300 calories per serving. The calories and grams of protein and fat for a recommended serving of all three groups of protein-rich foods are listed in Table 1-2 for quick reference.

TABLE 1-2.
SERVING SIZE, CALORIES, AND COMPOSITION OF
PROTEIN-RICH FOODS

CATEGORY (3 OZ./85 G SERVING)	CALORIES	PROTEIN (G)	FAT (G)	CARBO-HYDRATE (G)
Lean meats and meat alternatives	165	21	9	—
Medium-fat meats and meat alternatives	225	21	16	—
High-fat meats and meat alternatives	300	21	24	—

FOODS RICH IN FAT

This category of foods includes butter, vegetable oil, mayonnaise, and heavy cream. There is some overlap of foods considered high in fat and high in protein. Bacon, for instance, contains significant quantities of fat but still is considered a protein-rich food. Cheese, avocados, coconuts, nuts and seeds,

1-3. *Some foods are naturally rich in fats. Others become fat-laden after they are refined or processed. Heavy cream, coconut, and cheeses are high in saturated fats. Olive oil, nuts, and avocados are either polyunsaturated or monounsaturated.*

and olives are high in fat, as well as in other nutrients such as carbohydrates and protein. This makes them hard to categorize.

Cooking oils, butter, margarine, and shortenings provide 5 grams of fat or 45 calories per tablespoon. Heavy cream, mayonnaise, salad dressings, and nuts have about the same amount of fat and calories as cooking oils. Humans require only a very small part of the day's calories in the form of fats. Once the need is met, the body handles the overflow by turning it into body fat. Below is a list of different high-fat foods.

Nondairy creamers
Ice milk
Yogurt
Shakes, malted milks, and egg creams
Cream soups
Tahini
Peanut butter
Bacon
Ground beef, turkey, or lamb
Sausages, hot dogs, pâtés
Spareribs
Cheeses such as Cheddar, blue, Jack, Swiss

Biscuits

Granola

Snack chips (corn, potato, tortilla chips)

FOODS RICH IN EMPTY CALORIES

The human body needs more than just calories to maintain health. Any food source that has a good supply of nutrients in relation to the number of calories it contains is considered nutrient-dense. Whole grains, fresh fruits and vegetables, lean meats, fish, poultry, and low-fat dairy products are all nutrient-dense.

Foods and beverages with either a very limited number of nutrients or none at all in comparison to their caloric content have "empty" calories. Examples of these items include beer, wine, doughnuts, jams and jellies, candy, and "junk foods." High-fat foods eaten to excess are also laden with empty calories, even if they do contain additional nutrients.

1-4. *The baked potato topped with yogurt, served with a small salad dressed with a reduced-fat vinaigrette, has the same approximate calories as the potato chips in the background. Obviously, you get more to eat when you select the potato and salad. In addition, they offer more complex carbohydrates, vitamins, minerals, and fiber, and far less fat and salt.*

DETERMINING DAILY CALORIC NEEDS

It is important to know how many calories ought to be consumed on average throughout the course of the day. Dietary goals frequently express recommendations in the form of percentages. The day's calories are multiplied by the percentage to find the number of calories that should be supplied by each of three nutrients. For example, if the day's total calories equals 2,000, then 1,000–1,200 of those calories should be provided by carbohydrates, 300–400 should be protein calories, and no more than 600 should be from fats.

There is a distinct correlation between calories consumed and actual body weight. If just enough calories are available to meet the body's energy needs, weight is maintained. Too many calories results in weight gain. Cutting back on calories means that weight will be lost. Weight control is not just a matter of just eating less, however. A worksheet for determining daily calories is included with this chapter. As it is completed, many different factors—such as age, gender, and activity level—that play a role will be discussed.

DETERMINING A HEALTHY BODY WEIGHT

It is not a simple matter to decide the exact weight that is best for an individual. Recommendations found in tables such as those prepared by Metropolitan Life Insurance must accommodate a diversity of body frames and ages. More specific suggestions can be made by professionals able to measure the percentage of body fat and lean muscle tissue with special tests. In one such test, calipers are used to "pinch" areas of the body where fat is likely to accumulate. A more accurate test involves weighing a person while he or she is submerged in water.

The procedure outlined on Worksheet 1-1 requires a person to find a healthy body weight by first determining frame size. The wrist should be measured just below the wrist bone (toward the hand). A medium frame will show a measurement of 6 inches for women and 7 inches for men. Anything less indicates a small frame; a larger measurement means that the person has a large frame. Then the individual's height can be used to determine a healthy body weight by frame size.

No matter how a healthy body weight is determined, it is a good idea to remember that the actual amount a person weighs is only a part of the issue. The scales may say that a person's weight is well within an acceptable range. The presence of a "spare tire" or "love handles," or pants that refuse to zip up are often better indicators of how fat a person actually is. If an individual person has a high percentage of body fat, that person will look "fatter" than another person of the same gender, height, and weight with a lower percentage of body fat. This is true because fat tissue takes up more space but weighs less than lean muscle tissue.

WORKSHEET 1-1.

DETERMINING CALORIES NEEDED TO MEET OR

MAINTAIN A HEALTHY BODY WEIGHT

Step 1. Determine a Healthy Body Weight
Use height and weight tables, or calculate based on frame size:

FRAME SIZE	WOMEN	MEN
Medium	100 lbs. up to height of 5 feet. Add 5 lbs. for each additional inch.	106 lbs. up to first 5 feet. Add 6 lbs. for each additional inch.
Small	Subtract 10% from weight for same height as medium frame.	Subtract 10% from weight for same height as medium frame.
Large	Add 10% to weight for same height as medium frame.	Add 10% to weight for same height as medium frame.

Your height_____   Your Healthy Body Weight_____

Step 2. Calculate Basal Calories
Multiply healthy body weight by the appropriate factor:
>   Healthy Body Weight $\times$ 9 (women) = _____
>   Healthy Body Weight $\times$ 10 (men) = _____

Step 3. Calculate Activity Calories at Proper Level
Multiply healthy body weight by appropriate factor, determined by normal
daily activity level:

Sedentary	Healthy Body Weight $\times$ 3 = _____
Moderate	Healthy Body Weight $\times$ 5 = _____
Strenuous	Healthy Body Weight $\times$ 10 = _____

Step 4. Calculate Total Daily Calories
Add basal calories (from Step 2) and activity calories (from Step 3) to
determine total daily calories: _____

Step 5. Adjustments to Reach a Healthy Body Weight
If you already are at a healthy body weight, there are no adjustments
necessary, as long as you eat a well-balanced diet that provides all of the
essential nutrients in the proper ratio.

   To **lose weight**, subtract calories from results in Step 4:

   To lose ½ pound of body fat per weight, subtract 250 calories. (It is not
   safe to allow calorie levels to drop below the basal calories.)

To **gain weight,** add calories to results in Step 4:
A weight gain of about ½ pound per week is suggested, to avoid a weight gain that is primarily body fat. Increase calories by about 250–300 per day

Total Daily Calories (+ / −) Adjustment to Gain or Lose = _____

Determining Basal Metabolic Needs

There are two separate figures that are added to find the total calories needed by an individual. The first figure is based on basal metabolism. This is the energy expended by the resting body for involuntary activities such as respiration, digestion, circulation, and temperature regulation. The greatest part of the calories consumed in a day are used to meet basal metabolic needs.

Each individual's metabolism is influenced by gender, age, general body composition (mainly body fat or mainly lean muscle), and geographic climate. Women usually require fewer calories than men, and older people require fewer than younger people. Lean muscle tissue burns more calories than fat tissue. Colder climates force the body to expend more energy keeping warm, thus consuming more calories. Other factors that affect how quickly the body burns calories while at rest are stress, exercise, and general health.

The BMR (basal metabolic rate) is found by multiplying a person's healthy body weight by the appropriate factor. Men multiply that weight by 10; women by 9. The difference in the multiplication factor reflects the fact that men carry more muscle mass than women, as a rule.

Calculating Calories for Various Activity Levels

The amount of calories needed to perform voluntary activities will vary according to an individual's normal daily routine. Sedentary, moderate, and strenuous activity levels all require different energy reserves. Each category will have a multiplication factor assigned to determine how many calories are appropriate at that level, based upon healthy body weight.

Sedentary activity is typically considered to be office or desk work, little scheduled exercise, or "weekend" sports such as golf (when the person uses a golf cart) or tennis doubles played at a low-intensity level. A person who is sedentary should multiply his or her healthy body weight by a factor of 3.

Moderate activity is defined as some regularly scheduled exercise done approximately three to four times each week. Walking, jogging, swimming, and school sports are moderate-level activities. At this level of activity, an individual's healthy body weight is multiplied by a factor of 5.

Strenuous activity is regular, vigorous, and sustained. A person who engages in sports training or a daily workout conducted at a high-intensity level for an extended period, or whose job is considered manual labor, such as farming or construction work, needs far greater supplies of energy than a sedentary or a moderately active person. The factor used to multiply healthy body weight in this category is 10.

DETERMINING TOTAL DAILY CALORIES

The calories required for basal metabolism and activity level are combined to determine the calories needed each day to maintain weight. For example, a 200-pound man with a moderate activity level would need 2,000 calories per day for basal metabolic activity (200 pounds × 10) plus 1,000 calories for moderate activity (200 pounds × 5) for a total of 3,000 calories per day.

If the amount of calories consumed exactly matches the body's energy requirements, there will be no weight gain and no weight loss. Equilibrium is maintained, and body weight is kept constant.

MAKING ADJUSTMENTS

Gaining or losing weight is possible when the number of calories eaten in a day *and/or* activity levels are adjusted. Weight loss is accomplished by reducing the number of calories consumed in a day, or increasing the activity level while maintaining the same overall number of calories, or both.

Reducing intake by 500 calories a day will usually result in the loss of about a pound of fat in a week. A safe, effective weight-loss program will not allow calorie levels to fall below the amount required by basal metabolism: 1,200–1,500 calories per day for women and 1,500–1,800 calories for men. When the basal metabolism has its needs adequately met, the individual can be more certain that the weight lost is fat, not water or muscle weight. A woman generally can lose a maximum of 1 pound of fat per week on a safe program; a man can lose slightly more, up to 2 pounds a week.

To gain weight would require the reverse sequence. Instead of subtracting 500 daily calories to lose a pound a week, daily caloric intake should be increased by 500 calories to gain a pound a week. Extra calories should be those that provide high-quality nutrients, not the empty calories found in "junk foods" or alcohol. Exercise is important in a weight-gain program so that muscle mass and lean tissue are increased, not the body's stores of fat. When preparing a nutritional menu for groups, the chef and the nutritionist must select a daily calorie level as a framework. In the following discussion, nutrient requirements are based on an intake of 2,000 calories per day.

PUTTING THE GUIDELINE TO WORK:
CALORIES IN THE KITCHEN

Although the number of daily calories a patron eats is the responsibility of that particular person, the chef can be a significant underlying influence. A patron's intention to eat healthfully may be undermined by a menu that has either no low-calorie dishes or one on which the only such offerings are bland, boring items. By featuring a menu of carefully planned, enticing selections, the chef can encourage patrons to make healthful, calorie-wise choices. Low-calorie dishes that can be appreciated for their lively flavors and interesting combinations will assure guests that their healthful selection is not second-best. Any reduced-calorie version of a familiar dish that might not fare well in a taste comparison with the original should not be placed on the menu. Instead, the chef should create an altogether different item. Featuring foods that are low in fats also provides options that are low in calories. To help keep the total calories of a dish within a moderate range, the chef can use low-fat foods as the main ingredients and reserve small amounts of high-calorie foods for garnish or flavoring.

OFFER AN ENTICING SELECTION OF HEALTHY OPTIONS

Low-calorie dishes can be featured in all courses of a meal—from soup to salad, entrée, and dessert. A soup, for example, might be a richly flavored broth brimming with seasonal vegetables or a thick soup that is given its smooth, creamy texture by pureed vegetables, grains, or potatoes. Either of these would contain far fewer calories than a soup laced with a great amount of heavy cream.

Innovative, low-calorie salads can feature interesting, colorful ingredients, such as a variety of crisp, fresh greens; sweet peppers; jicama; mangoes; and slivers of grilled meat, seafood, and poultry. It is important to serve a dressing that sustains the low-calorie quality of a salad. To reduce the calories of an oil and vinegar mixture, replace most of the oil with a thickened stock, or fruit or vegetable juice. To create a creamy dressing, use low- or nonfat dairy products such as yogurt, pureed ricotta cheese, or buttermilk.

Low-calorie main courses can reflect the chef's culinary imagination. Creative uses of low- and moderate-fat meats, fish, and poultry in simple, grilled dishes appeal to broad audiences. Dishes inspired by Southwestern American cooking get most of their excitement from chilis and spices, not cheese and sour cream. Pasta dishes combined with such flavorful ingredients as sun-dried tomatoes, fresh herbs, and a delicate splash of extra-virgin oil are vast improvements over meat or cream sauces. Even pizzas can be prepared with such bold tastes and colors as grilled peppers, reduced-fat mozzarella or goat cheese, and wild mushrooms to replace high-fat pepperoni and sausage toppings.

Sometimes customers who refrained from ordering a calorie-laden en-trée they wanted are inclined to overcompensate and reward themselves with rich desserts. By offering a wide variety of low-calorie desserts, the chef can encourage patrons to resist tempting, high-calorie indulgences. There are a number of appealing alternatives to the standard, high-calorie fare. A beauti-fully presented selection of fruits, perhaps with a fresh sorbet or granita, is an excellent menu item. It is also appropriate to have a few more "sinful" dishes with carefully measured amounts of chocolate, nuts, and even a rosette of real whipped cream.

Fats

Fat has become the focus of countless articles, books, diet plans, and advertising claims. The potential for misunderstanding is enormous. When bombarded by an overwhelming amount of information—some of it contradictory—there may be a tendency to lump it all together and label any foods containing fat as "unhealthy." This is hardly appropriate to any sound nutritional program. It is important to realize the positive and negative roles that fat plays. Fat is considered an essential nutrient because it provides energy and fulfills other vital bodily functions. Although a small amount of fat in the diet is necessary, no more than 30% of one's daily calories should come from fat. No single type of fat ought to be completely eliminated from a healthy diet. However, it is a good idea to reduce the amount of saturated fats and replace them wherever possible with either mono- or polyunsaturated fats. For more on fat in the diet, see Focus 2-1: How Much Fat Do I Need?

Adhering to this guideline for nutritional cooking provides additional benefits related to several other guidelines. Moderating the use of fat and cholesterol tends to moderate not just high-calorie ingredients, but also total calories in meals, and to increase the serving sizes of foods such as fruits, vegetables, grains, and legumes.

This chapter discusses the three types of fat, as well as a fat-related compound, cholesterol. It also describes the functions of fat in food and in the body. Finally, suggestions are made to help the chef moderate the fat and cholesterol in menu items.

FOCUS 2-1   HOW MUCH FAT DO I NEED?

Calculating how much fat is appropriate for personal health can be confusing. Many nutrition experts suggest that the total amount of fat should be less than 30% of the day's total calories, roughly dividing them into saturated fats (less than 10%), polyunsaturated fats (10% or less), and monounsaturated fats (the remaining 10%).

Knowing the number of fat grams that a healthy diet can include is helpful information, because most food labels and nutritional composition charts list the item's fat content in grams. This means that the fat calories should now be converted into fat grams. The formula for calculating the amount of fat allowable in both calories and grams is:

Total Daily Calories $\times$ .10 = Maximum Calories of Saturated Fats

2,000 $\times$ .10 = 200

Total Daily Calories $\times$ .30 = Maximum Calories of Total Fat

2,000 $\times$ .30 = 600

To convert fat calories to grams, divide by 9:

200 calories (saturated fats) = 22 grams of saturated fat
600 calories (total fats) = 67 grams of total fats

A sample menu was developed using the exchange system. According to this diet plan, seven fat exchanges are allowed. Sweets and alcoholic beverages are included in the fat category, which means that the seven exchanges could be allotted differently to allow for a pat of butter or a glass of wine.

BREAKFAST

Orange juice
Toasted English muffin with peach or apple butter (1 fat)
Oatmeal with raisins and cinnamon
Coffee with milk

LUNCH

Grilled chicken burrito in a flour tortilla with sour cream (sour cream, 1 fat)
Brown rice pilaf
Steamed yellow squash with fresh herbs and jalapeños
Skim milk

SNACK

Whole-wheat crackers
Low-fat yogurt with fresh peach slices

DINNER

Cuban black bean soup
Tossed green salad with tomatoes and vinaigrette (1 fat)
Pan-seared pork on a bed of pumpkin pasta with a warm apple compote
(pork, 4 meat + 2 fat)
Broccoli with lemon glaze
Strawberry shortcake (biscuit, 1 grain + 1 fat; dollop of heavy cream, 1 fat)
Slice of whole-wheat baguette

WHAT ARE FATS, AND WHY ARE THEY IMPORTANT?

For purposes of simplicity, this section considers fats in a relatively narrow focus, as cooking fats. This is the form in which the fat has been "refined" from its original source, plants or animals. Fats as a component of foods will be discussed in the next section.

A single fat is actually a number of chains, each composed of carbon, hydrogen, and oxygen, linked together. The chains are known as fatty acids. The individual fatty acids may be saturated, poly-, or monounsaturated, depending on how many open sites there are for hydrogen atoms to bond with a carbon atom. Saturated fatty acids cannot accept any more hydrogen; monounsaturated fatty acids have one open site on the chain; polyunsaturated fatty acids have more than one open site.

Cooking fats and fats in foods are grouped into categories according to their degree of saturation. The predominant type of fatty acid will determine if the fat is considered saturated (e.g., butter, lard, coconut oil), monounsaturated (e.g., olive oil, nut oils), or polyunsaturated (e.g., corn oil).

Cholesterol is not the same thing as cooking fats and fats found in food, but it is a fat-related compound. There are two ways in which cholesterol is normally discussed. *Dietary cholesterol* is that contained in foods. *Serum cholesterol* is found in the bloodstream and is also known as blood cholesterol.

SATURATED FATS

Saturated cooking fats are usually easy to identify. They tend to be solid at room temperature and flavorful. Their smoking points are lower than those of other fats. Most saturated fats, including butter, lard, and chicken fat, are animal products. The exceptions to these general statements include coconut, palm, and palm kernel oils, often referred to as "tropical oils." They are liquid at room temperature, tend to remain stable even when heated to high temperatures, and are derived from plants.

Saturated fats are often perceived as the ultimate dietary villains. There is some basis for this perception. Saturated fats can increase blood cholesterol levels (known as serum cholesterol), as well as the build up of plaque in arteries that can lead to atherosclerosis.

There are several risk factors associated with atherosclerosis. People who are overweight or obese, suffer from hypertension, have high serum cholesterol levels, or diabetes are at greater risk. Those who suffer from excessive amounts of stress in their daily lives, smoke cigarettes, or are sedentary are also considered to be at risk of developing atherosclerosis. Estrogen has been linked with the suppression of plaque buildup. Men of all ages are at greater risk than women of developing atherosclerosis because they lack this hormone; once women pass menopause, their risk increases to match that of men.

2-1. *Most foods containing saturated fats are derived from animal sources. Butter, bacon, salami, cheese, chorizo sausage, and heavy cream are all examples. Tropical oils, such as palm kernel and coconut oils, are exceptions.*

MONOUNSATURATED FATS

Because monounsaturated fats are usually liquid at room temperature, they are considered oils. Plant products such as olives, peanuts, and walnuts are among the common sources of monounsaturated cooking oils. The flavors of these oils are usually considered appealing. Canola oil, made from the rapeseed plant, is a monounsaturated fat that is nearly neutral in flavor.

Some studies of eating habits in various cultures have shown that people with diets that rely upon a higher proportion of monounsaturated fats tend to have lower blood cholesterol levels and less incidence of heart disease. When the total amount of fat is kept within the recommended guidelines (no more than 30% of the day's total calories), and monounsaturated fats are used in preference to saturated fats, there appears to be a positive effect on levels of the "good" cholesterol, HDL, as well.

2-2. *Monounsaturated fats appear to help lower the level of harmful cholesterol, low-density lipoproteins (LDL), and to raise levels of good cholesterol, high-density lipoproteins (HDL), when used to replace saturated fats in a diet plan that keeps all fats at 30% of the day's total calories or less. Sources of monounsaturated fats include peanuts and peanut oil, avocados, olives, and olive oil.*

POLYUNSATURATED FATS

Polyunsaturated fats are usually liquid at room temperature and nearly flavorless. They are produced from plant sources and include the familiar corn and safflower vegetable oils. Polyunsaturated fats have been shown to lower blood cholesterol levels. Many shortenings and margarines are made from polyunsaturated or monounsaturated oils. The process of making a liquid oil into a solid fat is known as hydrogenation. During hydrogenation these oils are combined with additional hydrogen. The hydrogen bonds with the carbon at the place where a double bond exists, increasing the overall degree of saturation for the entire fat. Hydrogenation somewhat solidifies the liquid form

2-3. *Polyunsaturated fats are found in vegetable-based products such as corn oil, walnuts and walnut oil (as well as most other nuts, including almonds, hazelnuts, and pecans), and sesame seeds and sesame oil.*

of the oil at room temperature. The more solid the shortening or margarine is, the more saturated the oils have become. Hydrogenated shortenings do not necessarily have the beneficial properties of a nonhydrogenated oil, though they are usually less saturated than butter or lard.

CHOLESTEROL

Having cholesterol in the blood is essential to life. Among the crucial roles cholesterol plays is the production of hormones and Vitamin D. It is not essential to consume cholesterol, however, because human beings are capable of producing it from other dietary components. It is not exactly clear what the effect of cholesterol consumed in the foods we eat has on the levels of cholesterol in the blood. It appears that it is far more important to control the amount of fat, especially saturated fats, but there is no real consensus yet.

FOCUS 2-2   CONFUSING CHOLESTEROL WITH FAT

Nutrition has become a hot topic. People are eager for information, and many are equally eager to make some simple, healthful changes in their own diets. News stories that report links between our average diet and the likelihood of developing a disease are often the impetus behind a new marketing campaign for "Contains No Cholesterol!" peanut butter or "100% Vegetable Oil" margarines that are "Cholesterol Free."

No one is actually telling a lie. Of course peanut butter or vegetable oil-based margarine has no cholesterol, because cholesterol is never found in a plant food. This is true no matter what type of refining or processing the food has undergone. Still, the manufacturer is counting on the fact that we will remember that cholesterol is bad for us. Then, when we are walking down the aisles of the supermarket, we will automatically reach for foods that we believe will improve our health, or at least not hurt us.

The truth is, however, that most brands of peanut butter and margarines have been hydrogenated. The poly- and monounsaturated fats that naturally occur are now more saturated than they were to begin with, although they may still be more unsaturated than they are saturated.

Tropical oils such as coconut, palm, and palm kernel are saturated to start with, and consumers should be aware that they are best avoided. But a label that proclaims "Free of Tropical Oils" isn't necessarily a good nutritional bet either, if there is a hydrogenated shortening listed in the ingredients.

Anyone who has read about nutrition or carefully examined the findings of various studies knows that reducing serum cholesterol requires more than simply eating foods that do not themselves contain cholesterol. There are many risk factors associated with high levels of cholesterol in the blood. One key factor that can be controlled through the diet is reducing the total amount of fat to meet the recommended guideline: only 30% or less of the day's calories from all fat sources, and of that, less than one-third from saturated fats. Certainly it is also prudent to keep dietary cholesterol at or below the suggested maximum of 300 milligrams per day. This dietary change, when consistently applied, does appear to help reduce serum blood cholesterol levels in most individuals. Studies are still being undertaken to determine the exact links between diet and health in this area, as well as in others, such as cancer, diabetes, and hypertension. The results are not yet conclusive, but there is enough clear evidence to make a case for watching labels for both saturated fats and cholesterol so that, no matter what the claims, the consumer can make an educated choice.

Cholesterol is a sterol, which is a subcategory of lipids ("lipid" is the scientific name for all of the various substances commonly referred to as fats). Cholesterol is found only in animal foods. It does not exist in any plant products, including vegetables, fruits, nuts, and legumes. This means that companies who make products such as peanut butter or corn oil margarine and emblazon their labels with "Cholesterol Free!" are accurate, but these labels may be misleading to a consumer. For some further insight into the ways that clever marketing strategies can put up a smokescreen, read Focus 2-2: Confusing Cholesterol with Fat.

Certain foods contain greater amounts of cholesterol than others. A 3-ounce portion of braised veal liver, for example, has more than 300 milligrams of cholesterol, while a similar portion of grilled sea bass has only 45 milligrams. A maximum of 300 milligrams of cholesterol per day is recommended. Further recommendations for reducing blood cholesterol levels can be found in Focus 2-3: Changing a Cholesterol Profile.

FOCUS 2-3   CHANGING A CHOLESTEROL PROFILE

If a person's cholesterol screening shows high levels of serum cholesterol, a second blood test is usually performed to determine the exact levels of two lipoproteins that act as carriers for cholesterol: high-density lipoproteins (HDL) and low-density lipoproteins (LDL).

A high level of LDL in the blood is a fairly good indicator of increased health risk. LDL, the "bad" cholesterol, is a sticky substance that tends to deposit cholesterol on the lining of the arteries. These deposits may build up and eventually block the arteries so that blood cannot flow through them. Such a condition can lead to aneurysms, coronary and cerebral thrombosis, embolism, heart attack, and stroke.

A high level of HDL is desirable, because it usually indicates a reduced health risk. HDL, the "good" cholesterol, seems to remove LDL from the bloodstream. HDL carries LDL to the liver, where it is dismantled and either flushed from the body or reassembled into other compounds.

Several factors help determine an individual's serum cholesterol level and risk for heart disease. They are age, gender, heredity, glucose tolerance, blood pressure, stress level, cigarette smoking, activity level, weight control, and diet. Age, heredity, and gender are outside a person's control, of course, but one can make positive changes in the other factors.

A habit of smoking appears to raise the LDL level in one's blood. Ceasing smoking appears to lower one's LDL level, while maintaining or raising one's HDL level. Starting and maintaining a regular exercise program has been shown to reduce

continued ►

one's LDL level and increase the HDL level. Nearly everyone is capable of exercising enough to receive a benefit. A person who is overweight or obese can increase HDL and decrease LDL by losing weight on a safe, medically sanctioned program.

Some studies seem to show that moderate alcohol consumption might possibly lower LDL and increase HDL as well, but this is not a conclusive finding. To drink a cocktail, or a glass of wine or beer is an individual decision and should not be considered a "prescription" for a healthy heart.

Keeping total fat, and especially saturated fat, consumption at or below suggested maximums is important, just as is avoiding excessive consumption of cholesterol-rich foods. Diets built around a wide variety of foods containing generous amounts of carbohydrates and fiber (whole grains, oats, rice, fruits, vegetables, and starchy vegetables) also appear to help cleanse LDL from the blood. There is certainly no harm in increasing the amount and variety of carbohydrate- and fiber-rich foods in the diet, and there may be a distinct benefit.

FATS IN FOODS

In the preceding section, fats were considered in their more refined forms, as cooking fats. In this section fats are looked at as a component of foods. In some foods, the presence of fat is obvious. In others, fat may not be so apparent.

Adding butter, heavy cream, cheeses, and egg yolks to a dish has a distinct effect on both the taste and texture. These foods have instantly recognizable flavors that are almost universally appealing. Butter, for instance, gives dishes a sweet, fresh "buttery" taste, while cream adds a smooth, suave flavor. They have a tendency to coat the mouth as they are eaten, prolonging the taste experience. Because of their physical properties, they have a silky, rich texture that is highly desirable as well. Ice cream is a perfect example. Chocolate, another food high in fat, has the same characteristics. It has been suggested that people who find these foods irresistible have not so much a "sweet tooth" as a "fat tooth."

In addition to giving foods wonderful textures and appealing flavors, fats also act as a preservative. One way fats can help preserve food is by acting as an air-tight seal. For example, layering the top of a container of confit of duck or jugged hare with fat prevents the food's contact with air. This keeps the food from drying out and becoming stale.

Because saturated fat is quite stable, it can help preserve food in another way. Traditionally, fat was blended into sausage, pâté, terrine, and rillette mixtures to help preserve the meat. This same technique of adding a stable fat to food to preserve it is commonly used in processing crackers, cereals, snack foods, and convenience foods. Tropical oils and partially hydrogenated vege-

2-4. *Even though no direct evidence links the cholesterol we eat with elevated blood cholesterol levels, it is suggested that daily cholesterol consumption be kept at less than 300 milligrams. Egg yolks, a concentrated source of cholesterol, should be limited to about three per week. Organ meats, such as liver, sweetbreads, and kidneys, should be eaten only occasionally, in moderate amounts.*

table oils are used often; they are flavorful, shelf-stable, and inexpensive.

Cholesterol remains one of the most confusing issues in relation to a nutritionally sound diet. Most people, unless they have a particular sensitivity to the cholesterol in foods, need to be more concerned with the levels of fats in their diet than counting milligrams of cholesterol. Reducing saturated fats will almost invariably reduce dietary cholesterol intake, since cholesterol is generally found in foods with the highest concentration of saturated fats.

It is possible to completely eliminate all sources of dietary cholesterol by becoming a strict vegan, who consumes no foods that come from animals, including cheese, milk, and eggs. Other individuals can elect to control cholesterol in their diets by making wise food choices. Many foods that are rich in a variety of nutrients may also contain cholesterol, so even though it is a good idea to limit the amount of liver or red meats eaten each week, these foods still have a place in a reasonable menu or diet plan. A prudent amount of extremely high cholesterol foods is considered to be no more than three egg yolks per week, and a limit of no more than one or two servings a month of organ meats such as sweetbreads or brains. Table 2-1 provides a breakdown of the types of fats and the amount of cholesterol found in some selected foods.

TABLE 2-1.

FATTY ACIDS AND CHOLESTEROL IN SELECTED FOODS

	SATURATED (G)	MONOUN- SATURATED (G)	POLYUN- SATURATED (G)	CHOLES- TEROL (MG)
Milk, 1 cup:				
Whole	5.1	2.4	0.3	33
Nonfat, skim	0.4	0.2	tr	5
Egg, hard-cooked	1.7	2.2	0.7	274
Butter, 1 tbsp.	7.1	3.3	0.4	31
Margarine, corn,				
1 stick	2.0	5.5	3.4	0
Oils, 1 tbsp.:				
Coconut	11.8	0.8	0.2	0
Corn	1.7	3.3	8.0	0
Olive	1.8	9.9	1.1	0
Safflower	1.2	1.6	10.1	0
Fish, 3 oz.:				
Salmon, baked	1.2	2.4	1.4	60
Sardines, Atlantic	2.1	3.7	2.9	85
Tuna, chunk light,				
in oil	1.4	1.9	3.1	55
Meat, 3 oz.:				
Rib roast	11.7	13.6	1.0	70
Ground beef	7.6	8.5	0.7	88
Beef liver, fried	2.5	3.6	1.3	372
Ham, roasted	3.2	4.2	1.1	80
Veal cutlet	4.0	4.0	0.4	86
Chicken, 3 oz.:				
Dark meat				
baked, no skin	2.3	3.0	1.9	79
Fried, skin	3.9	5.7	3.3	78
Light meat				
baked, no skin	1.1	2.3	0.8	72
Fried, skin	2.8	4.1	2.3	74

Source: U.S. Department of Agriculture, "Provisional Table on the Fatty Acid and Cholesterol Content of Selected Foods," 1984.

FATS IN THE BODY

Fat is a concentrated source of energy for the body. A single gram of fat contains 9 calories. One ounce (28 grams) of pure fat contains about 250 calories. This is more than double the number of calories found in the same amount of carbohydrate or protein. It is easy to consume a lot of fat calories without eating a lot of food.

In the body, fat and cholesterol help to create various important structures, including hormones and components of cells and tissues. Fat helps transport nutrients through the blood to the sites where they are needed, and it surrounds organs to protect them from being damaged. Fat can be stored in the layer of adipose tissue beneath the skin.

Fat plays another important role in the body. During digestion, when foods are broken down into their components so that the body can absorb and use them, fats are forced to group together. They rise to the top of the stomach and are saved until last to be digested. This gives a person a lasting sensation of fullness known as "satiety," which delays the onset of hunger.

PUTTING THE GUIDELINE TO WORK: FATS IN THE KITCHEN

To successfully moderate the amount of fat used in cooking, the chef must realize what purpose the fat serves in a dish. Fats give foods flavor, richness, and sheen. They provide lubrication, so that foods can be cooked without sticking to the pan or grill. Fat also aids in emulsifying, creaming, and binding foods. After the chef establishes the purpose of fat in a particular dish, he or she may be able to alter the preparation to achieve a similar effect in a more healthful way.

REDUCING FATS WHILE INCREASING FLAVOR

Many Western palates have grown accustomed to the smooth, silky feel and rich taste of butter, cream, eggs, and cheeses. High-fat meats such as spareribs, pork chops, and USDA Prime steaks are a standard by which the flavors of other foods are judged. When moderating the amount of fat in a dish, it is essential to introduce plenty of flavor, otherwise the menu item may seem sadly lacking and be unsatisfying to eat.

One way to introduce moderation is to purchase ingredients that are lower in fat than their traditional counterparts. USDA Choice grade meats have less marbling than do Prime grade cuts and, therefore, are a better choice for a nutritionally oriented menu. Trimming and discarding surface fat is another way to reduce the fat on the entire plate. The skin of most poultry can be left in place for grilling, roasting, or sautéing. Because a substantial amount of the saturated fat in poultry is concentrated in its skin, it is best to remove the skin before service. For some additional purchasing tips, read Focus 8-3: Trimming the Fat from Birds in Chapter 8 of this book.

Dairy products used in a number of dishes should also be evaluated for their fat content. Evaporated skimmed milk can frequently be substituted for heavy cream. Yogurt is now available in both low- and nonfat versions. Mozzarella and ricotta cheeses are also available in reduced-fat versions. A form of fromage blanc made by draining low- or nonfat yogurt can be prepared and blended with a small amount of sour cream to get a rich flavor with far less fat than straight sour cream or crème fraîche.

Boldly flavored sauces to accompany meats can be made using ingredients such as tomatoes, a spicy bean stew, or a rich, thickened veal stock (fond de veau lié). These ingredients can give not only flavor but also an appealing body, which is achieved without the use of butter to "monter au beurre" and lightly thicken the sauce.

There is room for some fat in dishes, even in nutrition-oriented items. When an entire dish is infused with fat, it simply blends in with the overall taste. Instead, prepare the dish using low-fat ingredients and prominently place a small, carefully measured amount of a high-fat ingredient where it can be immediately identified and enjoyed.

One of the best examples of using a carefully measured amount of a high-fat ingredient in a dish, without going over the allotment of calories and fat for a menu item, is creamed soups. Traditionally, a roux made from butter and flour would be used to thicken the broth. In a modified approach to soup making, roux is replaced with pureed vegetables; starchy ingredients such as potatoes, rice, or beans; or a modified starch such as arrowroot. Evaporated skimmed milk is used to achieve the same result as adding heavy cream, without all of its calories and fat. The "net savings" from these changes to the traditional formula make it possible to indulge the guest with a small, carefully measured dollop of heavy cream as a garnish. All of the expected tastes, textures, and colors are found, without all the calories of the traditional version.

Complementing small portions of meat, fish, or poultry with generous amounts of flavorful vegetables, grains, and beans helps to satisfy the eye, palate, and stomach while moderating the use of fat.

No ingredient needs to be banned from a diet, unless there are specific medical reasons to do so. Instead, all foods can become an enjoyable part of a balanced diet when they are used in prudent, carefully measured quantities.

FAT AS A COOKING MEDIUM

It is possible to minimize the amount of fat used during sautéing by carefully selecting and preparing sauté pans. When sautéing foods that have a great deal of natural moisture (such as spinach, tomatoes, and mushrooms) or fat (such as duck and beef), it may not be necessary to add any fat to the pan. Even delicate foods (such as fish or chicken breasts) may be sautéed using just a light coating of oil. Careful regulation of moderate heat helps prevent food from drying out and sticking.

Some methods are particularly well suited to nutritional cooking. Grilling, roasting, smoke-roasting, steaming, poaching, baking, and microwaving are excellent examples. Foods cook through the application of either hot air, steam, or cooking liquids. These methods do not require added fat that may occur in basting liquids, marinades, high-fat glazes, or lubricating oils and butter. Intense heat can give the natural juices of meats deep, rich flavors. The use of added fat can be reserved for a garnish or accent flavor.

Foods remain juicy and moist if they are cooked just until they are done and no longer. Overcooked items lose their natural juices. Being attentive to proper cooking time can help eliminate the need to restore a food's original moisture with added cream or butter.

FORM FOLLOWS FUNCTION

Certain items are simply not suitable for tinkering. Dishes that would immediately be perceived as substitutes or low-fat versions should be given some careful thought. There is no way to make a hollandaise without butter and egg yolks. These ingredients have special chemical properties that allow this sauce to be prepared. A pale imitation of a béarnaise sauce is not going to be well received. It is probably better to remove such dishes from the menu. Instead, feature menu items that do not invite a comparison that might leave the guest feeling unsatisfied.

CHAPTER

3

Carbohydrates

Many societies are heavily dependent upon a single grain for most of their diet. Corn was the grain base of ancient Aztec, Incan, Mayan, and other native American cuisines. Rice is found throughout Asia. Wheat is predominant in the United States and other Western societies. Grains, including corn, rice, wheat, millet, barley, rye, and oats, are the foundations of various diets throughout the world.

The nutritional importance of these "peasant foods" is just starting to be appreciated. Until quite recently, foods like meats, fish, poultry, cheeses, butter, and cream, which are at the top of the food chain, were generally preferred. A great number of different foods from lower on the chain, such as grains, legumes, fruits, and vegetables, are rich sources of both complex and simple carbohydrates, as well as of fiber, a non-nutritive but essential component of a healthy diet. And, not least important to the chef, they include a broad spectrum of textures, flavors, and colors to give routine fare additional appeal. Focus 3-1: How Much Carbohydrate Do I Need? discusses the daily intake considered best for the diet.

Foods that derive the majority of their calories from added sugars are a nutritional dead end. These sweeteners are simple carbohydrates that have

FOCUS 3-1 HOW MUCH CARBOHYDRATE DO I NEED?

About half of one's total daily calories should come from carbohydrates. Based on a 2,000-calorie diet, 1,000 calories, or 250 grams, of carbohydrate should be consumed daily. This may seem like a large amount, especially to people who are more accustomed to meeting their caloric needs with meats and high-fat foods. To balance a diet and meet basic nutritional requirements, it is important to select a variety of carbohydrate-rich foods.

Four of the six exchange lists include foods that provide significant amounts of carbohydrates: grains and starches, milk, fruit, and vegetables. A day's requirements are divided among the groups, with the number of exchanges needed from each group determined by an individual's required calorie level. In the sample menu shown, there are two exchanges from the milk group, four from the vegetable group, five fruits, and ten starches and grains.

Foods selected from the exchange list should be varied to ensure that vitamin and mineral needs are met. In order to keep within other dietary guidelines, milk and milk products should be skim or low-fat. Dark-green, leafy vegetables such as spinach or kale; orange and red vegetables such as squashes, beets, or carrots; and members of the cabbage family such as brussels sprouts or broccoli should be included for their vitamin, mineral, and fiber contents. Whole-grain meals and flours are good low-fat, low-calorie ingredients that can add valuable nutrients to a side dish, bread, or pasta.

BREAKFAST

Orange juice (1 fruit)
Toasted English muffin with peach or apple butter (2 grain)
Oatmeal with raisins and cinnamon (1 grain + 1 fruit)
Coffee with milk

LUNCH

Grilled chicken burrito in a flour tortilla with sour cream (1 grain)
Brown rice pilaf (1 grain)
Steamed yellow squash with fresh herbs and jalapeños (1 vegetable)
Skim milk (1 milk)

SNACK

Whole-wheat crackers (1 grain)
Low-fat yogurt with fresh peach slices (1 milk + 1 fruit)

DINNER

Cuban black bean soup (1 grain)
Tossed green salad with tomatoes and vinaigrette (2 vegtables)
Pan-seared pork on a bed of pumpkin pasta with a warm apple compote
(1 grain, 1 fruit)
Broccoli with lemon glaze (1 vegetable)
Strawberry shortcake (1 fruit, 1 grain)
Slice of whole-wheat baguette (1 grain)

been refined and purified, and in the process, have been stripped of nearly all other nutrients. One hundred years ago, the average American consumed less than 20 pounds of added sugars annually. Today, that figure is approaching 100 pounds per year. Instead of keeping refined or added sugars to less than 10% of the day's calories, most Americans now consume nearly twice the recommended amount. Artificial sweeteners have been used for decades by dieters and diabetics to help reduce added sugars in the diet. For a more complete discussion of these sweeteners, read Focus 3-2: Sugar Substitutes.

It is not always easy to identify foods that contain large amounts of added sugars. These ingredients are much cheaper than they were a century ago. They have become an important part of food processing, making their way into a wide variety of foods including cereals, spaghetti sauces, and frozen entrees that might not strike the average consumer as "sweet." Most people would benefit from reducing their intake of all added sugars in favor of whole foods that provide not only carbohydrates, but also a good supply of vitamins, minerals, and fiber.

FOCUS 3-2   SUGAR SUBSTITUTES

Artificial sweeteners are found in many processed "diet" foods and in a host of other products such as sodas, candies, gum, and toothpaste. The application of sugar substitutes in the kitchen is limited, however, because they are chemically different from sugar and function differently when replacing sugar in recipes. In addition, some artificial sweeteners have an unpleasant aftertaste or take on an unpleasant flavor when they are heated during baking or cooking. Three sugar substitutes currently used are saccharin, aspartame, and a relatively new sweetener, acesulfame-K.

There has been significant controversy regarding the safety of sugar substitutes. The Food and Drug Administration has banned the use of cyclamates simply on the basis that it has not been proven whether or not they cause inheritable genetic damage. Aspartame had approval of use granted, then withdrawn for seven years, and then granted again.

The label of products containing aspartame must warn of the presence of phenylalanine, a substance that cannot be metabolized by people who have a medical condition known as phenylketonuria (PKU). Saccharin, the oldest artificial sweetener, remains under scrutiny even though its use is approved. Public concern over studies correlating a high dosage of saccharin with bladder tumors in some laboratory rats led to the passage by the U.S. Congress of the 1977 Saccharin Study and Labeling Act, which requires a warning label to appear on products that contain saccharin.

In an effort to help consumers who have concerns about the potential risks involved with artificial sweeteners, Acceptable Daily Intake (ADI) levels have been established by the FDA for aspartame and acesulfame-K, which are considered safe when taken daily over a lifetime. At this time, the ADI for aspartame is 50 milligrams per kilogram of body weight; the ADI for acesulfame-K is 15 milligrams per kilogram of body weight. These levels were once thought to be so high that there would be little chance of ever exceeding them. There is growing concern that these ADI levels are becoming easier to reach as artificial sweeteners are used in more products than ever, especially those foods intended to appeal to youngsters.

WHAT ARE CARBOHYDRATES, AND WHY ARE THEY IMPORTANT?

Carbohydrates are an excellent energy source. In fact, they are preferred by the central nervous system and the brain. Carbohydrates are composed of smaller units containing carbon, hydrogen, and oxygen, known as sugars. Simple carbohydrates contain one or two sugars, while complex carbohydrates are long, branched chains of sugars that form starch or fiber. Both types of carbohydrate are necessary for the body to work efficiently and to maintain a store of energy that it can draw upon in times of need. The systems used to regulate the availability of energy are interesting from a personal health standpoint, and are discussed in Focus 3-3.

FOCUS 3-3   FEAST OR FAST, FIGHT OR FLIGHT

As food is taken into the body, it is broken down into its components by enzymes found in the saliva and the stomach. Proteins are broken down into amino acids, fats into glycerides, and carbohydrates into a simple sugar known as glucose.

Glucose is absorbed by the body during digestion and released into the blood, at which point it is sometimes known as blood sugar. When one's blood-sugar level rises too high (the feasting state), the pancreas releases insulin, a hormone that makes it possible for the glucose to be absorbed into the muscles or the liver. The liver can transform the glucose into glycogen or store it as fat. Regulation of the blood-sugar level is important to an individual's overall health and well-being.

When the body requires energy to perform sustained physical activity, glycogen stored in the muscles is burned up. In an emergency or during extreme stress, a hormone (epinephrine) that has the opposite effect from insulin is released so that glycogen stores will rapidly convert to glucose and flood the bloodstream. This "adrenaline rush," or "fight or flight" reaction, enables people to lift a weight several times their normal capacity in an emergency, to deal with highly charged, stressful situations, or to run away from danger.

After stores of glycogen have been depleted, a state known as fasting occurs. The body can draw necessary energy from protein or fat supplies. This is not the most desirable situation, because protein is best reserved for purposes such as repair and replacement of tissues. Fats require a sufficient supply of carbohydrates to burn completely. Lacking these, fats are broken down only partially, and toxins known as ketones accumulate in the blood, resulting in the potentially harmful state known as ketosis.

SIMPLE CARBOHYDRATES

Fruits, vegetables, and milk are the best sources of simple carbohydrates. These compounds, occasionally called *simple sugars*, are quickly absorbed by the bloodstream, and therefore are available for immediate use by the individual cells. An apple, for instance, provides quick energy because it has a good supply of simple carbohydrates in the form of the sugar called *fructose*. It also provides significant amounts of vitamins, minerals, water, and fiber.

There is another form of simple carbohydrates, the refined or added sugars. These are formed by concentrating and purifying simple carbohydrates found in other foods. This process may be done mechanically by man—in the case of table sugar, molasses, corn syrup, or maple syrup—or naturally by

3-1. *The array of vegetables and fruits in this photograph demonstrates the diversity of carbohydrate-rich foods. Apples, onions, carrots, parsnips, and pears are all excellent sources. Potatoes are usually thought of as a source of complex carbohydrates, but the tiny new potatoes shown here actually supply both simple and complex carbohydrates.*

bees, which produce honey from the nectar of flowers. Refined and added sugars provide energy in the form of calories but few, if any, additional nutrients.

Calories that provide energy and nothing else are considered empty. Moderating use of refined and added sugars, whether granular or pourable, man-made or from honeybees, to less than 10% of the day's calories is recommended. An appetite for healthful foods may be suppressed if the empty calories of a candy bar quiet hunger pangs. The net result of an eating pattern that substitutes empty calories for nutrient-dense foods is a form of malnutrition. See Focus 3-4: Eating Away at a Sweet Tooth.

FOCUS 3-4 EATING AWAY AT A SWEET TOOTH

Most nutritional guidelines recommend that added sugars, in the form of table sugar, honey, jams, and jellies, be limited to 10% of the total daily calories. The Food and Drug Administration has estimated that Americans consume about 20% of their daily calories, or approximately 80 pounds of added sugars, over the course of a year.

Where does it all come from? Candies, cookies, cakes, and ice cream are obvious offenders. A pool of maple syrup on pancakes and waffles and a big dollop of honey in a steaming cup of tea are others. The amount of sugar in even "healthy" foods such as bran muffins or carrot cake would probably surprise the average consumer.

Sugar has been the focus of a great deal of research to discover a possible link between eating too many sweets and a higher incidence of diseases such as diabetes mellitus, coronary artery disease, blood glucose abnormalities, and obesity. So far, no convincing evidence has been found. Consuming excessive calories in the form of candies, cookies, cakes, and ice cream is easy to do and can lead to obesity. A further problem with sugars is that they frequently are combined with generous amounts of fat such as shortening, butter, heavy cream, and eggs.

Sugar consumption also should be carefully controlled because its calories don't provide very many additional nutrients to the body. Probably the worst that can be proven of eating too much sugar, however, is that it is definitely linked to a higher incidence of tooth decay. Bacteria naturally present in the mouth combine with sugars (both added sugar and those from nutrient-rich carbohydrates) and form an acid that eats away at teeth, eventually leading to cavities. The best defense against tooth decay is to avoid sugary snacks between meals and to brush teeth thoroughly after meals.

COMPLEX CARBOHYDRATES

The foods that supply a rich source of complex carbohydrates include starches and starchy vegetables such as cereals, rice, wheat, corn, squashes, pumpkins, breads, cereals, potatoes, and pasta. Meals that incorporate large servings of these foods are beneficial in many ways: they are filling and generally lower in total calories and fats than high-protein or high-fat offerings. A serving of whole-grain waffles, pancakes, or hot cereal fills the stomach up because these foods are bulky. The stomach then signals the brain that it is full; this is the state known as "satiety." Hunger is appeased by consuming only a moderate number of these nutrient-dense, but high-volume calories. Fried eggs, bacon, or sausage have many more calories packed into a smaller volume. A traditional breakfast of high-fat foods might make it easy to eat too many calories, without getting a good supply of nutrients, long before the brain is signaled that the stomach is full.

The process of transforming complex carbohydrates into glucose can take up to four hours. Throughout this time, enzymes break the long chains into progressively smaller units. As units of glucose are freed from the complex carbohydrate, they can be readily absorbed into the bloodstream and used as a source of energy. Any surplus of glucose is handled in one of two ways. The liver can convert it into glycogen, the "backup" reserve that is used to meet energy needs when there is no glucose available in the blood. Or, if glycogen stores are full, the excess is converted into fat, for more long-term storage.

3-2. COMPLEX CARBOHYDRATES

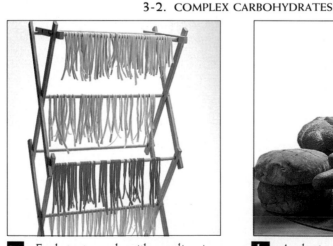

a *Fresh pasta made with semolina is an excellent and very popular way to introduce complex carbohyrates into the menu. Flavoring and coloring the pasta with (from top down) saffron, spinach, or beets is a good way to vary the basic recipe (shown on bottom).*

b *A selection of hearth-baked breads such as those shown here are another good way to boost the variety of complex carbohydrates offered to the guest.*

FIBER

Foods that contain simple and complex carbohydrates have been noted as energy sources that provide not only calories but also certain essential noncaloric elements such as fiber. Fiber has been referred to as nature's broom; a natural laxative, roughage, and bulk. Current studies have reinforced the notion that fiber is a valuable part of the diet. There are two types of fiber: soluble and insoluble. Both of them play important, and at times quite different, roles in human nutrition.

It is important to eat a variety of foods that are known to be sources of soluble and insoluble fiber. It is not normally necessary for a healthy individual to take fiber supplements. In fact, dietary supplements may cause some problems. It is easier to get too much when the fiber comes in the form of a pill or a drink. An excess of fiber could be responsible for nutrient depletion in individuals whose nutrient intake is marginal, as well as causing discomfort and bloating. A person who consumes high-fiber foods (whole grains, cereals, beans, fruits, and vegetables) instead of supplements will rarely be in danger of consuming an excess of it.

3-3. *There are two types of fiber: soluble and insoluble. Fiber is important in any healthy diet. Insoluble fiber found in various foods such as whole-grain breads, celery, beets, rye crackers, and lentils acts as a scrub brush, cleansing the digestive tract and speeding the passage of food through it. Soluble fibers swell, giving a feeling of fullness, and also help remove certain harmful substances from the bloodstream. Oats, strawberries, grapefruit, and apples are all good sources of soluble fiber.*

Insoluble Fiber

Insoluble fiber is the "roughage" that helps keep people "regular." Some sources of insoluble fiber include most fruits and vegetables, wheat bran, popcorn, nuts, and whole grain flours and meals. Rather than dissolving in water, insoluble fiber absorbs it like a sponge. Foods high in insoluble fiber often are considered "filling."

Insoluble fiber has the effect of speeding the transit of foods through the digestive tract. It has been theorized that insoluble fiber may cause high-calorie foods to be eliminated before all of their calories have been absorbed. Unfortunately, essential vitamins and minerals also may be lost to the body before they can be assimilated.

FOCUS 3-5   MIRACLE FOODS AND MEDIA MYTHS

Bran and bran products used to be sold primarily in health-food stores. Most people barely recognized bran as a good source of fiber. Few people went out of their way to purchase it, and the price that oat bran commanded was low indeed. When the media publicized a study that appeared to have found a link between an increased consumption of oat bran and lowered levels of blood cholesterol, consumer demand for this food grew dramatically.

Suddenly, supermarket aisles blossomed with new products that featured oat bran, such as cereals, prepared muffins, cookies, and cakes. Prices rose with demand. Serious research into the ways that diet can affect serum cholesterol levels had prompted a media field day. Oat bran was quickly put aside, however, when follow-up coverage seemed to disprove initial reports.

There aren't any miracle foods, of course, but marketing experts were aware that a healthy food would sell well. They had jumped on the bandwagon, promoting oat bran and related products, and leaving consumers with little guidance in sorting the good from the bad. A product may have contained large amounts of sugar, calories, sodium, cholesterol, and fat, but because the item contained oat bran it was declared healthful.

Claims on a label made by the producer can be misleading. Responsibility in advertising is an issue that will be debated for years to come. In the meantime, the best defense against misleading health claims is nutrition knowledge. The more educated consumers are about nutrition and its role in maintaining health, the less likely they are to blindly accept claims of "new and improved" products. The old saying, *caveat emptor* (let the buyer beware), is as wise advice today as it ever has been.

Soluble Fiber

Soluble fiber dissolves in water. Sources of soluble fiber include apples, beans, lentils, citrus fruits, potatoes, squashes, barley, and rice. Oat bran, an excellent source of soluble fiber, has received a great deal of attention because of its reputed ability to lower blood cholesterol levels. For a discussion of the way that this information was used to promote a variety of foods containing oat bran, read Focus 3-5: Miracle Foods and Media Myths.

Even though the human body cannot digest fiber, soluble fiber tends to slow the rate at which sugars are released into the bloodstream, so there is a delay before hunger returns. People on a weight-loss program can include soluble fiber in their meals to help curb hunger between meals, often making a sweet snack easier to resist.

PUTTING THE GUIDELINE TO WORK: CARBOHYDRATES IN THE KITCHEN

As side dishes and accompaniments gradually have gained importance on the menu, there is more awareness and use of fruits, vegetables, grains, and legumes. Because the variety and serving sizes of these foods is greater, the balance of the menu tends to be affected. The serving sizes of protein-rich foods gradually is being reduced. The nutritional benefit of this shift in emphasis is that patrons are offered more vitamins, minerals, and fiber in carbohydrate-rich foods and less fat and cholesterol and fewer calories in protein-rich foods.

FEATURING CARBOHYDRATES THROUGHOUT THE MENU

The chef may take several approaches, and many areas of the menu have potential for incorporating carbohydrates. Dishes such as paella, made with rice and vegetables and accompanied by a small "garnish" of lean chicken and shellfish, are appropriate for a number of different menu styles. An old standby such as spaghetti with tomato sauce is also an item suitable for featuring carbohydrate-rich ingredients. Additional possibilities include pizzas, Tex/Mex enchiladas or burritos, and Japanese simmered-noodle dishes. Vegetarian dishes can provide inspiration as well.

Sauces and accompaniments can increase the overall interest of the dish and increase the variety and quantity of carbohydrates provided. Some healthful choices include a vegetable-based sauce, a bed of a grain pilaf or risotto, a fresh salsa, or a chutney. Side dishes such as polenta or a pilaf of a "new" grain like quinoa can introduce a new flavor, color, and texture to guests. The bread basket is a fertile area for improving the carbohydrate content of a meal by offering breads, muffins, and crackers made with whole grains.

The chef can make appetizers from vegetables and grains, reserving high-protein or high-fat ingredients as garnish. Many soups are good vehicles for high-carbohydrate ingredients. For instance, a chowder may include potatoes, corn, and peppers; and garbures or potages may be created using grains, cabbages, peas, and other vegetables.

One carbohydrate source that receives a relatively smaller amount of attention is milk. If milk is offered as a beverage selection, low-fat or skim milk would be healthful menu additions. Lactose, the simple carbohydrate found in milk and milk-based products, is supplied by low-fat or nonfat yogurt, and ricotta, mozzarella, and cottage cheeses. Using these ingredients instead of higher-fat foods can help customers meet their carbohydrate needs without indulging in fats.

A dairy base made from pureed nonfat yogurt and ricotta cheese can be used to prepare frozen desserts and Bavarians. Desserts based on grains and fruits offer carbohydrates without necessarily introducing many added sugars. Some tips for boosting the sweetness of a dish without adding sugar are included in Focus 3-6: Sweetening without Adding Sugar.

FOCUS 3-6 SWEETENING WITHOUT ADDING SUGAR

The dietary guidelines from the U.S. Department of Agriculture recommend that consumption of added sweeteners and foods which contain them contribute less than 10% of the day's total calories. Added sugars are not the only substances that can make foods sweet. Simple carbohydrates found in fruits and milk products contain a certain amount of naturally occurring sugar that can satisfy the sweet tooth.

Sodas, sweet snacks, and even some processed foods such as spaghetti sauce are sources of much added sugar; however, desserts are probably the most challenging menu area for the chef when it comes to moderating the use of added sugar. It would be unreasonable for him or her to expect all patrons to completely forego sweet desserts. Humans universally like the sweet tastes featured in desserts. And there are some less tangible rewards, including a sense that the meal is finished, and that no one is getting up from the table "cheated" out of a special treat that everyone else gets to enjoy.

The following list of tips can help the chef maximize sweetness in foods, without boosting the amount of sugar, syrups, and other sweeteners.

- Use only the minimal amount of sugar, syrups, or other sweeteners necessary in a recipe to give it the desired flavor.
- Use sweet spices, such as allspice, cinnamon, cloves, nutmeg, and vanilla beans.
- Add ripe fruits, whole grains, and nuts for their sweetness and flavor.

- Use a puree of fruits as a base for soufflés, puddings, and dessert sauces. Ripe bananas, apple or pear purees, fresh or quick-frozen berries, and melons are a few suggestions.
- Use fruit juice concentrate as a sugar substitute. Apple, orange, and fruit juice blend concentrates are particularly flavorful choices.
- Use dried fruits such as raisins, currants, apricots, dates, figs, and prunes. If they are to be rehydrated, soak them in warm apple juice, and use the juice in the recipe, too.
- To sweeten a dessert, serve a small amount of a sweet sauce with it.
- Serve sweet dishes warm; warmth intensifies all flavors.

CHAPTER

4

Protein

In the United States, meat traditionally has been considered a primary source of valuable protein. In fact, many people in this country are accustomed to portions of meat that are considerably larger than is recommended for good health. Some patrons who believe that they require plenty of meat in their diets may be resistant to moderate-sized meat portions. To overcome such hesitancy, the chef may find it helpful to shift to recommended serving sizes in several stages. Gradual change is likely to be better received than an abrupt switch in menu items. One of the chef's goals should be to help customers consume 15–20% of their daily calories from protein without consuming excessive fat and calories. To calculate protein requirements according to the exchange system, read Focus 4-1: How Much Protein Do I Need?

The next step, and perhaps the hardest part of this battle, is to get the message across that humans don't eat pure protein, but foods that contain protein. Protein is contained in many foods; some are a better source than others. But a healthy diet would never rely upon any single food for any nutrient. Providing a variety of foods is the key to making sure that a person's protein needs are adequately met.

FOCUS 4-1 HOW MUCH PROTEIN DO I NEED?

It is important to maintain a balance of nutrients so that the body can properly metabolize each one and use it most effectively. About 15–20% of a day's calories should be supplied by protein. For a 2,000-daily-calorie diet that works out to 300–400 calories, or 75–100 grams of protein.

The exchange system considers a single exchange of lean meat to be 7 grams of protein, and 3 grams of fat. At the 2,000-daily-calorie level, just six exchanges are adequate to meet the guideline. Why isn't the number ten to twelve exchanges? The answer is simple: foods from other groups, especially the milk and grains groups, also contain some protein. The exchange system accounts for this.

A person following a vegetarian diet will need to make some different food choices from among the six food groups in order to adequately meet his or her protein needs. Strict vegans should substitute soy milk or other calcium-rich foods to replace the protein and calcium found in milk and milk products. Meat, poultry, and fish exchanges should be replaced with exchanges of protein-rich legumes, nuts, and grains.

The volume of food eaten by a vegetarian who conscientiously selects a varied, healthy diet from among the food groups will be far greater than that consumed by a meat-eating individual. One exchange of meat is a small, 1-ounce cube, while an exchange of whole-wheat pasta, cooked cornmeal or grits, or bulgur wheat is ½ cup. Beans such as lentils or black beans are ⅓ cup per exchange, as is an exchange of a baked yam or sweet potato.

BREAKFAST

Orange juice
Toasted English muffin with peach or apple butter
Oatmeal with raisins and cinnamon
Coffee with milk

LUNCH

Grilled chicken burrito in a flour tortilla with sour cream (2 meat)
Brown rice pilaf
Steamed yellow squash with fresh herbs and jalapeños
Skim milk

SNACK

Whole-wheat cracker
Low-fat yogurt with fresh peach slices

DINNER

Cuban black bean soup
Tossed green salad with tomatoes and vinaigrette
Pan-seared pork on a bed of pumpkin pasta with a warm apple compote
(4 meat)
Broccoli with lemon glaze
Strawberry shortcake
Slice of whole-wheat baguette

WHAT IS PROTEIN, AND WHY IS IT IMPORTANT?

Protein is one of the essential nutrients. Foods that provide significant amounts of protein include meats, fish, poultry, grains, dairy products, eggs, legumes, nuts, and seeds. Like carbohydrates and fats, protein provides calories that can be used by the body as a source of energy. There are, however, many vital functions that only proteins can perform. Ideally, the other nutrients should provide enough energy so that protein is spared to do the jobs it is uniquely able to perform.

The basic building blocks of protein are known as amino acids. The multitude of proteins found in human cells are composed of about twenty amino acids (see Table 4-1). Most of these are produced by the body. The

TABLE 4-1.

THE AMINO ACIDS

ESSENTIAL	CONDITIONALLY ESSENTIAL	OTHERS
Isoleucine	Arginine	Alanine
Leucine	Cysteine	Aspartic acid
Lysine	*Histidine	Cystine
Methionine	Tyrosine	Glutamic acid
Phenylalanine		Glutamine
Threonine		Glycine
Tryptophan		Proline
Valine		Serine

* Essential for infants and small children.

eight essential amino acids that cannot be produced in the body must be supplied by the diet. All protein-rich foods contain some of these eight and some contain all of them. Certain other amino acids are known as "conditionally essential." Normally, the body can produce them from the eight essential amino acids. When they are not consumed in sufficient amounts, a dietary source may become important for them. The presence or lack of the various amino acids makes it possible to categorize foods as either complete or incomplete proteins.

COMPLETE PROTEINS

The reason that meats have achieved such instant recognition as protein-rich foods is that they have a good supply of all eight essential amino acids in the correct ratio. Any protein that meets both of these requirements can be used most efficiently by the body to support the production of other proteins. Foods such as beef, chicken, pork, and lamb are referred to as "complete proteins" and "high-quality proteins." These terms tend to encourage people to falsely assume that the protein derived from animal sources is somehow "better for you" than that derived from plants. This is one of the reasons that there is so much initial resistance to menus that downplay the importance or size of a meat serving. Some people equate this change with incipient vegetarianism. They may actually be concerned that such a diet could be hazardous to their health.

Diets that exclude or limit animal proteins are far from being universally embraced. On the contrary, they are viewed with skepticism. A brief guide to vegetarianism is found in Focus 4-2: Themes and Variations in Vegetarianism.

Animal products provide good-quality protein in a readily digestible form. However, they also may contain saturated fats and cholesterol. Table 4-2 gives examples of protein food sources that are lean, medium-fat, and high-fat.

4-1. *Meats, poultry, and fish are recognized as good sources of complete proteins—containing sufficient amounts of all eight essential amino acids for the body to use to carry out necessary functions such as building or repairing tissues. From top, counterclockwise, are salmon, lobster, sausage, lamb tenderloins, calf's tongue. In the center are mussels and clams, beef tenderloin, scallops, and chicken.*

TABLE 4-2.

SOME EXAMPLES OF LEAN, MEDIUM-FAT, AND

HIGH-FAT PROTEIN-RICH FOODS

LEAN	MEDIUM-FAT	HIGH-FAT
Beef tenderloin, round steak	Corned beef, chuck	Hamburger; club or rib steaks
Chicken or turkey, without skin	Ground-round steak	Breast of lamb
Leg of lamb	Pork roast, liver, heart, kidney	Duck, goose
White-fleshed fish (flounder, halibut)	Fatty fish (salmon, tuna)	Cold cuts
	Eggs	Hot dogs
Cottage cheese, dry	Cottage cheese, creamed	Cheddar cheese

FOCUS 4-2   THEMES AND VARIATIONS IN VEGETARIANISM

As more and more Americans consider themselves vegetarians, the interpretation of what a vegetarian is varies from one person to another. The reasons for becoming a vegetarian are as different as there are types of vegetarians. Some people are vegetarians for religious, moral, and ethical reasons, believing that it is wrong to kill and eat another living being. Other vegetarians are more concerned with the health benefits they may receive by reducing their consumption of fat and cholesterol in foods like steaks or pork chops. Still others may choose such a diet because meats and fish as a regular part of their meals may be beyond their financial means. The motivating factors often tend to be a combination of concerns.

Vegetarians known as *vegans* have the most restrictive diets. They eat no foods of animal origin. Their diet consists of vegetables, fruits, grains, cereals, nuts, and legumes. This style of vegetarianism can usually provide a balanced supply of amino acids and other nutrients, with the possible exception of vitamin B-12, which is naturally supplied only by meats. Taking a dietary supplement of this vitamin can help maintain an adequate level.

Lacto-ovo vegetarians consume the same foods eaten by vegans, but also include milk, cheese, and eggs in their diets. The addition of these protein-rich foods increases the likelihood of getting a supply of all eight essential amino acids.

There are even further modifications of vegetarianism. Some people who refer to themselves as vegetarians occasionally eat small amounts of fish. Others eat virtually any food except red meats.

Whatever the reasons for and style of vegetarianism adopted by someone, these diets are not likely to be harmful. Unless there is an undue emphasis on moderate to high-fat ingredients such as cheeses and tofu, vegetarian diets may even be superior because they tend to be lower in fats than a typical diet that includes meat. Even children reared on vegetarian diets show no major deficiencies, as long as care is taken to select varied food sources so that the diet meets the general recommendations for healthy eating.

INCOMPLETE PROTEINS

Meats, fish, poultry, and dairy products are not the only good sources of dietary protein. Many vegetables, grains, dried legumes, and nuts also have significant amounts of protein. The difference is that they either do not have all eight essential amino acids, or they lack a sufficient supply of one or more of them. These proteins are referred to as *incomplete* proteins. When there are insufficient supplies of one or more of the essential amino acids in a protein, the other amino acids that are present cannot be used and are wasted.

A diet that over the course of a day includes a variety of protein-rich foods is likely to provide an adequate supply of the amino acids required by a healthy individual. The importance of including some source of a complete protein at every meal has been greatly exaggerated. In the next section on complementary proteins, this issue will be given additional consideration.

COMPLEMENTARY PROTEINS

Vegetarians have long been aware that the proteins present in grains can be made *complete* by eating legumes with them. This practice is sometimes called *mutual supplementation*. Properly combining foods so that there is enough of each amino acid may seem like an overwhelming task. It is not necessary to memorize the amino acid content of many different foods, however.

An easier way to make appropriate selections and combinations is to consider which plant foods are the best sources of protein. The three groups of plant foods that are the best protein sources are grains and cereals, beans

4-2. VEGETABLE SOURCES OF PROTEIN

a *Beans, an excellent source of protein, are generally lacking in sufficient amounts of one or more essential amino acids. Combining beans with either grains or nuts and seeds makes the proteins complete, which is known as "mutual supplementation." Shown here are (from top left, clockwise) navy beans, cranberry beans, lentils, black beans, pony beans, yellow soldier beans, kidney beans, split peas, and (in center) flageolets.*

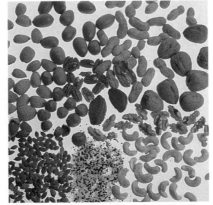

b *Nuts and seeds are also a good source of protein, as well as a concentrated source of energy in the form of fat. Shown here (from bottom left, counterclockwise) are pumpkin seeds, black and natural sesame seeds, cashews, walnuts, pecans, peanuts, almonds, hazelnuts (or filberts), and brazil nuts.*

c *In addition to their role as a good source of complex carbohydrates, cereals, grains, and meals offer a significant amount of protein. From top left, clockwise, are whole-grain bread, whole-wheat spaghetti, orecchiette, red bliss potatoes, spinach fettucini, cornmeal, bulgur wheat, couscous, kasha, whole-wheat crackers, wild and brown rices, and tricolor fusilli in the center.*

and peas, and nuts and seeds. When at least two of these three groups are represented in a meal, adequate supplies of the essential amino acids will be provided. Adding dairy products or eggs can also enhance the quality of the protein in a dish, making it complete.

The traditional dishes from cuisines that rely upon plant foods as their major (or only) source of protein are all excellent examples of this practice. Lentils and rice, pasta and beans, tortillas and beans, tofu and rice, or hummus and pita bread are a few examples. For further understanding, read Focus 4-3: Mutual Supplementation.

Recent studies have shown that the body does not insist upon having all eight essential amino acids consumed in the same forkful in order to use them properly. A diet need not be balanced at each meal, but rather should be balanced over the course of a day.

FOCUS 4-3   MUTUAL SUPPLEMENTATION

There is no mystery to getting adequate protein supplies in a vegetarian diet, even a strict vegan diet that includes no animal foods. A vegetable protein can be made nutritionally complete by mutual supplementation—simply selecting at least one component from two out of the three major sources of vegetable proteins. The three groups are grains and cereals, legumes, and nuts and seeds. A variety of dishes prepared from complementary protein groups is listed below.

DISH	GRAINS	LEGUMES	NUTS/SEEDS
Hoppin' John	Rice	Black-eyed peas	—
Pita and hummus	Bread	Chick peas	Sesame seeds
Pasta e fagioli	Pasta	Navy beans	—
Moors and Christians	Rice	Black beans	—
Peanut butter sandwich	Bread	—	Peanut butter

If one's diet permits, milk, cheese, eggs, or a very small amount of chicken or fish added to a dish can round out its amino acids. A stir-fry of vegetables served on rice will be "completed" by a very small garnish of chicken or fish. Milk poured over oatmeal will boost the cereal's protein level; low-fat cheese on a baked potato enhances its nutritional value; and an egg added to rice pudding will do the same for this grain-based dessert.

While cheese, eggs, and tofu are sources of good quality protein, they are relatively high in fat. Their use should be monitored so that the amount of fat in an individual's diet does not exceed the 30% of one's total daily calories.

GETTING ENOUGH PROTEIN

Protein-deficiency diseases can be extremely dangerous, even fatal, if allowed to continue without adequate treatment. Such diseases are usually not a problem for most Americans. As a matter of fact, health risks associated with the overconsumption of protein are more likely to be of concern. These problems include obesity, loss of calcium, and dehydration. Focus 4-4: Protein Intake and Osteoporosis further discusses a condition aggravated by a diet that places undue emphasis on protein.

The Food and Nutrition Board of the National Academy of Sciences has established a formula for determining the protein needs of adults. This formula, shown in Worksheet 4-1, assumes that a person eats a variety of protein-rich foods from both plant and animal sources.

Protein requirements for most adults average between 6 and 8 ounces per day. Many people eat more than that amount in a single meal, often without being aware that they have done so. For example, protein is found in bread, vegetables, grains, potatoes, beans, and nuts as well as in meat, poultry, fish, dairy products, and eggs.

The Recommended Dietary Allowance (RDA) for protein is considered more than adequate by many nutritionists. It allows 0.8 grams of protein for each kilogram of weight for healthy adults. They believe that most people could get along with less, possibly with greater benefits to their overall health. The problem with a diet that favors meats, eggs, and cheese is that along with too much protein come fats, cholesterol, and calories. Furthermore, the body is not equipped to use excess protein. Any excess amino acids are broken down and reorganized into fat, which can be stored with almost no limit. Excessive storage of fat can lead to obesity, one of Americans' major health hazards.

FOCUS 4-4   PROTEIN INTAKE AND OSTEOPOROSIS

The loss of height that many people experience as they grow old is the result of adult bone loss, also called osteoporosis. A number of risk factors are associated with osteoporosis, but one of the primary areas is a chronic shortage of calcium. Even though it is well known that children need milk to grow healthy bones and teeth, many people may not be aware that an adequate calcium supply is just as important to adults.

Calcium, along with phosphorous and fluoride, is critical to the development of bones and teeth, where nearly all one's calcium supply is concentrated. A small but important amount of calcium circulates in the blood and within the cells to carry

continued ➤

out regulatory functions related to blood pressure, blood clotting, proper nerve transmission, and muscle contractions.

When the calcium level in the bloodstream drops, this mineral is drawn from the bones. Storage in the bones is then replenished as the body absorbs a new calcium supply. A person's ability to absorb calcium is directly related to the body's needs. During times of rapid growth, infants and adolescents absorb about 60% of the calcium present in their diets. Fully grown adults might absorb only 10% (even with abundant supplies constantly available from their diets). An excess of protein-rich foods such as meats appears to impede calcium absorption because it encourages the body to excrete dietary calcium, rather than assimilate it.

Western countries, such as the United States and Canada, have set daily calcium requirements higher than those of other countries. This has been done partly to offset the higher animal protein diets that people in Western countries tend to have.

A diet should include an adequate calcium supply throughout one's lifetime. Cigarette smoking, drug and alcohol abuse, and prolonged drug therapy can compromise bone strength and calcium reserves. Drinking milk or eating foods such as dark-green, leafy vegetables and canned tomatoes (which are processed with calcium salts) are good practices. Although protein appears to inhibit calcium absorption, eating foods rich in vitamin C may increase absorption up to 50%. Other positive practices include performing regular weight-bearing exercises such as jogging or walking to work the bones. Women may consider estrogen therapy at the time of, or even before, menopause to help prevent osteoporosis, since it appears that decreased production of this hormone accelerates bone loss.

WORKSHEET 4-1.
CALCULATING PERSONAL PROTEIN NEEDS

The RDA (Recommended Dietary Allowance) for protein varies according to a person's age and weight. The formula shown here can be used by adults to determine their need for protein, based on body weight.

Step 1. Convert body weight to kilograms by dividing pounds by 2.2. For example,

$$154 \text{ lbs.} \div 2.2 = 70 \text{ kilograms}$$

Step 2. Calculate grams of protein needed per day by multiplying body weight in kilograms by 0.8 grams. For example,

$$70 \text{ kilograms} \times 0.8 \text{ grams} = 56 \text{ grams of protein}$$

Factors That Change Protein Needs

Protein requirements can be affected by several factors. Vegetarians may need to increase the suggested RDA for protein by about 15%. Those on a meat-and-potatoes diet should decrease the RDA for protein by 15%. Children, pregnant women, and nursing mothers require more protein to support growth. Illness, infections, attacks on the immune system, and malnutrition can have consequences on how much protein the body needs and how well it can use the protein it receives. Life-style, previous eating habits, and health history should all be taken into account if an individualized menu plan is being prepared.

PUTTING THE GUIDELINE TO WORK: PROTEIN IN THE KITCHEN

There is wisdom in introducing changes in portion sizes gradually rather than abruptly. A guest who is used to eating an entire Cornish game hen, for example, will most certainly feel unsatisfied if a plate with just a breast on it is served. The first suggestion, then, is to allow the staff as well as the patrons to become comfortable with the new portion size by making several intermediary changes.

Another way to serve smaller portions of animal-source proteins without alarming guests is to use new plating techniques. For instance, a pork tenderloin can be roasted, sliced thinly on the bias, and then fanned out on the plate. Chicken or salmon cutlets can be gently pounded to increase their surface area and make them look larger, even after they are cooked.

When the size of the piece of meat, poultry, or fish is kept at the recommended portion size (3½ ounces or 100 grams), the other elements need to lend a bountiful appearance to the plate. Grain pilafs, ratatouilles, "noodles" of summer squash, beds of pasta or wilted greens can provide generous plate coverage. The chef should combine foods to create effective presentations. Pleasing the guest's eye helps him or her feel satisfied. Many dishes that combine grains with legumes, nuts, seeds, and vegetables like potatoes or squashes can be made appealing, even to nonvegetarians. These types of protein-rich entrées tend to be low in fats and high in carbohydrates.

The chef should develop a variety of dishes that rely on meats that are naturally low in fats, such as pork or beef tenderloin, chicken breast, flank steak, and catfish. Fatty cuts like spareribs and organ meats such as sweetbreads should be used sparingly, as should typically high-fat fillings like forcemeats or sausages.

Salt and Sodium

Sodium is one of the minerals the body needs in order to function properly. Table salt, a compound of sodium and chloride, is the form of sodium with which most people are familiar, but there are many other food sources. Some foods—milk, meats, cheeses—contain significant amounts of sodium naturally. Sodium may also be added to foods during processing. In fact, there is so much sodium in so many foods and beverages that most people get several times the amount they actually need.

Salt and other sodium compounds, such as sodium citrate or sodium phosphate, are frequently used as additives in processed foods. Salt has the ability to preserve foods and protect them from a variety of pathogens.

Is reducing sodium important? For many years, it was considered an article of truth that diets high in salt and sodium would lead to high blood pressure (hypertension). Today, however, the relationship between sodium and hypertension is not regarded as conclusively understood. No single study has shown a positive correlation between a high-sodium diet and high blood pressure for the general public. Reactions to sodium may vary greatly from person to person.

In fact, there is no definitive prescription for preventing hypertension. Controlling dietary sodium, maintaining a healthy body weight, exercising, moderating alcohol consumption, and quitting smoking appear to help treat hypertension once it is diagnosed. This has led many medical authorities to recommend reducing sodium consumption to less than 3,000 milligrams, along with making other positive adjustments to life-style as a way to prevent hypertension's onset.

The task of moderating salt consumption involves more than just limiting what is added at the table. It also requires reducing the amount of salt added during cooking, and reducing the reliance on high-sodium processed and convenience foods. An important step is encouraging chefs to find new ways to flavor and season foods. Several techniques are discussed throughout this chapter.

WHAT IS SODIUM AND WHY IS IT IMPORTANT?

Sodium is a noncaloric mineral that is essential to the regulation of body functions. Sodium helps maintain the body's normal fluid balance. Its role in this balance has led researchers to note the possible link between sodium levels and the incidence of hypertension in some individuals. A more detailed explanation of the role of sodium in hypertension is found in Focus 5-1: How Much Salt Is Too Much? One of the many forms in which sodium is available is the compound, sodium chloride, also known as table salt. However, the salt that chefs add to foods during preparation of a dish and that guests add at the table is only a portion of the sodium one might consume. A list of kinds of salt follows.

Table Salt: Fine-grained sodium chloride is mixed with a trace amount of an anti-caking agent, such as calcium silicate.

Iodized Salt: Sodium or potassium iodide is added to table salt to prevent the formation of goiter, an enlargement of the thyroid gland caused by iodine deficiency.

Kosher Salt or Coarse Salt: Chemically identical to table salt, kosher salt contains no additives.

Sea Salt: The unrefined salt crystals left when sea water evaporates. Coarse- or fine-grained, sea salt contains trace amounts of minerals that may impart color or flavor.

Light Salt or Salt Replacements: These are salt substitutes partially or entirely formed from potassium chloride.

FOCUS 5-1   HOW MUCH SALT IS TOO MUCH?

If an individual were to develop a sodium deficiency, it would be a serious condition. He or she might lose his or her appetite, experience muscle cramps, and lose the abilities to concentrate, remember, and perform mentally challenging tasks. The chance of such a deficiency, however, is small. For most Americans, consuming too much sodium is of greater concern.

Normally, an excess of salt and sodium can be filtered out of the body through the kidneys. A salty lunch or a package of potato chips often stimulates a compelling thirst. After a person drinks fluids, the body produces a special hormone that helps the kidneys excrete sodium. When this normal sequence is interrupted, either through an inherited sodium sensitivity or through a temporary condition, the excess sodium apparently is transferred to the smooth muscle lining the artery walls. As a result, the muscles contract, constricting the arteries, which ultimately causes high blood pressure.

The exact sequence followed by the body when too much salt or high-sodium food is ingested is not perfectly clear. There is as yet no certain relationship between the foods eaten and the development of hypertension. It appears, however, that once hypertension is diagnosed, controlling sodium in the diet has a positive effect for most individuals, especially paired with weight loss and stress management.

Sodium intake should be limited to 1 gram per 1,000 daily calories, up to a maximum of 3 grams in a day.

Restricting sodium, especially salt, and losing excess weight helps to lower even mild cases of high blood pressure. A basic step in controlling sodium intake is

continued ►

to base one's diet on whole, fresh, unprocessed foods. In addition, the individual should strictly moderate consumption of canned and processed foods, and high-sodium foods such as smoked meats and fish, cheese, snack foods, olives, pickles, sauces, and prepared condiments such as mustard.

Salt is one of the most basic seasonings used in a kitchen. When it is added to foods in discrete amounts, it has the effect of heightening their flavors, usually with far less salt than many chefs are accustomed to using.

In addition to its role in maintaining body functions, sodium also is important in food preservation. When refrigeration was not readily available, various foods were commonly treated with salt so that they could be stored for long periods. This was due to the fact that salt inhibits the growth of molds and bacteria that cause spoilage by drawing out enough moisture to discourage that growth. For this reason, it is used as a preservative in canned, packaged, and processed foods. In addition, many people enjoy the taste of pickled, brined, corned, cured, and smoked foods.

Processed foods are likely to be the largest source of sodium, even if they don't taste salty. A list of the key terms to look for in the ingredients list is found in Table 5-1. Descriptive terms used on the label are defined in Table 5-2.

5-1. *Anchovies, pickles, Parmesan cheese, green peppercorns, miso paste, mustard, capers, salami, Edam cheese, and pickles all have a lot of sodium. These ingredients need not be excluded, but they should be handled with care.*

TABLE 5-1.

HIDDEN SODIUM SOURCES

TYPE	ROLE
Monosodium glutamate (MSG)	Flavor enhancer
Sodium benzoate	Preservative
Sodium caseinate	Thickener and binder
Sodium citrate	Buffer, used to control acidity in soft drinks
Sodium nitrite	Curing agent in meat
Sodium phosphate	Emulsifier, stabilizer
Sodium propionate	Mold inhibitor
Sodium saccharin	Artificial sweetener

TABLE 5-2.

MINIGLOSSARY OF SODIUM TERMS ON FOOD LABELS

Sodium free	Less than 5 mg per serving
Very-low sodium	35 mg or less per serving
Low sodium	140 mg or less per serving
Reduced sodium	Processed to reduce the usual level of sodium by 75%
Unsalted	Processed without the normally used salt
Low salt	Made with less salt than the regular variety of the same food

Today, salt is most desirable for its ability to make foods taste better. It is the taste of salt that many people have learned to like, even crave, in many foods. Canned soups, for example, could be made with even less salt than is found in "low-sodium" items, but such products are perceived as bland and dull by most consumers. In the following section, a number of different strategies for reducing sodium in cooking are given.

PUTTING THE GUIDELINE TO WORK: SALT AND SODIUM IN THE KITCHEN

One of the greatest concerns for chefs and patrons alike is that without salt, foods would be tasteless. Salt's major function in cooking today is to enhance flavor. Other capabilities of salt, such as preserving foods and inhibiting bacterial and fungal growth, can be fulfilled in other ways—refrigeration, freeze-drying, or vacuum-packaging. Therefore, the major focus of this section will be to describe alternative ways to season foods.

CREATING A PALETTE OF FLAVORS

If a nutritional menu selection is to achieve acceptance, it must be perceived as satisfying. Foods that are likely to be most appealing are those with rich, substantial flavors. Clearly, a menu description that boasts of fresh, crisp salad greens with a pungent dressing and grilled, marinated flank steak and a side dish of spicy green beans has more immediate appeal than a plate of plain boiled rice, poached chicken, and broccoli.

It is often helpful to think of menu items in terms of their flavor potential. Not every single offering needs to be big and bold. There should be a balance of flavors: some delicate and subtle, some more pronounced, still others to act as background flavors to carry other ingredients. The best way to achieve a good flavor mix is to select a good variety of foods. The chef should inspect foods for quality before purchasing or accepting an order.

HIGHLIGHTING NATURAL FLAVORS

When herbs, spices, and sauces are poorly chosen or too liberally used, they can obscure the natural taste of foods. Similarly, an excessive use of salt can overwhelm the natural flavors of ingredients. Over an extended time, heavy use of salt can even kill one's taste sensitivity. As the tastebuds are weaned from salt, an appreciation for foods' natural flavors returns.

5-2. High-acid foods have bright, sharp flavors that often can replace salt. Apple cider and red wine vinegar; dry red and white wines; citrus fruits such as limes, oranges, lemons, tangerines, and grapefruits; and tomatoes are all naturally high in acid.

FOCUS 5-2   SPICES AND HERBS FOR FLAVOR

The wide range of available spices and herbs can be used to great advantage in nutritional cooking. To enhance foods that seem lackluster, one can add a savory herb such as basil, dill, oregano, thyme, bay leaf, sage, lemon balm, savory, epazote, or coriander. Fresh herbs can give a new, different accent to familiar foods. Sage, for example, gives a lift to simple bean dishes. Coriander has become essential to salsas and relishes that accompany Oriental and Mexican dishes.

Any of the numerous chilies can add heat to a dish. Varieties such as anaheim, ancho, pasilla, and habañero are increasingly available in both fresh and dried forms. Other spices that can enliven dishes include fresh or powdered gingerroot, garlic, peppercorns (black, green, or white), paprika, chili and curry blends, and cayenne pepper. Mustard in any of its forms—including powder, seeds, and a prepared condiment—is a well-liked, pungent flavoring. Freshly grated horseradish or a prepared condiment made from brined horseradish can add a noticeable kick to menu items.

Herbs that offer intense, unique flavors include tarragon, fennel and anise seeds, marjoram, cilantro, and chervil. Rosemary is another intense, almost "piney" taste that complements richly flavored foods. These herbs are likely to have a strong impact, so it is important to pair them with foods that have pronounced flavors. The chef should use these herbs frequently, but add them sparingly, lest other flavors in a dish be overwhelmed. Herbs are particularly delicious when used in grilling and roasting.

Citrus fruits, including lemons, limes, oranges, tangerines, and grapefruits, and flavored vinegars are superb at giving a refreshing taste to foods without increasing their sodium levels. Onions, garlic, shallots, scallions, and chives lend a sharp taste and aroma to dishes. Combining and contrasting spices, herbs, and other distinctive flavoring agents can help the chef moderate the sodium level in dishes while enhancing the robust flavors of their ingredients.

Reducing salt in cooking, unless for a sodium-restricted clientele, should be a gradual process. An abrupt change could unexpectedly and unpleasantly shock the taste buds of diners. Ideally the chef will allow both the kitchen and wait staffs and the customers to become used to moderate taste changes in incremental stages, rather than impose a new, stringent philosophy on them. While salt content is being reduced, new strategies for seasoning foods and combining flavors can be introduced.

Spices and herbs, aromatic ingredients, citrus juices, vinegars, and cooking techniques are appropriate ways to accentuate flavors. The accompanying Focus 5-2: Spices and Herbs for Flavor describes some specific ingredients and the range of flavors that they can contribute to foods.

GETTING THE MOST FROM THE LEAST

Salt and high-sodium ingredients such as soy sauce, olives, and capers need not be eliminated from use in cooking. The chef simply needs to maximize the impact that can be achieved with a small amount of these flavorful ingredients. This was true for fats and protein; it is just as true for salt.

The following is an example of how to modify a dish to lower its salt content. A traditional approach to preparing a grilled tuna steak with capers would probably be similar to this one: Make a marinade of oil, vinegar, lemon juice, capers, and salt and pepper. Add the tuna and let it marinate briefly. Blot the steak to remove the excess marinade, and grill it to the correct doneness. Add salt and pepper to taste, and top with a compound butter (a mixture of butter, capers, lemon juice, salt, and pepper). Moderating salt (and fat) in this dish is not difficult. Consider the points at which salt is used, and identify their relative importance. The salt in the marinade is probably not important, nor is it necessary to add a lot of salt to taste if the customer has a shaker on the table. The compound butter should be replaced by another sauce—for example, ratatouille. The amount of sodium in the capers is sufficient to flavor this sauce without requiring additional salt.

When salt is added to foods early in the cooking process, some of its flavor effectiveness may be lost. Often the chef adds more salt just before the dish is served. Less total salt is used when salt is eliminated from the cooking process and is added by the chef just before serving to adjust the flavor to taste, or by the patron after the dish is sampled.

Because many patrons have come to expect food to be salted before it is served, seasoning should be checked before a dish leaves the kitchen. There should never be the impression that the chef forgot to add salt.

High-sodium ingredients may be used to replace some or all of the salt called for in a recipe. Examples of such foods include Parmesan or Romano cheese, green peppercorns, capers, anchovies, pickles, olives, and mustard. These salty ingredients should be added first so that the chef can check the taste before deciding to add more salt. Sodium may be heavily concentrated in the brine surrounding ingredients such as pickles, olives, capers, and green peppercorns. The chef may prefer to rinse away the brine. If this brine is rinsed off, there will still be plenty of saltiness in the foods.

CHAPTER

6

Vitamins and Minerals

There is no "wonder" food that contains every essential nutrient in the right proportions. And there is certainly no single pill or supplement that can make up for a diet that is not well balanced. The best way to ensure that an individual diet is healthy is to consume a variety of foods. A menu or diet plan that offers a wide array of choices is certainly more interesting than taking pills or supplements, and it is also a good way to make use of seasonal items, special products, and unusual ingredients.

Fresh, high-quality, properly prepared foods are the best. The ideal is to keep refined, processed convenience foods to a minimum. Food purchasing and preparation techniques should be adapted to the different needs of specific operations. Large-scale foodservice establishments may rely upon frozen or canned foods more than a smaller bistro might. In all situations, the chef has a responsibility to provide the most nutritious food possible. Cooking techniques should be chosen for their ability to retain as many nutrients as possible.

Foods differ in the types and quantities of vitamins and minerals they contain. While research is still being conducted to determine the optimum levels for the different nutrients, it is clear that a varied diet helps achieve a balance and usually eliminates the need to be concerned with either deficiencies or excesses. In fact, there is no particular benefit in vitamin and mineral supplementation if an individual is making wise food choices, unless there is a specific medical reason to do so. Vitamin pills often lull people into a false sense of security, and they may feel that the pills are taking care of their nutritional needs. Read Focus 6-1: Vitamin and Mineral Supplements: Help or Hoax? for a more in-depth discussion.

WHAT ARE VITAMINS AND MINERALS, AND WHY ARE THEY IMPORTANT?

Cereal boxes with labels that proclaim "Fortified with Eight Essential Vitamins and Minerals" are so much a part of the American food scene that most people seldom stop to consider that it hasn't been such a long time since vitamins as such were first identified. However, folk medicines and cures were used long before the existence of vitamins and minerals was known. These age-old treatments included poultices, teas, and elixirs made from roots, herbs, and other vitamin- and mineral-rich foodstuffs. As scientists learn more about the specific qualities of vitamins and minerals and their roles in maintaining health and promoting healing, much of this folk wisdom has become verified.

Vitamins and minerals, like water, are noncaloric nutrients. Although they are important to overall health, they are generally needed in smaller quantities than the energy-providing nutrients. Recommended Dietary Allowances (RDAs) have been established for many, though not all, of the vitamins and minerals known to be important for good health. These levels are normally sufficient to maintain health and to prevent any deficiency diseases from devel-

FOCUS 6-1   VITAMIN AND MINERAL SUPPLEMENTS: HELP OR HOAX?

Throughout most of this book, satisfying normal nutrient requirements through a diet containing a variety of foods is urged. Recommended daily allowances for several nutrients have been developed. These allowances are considered sufficient to maintain health and avoid deficiency diseases. Yet, many Americans take additional vitamin E to help heal dry skin, a cut, or burn, and additional vitamin C to either ward off or cure a cold. Do such tactics work?

A great deal of research still needs to be done before anyone can say with certainty that there are some absolute guidelines for vitamin and mineral use. There is, however, enough evidence to form some opinion about the value of vitamin and mineral supplementation. For most people, there is no strong evidence that taking a once-a-day multivitamin with minerals makes a big difference in their health, as long as they are eating properly. A pill or capsule will not make up for a poor diet, no matter what the supplement's label may claim. After all, these pills offer only vitamins, minerals, and some amino acids. They do not provide carbohydrates, fiber, water, and other nutrients that may not fit into the formulation of a pill.

There are some cases in which supplementation is advisable. For strict vegans who eat no animal foods and may be deficient in vitamin B-12, the only way to get this vitamin is to take it as a supplement. Certain health conditions may indicate the need for supplements of minerals such as iron or calcium, if it is not possible to obtain enough of that nutrient through the foods that are consumed. Pregnancy, for example, greatly increases one's need for iron, and there is a definite benefit to getting the additional stores needed through supplementation.

But can megadoses of vitamins and minerals cure or prevent diseases? No one knows the answer to that question. What is understood, however, is that megadoses can cause a buildup of toxic levels of vitamins and minerals in the body. Once that happens, one may suffer a number of related illnesses, from nausea to depression, and possibly death.

oping. The RDAs have been generalized to suit an entire group from within the total population. This means that some people within that population might fall outside the standards established as normal. This has led to speculation by members of the scientific and health communities that the optimal levels for some vitamins and minerals may actually be higher than the established RDAs for individuals whose diets supply only marginally adequate levels of specific nutrients. There is a strong possibility that indiscriminate supplementation of certain vitamins and minerals could be hazardous to one's health. For a listing of the various vitamins and minerals, food sources, as well as a listing of symptoms and conditions indicating both deficiencies and excesses, refer to the Appendix.

In the following section, the two categories of vitamins are described. These distinctions are important to the individual as well as the chef. Minerals also are discussed. Proper purchasing, handling, and cooking of foods to help prevent loss of these valuable nutrients is the final section in this chapter.

WATER-SOLUBLE VITAMINS

The B-complex vitamins and vitamin C are water-soluble. They are found in a variety of food sources, including fruits, grains, vegetables, and meats. The fact that they can dissolve in water means that they can be easily transported throughout the body in the bloodstream. It also means that they can be cleansed from the body along with waste water when there is an excess present. A small amount of these vitamins can be stored briefly in muscle tissue, but it is important to replenish the body's supplies every day through the diet. It is unlikely that a toxic level could accumulate, unless there is massive supplementation in addition to dietary sources.

The B-vitamins are critical for the proper release of energy to the body. A deficiency of a B-vitamin may result in a condition such as beri beri, anemia, or pellagra. Because vitamin B-12 is found only in animal foods, strict vegans may need to supplement their diets to obtain enough of it. However, vitamin supplementation should be carefully done, because self-administering large doses of B-vitamins can cause a toxic reaction that is as bad, or worse, than the condition being treated.

Vitamin C was the subject of one of the first vitamin studies, in which the British Royal Navy tried to determine the foods that might help cure scurvy. Eventually, citrus fruits were identified as the best cure and the navy issued limes to its sailors; thus came their nickname, "limeys." Vitamin C increases the absorption of iron by the body and promotes the production of collagen, the protein substance that helps tissues hold together.

One of the biggest problems facing the chef when preparing foods that contain the water-soluble vitamins is selecting techniques that retain as many of the vitamins as possible. Vitamin C and the B-complex vitamins are quickly destroyed in the presence of air, heat, light, and enzymes. As soon as foods are cut, they lose some vitamins. When they are cooked, they will inevitably lose more. As long as care is taken to minimize these losses, the vitamins retained in most foods will be kept at reasonable levels.

FAT-SOLUBLE VITAMINS

Vitamins A, D, E, and K are fat-soluble. They are found in a variety of food sources, and often will occur together in plant and fish oils. Unlike the water-soluble vitamins, fat-soluble vitamins are not easily removed from the body once they are ingested. For this reason, it is very important to avoid greatly exceeding RDAs for A, D, E, and K vitamins. The body can store virtually limitless amounts of them in its fat tissues, making it easy for toxic levels to accumulate. Once that happens, a variety of conditions may develop, some of which are dangerous and some of which may be fatal.

Vitamin A has been closely identified with vision. The form of vitamin A found in animal foods is known as retinol. Vitamin A itself is not found in plant foods, but a substance known as carotene, which the body can use to produce vitamin A, is contained in orange, yellow, and dark-green, leafy vegetables. Foods containing carotene and retinol (except possibly liver) cannot normally be converted to vitamin A quickly enough to reach a toxic level. Carotene can cause a person to appear jaundiced, however, because its yellow pigment may be stored in fat layers just beneath the skin.

Vitamin D is closely associated with the proper formation of bones. In fact, the disease that results from a lack of this vitamin is rickets, a condition in which bones grow abnormally. Sunlight on a person's skin can produce vitamin D from cholesterol. However, people who are rarely exposed to sunlight might need to evaluate their diets to be certain that they are consuming enough. Milk, cereals, and other foods are frequently fortified with vitamin D. Other food sources for this vitamin can be found in the Appendix.

Another fat-soluble vitamin, E, is an antioxidant, which means that it can "save" other cells from being lost through exposure to oxygen by "sacrificing" itself. This is especially important to cells in the lungs, which otherwise might be destroyed by high concentrations of oxygen. It would be difficult to eliminate vitamin E from the diet, because it is found in virtually all food groups. However, it is possible. If an extremely low-fat diet or one that included mainly highly processed fast foods were followed for an extended period, a deficiency could occur.

Vitamin K, associated with the proper formation of blood clots, is produced by bacteria found in the intestines of healthy individuals. Still, about half of a person's RDA for this vitamin is normally provided by food, particularly dark-green, leafy vegetables.

Fat-soluble vitamins in foods are less likely to be affected by cutting these foods ahead of time or cooking them in water far in advance. They can be destroyed by exposure to high temperatures, light, or air and by being cooked in fat.

Many vitamins, both fat-soluble and water-soluble, are lost when foods are processed or heavily refined. Some vitamins may be reintroduced in a process of fortification or enrichment. Read Focus 6-2: Enriched with Eight Essential Vitamins and Minerals for more information.

MINERALS

The body needs minerals in varying amounts. Some, such as calcium, fluoride, magnesium, and potassium, are called macro-minerals because they are required in large amounts. Others, such as copper, iodine, iron, and tin,

FOCUS 6-2   "ENRICHED WITH EIGHT ESSENTIAL VITAMINS
            AND MINERALS"

This phrase has been a common sight on packages of cold cereals for so long that many of us may not even think twice about how enriched foods first came about. The story of their origin begins in 1936, when a survey revealed that the incidence of deficiency diseases resulting from inadequate supplies of certain nutrients was increasing. About that time, improved milling machinery had made it possible to make a whiter, smoother-textured flour that produced a softer, whiter bread.

Until then, whole-wheat bread had supplied the majority of the daily requirements of not only iron, thiamine, niacin, and riboflavin, but also magnesium, zinc, vitamin B-6, folacin, and dietary fiber. Refined flours lost significant amounts of these nutrients, as well as others that weren't identified until years later. Niacin levels in unenriched white bread, for example, are only 2% of those found in whole-grain bread. Unfortunately, as white bread became readily available, the demand for whole-grain breads dropped. The prevalence of deficiencies made it obvious that something needed to be done to boost people's nutrient supply. Thus, foods "Enriched with Eight Essential Vitamins and Minerals" were created.

The Enrichment Act of 1942 required enrichment of all grain products, including cereals, pastas, and bread, which were brought across state lines. Iron, thiamine, niacin, and riboflavin levels have to be close to what they had been in the whole-grain versions. Other nutrients are added as part of the enrichment process, but it is not mandatory that their levels be raised to match those in whole-grain products. There is no requirement for replacing dietary fiber.

Enriched products are certainly a better nutritional bargain than nonenriched, bleached, and refined ones. However, they are no match for whole grains and meals. Adding back some of the nutrients doesn't make the product nutritionally complete, even if the label claims that a cereal offers 100% of eight, ten, or eleven essential nutrients. The possible side effects from a diet that relies heavily upon highly processed grains and flours are still coming to light as scientists and nutritionists uncover more about the special roles played by each of the nearly fifty known essential nutrients.

are known as trace minerals or micro-minerals because the body needs only minute amounts of them. It should be noted clearly that the two terms reflect the amounts needed, and not their relative importance to health.

A diet that includes a good variety of foods, especially whole or minimally processed ones, will almost always meet the body's need for all minerals.

6-1. VITAMIN- AND MINERAL-RICH FOODS

a *Whole and dried fruits, and fruit juices, offer impressive amounts of various necessary vitamins and minerals. They should be included in menu planning not only for their nutritional value, but also for their bright colors and flavors. Strawberries, bananas, grapes, pineapple, apples, peaches, and cherries are hard to resist. Dried figs, apricots, dates, and golden raisins can give a wonderful sweetness to desserts and fruit compotes. And what would breakfast be without orange juice?*

b *More than a colorful selection of vegetables, this photograph also shows an immense warehouse of vitamins and minerals. Peppers are as rich in Vitamin C as oranges, for example. A crisp salad of Boston lettuce and cherry tomatoes, an artichoke appetizer, tender carrots, grilled endive, roasted potatoes, pan-steamed asparagus, several leaves of radicchio as a bed for a salad, or lemon-glazed broccoli or cauliflower would never be mistaken for bland, boiled "veggies."*

Even people who do not drink a lot of milk can get enough calcium from a varied diet without necessarily relying on supplements.

While vitamins are often quickly destroyed during cooking, minerals appear to remain stable. For additional information about minerals, their food sources, and possible health complications from deficiencies or excesses, consult the chart included in the Appendix.

PUTTING THE GUIDELINE TO WORK: VITAMINS AND MINERALS IN THE KITCHEN

Although no one can force a guest to eat a healthy diet, having a varied selection of fresh, intriguing, properly prepared foods on a menu can help encourage wise choices. This section describes the ways the chef can maintain the quality and integrity of foods at various points: ordering and purchasing; storing and handling; and advance preparation, cooking, and serving.

ORDERING AND PURCHASING

The seasons play a big role in determining what fresh produce is available and how much it will cost. A foodservice operation with a large budget can probably procure nearly any item at any time of the year, enabling it to feature asparagus in November and strawberries in October. A better alternative might be a menu that the chef is able to adapt often enough to reflect the change in seasons or to make use of a special item. For example, if the fresh peas usually featured with a fish entrée cannot be found, then perhaps another green vegetable, such as broccoli, might be ordered instead.

Not every menu is designed to be so flexible, however, and most operations must keep their food costs as low as possible. There are some foods that may be better in a frozen or canned form. Frozen corn kernels, peas, berries, and spinach are all good alternatives when the fresh version is either of poor quality or too expensive. Canned tomatoes frequently have a better flavor, color, and texture than the pale watery versions available when the local growing season ends.

The chef should read carefully the labels of processed, packaged foods to find out what ingredients may have been added and the purpose they are supposed to play. Not every additive is harmful; some are actually beneficial. It is a good idea to be on the lookout for hidden sodium, monosodium glutamate (MSG), dyes and colorings, or preservatives. Low-sodium and low-fat products should be selected whenever possible, and an adjustment to the recipe might be a good idea as well. Random taste tests should be performed from time to time to make sure that the food is providing the best possible flavor and quality to the finished item.

Some kitchens use prepared bases for soups and stocks. These items are often very high in sodium. Brands that have the best quality and the least amount of sodium should be selected. Chefs also should read the directions carefully so that these prepared bases are properly diluted for use as an ingredient in soups, stews, and sauces.

STORING AND HANDLING

Most fresh, perishable foods should be refrigerated as soon as they are received. Meats should be wrapped loosely with butcher paper, or held in the vacuum packaging in which they were received. Meats stored on the bottom racks of the cooler will not drip onto other products. Sheet pans placed underneath meats will catch drippings. Fish should be properly iced, and live shellfish should be kept in damp burlap sacks or paper.

Ripe fruits and vegetables should be refrigerated and wrapped only loosely, especially lettuces and other leafy vegetables. Circulation of air helps inhibit bacterial growth. Uncooked vegetables should not be stored in water. Produce should be rinsed and cut just before it is used so the greatest amount of vitamins and minerals are retained.

6-2. *As long as they are handled with care, fresh seasonal vegetables can be a great way to boost the nutritional profile of a dish. Overcooking, cooking in water laced with too much salt or an acid such as lemon juice, cooking too far in advance, and holding vegetables in water are just a few of the improper cooking procedures that can rob a vegetable not only of its vitamins and minerals, but also its color, flavor, and texture. The beans on the right have been properly cooked, and they look crisp, bright green, and appetizing. Those on the left have turned a dull olive color, and look waterlogged, limp, and wrinkled.*

Foods lose their nutritive value when they are kept for long periods. For this reason, stock rotation is important to help keep the food supply fresh.

PREPARATION AND COOKING

Nutrient levels are diminished when foods are overcooked, or cooked at too high a heat, in too much liquid, or in the presence of acids (vinegar, lemon juice, etc.) or alkalis (baking soda). The presence of copper or iron in cookware may lower the levels of some vitamins and minerals in food. The briefer the exposure is to any of these conditions, the greater the nutrient retention.

Foods cut into small pieces will cook more quickly than those that are left whole, thus helping to retain some nutrients. On the other hand, whole foods will lose fewer nutrients due to direct contact with air, heat, and moisture, but overall cooking time will be longer. These two concerns may seem like a big stumbling block. The choice between the two procedures should be made according to the dish, the cooking equipment available, the time allowed for preparation and cooking, and the overall presentation of the dish.

Dry-heat cooking methods (roasting, grilling, broiling, and baking) help retain more of the water-soluble nutrients. Methods that avoid direct contact with liquids and rely instead upon steam (steaming, en papillote, microwaving, and to a lesser extent, shallow poaching) also retain nutrients.

Moist-heat techniques that incorporate any cooking liquid as a part of the finished dish tend to recapture nutrients that were lost to that liquid. This improves the nutritive value of the dish. Stewed, braised, and shallow-poached foods all have this advantage.

As a general rule, time, heat, and exposure to air should be kept to a minimum. Most food looks and tastes best when it is cooked just until it is properly done, and served as soon as possible after that. Many dishes, such as a plate of grilled vegetables, are most appealing when they are served immediately after being cooked. There are some dishes, like a stew, that may be stored for a few days after they have been cooked.

Often the discussion of nutrient retention focuses primarily on vegetables. It should be remembered that an overcooked piece of pork has lost its B vitamins just as surely as has a serving of limp, gray broccoli.

There is no perfect cooking method that will retain every nutrient contained in raw food. Nutritionally cooked dishes should be prepared according to a number of considerations. Not every dish can fulfill every possible requirement for healthful cooking.

Cooking techniques should be selected to deliver the best flavor, texture, and appearance in the finished dishes. This must be the chef's primary concern, because foods that are not appealing do not get eaten and, therefore, provide patrons no nutrition.

Beverages

The owner of any establishment that does have a full bar or that serves wine and beer is faced with something of a dilemma. Wine, beer, and cocktails are big money-makers; curtailing their sales can put a dent in the overall profit margin of an operation. Various strategies have been proposed to bolster profits without "pushing" a substance that is without doubt one of our society's most insidious and misunderstood drugs. The first section of this chapter will outline some of them.

Drinking has become universally associated with wine, beer, and hard liquor for many individuals. When someone is asked for a drink choice, then, it is important to give them the opportunity to select a nonalcoholic beverage or water without making them feel odd. The body needs to have its stores of water replenished throughout the day, and encouraging people to drink water, and/or fruit and vegetable juices is a good idea.

Growing concerns with health and well-being have revolutionized many concepts about what alcoholic beverage to have and when it is appropriate. For many people, a cocktail before dinner or a glass of wine with a meal is a pleasant "extra" that enhances their dining experience. They have no difficulty handling a single drink, and also no difficulty stopping themselves before they have had too much.

Despite evidence indicating that a little alcohol may actually be good for a person, there is no serious proposal that non-drinkers should adopt the habit for their health. Numerous studies have documented the negative effects of alcohol on the body. It seems wisest, therefore, to follow a course of moderation. See Focus 7-1: What Is Moderation? for further discussion of this topic.

FOCUS 7-1   WHAT IS MODERATION?

Each of the USDA dietary goals for Americans has been carefully phrased. The goal for alcohol consumption now says: If you drink alcohol, do so in moderation. What is moderation? The answer depends on many factors. The liver is responsible for processing the alcoholic beverages a person drinks. Under normal circumstances, the liver can produce enough of the appropriate hormones to metabolize one drink in about 90 minutes. This means that a glass or two of wine or beer, or a single mixed cocktail is within the range of what might be considered "moderation" for most people. Several factors can change this range, however.

Body size is one; the larger a person is, the more alcohol they are likely to be able to handle before exhibiting any noticeable impairment. If the person has not eaten recently, that will slow the rate at which the liver can handle liquor, increasing the effect that the alcohol has on the body. When a person has more than one drink an hour, the alcohol accumulates in the body. Two drinks taken within an hour will affect judgment. After four drinks, a person's emotional control is impaired. Eight drinks will have an effect on one's vision. If more than that is drunk, the person will become totally out of control, or sink into a stupor.

Ounce for ounce, beer contains less pure alcohol than a blended whiskey. Remember, however, that a typical serving of beer is 12 fluid ounces. Whiskey is normally served in 1½ ounce *shots* or *jiggers*. Table 7-1 lists various alcoholic beverages and the amount of calories they contain. The calories have a direct relation to the amount of pure alcohol in a drink.

BEVERAGE PROMOTION

TURNING WINE (SALES) INTO WATER (SALES)

Alcohol does provide the body with calories, but not with any essential nutrients. There may be no indication that the body needs alcohol, but it most certainly has a need for water. Body cells are composed mostly of water. The body relies on water to perform several vital functions and needs to have its fluid level replenished throughout the day (see Focus 7-2: The Forgotten Nutrient). Thirst does not always prompt a person to drink enough water. For some patrons, the cachet of a bottled water or the taste of their favorite brand of water may encourage them to drink another glassful. They eventually may come to prefer water over other beverages.

There has been an increase in the consumption of bottled waters. Although Americans used to drink far more hard liquor than bottled water, today they drink about equal amounts of liquor and bottled water. When a selection of mineral waters is offered, the patron will come to rely on it as a part of the dining experience.

BET YOU CAN HAVE JUST ONE

For various reasons, including health and driving safety, many patrons are moderating their alcohol consumption. When they do have a drink, these patrons tend to indulge in premium products. They select higher-priced name brand liquors and vintage wines from distinguished growers. Such a behavior pattern may help operators to simultaneously boost profits and serve alcohol responsibly.

Wines can be offered by the glass, if there is a storage system in place to keep wine from losing quality once it is opened. There is a greater likelihood that patrons may select a single full-sized glass of wine with their entrée when they have several excellent wines to choose from and can have a "tasting-size" or a full-size glass. Another option would be to offer customers a "tasting" of

FOCUS 7-2   THE FORGOTTEN NUTRIENT

Humans need water to live. It is in all of our cells, in our blood, in our bones, our teeth, our hair, and our skin. In fact, we are nearly 60% water. The roles that water plays in sustaining life are impressive, to say the least.

Water is a nearly universal solvent that can dissolve minerals and other compounds and carry them throughout the body. Water transports nutrients and necessary building materials to each cell in the body, and forms an integral part of the cells themselves. Water is critical to the body's chemical reactions; it also removes impurities from the bloodstream and the body.

Because water cannot be compressed into a smaller space, it can cushion joints, organs, and sensitive tissues such as the spinal cord. Water maintains pressure on the eyes' optic nerves so that one can see. Water also helps stabilize blood pressure.

Maintaining an adequate supply of water is important to help regulate body temperature. Excess heat, which builds up during physical exertion or when people are in a hot climate, transforms water into a vapor through sweating. This energy exchange cools the body by carrying heat out and away.

The human body generally loses about a quart of water daily through cleansing and cooling processes. That amount also needs to be replenished daily, by drinking fluids and eating foods that contain water.

TABLE 7-1.
ALCOHOLIC BEVERAGES AND AVERAGE CALORIES

BEVERAGE (PER SERVING)		CALORIES*
Scotch, whiskey, gin,	80-proof	97
vodka, tequila,	86-proof	105
and rum (1.5 oz.)	90-proof	110
	94-proof	116
	100-proof	125
Brandy (1 oz.)		65
Liqueurs (1 oz.)		75–100
Dry wine (3½ oz.)		87
Sweet wine (3½ oz.)		142
Beer, lager-style (12 oz.)		140–165
Beer, light (12 oz.)		95–105

* The number of calories in an alcoholic beverage is directly related to the amount of pure alcohol (ethanol) it contains.

7-1. *Selling wine by the glass has many advantages, for both the restaurant operator and the guest. Those who wish to sample a special wine might try a tasting size while a full-sized glass would accompany an entrée.*

7-2. *Many special systems are available that allow the restaurant owner to offer several wines by the glass. These systems keep a wine at its best even after it has been opened for several hours, or even several days. The system shown here replaced oxygen, which could cause the wine to sour, with nitrogen, which protects the wine without affecting it.*

7-3. NON-ALCOHOLIC BEVERAGES

a *In addition to bottled waters and sodas, a selection of beverages made from freshly squeezed juices can add interest to the standard drink list. The spicy vegetable juice cocktail shown here is made with an automatic juicer.*

b *Quality "virgin" cocktails, such as the Madras shown here at right, are made from fruit juices without any liquor, or are nonalcoholic versions of wine or beer (also shown). It is critical to conduct taste tests to be certain that nonalcoholic versions of familiar drinks will meet customer expectations.*

one wine with their appetizers and a tasting of a different wine with their entrées. This trend has become more widespread with the increased availability of moderately priced wine-dispensing and storage systems.

Serving beer may assume a more upscale image when different beers are featured to complement specific dishes. For instance, certain brands may be paired with the spicy flavors of Chinese or Mexican menu items. Service is also enhanced when beer is stored at optimal temperatures and served in chilled glasses.

The decision about whether or not to have some wine or beer with a meal is a personal one, as are the decisions to have french fries with a sandwich or chocolate cake for dessert. The most effective way to moderate guests' alcohol consumption is to serve all beverages—alcoholic and nonalcoholic—properly and with the same degree of concern for quality. In addition, the establishment should offer nonalcoholic alternatives to traditional cocktails that are not pale imitations of original drinks. It is challenging, but possible, to create a repertoire of alcohol-free beverages that are appealing.

PUTTING THE GUIDELINE TO WORK:
ALCOHOL IN THE KITCHEN

Even restaurants that do not offer wine, beer, or liquor to their guests may keep alcoholic beverages on hand for preparing menu items. A number of dishes, including entrées, sauces, and desserts, may be enhanced by flavorful spirits.

The caloric content due to the use of alcohol in a dish depends on how much, if any, of the alcohol evaporates before the dish is served. If spirits are heated for a long time, a large portion of their pure alcohol evaporates and *many* of the calories, therefore, are lost. Careful studies have dispelled the notion that *all* of the alcohol and calories are lost; there is always at least a small residual amount. In cases when spirits are added at the last moment, or when a liqueur is added to a cold preparation, virtually all of the alcohol and its calories are retained.

II

The Guidelines at Work

Each of the seven guidelines for nutritional cooking concentrates on a single area: calories, fats, proteins, carbohydrates, salt and sodium, vitamins and minerals, and alcohol. Having knowledge of the individual nutrients and their roles in maintaining a healthy diet is important. A sound nutritional education requires that the chef also be familiar with the key food-related terms used by nutritionists. Being able to communicate effectively and understand each other will help make it easier for chef and nutritionist to develop a menu together.

Taking theory out of the textbook or the classroom and bringing it into the kitchen can create some difficulties. The major problem often is taking the knowledge learned about individual nutrients and attempting to incorporate this into a comprehensive program. For example, the inspiration for a recipe usually doesn't come from nutrient categories, but rather from a particular food, such as scallops, Cornish game hen, venison, or pork tenderloin. The chef needs to be able to see that a particular food item may provide more than one nutrient, and may add undesirable elements, such as fat. Chapters in this section address several issues that focus on the importance of food as the source of all nutrients, rather than dividing cooking and nutrition into two separate concerns.

Foods are examined in terms of the ways in which selection may be used to achieve the maximum nutritional impact. The value of fresh fish, fruits, and vegetables; lean meats; dairy products that are low in fat; and flavorful seasonings and flavoring ingredients can hardly be overemphasized. Any good cookbook invariably begins by instructing the cook to seek out seasonal items whenever possible, using the market as the guide for preparing a menu.

These special injunctions do not vary from one style of cooking to another, but apply equally to fine French cuisine, the cooking of provincial Italy, and contemporary nutritional preparation. Foods already as fresh and full of nutrients as possible will look appealing and taste delicious. Even when the purchasing parameters of a particular establishment dictate the use of frozen or canned goods, the chef should obtain quality.

There is a great deal of value, too, in learning about the wealth of available ingredients. Grains such as barley, quinoa, couscous, and bulgur, for example, are showing up on more menus. These foods are often new to both the guest and the chef. Chapter 8 on ingredients provides basic information about a variety of foods from all categories.

Making a transition to nutritional cooking is often an overwhelming task if the chef believes it will be necessary to learn how to cook in an entirely new way. Chapter 9, *Cooking Techniques* refutes this idea by demonstrating how, in most cases, traditional methods are well suited to the preparation of a nutritional menu item. For example, grilling and roasting are, by definition, cooking methods that do not introduce additional oils or fats during cooking. Sautéing traditionally calls for foods to be cooked very quickly, over high heat, in a *small amount* of oil or clarified butter. Simply by taking a more literal approach to applying classic cooking standards and resisting the tendency to add a little more butter, a little more cream, or a little more salt, the chef can begin to incorporate the many small changes that will, over time, result in a big change for the better. Pan-frying and deep-frying don't fit nutritional standards. Therefore, these two methods are not included here.

The biggest nutritional concern in cooking is not so much the actual method, as the "added" components such as stuffings, sauces, thickeners, coatings, and garnishes. Throughout the discussion of each cooking method, the foods, flavorings, and garnishing ingredients are also scrutinized to ensure that the best possible value is derived, nutritionally and in terms of flavor, appearance, and texture.

The purpose of quality purchasing and careful preparation is to create dishes that the customer will enjoy. The final chapter in this section discusses some topics related to creating a menu and developing recipes to support it. It isn't enough to decide one day that an establishment ought to offer one or more nutritious items. The time and energy that goes into preparing new menu selections is a valuable commodity. It should not be squandered on creating a new menu in which the customer will have no interest.

Different establishments have different needs and different capabilities. A fast-food restaurant certainly cannot incorporate nutrition in the same way as a hospital kitchen. Both of these operations should take the time to assess which changes can be made easily and with as little cost as possible, and which ones will require a bigger investment. The hospital kitchen may take more time to develop a nutritionally oriented menu cycle. Recipes may need to be specifically developed and special products ordered. Additional training may be necessary so that the staff can prepare and portion the foods properly.

The fast-food restaurant, on the other hand, will take a different approach. The new item will be developed in a test kitchen, then analyzed. A marketing strategy, involving surveys and sample markets to determine the new selection's viability, will probably be part of the overall plan. The process changes for spas, bistros, cafeterias, and family and "white tablecloth" restaurants.

Good recipes are the foundation of any nutritional program. Some traditional recipes do not require any changes. The ways that these recipes can be identified are discussed in Chapter 10. In other cases, it may only be necessary to moderate those ingredients of concern because of calories, fat, cholesterol, or sodium contents, or to find substitutes that will produce a finished dish with an acceptable flavor, texture, and appearance.

Once the initial reluctance to learn a new way of thinking about food is overcome, many chefs find the challenge of nutritional cooking to be an intriguing and welcome spur to their own creativity. By taking cues from the market, the season, or from other cuisines, the chef can open up a whole new avenue for recipe development. After the recipe is designed, the process becomes one of refinement, until the finished dish achieves all of its goals: brilliant flavors, a beautiful appearance, the correct portion size, and, of course, the best possible nutritional balance.

Ingredients

The starting point for nutritional cooking is the list of goods the chef orders from purveyors, handpicks from markets, contracts from smaller farmers, or grows in on-premise kitchen gardens. All good cooking demands the best possible foods. The requirement is perhaps even more obvious in nutritional cooking because there are no buttery, cream-laden sauces to hide a piece of fish or dress up a plate of pasta.

Throughout this chapter there will be an ongoing discussion of the ways in which every chef can apply the basic rules of proper purchasing to meet the seven guidelines for nutritional cooking. The needs of each kitchen should act as the pattern for adjusting and modifying the basic information.

Following is a brief review of some key points for an effective purchasing program.

- Purchase the freshest, highest-quality foods available.
- Maintain a respect for, and awareness of, foods' seasonality.
- Develop an accurate list of required items for the preparation of all dishes listed on the menu.
- Remain flexible so that special purchases or windfalls can be used to advantage.
- Avoid overpurchasing as much as possible.

8-1. *As the centerpiece of an entrée, the meat, poultry, or fish chosen must be of the best quality. This selection shows a small sampling of the variety available to the chef in planning a menu. From top left, clockwise, clams, chicken breast, mussels, oysters, and beef tenerloin.*

In addition to these basic rules, the chef should also be conscious of various foods' nutritional strong points and shortcomings. This requires a basic understanding of which foods are rich in complex carbohydrates and fiber, which offer a good source of protein with the least fat, and which are the best sources of vitamins and minerals. When possible, a preference should be given to selections that are low in overall calories, fat, cholesterol, sodium, and refined sugars.

MEATS, POULTRY, AND GAME

The centerpiece of most meals is still a serving of meat, poultry, or game. When the portion size is down-scaled to meet the suggested guidelines of around 4 ounces per serving, it becomes even more important to select the best cuts. As previously mentioned in Chapter 4, there are three categories of meats: lean, moderate-fat, and high-fat. Specific examples of relatively lean meats, poultry, and game are listed below.

BEEF
  Well-trimmed cuts from the loin and top round
  Tripe, tongue, and heart
VEAL
  Rib and loin chops, roasts, steaks
PORK
  Tenderloin, loin, center cut ham (fresh and cured)
LAMB
  Leg, arm, and loin cuts
POULTRY
  Turkey and chicken, light meat
  (Duck breast, well-trimmed, is also acceptable)
GAME ANIMALS
  Venison, rabbit, buffalo
GAME BIRDS
  Pheasant, grouse, quail, partridge
  (Breast meat, well-trimmed, from duck and goose may be acceptable)

PURCHASING

The chef may need to adjust the standard meat order in several ways. For example, instead of selecting the highest USDA grade, it may be more nutritionally correct to choose a slightly lower grade. The standards for grading rely upon a number of different factors. One is the amount of marbling—

8-2. Meats are given a quality grade based on a number of factors, one of which is the degree of marbling (the fat found within the muscle itself). Select grade (left) has the least amount; Choice (center) has only a moderate amount and is considered suitable for inclusion in a healthy eating plan; Prime grade (right) has the most internal marbling. Choice meats are the preferred choice for a diet or menu aimed at moderating the overall amount of fat in the diet without sacrificing flavor or quality.

the streaks of fat found within the "lean" meat. In the case of beef, Choice may be a better selection than Prime. The quality is still excellent, but there is generally less marbling throughout all the cuts. The difference between three grades of beef is shown in the accompanying photograph.

In addition to paying attention to the grade, the chef should also become familiar with the relative fattiness or leanness of different parts of the animal. For example, a piece of beef top round is less fatty than the bottom round or the rib. The pork tenderloin is a moderate-fat meat, while spareribs or chops may have a far higher fat content. The chef should also keep in mind the option of using game instead of a "traditional" meat as explained in Focus 8-1. As the analysis in Table 8-2 shows, most game animals are substantially leaner and lower in cholesterol than their domestic counterparts. Wild animals simply do not accumulate the fat that farm animals do. The end results are clearly a boon for the nutritionally oriented restaurant.

Poultry is popular for use in a variety of menu items because of its wide availability and nearly universal appeal. The chef should not assume, however, that using poultry instead of a red meat is always nutritionally sound. For example, if ground turkey meat is used to replace ground meat, it is a good idea to investigate the composition of the ground turkey being purchased. The breast meat of most birds is leaner than the leg meat. For every 100 grams of ground light meat (skin removed), there is slightly more than 4 grams of fat;

TABLE 8-1.

COMPARISON OF DOMESTIC AND GAME ANIMALS

	SPECIES											
	DOMESTIC				WILD							
	DUCK†	USDA BEEF (TOP, BUTT, BROILED)	RABBIT	CHICKEN (ROASTED LIGHT MEAT)†	PHEASANT BREAST*	SQUIRREL	RABBIT	DEER (VENISON)	ANTELOPE	BISON	ELK	MOOSE
Fat (in g)	11.2	9.4	8.4	4.5	3.6	3.65	3.51	3.19	2.67	2.42	1.9	0.97
Cholesterol (in mg)	89	76	86	85	N.A.	95	123	112	126	82	73	78
Calories	201	207	206	173	133	136	173	158	150	143	146	134

Note: These values are based on a 100 g (3½ oz.) cooked portion. Adapted from *Mayo Clinic Nutrition Letter*, November 1989.
* All values for pheasant based on raw meat. Cooked values would be about 25% higher.
† Skin removed.

FOCUS 8-1   LOW-FAT GAME MEATS

Bison bourguignonne may not be the most familiar offering on a menu, but it could signal a change to a lower-fat meat source that has been relatively underexplored in many American restaurants. The accompanying table shows that the so-called "exotic" game meats are substantially lower in fat than their domestic counterparts.

Animals in the wild rarely become fat. The limited fat stores they accumulate to see them through the winter are usually deposited in layers just below the skin to act as both insulation and as an energy reservoir. There is relatively little marbling found in the meat, a fact the chef should keep in mind. The traditional culinary approach to most game has been to bard or lard the cuts before cooking them to counteract the meat's natural dryness. Today, it is best to remember that overcooked meats will have a dry texture, whereas those cooked just to the desired doneness will usually have a moister, juicier feel.

Other points in game's favor are the bolder, more interesting flavors. The tender portions such as the loin and the rib of deer, elk, bison, or antelope can be successfully grilled, roasted, or broiled. A rich variety of flavoring ingredients may also be used. Juniper berries, peppercorns, capers, and roasted garlic are just some of the delicious options.

FOCUS 8-2   FREE-RANGE BIRDS

To anyone who still remembers old-time barnyards, the notion of free-range birds commanding special attention, meriting note on a menu, and costing anywhere from half again to twice as much as a factory-raised bird must seem peculiar.

Poultry farming had a moment of special importance in the history of the American life-style. Families looked to this enterprise as a way to bring in additional money. Just as the idea was cresting, and some people were actually making a go of it, the movement toward factory-style chicken farms was getting stronger. Eventually, family-owned chicken farms were no longer able to compete with the greater supply and lower prices of large poultry-farming operations.

Modern poultry-raising techniques employ a whole host of practices that some people find suspect. The birds are carefully bred to produce a greater percentage of breast meat to meet consumer demand for white meat. They are confined to a space that measures about one square foot. Their diet is liberally doused with antibiotics, growth enhancers, and other ingredients intended to ward off the numerous diseases to which poultry are prone, as well as to promote rapid weight gain. Although no one has documented evidence that the residues of hormones, steroids, and antibiotics in the birds' flesh have actually caused cancer or other illnesses in humans, there is growing public concern.

Bart Ehman, a chicken farmer who decided to raise his birds without antibiotics and steroids, is considered the modern-day pioneer of free-range birds. They are often slightly different breeds than those found in large-scale operations. In addition to the chemical- and hormone-free feed they receive, the birds are allowed access to outdoor running space.

Many people prefer the flavor of free-range birds and believe that they have a more definite texture and taste. These birds do appear to be lower in fat than their confined counterparts. As to whether or not allowing these birds to range lowers stress, resulting in a richer flavor, there is no definitive answer. Free-range birds are appealing to certain parts of the market. If they are included on a menu, they should be clearly identified.

thus, 25% of its calories come from fat. But, if the ground turkey that is used is leg meat, there are around 9 grams of fat per 100 grams used, which boosts the fat calories to nearly 36% of the total. Free-range birds, though often more expensive, may be a good choice for some restaurants. Their nutritional and flavor benefits are discussed in Focus 8-2: Free-Range Birds.

Variety meats (also known as organ meats, or offal) are a special category that includes liver, brains, sweetbreads, and kidneys. Many of these items may be prohibitively high in fats and cholesterol for more than an occasional indulgence. It is sometimes possible to use a carefully controlled amount of liver, because of its value as a source for iron, zinc, and vitamin A. Some other meats, such as calf's tongue and heart, that fall within this group may be unfairly neglected, although they are a good low-fat source of protein, vitamins, and minerals. It is important to carefully evaluate the nutritional composition of variety meats to avoid inadvertently adding a menu item that is too high in fat and cholesterol.

PREPARATION

The first preparation step for most meats and poultry usually is to trim away any surface fat. There may be some benefit in leaving the surface fat on meats and poultry to be grilled, broiled, or roasted, as long as it is removed before it is served. If the skin remains on a bird as it roasts, the chef must remove the fat from the pan drippings before making a pan sauce. Read Focus 8-3: Trimming the Fat from Birds for a more detailed discussion of when and why the skin on poultry and game birds should be removed.

Once the meat has been trimmed of visible fat, sinew, gristle, or silverskin, the next step usually is to cut and portion the meat, poultry, or game correctly for the cooking technique. The suggested portion size for meats, poultry, and game is 3.5 to 4 ounces in raw weight. Cuts which include bone, such as chops, will weigh more.

The chef can use some special cutting and plating techniques in order to "feed the eye." When portion sizes drop from the typical 8 to 10 ounces to around 4–6 ounces, there needs to be some thought given to how the finished plate is going to look. Certain cutting techniques can give a big boost to the plate's appearance. Cutting veal into "émincé," for instance, will give the impression of greater amounts of meat than a single scallop. Pounding cutlets or poultry breasts to give them more surface area will make them look larger. Slicing grilled, roasted, or braised items and fanning or shingling them on the plate is another way to give the impression of bounty.

Special preparation techniques may be required to produce foods that are highly flavored and have a good degree of color and texture interest. Chief among them are the use of glazes, marinades, stuffings (avoid high-fat forcemeats), sauces, relishes, compotes, and stews of vegetables, grains, and legumes.

FOCUS 8-3   TRIMMING THE FAT FROM BIRDS

Most of the fat (including saturated fats) found in poultry is concentrated in the skin and in pockets inside the cavity of the bird or surrounding the joints. For the chef, the question is whether or not the fat and skin should be removed before cooking.

It was thought that a substantial increase in the amount of fat in lean meat would occur if the visible fat and skin were left on during cooking. However, repeated studies have failed to measure a marked difference between the fat in birds that are skinned and trimmed before cooking and those that are roasted, sautéed, or grilled with the skin intact.

There may be some benefits to leaving the skin on during cooking, in some cases. Grilled poultry breasts or spit-roasted birds may shrink less and retain natural juices better if the skin is left to act as an insulation and protection. If the chef wishes, some aromatic ingredients may be placed under the skin to gently flavor the meat during cooking. It is usually easy to pull away the skin before plating.

The same is true of birds that are to be roasted whole. However, the chef must keep in mind the amount of fat in the roasting pan when making a pan sauce. If the drippings include a great deal of rendered fat, that fat will need to be skimmed completely away before using the flavorful fond in a sauce.

When baking, grilling, roasting, or broiling poultry, the chef has the option of replacing the skin with a crust of bread crumbs, herbs, shredded potatoes, or vegetables. This layer will help protect the meat against drying out while it cooks, just as the skin might have done, without adding fats. Other strategies might include using basting or glazing sauces that are naturally low in fats. The added benefit of these techniques is that they add a special flavor, color, and texture to the dish.

Leaving the skin on does not help when cooking with the moist-heat techniques. The best approach when steaming, poaching, or simmering poultry is to remove the skin before cooking. This is done not so much to prevent the fat from being transferred to the meat as it is to avoid incorporating it into the steaming liquids, which might eventually be served with the bird.

An attractive plate of food can do a great deal to counter resistance to the notion that a nutritional meal is going to necessarily leave one feeling hungry. Additional elements on the plate may also contribute to a sense of largesse. A bed of wilted greens makes a portion of sliced duck look more filling, and a pool of sauce fills in the blanks for a sliced pork tenderloin.

Meats and poultry, which along with fish and seafood are normally the most expensive dishes produced in the kitchen, can be prepared so that they will create the greatest possible degree of customer satisfaction. The recipes in Part Three are a good place to look for inspiration, and the chef should use them as a starting point for developing a repertoire of special dishes.

FISH AND SHELLFISH

Fish and shellfish entrées have always been important on most menus, and are most certainly at home on a nutritional menu. A selection of fresh fish is shown in the accompanying photo. There are many benefits to including a variety of fish and shellfish on the menu. For example, they are often perceived as being nutritionally superior because they are naturally low in calories and saturated fats. They are a desirable option for people who already have an interest in eating in a healthy fashion. Some fish are excellent sources of a group of essential fatty acids—the omega-3 fatty acids—which have been the subject of research to determine if and how they lower overall blood cholesterol levels. Current research has shed some light on this subject, which is discussed in greater detail in Focus 8-4: Omega-3 Fatty Acids.

8-3. *Fish and shellfish are becoming more popular and the number of available varieties is increasing. Be sure to check all fish and shellfish for impeccable freshness and quality when they are purchased. The varieties shown here (from upper left, clockwise, salmon, Dover sole, frogs' legs, clams; oysters and mussels in center) offer a good example of some of the options the chef might with to include on a menu.*

FOCUS 8-4   OMEGA-3 FATTY ACIDS

Eskimos in Greenland have a diet that is very high in fat. From what we know of dietary fats, it would be reasonable to assume that they should have a high number of deaths due to heart disease. They don't, and that made scientists curious. Investigations eventually led those scientists to the omega-3 fatty acids. As continued studies unravel the ways in which these fatty acids work in the body, some answers to this mystery are beginning to appear.

The body needs certain fatty acids, many of which it can produce on its own, provided it gets the appropriate raw materials. We have known for some time that at least one of these acids, linoleic, must be part of the diet. Linoleic acid belongs to a group known as the omega-6 fatty acids. Conventional wisdom held that all of the other necessary fatty acids could be synthesized in the body, as long as linoleic acid was available. Current evidence seems to indicate that, although the body can and does use the omega-6 fatty acids, more positive benefits may be obtained by introducing a good supply of omega-3 fatty acids. The differences in body activity when omega-3 fatty acids are present appear to be subtle, but may be enough to make a difference in the health of someone who is already considered at risk.

Dietary supplements of the omega-3 fatty acids are not thought to be a good way to increase their supply to the body. For one thing, refined fish oils—a source of these acids—are high in calories and do not have the added nutrients that would be available instead by including more fish in the diet. Another point to keep in mind is that fish oils can be dangerously concentrated sources of numerous contaminants and pesticides found in many bodies of water.

The most prudent course is to replace two to five meat-based meals each week with fish. Some of the fish species known to be high in omega-3 fatty acids include herring, mackerel, sablefish, salmon, tuna, sardines, and anchovies. Moderately good sources include oysters, bluefish, halibut, ocean perch, trout, smelt, bass, pollock, hake, and mullet.

Certain types of shellfish are known to be quite high in cholesterol. This does not necessarily mean that they should be removed from the menu. The cholesterol levels in squid, lobster, and shrimp may be higher, ounce for ounce, than some other finfish, poultry, or even some cuts of meat. However, people who are not sensitive to dietary cholesterol may safely eat prudent amounts of these foods once or twice a week, as long as maximum levels of dietary cholesterol are kept at approximately 300 milligrams per day. Table 8-3 compares the total cholesterol and fat content of some common varieties of fish and shellfish with that found in a comparable serving of USDA Prime beefsteak from the rib.

TABLE 8-2.

COMPARISON OF FAT AND CHOLESTEROL CONTENT OF
USDA CHOICE GRADE BEEF VERSUS FISH AND SHELLFISH

ITEM	TOTAL CALORIES (PER 100 G)	FAT (G)	CHOLESTEROL (MG)
Beef, sirloin	200	9.2	74
Salmon	183	9.0	74
Trout	129	4.0	62
Flounder	99	1.0	58
Mussels	86	2.2	28
Scallops	88	.8	33
Squid	92	1.4	233
Lobster	90	.9	95
Shrimp	106	1.7	112

The immediate perception of fish as being "good for you," i.e., low in fats and cholesterol, can work to the restaurant's advantage, but it is crucial that the inherently healthy qualities of fish and shellfish not be allowed to fall victim to improper selection, handling, and advance preparation. Some typical preparation methods may call for excessive added fats and oils, especially pan-fried and deep-fried dishes. These methods can be replaced by techniques such as poaching, grilling, steaming, or roasting. The special care taken in selecting an appropriate cooking method that best highlights the fish's natural flavors should be complemented by equal care in choosing accompanying side dishes to add texture, flavor, color, and nutritional value.

A sauce is also acceptable in a nutritional preparation of any fish or shellfish, as long as that sauce doesn't introduce a great quantity of butter. Several recipes in this book provide good examples of how careful purchasing and wise application of cooking methods can be applied with excellent results.

An equally important reason to shift a menu's organization slightly to embrace a greater number of fish offerings is that there are so many different available kinds. Increased demand may make it difficult to find some of the more familiar and popular fish, but this same demand has coincided with a rise in consumer interest in more variety. This consumer sophistication opens the way for experimentation with unfamiliar fish. Orange roughy, sablefish, and grouper are examples of newly-appreciated fish varieties.

PURCHASING

Fish and shellfish can be purchased in a number of different forms, depending upon the needs of the kitchen and the menu. For the best quality, fish should be purchased whole, and if possible, shellfish should be purchased live. The chef should buy these food items as frequently as the location, budget, and other requirements of the kitchen allow, in order to avoid having to store fish for extended periods.

The major concern with handling fish and shellfish prior to cooking is to make sure that they are kept well-chilled. In the best of all possible worlds, fish and shellfish would arrive at the kitchen daily, fresh from the market, whole or live. In reality, this purchasing schedule may not be possible. Geographic location, local purveyors, and the number of patrons that must be accomodated each day may mean that the chef needs to purchase fish in quantities designed to last from one week to a month.

High-quality drawn, filleted, or even portioned fish can be found to suit the needs of an individual operation. Shellfish may be purchased frozen (raw or cooked), shucked if this market form is more suitable. The concern must always be to purchase the freshest, best-quality product available.

Fresh fish in any form should be carefully iced down during storage, and the ice should be replaced daily. Chipped ice keeps the fish drier, better chilled, and free from punctures, thus preventing a large loss of fluid from the fish. Frozen items should be gently thawed under refrigeration before they are cooked. Rapid thawing can cause the fish or shellfish to lose a great deal of moisture. This liquid carries away not only the flavor, but also a high percentage of the fish's nutritional value.

8-4. In order to maintain a fish's quality, it must be stored carefully. In this photo, fish has been properly iced down in a container filled with chipped ice. The ice should be changed daily until the fish is cooked. Use a perforated container to hold the fish and the ice, set into a large container, so that the melting ice will drain away from the fish.

PREPARATION

Any advance preparation, such as cutting or filleting, should be done as close to the time of cooking as is reasonable. To give the impression of bounty on the plate, the chef can use cutting and presentation techniques that "trick" the eye into seeing a generous portion size. One way is to cut fillets on the diagonal to create a large surface area for fish that will be grilled. Cutting fish into strips or émincé can make it appear more bountiful, as well. Shellfish that is presented on a bed of vegetables, grains, or pasta appears more bountiful than the same portion left to swim in a pool of sauce.

FRUITS, VEGETABLES, AND FRESH HERBS

Fruits, vegetables, and herbs are powerhouses of nutritional value, providing impressive quantities of complex carbohydrates, fiber, water, vitamins, and minerals. With relatively few exceptions, they offer this nutritional ban-

8-5. *Both the seasons and the menu should play complementary roles in determining what fresh produce appears in the kitchen. Certain items have no strict season; others are at their peak for only a short time, unless they are to be shipped in from another part of the world. Shown here are (from top left, clockwise) fennel, eggplant, raddichio, yellow squash, broccoli rabe, onion, oranges, apples, asparagus, carrots, strawberries, turnip, star fruit (carambola), lime, mango, kiwis, and bananas.*

8-6. *Herbs can provide an enormous flavor boost to nutritional dishes. Some herbs provide sharp, almost citrus-like flavors; others are mellow and sweet; still others are pungent and highly aromatic. Shown here is a sampling of herbs that can add life to a dish, when chosen with care and handled properly: (clockwise beginning from top left) mint, dill, chervil, oregano, rosemary, chives, sage, lemon grass, and cilantro. Center from top: thyme, basil, and tarragon.*

quet with very small amounts of fat. These fats are seldom saturated, and of course, they have no cholesterol. In addition, the fresh, bright colors, textures, and flavors of fresh produce make these foods an integral part of any successful nutritional cooking program.

For the most part, fruits, vegetables, and herbs will not require the same careful budgeting that is necessary when dealing with meats, poultry, and fish. For this reason, they play a key role in producing the necessary flavor boost and eye appeal that can help dispel the image of nutritional cooking as "uninteresting and tasteless."

PURCHASING

There is a wide range of options in purchasing fruits, vegetables, and herbs. They may be found fresh, frozen, dried, or canned. In terms of nutritional value, fresh produce is almost always preferred, but it is important to keep in mind the dictates of common sense concerning quantity, delivery, and storage capability. Produce should be purchased in sufficient quantities to last between deliveries, with care taken not to buy too much. Overpurchasing will result in a loss of raw material, which eventually cuts into the profits. Some chefs may prefer to purchase fruits, vegetables, and other foodstuffs that have been organically grown. There are different regulations regarding what may be sold as "organic." It is normally assumed that these foods are grown free of chemical fertilizers, growth enhancers, or pesticides. Beyond that, there is no real guarantee of any special claims to be more healthy, natural or safe. For more information, read Focus 8-5.

FOCUS 8-5 ORGANICALLY GROWN

When the words "organically grown" appear in the produce section, on the label, or anywhere in the advertising copy for a product, the savvy consumer should ask some pointed questions. Has the farmer been certified by a state or independent organization? If so, what are the particular certification requirements? Are there any state requirements governing who is allowed to call their products organic?

The general assumption about organic products is that they have been grown without any chemicals, including synthetic herbicides, pesticides, and fertilizers. Organizations that certify farms require that the land and crops be free of chemicals for a specified period. For instance, the Natural Organic Farmers Association requires that no chemical pesticides or herbicides have been used within the past three years. Other organizations may specify periods ranging from 12 months to five years. Some organizations require on-site visits to ensure that the standards are being met consistently. Others provide literature detailing the regulations and leave compliance to the individual farmer.

Purchasing organic produce, meats, poultry, and fish is not a simple matter. There is a relatively limited supply of certified organic goods, and usually these items cost more than those raised under more typical growing conditions. Increased consumer demand is starting to have an effect on farming methods, but a complete change is unlikely in the near future. Current farming practices rely upon synthetic fertilizers, herbicides, and pesticides to a great degree. Changing methods will increase costs to the consumer, at least initially.

continued ▶

Public awareness of the potential dangers of an agricultural system that has tended to rely upon only a few breeds or strains of animals and produce, coupled with increased reliance on antibiotics, steroids, growth enhancers, and other substances, is on the rise. More states are beginning to regulate the proper application of the label "organic." More stores and purveyors are selling organic produce. And more restaurants will be able to feature these items on their menus.

Tomatoes offer a good example of some of the factors that need to be taken into account when deciding in what form produce should be purchased. Fresh tomatoes, when in season locally, have an incomparable taste. After the local growing season is over, the chef may prefer to use good-quality canned tomatoes, because they may have better flavor than the pale, watery versions that are engineered to survive early picking, ripening rooms, and long-distance shipping.

Deliveries should be scheduled so that the produce used in the kitchen will be as fresh as possible. Storage capabilities should also be taken into account. For example, limited refrigeration space should be accommodated with more frequent deliveries. If frozen items are used, then adequate numbers of properly functioning freezers should be available.

The loss of nutrients during storage and advance preparation can be avoided if the chef remembers that vitamins and minerals are lost when produce is exposed to light, air, moisture, heat, acids, and metals. Additionally, nutritional value will start to decline immediately after harvesting, and this loss will continue the "older" the produce becomes. Delicate greens, herbs, lettuces, and other produce that tends to lose natural moisture rapidly should be stored in containers that will help minimize this. No free water should be allowed to collect in the bottom of storage bins.

PREPARATION

Produce should be rinsed, trimmed, and cut as close to cooking time as is practical. Except for those fruits and vegetables that tend to discolor when exposed to air, the practice of holding vegetables in water, before or after cooking, should be strictly avoided.

Kitchens that cook menu items à la minute may be able to devise practical methods for cooking many different types of vegetables to order. Or they may elect to prepare small batches several times throughout a service period so that a fresh supply of cooked items is constantly available. This second approach, which may at first seem time-consuming and "wasteful," might actually help control costs. The kitchen work must be properly organized so that it can be done easily, without an undue amount of scrambling during a service period to get the vegetables and fruits ready to cook. The consumer will enjoy the fresh taste of the vegetable or fruit most fully because there will be no unnecessary loss of flavor, texture, or color. There also will be less waste, because vegetables and fruits are cooked as needed and not in single huge batches.

The chef should also try to take advantage of cooking techniques that allow the vegetable or fruit to be cooked quickly and with as little added liquid as is reasonable. Baking or roasting whole in the skin, steaming and pan-steaming, and cooking in the microwave are all excellent options.

DAIRY PRODUCTS AND EGGS

Milk-based foods and eggs play many different roles in cooking and baking. They have particular chemical and physical functions, some of which cannot be duplicated in any way by a substitute. They also contribute to the flavor, texture, color, and overall appearance of many foods. Dairy products and eggs are excellent sources of protein, vitamins, and minerals, but they are also frequently the source of significant quantities of saturated fats and cholesterol. Wherever possible the chef should opt for low-fat versions of milk and cheese products.

8-7. Increased demand has been met with the development of a number of dairy items that are extremely low in fat, making it easy not only to substitute for traditional high-fat ingredients, but also to meet dietary goals for calcium, an essential mineral. The items shown here all have use in the nutritional kitchen.

A variety of lower reduced-fat alternatives is shown here. There has been a great deal of confusion over the role of dairy products and eggs in personal health. Butter is not necessarily excluded from the nutritional kitchen, but it is important to carefully evaluate the end result. The same is true of heavy cream and a variety of cheeses. The wisest course at this point is probably to adhere to the old injunction, "moderation in all things." In those instances where the texture, taste, or appearance of a food is most important, there are ways to lessen the overall level of calories from fats found in dairy products. See the section on "Substitutions" for ideas.

PURCHASING

The quality of dairy products and eggs has come under strict scrutiny, and the grading of most products is carefully controlled. Milk and milk-based products are carefully monitored at several stages of their production. The operator should be equally careful to store dairy foods at the correct temperature (35°–40° F). Eggs must be refrigerated when not in use. This is vital to keep these perishable items safe and wholesome. For a more in-depth look at some of the concerns over potential infection or intoxication of foods, read Focus 8-6: Food Safety and Salmonella.

Milk can be purchased in a variety of forms, including bulk, dried, or tinned. Evaporated milks (whole, skim, and condensed) are also available.

FOCUS 8-6   FOOD SAFETY AND SALMONELLA

Eggs are among the most versatile foods found in any kitchen. They are also an excellent example of the kinds of dangers that can appear in foods that aren't properly handled, stored, and cooked. News reports of deaths resulting from eating eggs infected with the salmonella bacteria caused authorities to take a closer look at the rules for safe handling of eggs and other "potentially hazardous" foods.

A potentially hazardous food has a bacteria-friendly environment. Bacteria need protein, moisture, and a moderate pH level. Eggs, meats, chicken, cooked beans and rice, and a host of other foods all fit this basic description. If these items remain in temperatures between 45 degrees F and 140 degrees F, the probability increases that many types of pathogens (bacteria, molds, yeast, and parasites) will thrive and multiply. Many kinds of bacteria are extremely adaptable to changes in their living conditions, once they are well-established, and can live on as either active or dormant contaminants for days, weeks, months, and even years.

The primary concern when it comes to eggs and poultry is the salmonella bacteria. Outbreaks of salmonellosis during 1988–1992 throughout New England, New York, and Tennessee led to the discovery that entire flocks of chickens, as well as the eggs that they produced, harbored the potentially harmful bacteria. Sanitation codes that had previously allowed eggs to be stored at room temperature were changed to state that eggs should be refrigerated. Any eggs with broken shells should be discarded, because the shells are often the site of additional contamination. It was further recommended that any dish requiring egg yolks that would not be cooked to a temperature greater than 165 degrees F should be prepared with a pasteurized egg product. Mayonnaise, Caesar salads, eggs-over-easy, and lightly poached eggs should be avoided.

The importance of cooking all foods properly, storing them correctly, reheating them quickly to a safe temperature, and keeping all tools, work surfaces, and storage containers scrupulously clean cannot be overemphasized. This injunction applies to personal hygiene as well. Cross-contamination is one of the most insidious means of spreading food-borne illnesses such as salmonellosis. Foods must be more than nutritious; they must also be wholesome and safe to eat.

SUBSTITUTIONS

Evaporated skimmed milk plays an important role in nutritional cooking; its color, flavor, and texture are used to duplicate the effect of adding heavy cream to soups and sauces without adding fats and cholesterol to the dish. Evaporated skimmed milk can also replace heavy cream as a coffee lightener, as it gives a pleasing flavor and "mouthfeel" to coffee. Skim milk can also be used to replace whole milk in many recipes. Part-skim mozzarella or ricotta may substitute for whole-milk cheeses.

Nonfat or low-fat yogurt can be drained to give it a texture similar to that of sour cream. This is done by placing the yogurt in a cheesecloth-lined strainer in a refrigerator (to keep the yogurt wholesome) and allowing the whey to drip away overnight as shown here. A small quantity of sour cream can then be stirred into the drained yogurt to give it a more desirable taste.

A list of acceptable substitutions can be found in Table 8-3. One of the questions often facing an operator is whether or not a switch to margarine in preference to butter is desirable. This issue is addressed in Focus 8-7: Butter versus Margarine.

Whole eggs do have a place in the nutritional kitchen. There are certain specific functions for which whole eggs have no replacement. However, if the needs of a particular kitchen should so dictate, the person in charge of purchasing should explore the feasibility of purchasing bulk egg whites, which are sold in liquid or frozen form. Egg substitutes may be a good idea on certain menus. The needs of the consumer should be kept in mind when making the determination whether or not omelets or scrambled eggs should be prepared from these substitutes.

FOCUS 8-7   BUTTER VERSUS MARGARINE

Nowhere does the issue of flavor versus health come more into play than in a typical discussion of whether margarine is "healthier" than butter. Just to set the record straight, the following list will compare the nutritional composition of a typical stick-style margarine with butter.

A pat of butter (about 1 teaspoon) = 34 calories = 4 grams of total fat = 2.5 grams saturated fat = 1.2 grams monounsaturated fat = .2 grams polyunsaturated fat = 11 milligrams cholesterol

A pat of vegetable oil margarine = 36 calories = 4 grams of total fat = .8 grams saturated fat = 1.8 grams monounsaturated fat = 1.3 grams polyunsaturated fat = 0 milligrams cholesterol

This comparison shows that the calorie and total fat measure are nearly identical. Butter does contain more saturated fat and cholesterol. In nutritional cooking the point is to moderate the use of all fats, so whenever butter is used, it must be carefully measured. The amount of cholesterol and saturated fat in a single teaspoon is not likely to upset the day's balance very dramatically. On the other hand, a person with an extreme sensitivity to cholesterol may have been advised by a doctor or nutritionist to replace butter with margarine.

The basic point is to keep in mind the relative merits of butter versus margarine. Because the use of discreet amounts of these ingredients should preclude any major dietary imbalance, the varying benefits of butter and margarine should be the basis for deciding, in accordance with the intended use. For example, is the product being used for flavor, as an ingredient in a batter or dough, as a cooking medium, or as a table-top spread?

Butter has a sweet, creamy taste and a "mouthfeel" that most margarines cannot duplicate. If butter is being used to achieve a special flavor, there really is no substitute. When used as a cooking medium, butter can be replaced by margarine, or better yet, by a wide variety of cooking oils, including olive oil, corn oil, or nut oils. A batter or dough can also usually be prepared with margarine or vegetable shortenings with no loss of quality, although the taste might be slightly different. The choice of butter or margarine as a spread for breads, rolls, and toasts should ideally be left to the individual. Try offering both, so that personal preference can be accommodated.

TABLE 8-3.
SUBSTITUTING LOW-FAT DAIRY PRODUCTS

HIGH-FAT PRODUCTS	LOW-FAT SUBSTITUTES
Heavy cream	Canned evaporated skimmed milk
Whole milk	Skim milk
Sour cream	Buttermilk and/or plain lowfat yogurt
Whole milk ricotta or mozzarella	Reduced fat versions made with either part or all skim milk
Sour cream as a garnish.	Drained low- or nonfat yogurt blended with a small amount of sour cream
Cream sauces	Velouté-based sauce

8-8. *Yogurt can often be used as is when substituting for sour cream or crème fraîche in certain recipes. However, a more pleasing texture is achieved when the yogurt is allowed to drain for 24 hours under refrigeration. The resulting yogurt "cheese" can be used in place of sour cream or crème fraîche as a garnish, or it can be seasoned and flavored with peppercorns, fresh herbs, and spices to make a low-fat, low-calorie spread or dip to serve with crudités or whole-grain breads. Note the amount of liquid (shown in the measuring cup) that drained from the yogurt.*

PANTRY ITEMS AND DRY GOODS

A great deal of emphasis has been placed on purchasing fresh meats, fish, poultry, and produce, and that is naturally a very important part of maintaining a kitchen's supplies. Equal care should be taken to stock the pantry with such staple items as dried beans, pasta, oil, flours, grains, and flavoring ingredients. The variety of foods purchased will depend upon the menu items being prepared. The following section discusses a broad array of items, with particular attention paid to any purchasing factors that should be taken into account for the nutritional kitchen, as well as directions for storage so as to maintain the best possible quality.

GRAINS, WHOLE MEALS, CEREALS, AND FLOURS

With the shift in emphasis from protein-rich foods to those offering a good source of complex carbohydrates, the benefits of a variety of grains, meals, cereals, and flours has come to the fore. The number of grains typically prepared in a kitchen today is substantially greater than would have been the case several years ago. In addition to the standard offering of rice and perhaps barley, today's chef has become increasingly familiar with previously unknown or exotic grains such as couscous, quinoa, millet, and amaranth. A selection of these foods is shown in Figure 8-9. Tess, a finely-textured grain, and Job's tears, are two additional grains that are becoming readily available.

Grains can be whole, cracked, or made into coarse or fine meals or flours. Whole grains usually have the germ and bran intact. They therefore are less stable under long-term storage than processed grains. The oils in the grain are concentrated in these parts of the grain structure. The more milling and/or processing a grain undergoes, the less likely it is to become rancid. There is some benefit to selecting grains that have been stone-ground, because this milling method is less likely to overheat the grain during processing; however, these grains carry a higher price tag. For more information read Focus 8-8: Stone-Ground and Whole-Grain Meals and Flours. All grains, meals, cereals, and flours should be kept cool, dry, properly covered, and away from exposure to direct light. Some whole grains may even need to be stored under refrigeration. These foods do last a long time, when properly stored, but they will eventually become stale and lose most of their flavor and nutritional quality.

Some people worry that a diet which incorporates a large amount of grains and cereals will lack the exciting tastes and flavors to which they have become accustomed. It is true that most grains and grain-based products have a subtle taste when served "as is." This characteristic makes them ideal for carrying the flavors of other foods and also enables them to act as the base for smaller portions of more pungent and highly flavored foods. The mound of

8-9. *Far from being dull and starchy, these foods are likely to be among those the chef will turn to more and more frequently to add some variety and interest to a nutritional menu. A selection of delicious foods with interesting textures and flavors that are a perfect accompaniment to a variety of entrées, or on their own with a savory sauce or condiment or plain includes (clockwise from top left): a selection of whole grain rolls and bagel (these renditions enriched with sunflower and sesame seeds), rolled oats for a hearty breakfast cereal; flour tortillas resting on whole-grain rye crisps, slices of a whole-wheat baguette; fusilli pasta; basmati rice; penne pasta; shredded wheat biscuits for a cold breakfast cereal selection; nests of spinach fettucini; and pearl barley.*

steaming couscous served with a spicy stew and piquant harissa sauce does more than fill up the plate. It also offers the diner a chance to calm a tongue burned from too many hot spices and chilies. A bed of fragrant basmati rice makes a serving of a seafood curry appear more bountiful, and each grain can carry the complex flavors of the sauce, without losing its own special savor.

FOCUS 8-8   STONE-GROUND AND WHOLE-GRAIN MEALS AND FLOURS

The basket of rolls, loaf of hot bread, or fragrant muffins a chef offers the guests has the potential to give them a great deal more than something on which to fill up while they read the menu. Baked goods are a good source of complex carbohydrates, dietary fiber, and other essential nutrients. The interested chef or baker has the opportunity to develop some special recipes or techniques designed to enhance the nutritional value of the average dinner roll.

Many baked products are made with bleached white flour that has been stripped of the bran, which contains a great deal of the grain's nutritive value. In addition, steel rollers are often used to mill flours. They normally operate at temperatures high enough to destroy heat-sensitive nutrients such as thiamine and niacin. The purchaser who is looking for ways to improve the value of breads and rolls should become familiar with some key terms.

Stone-ground means that the grains (often with the bran intact) are milled between stone wheels. The wheels may be operated by water power, and they seldom reach the same temperatures as steel rollers. The flours and meals produced in this manner will usually have higher levels of many vitamins, minerals, fiber, and natural oils. Stone-ground flours and meals should be stored carefully—away from heat, light, air, and moisture—to preserve their quality and to prevent them from staling or turning rancid.

To say that a grain or meal is "whole" means that the bran has not been stripped away before it is milled. This tends to give the flour a darker appearance, due to the specks of bran that will remain after milling. Items baked with whole-grain flours generally have a nuttier and more pronounced flavor than those made from white-wheat flour. The texture produced by whole-grain flours is generally chewier and denser.

Because they are not "diluted" with the bran content, white flours will have a higher ratio of gluten, the protein in wheat flour that enables yeast doughs to rise properly. Formulas for whole-grain breads frequently will require the addition of some white flour to help achieve a lighter texture. The greater the proportion of non-wheat flours, the denser the texture of the bread will be. Far from considering this a fault, today's health-conscious consumer appreciates the chewy texture and nut-like flavor of peasant-style whole-grain bread.

LEGUMES

Many of the world's cuisines that are built around grains, such as those of Japan or South America, have a complementary reliance on beans to round out the nutritional balance. The composition of beans is weighted more heavily toward protein than that of grains. Except when found in soups, dried beans and peas may be unfamiliar to many consumers. It therefore may take a little ingenuity by the chef to gain consumer acceptance for dishes that are based on these foods. The taste of many beans tends toward the bland side. If aromatics, herbs, and other ingredients are added judiciously, the perception of beans as uninteresting can readily be erased.

Various legumes can be obtained in the fresh state at certain times of the year. These include scarlet runner beans, fava beans, lima beans, and black-eyed peas. These foods should be treated in the same manner as any fresh produce. Dried legumes, which will last for long periods when properly stored, should be handled in the same way as other dry goods: They should be placed in an area that is well-ventilated, dry, cool, and dark. As beans and peas age, they will take longer to cook and require more liquid during cooking. The chef should check beans and peas before cooking to remove dried, moldy ones and small stones that sometimes find their way into the packages.

DRIED PASTAS

A pasta dish is often one of the most popular items on a menu. Consumers have increasingly accepted pasta and other noodles as a healthy alternative to standard fare. This perception is based in reality. Pasta and noodles offer a good source of complex carbohydrates. While it may be trite to restate that the problem is not the pasta but the sauce, it is a concept that needs to be understood before jumping on the pasta bandwagon. Offering dishes with butter, grated cheese, or high-fat meats such as bacon lessens the overall nutritional value of the dish greatly.

Dried noodles are made from a flour-based paste. Some special noodles, especially those from Eastern cuisines, may be based on a flour made from legumes. (For example, mung beans are the foundation for cellophane noodles.) Because they are dried, they will be suitable for storage in the same manner as other dried goods. The chief advantages to dried noodles, apart from their good keeping qualities, are that they tend to be less expensive than some other foods, they are available in a number of different shapes, sizes, colors, and flavors, and they usually have unassertive flavors that blend well with many sauces and garnishes, and with other tastes.

Fresh pasta has a definite place on certain menus, and a recipe procedure for preparing it is included in the recipe section of this book (Part Three).

OILS AND OTHER COOKING FATS

Cooking fats and oil are the culprits in sending many essentially nutritious foods and recipes over the brink into excess. They are also the very same elements that can lift an ordinary dish to new heights. The trick for the chef is to learn how and when to add a bit of butter or a droplet of oil. These ingredients are important in a well-balanced diet, and perform certain specific culinary functions. Careful control of the amount used, as well as an appreciation of how to get the most mileage out of the oils is important. For more discussion of the function that fats perform in the kitchen, read Focus 8-9: How to Spare the Oil and Spoil the Guest.

The majority of oils used in a nutritional kitchen will fall into the mono- and polyunsaturated categories. They are generally stable when stored at room temperature around 60-70 degrees F. Any oil will become rancid, take on an unpleasant odor, or smoke when heated, if proper storage procedures are not followed. Oils are best stored in glass or metal containers, out of direct contact with heat, light, air, and salts. Some very fragrant oils used for adding a particular taste (hazelnut oil, dark sesame oil, or extra-virgin olive oils) are especially prone to loss of their flavors if they have been carelessly handled. These kinds of oils usually carry the highest price tag, so it is doubly important to exercise care. Some chefs prefer to keep these oils refrigerated when not in use.

Some other cooking fats that bear mentioning include bacon, aerosol fats, and butter, an ingredient discussed previously in the section devoted to dairy products and eggs.

Bacon, and similar items such as sausages or salt pork, need not be banned from the kitchen. It is true that they are high in fats, cholesterol, and sodium, and possibly in nitrites or nitrates as well. There is no substitute for their special flavor in some dishes, however, so the chef may wish to have small quantities available to use as a seasoning. These products can generally be stored under refrigeration for a few days or frozen for longer periods. When using small amounts, the best way to extract their flavor is to chop them very fine and allow them to render gently over low heat. If possible, a dish including these ingredients should be prepared in advance, cooled, and then refrigerated. Any excess fat will then come to the surface, where it can be more easily lifted away.

Aerosol fats are popular because a very small film of oil can be applied evenly and easily to the entire surface of a pan. There is some environmental concern over their use because of the presence of polyfluorocarbons (PFCs), which are necessary for certain types of aerosol sprays to work. It is possible to achieve the same results with different tools, however. Alternative methods which achieve the same effect include placing the appropriate oil in a pump-spray bottle, or using a pastry brush or soft cloth to gently wipe an oil onto the surface.

FOCUS 8-9   HOW TO SPARE THE OIL AND SPOIL THE GUEST

Amidst all the confusion over fats, it is easy to lose sight of the fact that there is room in the diet for carefully monitored amounts of oils and other cooking fats. A basic rule of thumb is that a diet based on approximately 2000 calories per day can usually include 2-3 tablespoons of added fat or oil. This is still not a very large amount. By making careful selections and emphasizing mono- and polyunsaturated oils, an individual can find a number of ways to get the maximum benefits out of the least amounts.

Olives, hazelnuts, avocados, walnuts, peanuts, sesame seeds, and other oil-rich foods are the source of many special oils. The method often used to extract these oils is known as "cold pressing." This method, which is not totally efficient, may leave up to 20% of the available oil in the source. However, cold pressing's benefit is that the natural flavors remain in the oil, contributing wonderful aromas and flavors to any dish in which they are used.

Olive oil grading is done in accordance with an international grading system. When the term "extra-virgin" appears on the label of olive oil, it means that the oil has been prepared from the first pressing of the fruit only (the pits must be removed), and that there is less than 1% acid by weight. Virgin olive oil is the next best quality. It may have from 1% to 3.3% acid by weight, and is made from the second pressing of the fruit. Oil made by treating the fruit and the pits with a chemical solvent before pressing can only be designated as olive oil.

Sesame, peanut, hazelnut, walnut, and almond oils are not currently as carefully regulated as olive oil. Still, many producers use the same terminology because knowledgeable consumers equate cold pressing and extra-virgin with top-quality oils.

The more flavorful the oil, the more expensive it will usually be. These costly oils also will not last a long time. They rapidly lose their flavor and become stale or even rancid if they are held improperly or for too long. Keep them away from heat, light, air, salt, and moisture by storing them in dark containers in a cool area or under refrigeration.

The chef will find that these oils have a range of applications. Their most obvious use is as a dressing for a salad or a plate of vegetables. In addition, a small bowl of fruity olive oil can be offered as an alternative to butter or margarine on bread; a few drops of walnut oil on top of a bowl of soup, or drizzled on a grilled tuna steak, can impart a wonderful taste without adding significantly to either the fat content or the overall calories. The important thing is to apply them sparingly, at the last moment.

SUGARS AND SYRUPS

One suggestion for adjusting the typical American diet is to reduce the percentage of calories consumed in the form of refined sugars. The current estimates of an average daily intake ranges from around 20% to 25% of the day's total calories. Most dietary goals suggest reducing this percentage to 10% or less.

This does not mean that the chef must ban sugar, corn syrup, jams, jellies, honey, molasses, and other sweeteners from the pantry. Instead, he or she should evaluate recipes to determine where and when it is possible to reduce or eliminate the amount required. The recipes in this book do make use of a number of different sweeteners, and a well-stocked pantry should have a selection of sugars, including white, confectioners', and brown; syrups such as maple syrup, corn syrups, honey, and molasses; and items such as marmalades, jellies, and jams.

Sugars and syrups may be purchased in many forms. Brown sugar, superfine, granulated, powdered, demerrara, and turbinado sugars are all available, either in individual packets, one-pound boxes, or bulk. They should be kept in dry storage, away from moisture and heat. While there is little chance that they will lose their flavor over extended storage, moisture and heat could destroy their crystal formation and cause caking and lumping. Brown sugar is usually best stored under refrigeration in a closed container to prevent it from drying out and hardening.

Syrups, honey, and molasses may be purchased in different-sized containers, and should be kept in dry storage until opened. Maple syrup should be stored in the refrigerator once it is opened, but other forms of pourable sugars can usually be stored at room temperature. Be certain that they are kept carefully covered to avoid crystal formation or contamination.

AROMATIC AND FLAVORING INGREDIENTS

Reading through the recipes in this book should clearly demonstrate the importance placed on using good quality ingredients. This is as true of the "garnish" and "flavoring" ingredients as it is of the fruits, vegetables, and meats. Purchase these ingredients with an eye to quality. Some of them should be kept under refrigeration to prevent a loss of quality. Others should be purchased in small quantities so that prolonged storage will not rob them of flavor. Table 8-5 shows the range of ingredients, and the forms in which they are available, to help the chef increase the range of flavors in each dish. When a well-stocked pantry is at the chef's disposal, it can act as a source of inspiration.

Many of the recipes included in this book make use of specialty ingredients such as dried fruits and vegetables. Tomatoes, mushrooms, chilis, ba-

TABLE 8-4.

FLAVORING INGREDIENTS

INGREDIENT	HOW AVAILABLE
Herbs	Fresh, dried
Spices	Usually dried, available whole, ground, or as blends
Vinegars	Bottled in a variety of sizes
Balsamic	
Herb-flavored	
Red wine	
Rice wine	
Fruit-flavored	
Apple cider	
Distilled white	
Mustards	Whole seeds (white and black), powder, and
Whole-grain	prepared condiment
Dijon-style	
Creole-style	
Bavarian-style	
Peppercorns	Dried, freeze-dried, or packed in brine
Capers	Packed in brine
Horseradish	Fresh as root or prepared in a brine
Pickles	Packed in brine (jars or bulk containers)
Wild mushrooms	Fresh (depending upon season), or dried; truffles are also available tinned
Tomatoes	Fresh (may be oven roasted or pan-smoked for additional flavor; sundried (may be packed in oil); canned paste, puree, whole, crushed; juice
Chocolate	Cocoa powder—Dutch-processed has been treated with an alkali to mellow flavor and give darker color; unsweetened, baking, or eating; bitter, bittersweet, sweet; milk chocolate or white chocolate; chips, bars, or blocks; syrups
Sweeteners	Syrups, crystals, cubes, or powdered
Extracts and essences	Aromatics are steeped in either alcohol or oil and used in a variety of dishes. One of the most common is vanilla, but fruit-flavored, rum-flavored, and seed-flavored (anise or fennel) are also available
Wines, liqueurs, and cordials	Used to add flavor, to deglaze pans, or to act as a cooking liquid.

nanas, pineapple, raisins, currants, figs, and cranberries are among some of the numerous products available in a dried form. Drying any food tends to intensify the flavor. It may also concentrate the natural sugars; raisins and apricots, for example, contain a great deal more sugar than their fresh counterparts, but

8-10. *The judicious use of a commonplace spice such as pepper-corns can bolster the taste of a traditional dish that seems to be missing something. Adding a dash of something unexpected such as allspice or cumin might add a new dimension and a special flair to a dish. Some of the whole spices and spice powders that should be available to give the chef a wide palette of flavors with which to work are shown here: (clockwise from top left corner) powdered mustard and paprika to add some "heat"; whole allspice berries for an intriguing blend of flavors in one spice; fennel seeds (also known as anise); cumin seeds; whole nutmeg to grate di-rectly into dishes for a fresh, mellow taste; bay leaves to add a subtle aroma to long-simmering preparations; whole cloves; cin-namon sticks; an array of peppercorns, including red, green, black, and white to use singly or as a blend; and a whole vanilla bean.*

normally a far smaller measure is needed to get the desired flavor. It is normally a good idea to rehydrate dried foods by briefly soaking them in a hot liquid. In most cases, this liquid is incorporated into the finished dish to get the maximum flavor value.

FOCUS 8-10   CHOCOLATE WITHOUT FAT

Chocolate is one of life's greatest pleasures for many people. Unfortunately, the largest percentage of calories in a typical chocolate bar comes from cocoa butter. It is possible to get the special flavor of chocolate without all those fat calories. The trick is to replace chocolate with cocoa powder.

Cocoa powder contains approximately 1 gram of fat in a tablespoon and almost 14 total calories. Although it isn't usually recommended as a significant source of any particular nutrient, cocoa powder can be the chef's ally in developing a repertoire of chocolate-flavored dishes. Nowhere is this ability more appreciated than in the sometimes perplexing job of developing desserts that taste good but don't rely upon fats for most of their flavor and texture.

Cocoa powders should be chosen carefully. The best-quality brands will have a full, rich flavor with no harshness or bitterness. Dutch-process cocoa has been treated with an alkali in order to mellow the flavor and give the cocoa a deeper color. Another thing to watch is the amount of fat in a particular brand. The fat content can range from 10% to 20%, depending upon the way in which a manufacturer handles the chocolate during processing.

A steaming cup of hot chocolate is a treat that calorie-conscious diners may not think they can have. Replacing milk or cream with a combination of skim milk and evaporated skim milk is one way to reduce the fat. It is possible to produce in-house a pre-blended drink mix that has less sugar than most commercially available versions. Not only does it taste good, it is a great way to get a little extra calcium into the diet. Chocolate does interfere slightly with calcium absorption, but there is not enough chocolate in a cup of cocoa to completely wipe out the positive benefits from the calcium.

Other ingredients are selected for their special piquant flavors. Capers, pickles, olives, and brine-packed green peppercorns are high in sodium, by themselves. However, rinsing away the excess brine and using carefully measured amounts are steps the chef can take to assure that these ingredients can be used without upsetting the nutritional balance of a dish.

Special oils and vinegars are used frequently in the nutritional kitchen. These items should be of the best available quality. It is easy to infuse the flavor of herbs, spices, peppers, chilis, and garlic into oils and vinegars, or the chef may prefer to purchase flavored versions. Because they can lose flavor rapidly, it is a good idea to avoid overpurchasing. Once oils and vinegars lose their freshness, they assume a musty, unpleasant aroma and taste.

Various extracts and essences are frequently used to give a sauce, baked item, or frozen dessert a special flavor. Vanilla extract is probably the most common example. The best quality should be selected so that the most round and mellow flavor can be achieved with the smallest amount. Vanilla extract, as well as other extracts based on ingredients such as almonds, mints, and citrus fruits, do contain alcohol. However, it is usually such a small part of any recipe that there is little impact on the overall recipe.

Another important pantry basic is a supply of good quality chocolates and cocoa powders. Chocolate desserts are among the most popular offered by any restaurant. In a nutrition-conscious kitchen, it becomes important to offer at least a selection or two that can satisfy the craving for chocolate without sacrificing nutritional cooking guidelines. As Focus 8-10 describes, this seeming miracle can be accomplished with cocoa powder and a little imagination.

Cooking Techniques

The image of nutritional cooking is one of the major obstacles preventing its widespread acceptance. It will take more than magazine articles, high-tech television programs, and glossy coffee-table books to shatter the mental picture many people still harbor of a dietitian dressed in white, instructing us to eat unfamiliar foods with unpleasant textures and tastes, all without benefit of butter and salt. Much of the burden for changing this negative perception will rest on the shoulders of the chefs who decide to incorporate nutrition into their menus.

For chefs the problem boils down to two closely joined concerns. The first is a reluctance to change cooking styles. The second is a genuine concern that nutritionally prepared foods simply will not taste as good as those prepared using a more traditional approach. This chapter of the book will concentrate on dispelling the image of nutrition as punishment for either the chef or the guest.

Actually, many of the techniques already familiar to the chef are perfectly suited to a menu built around the nutritional cooking guidelines. Some techniques may require a few minor adaptations or modifications. Others will work "as is." Only two techniques, pan-frying and deep-frying, are outside the parameters of the guidelines discussed in the first part of this book.

A properly cooked food should have a lot of flavor and texture. It should look appealing also. The incorporation of nutrition does not necessarily require the chef to completely give up the high-fat, high-sodium, and high-calorie ingredients that many people crave.

In the first section of this book, the key terms were "moderate" and "increase." They are no less important here. In each technique there are several ways to increase the quality of the finished dish by selecting the highest-quality ingredients and preparing those ingredients in the best way. When ingredients and preparation are handled properly, it becomes much easier to moderate any procedures and eliminate or substitute for any ingredients that might have a negative impact on the nutritional value of a dish.

DRY-HEAT METHODS

The dry-heat methods of cooking that are suitable for the nutritional kitchen are essentially the same as those used in the traditional kitchen: sauté, grill, broil, and roast. Two techniques that are not appropriate are pan-frying and deep-frying. However, it is possible to duplicate some of the effects of these techniques, and these tricks will be explained, where appropriate.

SAUTÉ

Sautéed foods are prepared quickly in a small amount of fat or oil, over high heat. They are frequently cooked "à la minute," which means that the food is not prepared until an order arrives in the kitchen. Naturally, sautéed foods can be prepared in larger batches for service in a number of different dining situations, such as a cafeteria or dining hall.

For nutritional purposes, there is little need for any dramatic changes in the actual application of this technique. Traditional kitchen standards are well within acceptable ranges for nutritional cooking. The chef will need to pay more attention to the selection and preparation of foods that will be sautéed and must be more judicious in the use of cooking fats and oil. Foods should be naturally tender, of a shape and size to allow them to cook rapidly in a very small amount of fat over high heat.

As examples of adjustment in food selection and cooking fat use, for a nutritional sauté, the chef might use the Choice grade steak, instead of Prime, because Choice has less marbling. Sautés of beef, duck, or other meats that have a good quantity of natural fats and oils may not need any additional oil in the pan. More delicate meats, fish, or poultry may benefit from a light coating. Pre-seasoning pans can also help. The pictures in Figure 9-1 demonstrate how to properly pre-season pans for sautéing, which can be done before service. If the sauté pans are already oiled, the chef won't have to stop in the middle of a busy dinner or lunch to get pans ready, and the temptation to simply pour a ladleful of oil or butter will be eliminated.

To further reduce the amount of additional oil or other cooking fat, the chef might consider some different equipment options some of which are shown here. Nonstick pans, although not always the best choice for a high-volume operation, may be acceptable for certain smaller places. A tilting kettle (or Swiss brazier) made of stainless steel tends to release foods properly—with little sticking—if they are not disturbed during the first part of cooking. This kettle may require only a very small amount of oil, and in some cases, none at

9-1. PRESEASONING A PAN FOR SAUTÉING

a *The pan is first scoured with salt to remove any lingering debris and to give the interior of the pan a smooth surface.*

b *A light film of oil is sprayed into the pan to coat it evenly.*

c *The pan is rubbed with a piece of absorbent toweling to remove any excess and coat any bare spots.*

9-2. *Cutting back on the amount of oils and other fats added during the cooking process is an important factor in adjusting to a healthy style of cooking. The right pan can make a big difference when sautéing foods. Nonstick skillets (top right) are a good choice for use in the home, but for most restaurant operations, many chefs prefer to use cast-iron skillets that have been properly seasoned. A properly seasoned pan has been treated with enough oil to permeate the relatively porous metal. There is usually no need to add more fat, even when sautéing a delicate meat. Note the difference in appearance between the seasoned pan (bottom) and the untreated pan (top left).*

all. This is an excellent way to prepare sautéed items in larger amounts. Stainless-steel-lined sauté pans are very desirable for "white tablecloth" restaurants for the same reasons. Another excellent option is a cast-iron pan that has been properly seasoned and maintained. For more information, see Focus 9-1: Choosing, Preparing, and Maintaining a Sauté Pan.

Method

1. Select and prepare the food.

Sautés automatically require foods to be tender, portion-sized or smaller, and thin enough to cook quickly over high heat without toughening (although some thicker items may be finished in a hot oven without sacrificing quality).

FOCUS 9-1 CHOOSING, PREPARING, AND MAINTAINING A SAUTÉ PAN

The pan chosen for a sauté will have a great influence on the outcome of the dish. The shape of the pan, the material used, the surface treatment (if any) of the interior of the pan all play a role.

Over the course of centuries of cooking, the traditional shape of a sauté pan has evolved. The flat bottom provides a cooking surface. The shallow, sloping sides of the pan encourage any juices released into the pan to reduce rapidly, forming a flavorful base used to create the accompanying sauce.

The metal should be of a gauge heavy enough to prevent warping or hot spots and it should be responsive to rapid changes in heat. One of the best choices when the amount of oil is being reduced is a stainless-steel-lined aluminum sauté pan. Other good choices include a stainless-steel-lined copper sauté pan, a nonstick pan, and a cast iron sauté pan (also known as a griswold or a spider).

Each of these surfaces requires careful treatment. Nonstick surfaces are generally the least durable, and because of the extensive use a pan will undergo in a restaurant kitchen, they tend to be more appropriate for use in the home. Metal spoons, spatulas, and pot scrubbers will eventually destroy the nonstick coating. Stainless-steel-lined pans tend to hold up well with the least amount of special care. The surfaces should be scoured with salt rather than stainless-steel scrubbers to avoid unduly scratching the surface however.

For sautéing without any additional fats or oils, many chefs like to use cast iron pans. These pans must be properly seasoned before they can be used for cooking. One technique for seasoning a pan is illustrated in the step-by-step sequence shown here. After the pan is properly seasoned, it should be wiped clean rather than washed to maintain the protective seal on the pan's interior surface.

The preparation of foods for sautéing includes slicing, butterflying, or pounding in order to increase the surface area and shorten overall cooking time.

The decision to remove or retain poultry skin is one that should be made with respect for the demands on the kitchen. It may make more sense to take the skin off for sautéing and for service of great quantities, but for an à la minute kitchen, the chef may prefer to retain the skin to help prevent drying and to allow the skin's fats to act in place of any additional cooking oil. For further information about selecting and preparing a variety of foods, refer to Chapter 8, *Ingredients*, as well as specific recipes.

2. Add oil to the pan, if necessary.

The need for oil is determined by the nature of the food being cooked. Lean, delicate meats, fish, and poultry will need the added lubrication. The oil should be applied before placing the pan on the heat, using one of the following procedures: Spray a thin film on the inside of the pan (using a spray bottle); brush a thin film on with a basting brush; or pour in a small amount of oil, or other fat, and then use a piece of paper towel to spread it evenly and remove any excess. There should be only a very thin film, enough to lightly coat the pan. A rule of thumb is to use no more than about one half teaspoon (3 to 5 grams) of oil or other fat per order.

3. Preheat the pan until it is hot, but not smoking.

This step is essential in developing the best flavor in a sautéed dish. The juices released from the food will begin to reduce properly so that they will coat both the item and the pan. Reducing drippings in the pan is important when preparing a sauce. The chef must be careful not to allow the pan to get too hot (there will be a smell of hot metal), because of the danger of scorching.

4. Add the food to the pan.

For the best finished appearance of the dish, the food should be added so that the neatest side, known as the "presentation" side, is placed in contact with the pan first. Initially, the food will stick to the pan. It is important to allow the food to continue to cook, undisturbed, until its fats and juices start to render. As they are released, they will also release the food from the contact points with the pan. It will be easier then to turn the food without tearing it.

5. Turn the food once and complete cooking on the second side.

Ideally the food should be turned only once; this is done to create a good-looking exterior that is not speckled with reduced drippings. There are exceptions to this guideline, however, and experience as well as the nature of the food being sautéed will determine how often it should be turned. If the food is thick, it may be preferable to complete the cooking by placing it on a rack, uncovered, in a hot oven. This finishing is usually less drying than continuing to sauté over high heat.

6. Remove the food, and deglaze the reduced drippings in the pan.

The food's natural flavor is concentrated in the drippings that have cooked down in the sauté pan, forming what is referred to as the *fond*. The fond is almost invariably used as the basis of a sauce, so the flavor is recaptured to become part of the finished dish. Deglazing can be done with a variety of liquids, but if alcohol-based ones are used, there may be an increase in calories in the finished sauce, because some, *but not necessarily all*, of the alcohol will be cooked away. Very often, the amount of fond released by leaner meats, fish, or poultry is not sufficient by itself to prepare a sauce. In that case, it is

9-3. SAUTÉING PORK

a *Properly portioned medallions of pork are shown here being dry-sautéed. The fats naturally present in the pork act as the lubrication, and no additional oil is added to the pan. As the meat sautés, fats and juices that render into the pan release the meat so that it can be easily turned. Note the color change on the edges of the unturned medallion; this indicates that the meat is ready to be turned to complete cooking.*

b *A brown pork or veal stock is added to the pan once the pork is properly cooked to deglaze any of the drippings that have reduced in the pan. They will then become a part of the finished sauce, recapturing as much of the flavor as possible.*

c *Additional stock is added to the pan and allowed to reduce along with a variety of dried fruits and other garnish ingredients. This picture shows the correct consistency for the sauce. Once it has properly reduced, the medallions may be returned to the pan briefly to reheat gently as well as to be evenly coated with the sauce.*

important to use a richly flavored jus, stock, bouillon, or other sauce base to make up for the lack of fond.

7. Finish the sauce as indicated by the recipe, or as desired, and plate the sautéed food.

There are so many different ways to sauce a sautéed food that there is little benefit to giving general guidelines. The important thing to remember about a sauce for a nutritional sauté is that the choice should be one that will not introduce additional fats in the form of butter, cream, egg yolks, or cheeses. Better choices would be sauces based on vegetables, vegetable or fruit purees, fond de veau lié, or reductions. These are all good examples of sauces that are complementary to the intended effect of nutritional sauté.

GRILLING

Grilling has become so firmly associated with nutritional cooking that it is now a standard used to judge the nutritional qualifications of other techniques. There are several reasons for its popularity as a nutritional cooking technique: Additional oil or fat does not need to be added during cooking, foods prepared by this technique are generally lean, and the flavor is highly developed. The last is due to the slight charring and the reduction of drippings directly on the food's surface. No adaptions to the actual grilling techniques are necessary, but it is important to remember that some components typically associated with these techniques might require a careful evaluation before they are used. Oil-based marinades should be replaced with ones that rely more on citrus juices, vinegars, or other aromatic liquids. Rather than rely on oils' "moisturizing" effects, the chef should carefully select foods to provide moisture. Where necessary, it may be a good idea to protect the food from drying by wrapping it in a protective coating such as lettuce leaves or dampened cornhusks.

The choice of sauce is also an area where the chef can exercise some control over a grilled dish's ultimate nutritional value. Traditional selections have tended toward emulsified, butter-based sauces or compound butters. Some classic and contemporary examples of this tradition include a grilled steak served with béarnaise sauce or a grilled tuna steak served with a ginger-lime butter. These sauces have been used because chefs have believed they will lend moisture and richness to foods that might have dried out due to the intensity of the grill's heat. Nutritional grilling will challenge the chef to cook the food so that it remains moist and succulent and to select a sauce that will further promote flavor and texture without sacrificing nutritional benefit. For example, replacing a compound butter with a cold or warm salsa might provide a refreshing counterpoint on a variety of levels: color, texture, temperature, and flavor.

9-4. SEASONING THE GRILL

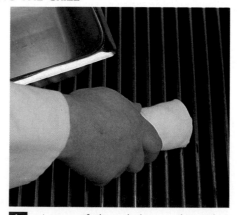

a *The rods for a grill must be carefully cleaned before you start to cook. A wire brush is scrubbed over the entire surface of the grill to remove any charred particles and to smooth the entire surface. This is done before the grill is heated, and as needed throughout cooking to prevent a buildup from forming.*

b *A piece of cheesecloth is used to rub a light film of oil onto the rods. This makes it easier to turn foods as they grill, since they are less likely to stick. Be sure not to apply the oil too liberally, since it could ignite.*

The preparation of the grill is also important. The rack needs to be scrupulously cleaned, and the rods should be seasoned as shown in the accompanying photographs so that the food will not have such a tendency to stick and tear when it is turned. The rods may be brushed with a small amount of oil while they are cool and then rubbed with toweling to remove any excess. Delicate foods such as fish or vegetables may require hand racks for successful grilling.

The use of special woods, stems, or leaves of herbs, or grapevine trimmings is one of the ways in which a grilled item can be given a special flavor. Some thought should be given to the food being prepared before deciding to add this intense taste. Not all foods can stand up to the strong aroma of mesquite, for instance.

Method

1. Select and prepare the food.

The types of foods suitable for grilling are similar in many respects to those used for sautéing. They should be naturally tender and thin enough or properly shaped to cook rapidly in the presence of intense, direct heat. The range of choices for grilling can be extensive. For some ideas, read Focus 9-2.

FOCUS 9-2   GRILLING THE UNUSUAL

Grilled foods of all sorts are showing up on menus across the country. Chops, steaks, and chicken prepared with a smoky, lightly charred coating have always been relished. But today's chef is grilling things that would have seemed outrageous, even a few years ago.

For example, all sorts of fish are sharing space on the grill with the traditional meats and poultry. Tuna, shrimp, scallops, swordfish, and shark are all popular, and some menus feature even more interesting items: squid, octopus, pompano, or lobster. Most fish and shellfish that will be cooked this way benefit from a brief marination in an acidic bath flavored with chopped shallots, cracked peppercorns, garlic, ginger root, and citrus zest. Obviously, a marinade could contain different ingredients, and the choice of particular items should be made with an awareness of the expected taste of the finished dish.

Grilled pizza seems to have achieved tremendous popularity overnight, and grilled breads are not far behind. These simple, rustic dishes are excellent as light appetizers or entrées. They can be offered in two sizes, increasing the options for the guest and encouraging him or her to sample something new. Grilled tortillas

continued ▶

served with fresh salsa and other vegetables is a great alternative to cheese- and sour cream-laden nachos and quesadillas.

Vegetables cooked on the grill are becoming familiar in most parts of the country. While peppers, mushrooms, and summer squashes are all well-suited to this method, other vegetables can be used with equal success: eggplants, sweet potatoes, fennel, leeks, red onions, winter squashes, and even some lettuces such as raddichio and romaine. These vegetables can gain a little additional flavor, through the use of a modified vinaigrette liberally seasoned with herbs and spices. (Note: Dense vegetables should be parcooked by steaming or boiling before they are grilled.)

Fruits are getting some attention as potential fodder for the grill, as well. A sizzling piece of grilled mango or banana makes a wonderful accompaniment to grilled or roasted fish. Pineapple can be lightly coated with a honey or maple syrup glaze and grilled before being served with a scoop of ricotta-based ice cream, offering the guest an unusual dessert item.

Tender or delicately textured items may need some additional advance preparation. They may be marinated briefly in a vinegar-, wine-, or citrus-based bath and brushed with some additional marinade during cooking; the acids will tend to firm the texture of the proteins by "cooking" them, in addition to giving them a brighter flavor. The use of marinades with more substantial foods is commonplace, and is a technique generally intended to add flavor, not moisture. The zucchini as well as the flank steak shown here has been allowed to marinate in a reduced-oil vinaigrette.

Another way to protect foods during grilling is to place them in a hand rack or wrap them in a protective coating such as dampened grape or banana leaves. For further information about selecting and preparing a variety of foods, refer to Chapter 8 and to specific recipes in this book.

2. Preheat the grill until the rods are hot enough to immediately sear the food.

As noted previously, part of the grill's preparation requires that any debris or food particles that may be stuck to the rods be scrubbed away. The rods should be cleaned and lightly oiled, and any excess should be wiped away before preheating the grill. The grill should be very hot before the chef starts to cook.

If special hardwood, chips, or herb branches or leaves are being used, they should be soaked in cold water while the grill pre-heats. Then, when the grill is hot, they can be thrown on top of the coals or firestones, where they will smoke, creating a smoke-bath to envelop the food.

3. Place the food on the grill.

The presentation side of the food should be placed down first so that it is in contact with the heated grill rack. Allow the food to grill long enough for it to release itself from the rods. If the food is turned too quickly, it will stick and tear. If desired, the food can be "marked" by turning the food 90 degrees, without turning it over. This will produce crosshatch marks, a purely decorative step that can be eliminated if desired.

4. Turn the food once, and complete cooking on the second side.

Turning the food repeatedly is generally not necessary and may cause it to lose more juices than might be desirable. The exception to this procedure is when the chef is going to use a glaze or sauce to coat the food. The sauce is frequently brushed on the food, then the food is turned so that the sauce will reduce, until all sides are evenly and properly coated. A number of items are receiving a coating of a spicy barbecue sauce in the accompanying photographs.

Many chefs will mentally divide the grill into a number of zones so that they can keep all of the fish in one portion of the grill, all the beef in another, the poultry in another, and so forth. There should also be a holding zone, which should not be as hot as the cooking area, to give the chef some control over the cooking rate. If a food is cooking too quickly, it may be pulled away from the more-intense heat to adjust cooking time as appropriate. The grill shown here provides a good example of the way a busy grill might look during the middle of dinner service.

9-5. *Kebabs of yellow squash, zucchini, and eggplant slices are grilled over hot coals until they are crisp on the outside, and tender on the inside. A light coating of a reduced-oil vinaigrette is brushed onto them as they cook for additional flavor.*

9-6. *Flank steak is a good choice for grilling. It has a naturally rich flavor that is enhanced by the slight smoking and charring of the grill, and it is naturally lean. The marinade shown here bathes the meat in an aromatic bath that includes pungent ingredients such as garlic and cracked peppercorns.*

9-7. *The grill station is among the busiest in many restaurants. With the wide variety of grilled foods featured on many contemporary menus, it is important to keep the grill organized so that flavors don't mix. On this grill, the top half is reserved for beef, chicken, and vegetables, while the lower half is used for fish and shellfish.*

It may be necessary or desirable to remove foods from the grill after they are marked on both sides and to finish cooking them in a hot oven. If this is done, the food should be placed, uncovered, on a rack in a roasting pan or sheet pan. Larger operations may find this a more effective way to grill foods that must be prepared in large batches. Another reason to finish grilled foods in the oven is to prevent drying. A thick chop or steak might dry out too much if it were to cook completely on the grill.

5. Remove the food, plate it, and serve immediately.

The number of sauces suitable to grilled foods is great. Compound butters, hollandaise, and béarnaise are so firmly associated with grilled appetizers and entrees, that alternative accompaniments can be hard to devise. Grilled foods have a strong, pronounced flavor that will find the best complement in robust, savory sauces such as chutneys or bean stews. Including a sauce that is based on fruits, vegetables, grains, or beans will increase the nutritional value of the entire meal.

BROILING

Broiling is quite similar in many respects to grilling. The major difference is that in a grill the heat source is located below a rack, whereas in a

9-8. *Unlike a grill, broilers have the heat source located above the rack. The rack can usually be raised and lowered to control the cooking temperature. The foods (swordfish is shown here) cook from a combination of radiant heat from above, and also direct contact with the hot rods of the rack. They are normally turned during cooking, although very thin items may not be turned at all.*

9-9. *Not every dish designated as "broiled" on the menu is a true broil. The gratin of salmon shown here is actually more similar to a baked dish. The salmon is placed on a sizzler platter, coated with a sauce, and then baked in the hot environment of the broiler without turning, until the sauce browns and the salmon is cooked through.*

broiler the heat source is above the rack. The same steps for preparing foods and equipment, outlined above in the section on grilling, will apply. Foods are cooked directly on the rack, and are marked, turned, and finished as for a grill. Swordfish steaks are shown here in the process of broiling.

Virtually any item that can be grilled can also be broiled. The difference has more to do with the words used than any significant difference in technique. Professional-quality broilers can generate far more heat than the typical home oven's broiler. This means that the effects achieved in a restaurant are often difficult to duplicate at home.

There is an additional application for broilers, however. They can be used to prepare delicate foods such as flounder, and broiled stuffed vegetables, or to achieve an effect known as a *gratin*. In this case, the food is not cooked directly on the broiler rack. Instead, it is placed on a sizzler platter, coated with bread crumbs or other appropriate ingredients, and broiled until a lightly browned crust has formed. The food is not turned; the cooking action is really more similar to that of baking, because the heat comes through the sizzler platter, cooking the bottom of the food at the same time that the heat source above the food cooks the top. The salmon gratin shown here is a good example of this style of broiling.

Method

1. Select and prepare the food.

The term "broiled" is firmly associated with "in butter" in the minds of both chefs and guests. It may take a bit of rethinking to adjust the standard broiled dishes. Instead of relying on butter to act as a flavoring ingredient, lubricant, cooking medium, and insulation from the drying effects of direct heat, the chef must modify the approach slightly by choosing naturally tender, lean foods such as fish, shellfish, or vegetables. Butter usually can be replaced with a light coating of bread crumbs, or a bath of low-fat vinaigrette, stock, wine, or other ingredients.

2. Properly heat both the broiler and the sizzler platter.

This step will help shorten overall cooking time, so that the food can cook quickly without losing a great deal of its natural moisture and nutritional value.

3. Broil the main item until just cooked.

Adjusting the broiler rack properly so that the food will cook quickly but not char is as important as removing the food from the broiler when it is cooked to the exact degree of doneness. These two factors are certainly important in traditional cooking, and for nutritional cooking they are the key, because there is no butter, glaze (a mixture of hollandaise sauce, whipped creams, and velouté sauce), or cheese coating to mask an overcooked, dry dish.

To prepare items by this method on a larger scale, use a sheet pan.

ROASTING/BAKING

Roasting may be one of the first cooking methods to come to mind when the interest is in preparing foods with as little additional oil or other cooking fat as possible. There is generally no need to add any oil during the process itself. Foods are cooked by the hot air trapped inside the cavity of an oven. This is a relatively gentle cooking technique. The concern many people have that roasted or baked foods tend to be dry is a genuine one. However, the best way to avoid dry roasts is to be certain that foods are cooked just to the point of proper doneness and no further.

Roasting is really the same general procedure as baking, but common usage has come to mean that roasted foods are cooked whole or in large pieces —a whole chicken is roasted, while the same chicken cut into pieces is baked.

The problem with roasting is that some of the occasionally applied optional steps have come to be considered essential. These are barding, basting with butter or released fats, and using stuffings made from high-fat forcemeats and gravies that retain a substantial amount of fats. These are not necessary, and can readily be eliminated without sacrificing moistness, flavor, or juiciness. In those cases where there is the possibility that the food, due to its delicate or lean nature, might dry out during cooking, other steps can be employed to mitigate any potential drying effect from the oven without sacrificing nutritional quality. These include using a bread-crumb coating to protect the surface, adding a filling or stuffing of vegetables or grains, or using a moist accompaniment such as a jus-based sauce, a creamy risotto, or a vegetable coulis.

Method

1. Select and prepare the food.

The types of foods generally cooked by this method include whole birds or fish; large "roasts" cut from the relatively tender primals such as the rib, loin, and sections of the leg; whole vegetables with protective skins such as potatoes and hard-skinned squashes, and fruits such as apples or figs.

There is some controversy as to whether or not leaving the skin on during cooking will increase the amount of fat present after cooking. The chicken shown will be roasted whole, with the skin on. Any increase in the amount of fat is minimal. It is important to remove the skin before serving. It

9-10. *The chicken shown here is trussed and ready for roasting. Because the skin will remain on the bird as it cooks, it is not necessary to baste as it roasts. The interior of the bird may be stuffed with a variety of aromatics, such as the fresh herbs shown here, to very gently "perfume" the meat. Other suggestions include whole cloves of garlic, sliced oranges, lemons, or limes, or quartered onions.*

may be acceptable to leave a little surface fat on cuts of meat to keep the surface from drying out, but it should be trimmed away before the meat is sliced and served. All of the rendered fat must be removed from the pan drippings before using them to make a sauce.

"Baked" fish fillets or poultry breasts are good candidates for the use of a "robe" of shredded potatoes or a bread-crumb coating. Other meats are occasionally treated to such a step as well; see, for example, the suprêmes of chicken coated with seasoned bread crumbs shown in the accompanying photographs. Consult specific recipes to get additional ideas and exact methods for these advance-preparation techniques. Any coating should not overwhelm the food itself (that is, it shouldn't be applied in a very thick coat). The coating should reach the correct stage of doneness at the same time as the main item. It serves no purpose to coat something to help retain moisture only to have the item overcooked and dry by the time the coating is done.

The nature of the food and the intended flavor of the finished dish will determine whether or not it should first be seared. Searing is done not so much to "seal in the juices" (a technical fallacy) as to develop the flavor of the finished dish more fully. This is one of the more important considerations in nutritional cooking because no additional butter or cream is used to bolster a weak or underdeveloped flavor.

2. Place the food in a pre-heated roasting pan.

A rack is commonly used to elevate the food so that it will cook from all sides; in some cases, it may not be necessary or desirable. A bed of aromatic ingre-

9-11 BAKING CHICKEN SUPRÊMES

a *The skin has been removed from these chicken breasts, and a layer of seasoned bread crumbs is being applied to act as protection against the dry, hot air of the oven, which could easily toughen the unprotected meat.*

b *To get the best finished product, the chicken breasts are placed on a rack on a baking sheet. This will allow the chicken to cook more quickly, since it is exposed to heat on all sides.*

dients such as vegetables, garlic, spices, or herbs may be included to act as a rack or simply to add flavor as the food roasts.

3. Roast (or bake) the food to the correct doneness.

The test of doneness will vary, depending upon the food being prepared. It is crucial to remember that there will be some carryover cooking, especially for meats, poultry, and fish. If the food is to be served at its best, then this must be taken into account, or the food will quickly overcook and lose moisture. Carryover cooking will also allow the natural juices in larger roasts to redistribute, spreading more evenly throughout the interior.

An optional step is the application of a glaze or basting sauce. The glaze should be applied early enough to allow it to properly coat the roasted item. Care must be taken to prevent it from scorching.

Yet another way to prepare roasted foods so that they have the greatest possible flavor is to smoke-roast them. The duck breasts shown here are being

9-12. Smoke-roasting, or pan-smoking as it is also known, requires the setup illustrated in this photograph. A layer of fine hardwood chips is scattered in the bottom of a roasting pan (disposable aluminum pans are shown here, but a hotel pan reserved for pan-smoking could also be used), then the food (duck breasts shown here) is arranged on a rack suspended above the chips. A second roasting pan is inverted over the bottom pan, and the whole setup is placed over direct heat. Some smoke is rising from the chips here. During actual pan-smoking, the top pan should be tightly covering the bottom pan, of course, to keep the smoke bath in contact with the food.

smoke-roasted in a bath of hickory-wood smoke. For additional information about this technique, read Focus 9-3: Smoke-Roasting Foods.

4. Prepare a sauce from the drippings, or prepare a sauce separately.

Any sauce should always be chosen so that it will complement both the flavor of the food and the overall nutritional quality of the dish. It is only good sense to use the juices released from the food itself as the basis of a sauce, when they are available. If there aren't enough juices, the chef may decide to prepare a separate sauce, relish, or other accompaniment for the item.

FOCUS 9-3   SMOKE-ROASTING FOODS

A cooking method referred to as "smoke-roasting" or "pan-smoking" can add a great deal of excitement to any menu. Foods emerge from the pan flavored with the special tastes that result from using hardwood chips such as hickory. Because no fats are added during cooking, smoke-roasting is an ideal nutritional cooking method.

Foods smoked by traditional methods are normally high in sodium because they are treated with a brine or a dry cure composed primarily of salt before smoking. This is done to draw moisture out. Before refrigeration was commonly available, this was one of the ways of assuring that smoked foods would not start to spoil as a result of the relatively long periods they would require in the smokehouse, usually at temperatures considered optimal for the rapid growth of bacteria and other pathogens. Smoke-roasted foods, however, are cooked at high temperatures, so there is no reason to be concerned about contamination during preparation.

The food item to be smoke-roasted is usually trimmed, peeled, and prepared as it would be for traditional roasting. Marinades, herbs, and other seasonings can be used as desired, or as a specific recipe indicates. Then, the roasting pan is prepared. A layer of hardwood chips is spread in the bottom of the pan. The food is arranged on a rack set in the pan, and a second pan or aluminum foil is used as a tight-fitting lid.

The pan is put over direct heat, on a burner or flattop. A smoke aroma will become apparent fairly soon. The foods should be kept in the pan for a few minutes, or until they have a browned exterior. It isn't a good idea to cook thick items, such as duck breasts, from start to finish by this method, however. The smoky taste can overwhelm a food's natural flavor. The ideal is to flavor the food and then complete the cooking process in a hot oven.

Several interesting applications for this method can be found in the recipes in this book, including Lightly Smoked Corn Chowder, and an appetizer of Duck Salad with Bitter Greens.

MOIST-HEAT COOKING METHODS

The moist-heat methods used in the typical professional kitchen are all well-suited to the nutritionally focused kitchen as well. The important points to keep in mind are careful selection of the main ingredients and judicious monitoring of any additional ones that might tend to be high in calories, fats, or sodium. Many of the traditional recipes for shallow-poached, steamed, stewed, or braised items call for liberal quantities of cream, butter, bacon, and other high-calorie, high-fat, high-cholesterol, or high-sodium ingredients. Sauces such as hollandaise, which is often paired with a poached salmon fillet, or ingredients such as the salt pork in coq au vin need to be either replaced or reduced.

The section that follows will outline the steps and explain the procedures for each of the moist-heat cooking methods: steam, shallow-poach, poach/boil, stew, and braise. Another technique has proven useful when correctly done; therefore, to this standard list of cooking methods we will add microwave cooking.

STEAM

When most people first think of cooking low-fat foods, they tend to look at steaming. This technique is admirably suited to achieving the guidelines for nutritional cooking. The food is prepared without the addition of any fats or oils, and a greater number and quality of nutrients remain in the food because they do not come into direct contact with the cooking liquid. Instead, the liquid is allowed to come to a boil in a closed vessel so that a bath of moist vapor surrounds the food and performs the actual cooking. One interesting approach to steaming foods is discussed in Focus 9-4: Cooking En Papillote.

The primary concern with most steamed dishes is not so much in modifying the technique as it is in making certain that steamed foods do not taste dull, bland, or insipid. This is all too often the case, because foods that are steamed are generally delicate, of a texture and shape that will allow them to cook in the gentle steam bath. Some special measures can be taken to counteract this potential problem, and they will be mentioned as appropriate in the step-by-step discussion that follows.

The second stumbling block is that steamed dishes very often rely heavily upon accompanying sauces and side dishes for textural, color, and flavorful interest. If these are chosen with care, they will not sabotage the desired result. For example, a piquant tomato coulis might be the perfect foil for a dish of steamed seafood. Dipping sauces made with small quantities of reduced-sodium soy sauce, blended with lime juice, ginger, and other seasonings can elevate a steamed snapper to new heights. These are just two examples. Recipes included in this book can provide additional inspiration. It is not necessary to fall back on the triumvirate of salt, sugar, and fat.

FOCUS 9-4 COOKING EN PAPILLOTE

There is something mysterious about cooking foods en papillote. The sudden release of a cloud of steam from the billowy package gives the dining room staff a chance to engage in a little showmanship. For the chef, it is a wonderful way to introduce new ideas. En papillote is a cooking method that is akin in most respects to steaming. The careful selection of ingredients and meticulous attention to the combination of flavors and textures will result in a dish that could become a cornerstone of a nutritional menu.

Foods that are most successfully prepared by cooking en papillote are those which are naturally moist and tender, such as fish. If the food can be cooked in a relatively short time, or is a candidate for steaming or shallow-poaching, chances are good that it can be prepared en papillote.

Numerous other dishes can be prepared this way. One example is pasta. Pasta and grains, which cannot be cooked quickly in a small amount of liquid, must be prepared in advance. The pre-cooked grain or pasta is combined with a sauce and garnish, and finished by marrying the flavors as the dish is rapidly steamed in its paper package.

Once the foods have been selected and prepared (in some cases they are fully or partially cooked), they are assembled into a package. Usually a layer of aromatic ingredients (such as shallots, leeks, or ginger cut into small dice or julienne) is arranged as a bed on one half of a large parchment-paper heart. The main item is added, and if necessary, a dash of a flavorful liquid such as stock, wine, or court bouillon. The paper heart is folded in half, and the edges are crimped to make a tight seal.

Directions for preparing foods en papillote will often indicate that the paper should be lightly oiled. This is not truly essential, but because the diner won't eat the paper, it is acceptable if the chef believes that it helps in the cooking process.

The package is then placed in a very hot oven and allowed to puff up. Because the package can't be opened before service, a few trial runs may be necessary to determine how long is long enough, and how hot is hot enough to fully cook the dish. Timing is crucial to the effective presentation of these items. The inflated package will stay that way for a short time, but it is best to get it to the guests as soon as possible.

Method

1. Select and prepare the food.

Foods most suited to steaming are those that have a delicate texture. Items such as fish, seafood, poultry breasts, vegetables, and fruits are all successfully prepared by steaming. If the food is not naturally of a shape and size that will allow it to cook quickly, then it should be cut, pounded, or trimmed.

It is important to give some thought to the ways in which aromatic and flavoring ingredients can be introduced. The methods for accomplishing this will vary, depending upon the size and type of steamer being used. A coating of herbs, or a bed of herbs or aromatic ingredients is one way. If a tiered steamer (aluminum, bamboo, or stainless steel) is used, then it is possible to add a variety of aromatics to the steaming liquid. The liquid may be more aromatic than plain water, and any flavor lost from the main item will be recaptured in the liquid. Thus, it may be used as a sauce or as the part of a sauce. Pressure steamers do not allow this option, so it becomes more important to carefully season the product to introduce additional flavor by using methods such as wrapping it in herbs.

2. Bring the steaming liquid to a full boil, or properly heat pressure or convection steamers.

Steam can only work efficiently when it is allowed to build up a good "head" by being contained in a closed chamber so that pressure will increase. Each time a steamer is opened, pressure is vented away and the cooking process is slowed down.

3. Steam the items, without disturbing them, until the food is properly cooked.

As in roasting, carryover cooking is a factor in steaming. The effects can be significant if the chef has not paid close attention to the cooking times of certain foods. It may take only a few seconds for shrimp to go from sweet, tender, and delicate to overcooked and rubbery.

Steamed foods may be served cold in some presentations. When this is desirable, the food should be slightly underdone, to allow carryover cooking to complete the cooking.

4. Served steamed foods at the correct temperature, with the appropriate sauce and other garnish.

Shallow-Poach

Shallow-poaching has become a very popular form of cooking. The biggest drawback is that the typical shallow-poach recipe calls for a beurre blanc to be made by reducing the *cuisson* (cooking liquid), and finishing of this sauce by blending in a substantial amount of whole butter. There is no actual difficulty in adjusting the technique to suit the dietary guidelines, as long as the automatic pilot is turned off long enough to select a sauce that does not rely on butter.

The selection of foods for shallow-poaching will follow most of the same standards as those for steaming. The item should be tender, easy to cook in a relatively short amount of time, of an even thickness and shape to promote even cooking, and finally, low in naturally-occurring fats. Unlike steaming, shallow-poaching is not often thought of as producing foods that have a too subtle flavor, because the item is prepared in direct contact with an aromatic cooking liquid such as a fumet, court bouillon, or broth bolstered with the addition of appropriate herbs, spices, vegetables, or fruits.

Whenever possible, the accompanying sauce should incorporate the cooking liquid in some way. The flavor as well as any nutrients transferred from the item to the cooking liquid is saved and presented as a part of a finished dish. There are a number of attractive options suitable for nutritional cooking. Instead of a traditional reliance on butter to thicken the sauce, the chef may want to use a modified starch. The approximate "mouthfeel," flavor, and color of sauces usually prepared with cream and/or butter can be achieved with evaporated skimmed milk. Reduction is an excellent means of intensifying flavors without resorting to butter.

Method

Some key steps for a nutrition approach to shallow-poaching are illustrated in the photographs accompanying this section.

1. Select and prepare the food.

Some examples of foods well-suited to this technique include fish fillets, paupiettes, and suprêmes of poultry. These foods have a delicate texture, and will tend to cook quickly even at moderate temperatures. The other necessary ingredients include a fully flavored poaching liquid, such as a stock or court bouillon, and the appropriate additional aromatics (diced or minced onions, shallots, carrots, celery, or other vegetables; herbs; spices; and wine). Unfortunately, the ingredient most often associated with shallow-poaching in a traditional kitchen is a large quantity of unsalted butter. Its elimination from this technique should in no way compromise the quality of the finished dish. Careful selection and handling of all food items to preserve the greatest possible flavor is the key.

2. Smother/sweat the bed of aromatics.

This step is undertaken to begin to release the flavors of the ingredients. The degree to which the aromatics are cooked will depend upon the total cooking time for the main item and the nature of the aromatic being smothered. Aromatic ingredients should be leveled into a "bed" in order to slightly elevate the main item from the pan.

9-13. SHALLOW-POACHING FISH

a *A usual first step for any shallow-poached item is to smother the aromatics so that they will release their flavor into the cooking liquid. Then, the item being poached (flounder fillets are shown here) is placed in the pan and covered loosely with parchment, cut to fit the shape of the pan.*

b *An alternative to a parchment coating is shown here: The flounder has been spread with a layer of a mousseline forcemeat, and then thin slices of zucchini are overlapped on the fish to act as a coating that will trap the steam enough to gently cook the fish and the forcemeat.*

c *Once the fish is cooked, it is removed from the pan, and the cooking liquid is allowed to reduce very quickly. Instead of the butter and heavy cream traditionally used to finish the sauce for a shallow-poached item, a velouté made by thickening fish stock with arrowroot, and then "creamed" with evaporated skimmed milk is used here.*

3. Add the main item and the poaching liquid. Bring the liquid to a gentle simmer over direct heat, and then cover the pan loosely.

By definition, shallow-poaching is a gentle cooking technique. In order to make sure that it does not take too long, the chef should bring the cooking liquid quickly to the correct temperature over direct heat. It is equally desirable to keep the pan uncovered until the correct cooking speed is reached. If the pan were to be covered before that, the liquid might readily come to a boil, which is too violent an action for shallow-poaching and might cause the food to overcook, burst during cooking, or become tough. The covering should remain loose so that steam released during cooking will not build up pressure, raising the overall cooking temperature and cooking the food too quickly. A loose cover will also prevent the food from releasing too much liquid into the pan. The cooking liquid is normally reduced and then used as a sauce base. If there is too much of it, the time needed for reduction will be increased, and there is a greater chance that the food will overcook as it is kept warm or that it will become too cold during the lag time between finishing cooking and plating.

4. Remove the main item from the pan at the correct doneness, moisten lightly, cover loosely, and keep warm. Then, prepare and/or reheat the sauce.

When selecting a sauce for a shallow-poached dish, the chef should keep in mind the needs and capabilities of the kitchen. An operation that must serve batches of food in large quantities will probably prefer to select a sauce that can be prepared in advance and then heated to the proper serving temperature. In this case, the cooking liquid can be reduced and used as the basis of sauces prepared at a later point in time. Kitchens that have à la minute menus may prefer to simply proceed by reducing the cooking liquid directly in the pan and then adding the appropriate ingredients or appareils, such as a coulis of vegetables, a stew of lentils or beans, or other such ingredients.

5. Serve the item at the correct temperature, with the desired and appropriate garnish, sauce, and accompaniments.

POACH/BOIL

Terms used to discuss this cooking method can become confusing. The differences between a poached food, a simmered one, and a boiled item are genuine but not always easy to pin down. The first way to draw a distinction is in temperature ranges for each of these methods. Poaching occurs at 160 degrees F to 180 degrees F (70 to 82 degrees C); simmering is done at 180 degrees F to 200 degrees F (82 to 95 degrees C); boiling is normally understood to occur at 212 degrees F (100 degrees C) at sea level. Boiling, however, has gradations ranging from a gentle boil to a rolling boil.

Foods that will be prepared by one of these three methods can come from a wide number of categories. In most cases, poached items will be more tender and require shorter overall cooking times than those to be simmered or boiled. Typical selections include fish (whole, fillets, or even steaks), poultry breasts, fruits, and eggs. Boiled and simmered meats are usually more mature and tougher, with greater amounts of connective tissue. They often require lengthy cooking times. Some examples of foods that are often boiled or simmered include whole birds (especially stewing hens), grains, beans, vegetables, and cuts of meat from the shoulder, shank, or more exercised portions of the animal.

It is a good idea, though, to remember that semantics have played a much larger role in determining whether or not a food is considered boiled, poached, or simmered; in some cases, the term used may not be the most accurate. A good example of this is eggs cooked in the shell. They are referred to in most cases as being hard-boiled, but in reality the water should be brought up to a temperature range that would be considered a simmer, according to the standards previously discussed.

The problems encountered in this technique are quite similar to those encountered in steaming. These items are perceived as being bland, unless there is a rich, strongly flavored sauce to accompany them. The test of a chef's skill is to give the maximum appropriate flavor without falling back on large quantities of flavorings that are high in calories, fats, cholesterol, and/or sodium. Emphasis should be placed on the foods' natural flavors through the use of herbs, spices, and other aromatics, reductions, and similar approaches.

Method

(For the sake of convenience, the term "poach" will be used throughout this explanation of method.)

1. Select and prepare the foods.

Foods for this technique fall into a variety of categories. There are no hard and fast rules stating that the food must be either very tender or very tough. Almost all foods can be prepared this way. Moist-heat cooking methods as a group all require special attention to prevent the foods from losing their flavor and texture. The selection of fresh, flavorful foods and properly seasoned cooking liquids, along with the use of aromatic vegetables, fruits, spices, and herbs, is essential. The pears shown here are being poached in a bath of a dry red wine.

2. Combine the food and poaching liquid at the correct temperature, and then establish the correct cooking speed.

Some foods, such as stewing hens, are best when combined with a cold liquid and brought slowly to a boil; others, such as a chicken suprême, respond when the poaching liquid is already at a simmer before the food is added. The more tender the product, the more likely it is that it should be combined with an

9-14. Many fruits can be poached for use in desserts or as an accompaniment to other dishes. The pears have been completely submerged in a bath of red wine to assure that they will cook evenly. A variety of spices could be added, as desired, to impart a special flavor to the fruit, such as cinnamon sticks, whole cloves, allspice berries, or sliced gingerroot.

already simmering liquid. In all cases, it is important to establish the correct cooking temperature and to maintain it consistently throughout the entire cooking period. Various ingredients may be added for flavor or as a garnish. They should be added in such a way that they are properly cooked without being overcooked and have the best flavor, color, and texture.

3. Poach the food until it is fork-tender (allowing for some carryover cooking).

Poached foods that are served hot should be fully cooked, then removed from the poaching liquid and served. A brief resting period may be beneficial for items that need to be sliced, or in those cases where the poaching liquid will become part of the sauce. Very often, however, poached items are served with a sauce that has been selected for its capability to be prepared independently of the cooking method.

When a poached food is intended for cold service, it is better to stop the cooking slightly before the food is properly done, allowing it to cool in the cooking liquid. The cooking will be completed very gently, without over-cooking, toughening, or loss of moisture.

4. Serve the food at the correct temperature with the desired and appropriate sauce, garnish, and accompaniments.

STEW/BRAISE

Stewing and braising have definite appeal, but are not always immediately obvious choices as suitable techniques for a nutritional approach. This perception is probably due to a number of different factors: The sauce in a stew or braise is thick and rich, giving the impression that it may be high in calories and fats; the general texture and flavor of braised or stewed foods is usually quite substantial. Finally, the classic recipes for many braised and stewed dishes do rely on foods that have a significant amount of naturally occurring fats, and furthermore, may indicate the use of cooking oils, salt pork, and similar ingredients.

It may surprise both chefs and patrons that these methods are actually very appropriate for nutritional uses with practically no modification.

The selection of foods can range from very delicate fish or vegetables to cuts of meat such as the brisket or shank. Care should be taken to remove excess surface fat, and the chef must avoid the extravagant use of items such as salt pork, bacon, or oils. These ingredients need not be entirely avoided however; the braised or stewed dish can be left to cool, and when that happens, the fat will rise to the surface and harden, making it possible to lift it completely away. This easy "degreasing step" makes potentially high-fat dishes fall within more appropriate ranges.

Another positive point is that any nutrients or flavor transferred from the food to the cooking liquid will become a part of the finished dish. The use of modified starches instead of roux to thicken the sauce, and the use of reduction as a means of concentrating flavors are additional steps that can be taken to produce high-quality braises and stews without sacrificing the looked-for texture and taste.

Method

For the sake of convenience, the term "braise" will be used throughout this section to indicate both braising and stewing. The accompanying photographs of a chili stew are intended to illustrate the basic steps of these techniques.

1. Select and prepare the food.

Tradition has inclined chefs to view more mature (and sometimes fattier) cuts of meat as the best for braising. The nutritionally minded chef will want to select naturally lean meats and accompanying ingredients that will produce a dish that is as full of flavor as possible while staying within suggested guidelines. Other foods that are delicious as braises include beans, vegetables, and fish.

Foods should be trimmed and seasoned. There may be a number of different optional steps included in various recipes, including a coating of some

9-15. PREPARING CHILI STEW

a *In a traditional recipe for a stew or a braise, the meat would be seared in hot oil. However, for this recipe, the cubed meat is quickly seared in hot stock so that it takes on a brown color, without taking on added fats.*

b *Once all of the additional ingredients are added, and the stew is brought to a simmer, it is covered so that it can finish cooking. Stews can be cooked on top of the stove. It is a good idea to check the cooking speed frequently since it is easy for a covered pot to come to a boil and scorch quickly. A better alternative might be to finish cooking in the oven, where the heat is gentler and more even.*

c *To bring the stew to the correct consistency, remove the lid during the final stages of cooking so that the liquid can reduce properly. The chili stew shown here has the ideal consistency: still moist, but not runny.*

sort, a filling or stuffing, or a marinade. Consult the recipes in this book for specific examples. The cooking medium and aromatics are of major importance in the success of the dish. These should be carefully prepared as well.

2. Sear the food to begin developing the flavor, if appropriate.

Instead of using fat to sear meats, they can be broiled, dry-sautéed, or cooked in a small amount of a stock or jus. This step is optional; not all stews and braises will require it.

3. Add the aromatic vegetables or other ingredients and properly sauté until a good color and aroma are developed.

Special care should be taken at this stage to be certain that the eventual flavor of the dish will be as full as it possibly can be. Braising and stewing are long processes, and sufficient time should be allowed to complete each step properly.

4. Add the braising liquid, and any aromatic ingredients not already added, and bring it up to the proper temperature.

If braising is to be effective, the cooking process should be slow and gentle. However, it is crucial to bring the liquid to a simmer, and then adjust it so that the simmer is maintained. Once the correct heat is reached, it may be a good idea to put braises (and stews) into the oven. This will keep the food from sticking and scorching on the bottom of the pot. The more gentle, even heat of the oven promotes a more tender finished product.

5. Cook the food until it is fork-tender, and finish the sauce as appropriate.

One of the major advantages of braising is that the sauce is prepared along with the main item. It may be a good idea to take the time to further refine the sauce and intensify its flavor by reducing it, or to add special garnishes or flavoring ingredients. Consult specific recipes for examples.

MICROWAVE COOKING

The chief advantage of using a microwave to prepare foods is that the food is cooked very quickly, with a high degree of nutrient and color retention. The primary drawbacks or complaints about microwaved foods are that they may cook very unevenly so that some portions become rubbery and tough before others are properly cooked, that the texture may not be pleasant, and that the expected flavor may not be fully or even partially developed.

Although microwaves have been in use for many years in both professional and home kitchens, many people hesitate to rely on them as a means of actually cooking foods. This is probably due in large part to the fact that there is often some difficulty in comprehending how a microwave works. The second inhibiting factor is that not all foods are suitable for microwave cooking. If, for example, a vegetable such as green beans or peas is prepared from the raw

9-16. USING THE MICROWAVE TO COOK FOODS

a *Many types of vegetables can be successfully prepared in a microwave. The vegetable (broccoli is shown here) is arranged on a plate or other microwave-proof dish, and a small amount of liquid is added. The plate should then be covered to trap the steam from the liquid. If plastic is used, it should be pierced in one or two places so that the steam doesn't build up too much pressure.*

b *To increase the flavor of a steamed dish of broccoli prepared in the microwave, it should be served with a piquant sauce or glaze. A Lemon Glaze is being brushed on the broccoli here.*

state in a microwave, the end result can be wrinkled, rubbery vegetables. On the other hand, some foods such as potatoes or hard-skinned squashes can be cooked easily and evenly in a microwave.

The best way to prepare vegetables and fruits is to place them in a relatively shallow container. The food should be arranged in a single layer so that the thickest portion is near the center. Add a small amount of liquid to the plate, and then cover it with plastic wrap, waxed paper, or parchment paper. Plastic wrap must be vented in a couple of spots by piercing it with a knife tip so that some of the steam will vent away. This is not necessary when waxed or parchment papers are used, since they do not form an airtight seal. Whole vegetables with thick skins do not need to be wrapped; their skins will act as a wrapper. They should be pierced in one or two places to allow the steam to escape from the interior.

Different microwaves have different power levels. It is important to become familiar with the particular model being used to determine the best power levels and cooking times. If the microwave does not have a turntable, it is a good idea to turn the plate or the vegetable at the halfway point so that it will cook evenly.

One of the most common uses in any kitchen for a microwave is to rapidly reheat cooked foods. This ability can be applied to great advantage,

9-17. *The microwave is a good way to reheat dishes such as grains, pastas, soups, stews, and vegetables that have been prepared in advance in large batches. To heat them evenly (Quinoa Pilaf with Red and Green Peppers is shown here), cover the food with vented plastic wrap, or with waxed or parchment paper, and microwave on the highest power setting until evenly heated. It is usually a good idea to stir the food halfway through the cooking time to be sure that all of the food is properly reheated.*

particularly in a kitchen where foods are prepared and then carefully portioned to assure not only consistency of portion size but also the consistency and accuracy of the nutritional balance of a dish or meal.

Foods to be reheated in the microwave should be placed in containers that are broader than they are deep. If necessary, a small amount of a flavorful liquid such as stock should be added to be certain that the finished dish has the correct moistness. Additional seasoning and aromatic ingredients may be added at this point and stirred into the dish. The container should be wrapped with plastic, waxed, or parchment paper. This helps the foods to reheat evenly. It is important to pierce plastic wrap in one or two places to allow any excess steam to escape.

Menu and Recipe Development

Through a menu, the chef tells the guests what the kitchen can prepare. Offering nutritional dishes in addition to the more usual fare or making nutrition the focus of the menu provides a new dimension. It can be a little confusing to keep nutrients in mind while writing menus, and the chef may often forget that nutrients can be found in foods and do not need to be added artificially. Putting nutrition together with food and keeping them properly married is a challenge for both the chef and the nutritionist.

The best menus are written by keeping the restaurant's customer base in mind. A coffee shop catering to professionals dashing to the office on the way from the train should offer foods that are easy both to serve and to eat. The owner of a cozy little bistro wants the items to have a different sort of appeal, inviting customers to spend a slow-paced evening lingering over the meal. For these two establishments, as well as for any other foodservice operation, making the customers' desires a priority at all times is the path to success. The first step in writing a nutritional menu is to learn as much as possible about what customers interested in nutrition would like to find on that menu.

Almost as important is making sure that all the staff members in the operation are aware of the nutritional goals that have been identified as the major focus of the menu. The cooks may need some training to help them get started. Kitchen practices, such as advance preparation of vegetables, may need to be revised or eliminated in favor of new ones. The dining room staff also need to be aware of changes or additions so that they can most effectively help the customers make selections.

Developing a new menu and the accompanying recipes is a process of evolution. As the changes are introduced, it is important to track how they are being received by the kitchen and dining room staffs, as well as the guests. These changes can then be modified or further changes made. This chapter will look at some of the fundamentals of building or adding to a menu.

TAKING THE MEASURE OF THE MARKET

When a manufacturer releases a new product or service into the market, it is a sure bet that a great deal of research has been done beforehand. Analysts will take countless surveys, make use of sample markets, and perform other studies. All of this is done to determine who makes up the potential market, and whether they will buy or subscribe, and how often. If the studies indicate that consumer interest is sufficient to cover the costs of developing the product, training personnel, buying new manufacturing equipment, creating advertising and promotions, as well as to make a profit, the product is released nationwide. If not, the company goes "back to the drawing board."

Market surveys are simply a way of asking someone if they might be interested in trying something new or how they feel about something they already have. When the commodity is nutrition, it pays to find out the public reaction. The actual survey can be quite informal. For example, the dining room staff may have a great deal of information already on hand. They often will know if there are many requests for dishes prepared without any oil, with the sauce on the side or the cheese removed.

Questionnaires are an excellent way to discover what the clientele would like to see on the menu. This is a more formal approach than a random opinion poll. It will take a little time and effort to set up a truly effective questionnaire. There are books available in most libraries that can offer assistance. In addition, the services of a marketing or public relations firm may be of invaluable help. The more time that is allowed to properly develop the questionnaire, the more likely it is that the results gathered will offer substantial help in determining what sorts of changes to the menu are desirable.

The second stage of any survey is an analysis of the results. This process is just as challenging as actually developing the survey. The responses need to be counted, and then categorized. A great deal of number-crunching is necessary to determine what percentage of the customers would welcome nutritional offerings, how often they believe they might order them, and what they believe a nutritional menu item ought to be.

The chef should be aware that there are no absolute guarantees that a survey will keep him or her from making any missteps. Trying to guess what will be a success is always a gamble, even if the homework has been meticulously completed. When the responses are combined with the impressions gathered from talking to the dining room staff about customer requests, they can point in certain directions. The higher the level of interest, the more nutritional offerings the menu should offer. As the general public becomes increasingly aware of the importance of nutrition to their overall health, interest will continue to rise. For this reason, periodic checks of the market are a good idea.

Some of the same tactics larger corporations use to generate interest in their new products could be employed by a foodservice operation to herald the arrival of new menu options or an entirely new menu. Press releases, interviews on local radio shows, flyers and posters, and table tents are all good ways to alert the guests to the new items.

MENU DEVELOPMENT FOR DIFFERENT KINDS OF ESTABLISHMENTS

Most restaurants, cafeterias, and other dining establishments usually have a typical customer. The menus, the style of service, the music, even the lighting and table-top settings are selected with the intention of making their particular patrons feel comfortable. When the formula works well, there is a natural tendency to resist any sort of change. This inertia can be difficult to overcome. Those establishments with menus that change frequently are usually more adaptable. On the other hand, places with established menus, menu cycles (such as those found in schools and hospitals), and prescribed diet plans are usually the least flexible.

Introducing nutrition can be a very simple process that won't inconvenience anyone, even when the menu is set. Small changes, such as using skim milk to replace whole milk in pancake batter recipes or cutting down the amount of sugar in a muffin recipe, will have a positive effect. More elaborate changes such as actually developing a large repertoire of specially developed or modified menus, creating a nutritious menu cycle, or purchasing software to help in the analysis of existing, adapted, or original recipes should be undertaken when the level of interest justifies the added time and expense.

In the following sections of this chapter, some of the basic kinds of establishments and their menu styles are discussed, along with a few suggestions to make dietary changes a part of any menu. Remember that small changes are the best way to incorporate nutrition gradually, almost without anyone noticing. The popularity of these changes is a very real way to gauge how successful a nutritional program might be.

FAMILY-STYLE RESTAURANTS

Family-style restaurants cater to a definite segment of the dining public: customers who are looking for familiar foods. They are interested in affordability, wholesomeness, and flavor. Rather than developing an entirely new menu, the chef may be able to make some minor modifications to include nutrition without making a big deal out of it.

For example, salad bars, which frequently are a feature of these restaurants, can be a better nutritional tool when they include a good selection of fresh vegetables and fruits, different lettuces, salads made with whole grains or pasta, and reduced-calorie versions of dressings. Menu choices that provide a good source of carbohydrates, dietary fiber, vitamins, and minerals could be "flagged" to make it easier for the guest to find them. The breadbasket could be modified a little to include a whole-grain bread, muffin, or cracker. Low- or nonfat milk products are likely to elicit a positive reaction, too.

Some of the current selections that may already be low in fats, cholesterol, and salt might be identified as such on the menu. If the kitchen is able to accommodate certain requests, it might be a good idea to let the patrons know that. A statement such as the following might be included on the menu or a table tent: "We will gladly try to accommodate special requests for foods prepared without added butter, oil, or salt."

Portion sizes for family-style restaurants can be a ticklish area. Even though in this book the standard portion size suggested for meats is around 3½ to 4 ounces, it is usually larger in a family-style menu, and an abrupt change in serving size might prove damaging to the restaurant's business. A more subtle approach would be to gradually cut back the serving size of meats by an ounce or two, allowing plenty of time for these changes to become so familiar that the customers will not readily comment on them. At the same time, increasing the variety and portion sizes of side dishes will help make the meal seem just as large.

If the small changes are accepted, then the next step might be to offer one or two specials that could form the nucleus of a new menu category featuring foods that are good, balanced sources of the various nutrients. Pasta dishes, broiled and grilled fish, and skinless chicken breast are generally popular and offer the chef plenty of opportunity to provide some variety.

WHITE-TABLECLOTH RESTAURANTS AND BISTROS

Restaurants that cater to a clientele composed mainly of business people and professionals can be relatively certain that their guests are likely to be nutritionally aware. These are the people who read about food and nutrition, join health clubs, and, at the same time, enjoy fine dining. They probably will be receptive to several menu options that are billed as "healthy." It might even be feasible to develop an entire menu built on nutritional principles.

Many restaurants of this sort offer menus that change seasonally, monthly, or even daily. A list of specials prepared from the best that the market and the season have to offer is a common feature. This environment is conducive to a great deal of nutritional creativity. Unusual foodstuffs such as wild mushrooms, different kinds of lettuces and greens, game, "new" grains, and other items can be included in dishes, to broaden the variety of tastes and textures. The chef can capitalize on this bounty by creating new dishes or revamping traditional recipes.

Nutritional cooking is at its best and most satisfying when the flavors in every dish are rich, big, and bold. This requires that the best features of any food be brought to the forefront. No customer would ever feel that he or she is missing something when tempted with foods that are at the peak of their season, fresh, and full of flavor. In order to do this, the chef may need to revise his or her thinking about food and flavors.

One way is to investigate dishes that borrow from different cuisines. The chef can tap into the nutritional strong points that each one possesses. For instance, a menu item inspired by Japanese cuisine might showcase quickly cooked fish accompanied by a variety of vegetables in a rich broth. The foods are cooked in such a way that they retain the most nutrients and crisp, interesting textures. Another example is American Southwest dishes that combine rice with beans and corn and add a burst of flavor with chilis and peppers. These items have several points in their favor: They have wonderful, earthy flavors that remain perennially popular, and are a great source of dietary fiber, complex carbohydrates, and protein. The chef can increase the number of nutritionally sound entrées and side dishes by looking to vegetarian cuisines for inspiration as well. Many other cuisines have something to offer the nutritional menu, especially peasant dishes, since they are bound to the foods that are grown widely and harvested at their peak.

10-1. *The selection of flavoring ingredients and condiments shown here would help the chef expand the nutritional offerings on a menu. They include such items as (from left, clockwise) fresh horseradish root, lemon grass, prepared mustard, tamarind pods, wasabi powder (a powdered form of horseradish used in Japanese cuisine), and fresh gingerroot.*

Chefs may find that the easiest areas in which to start may be portion sizes, sauces, and accompaniments. The portion size of an entrée, for example, can be gradually reduced to meet the recommended standard. If the normal steak cut is 8 to 10 ounces, it might be a good idea to introduce a few menu options that reduce it to around 6 ounces. This will automatically reduce the total calories, fat, and cholesterol on the plate, even without making any other change.

A French restaurant with a menu that relies heavily on sauces such as beurre blancs, hollandaise, or cream sauces might want to introduce a few selections with sauces made from vegetable purees or clear broths lightly thickened with a modified starch. The rich Alfredo sauce used with many pasta

10-2. *A variety of chilis and sweet peppers are added to dishes from all cuisines to give them a burst of color, flavor, and in some cases, a blast of heat. The availability of these ingredients has increased greatly in the past several years. Shown here, Szechuan dried chilis in the back row, dried pasilla chilis below them (from the left), a selection of sweet bell peppers of various colors, long green frying chilis (center), and (bottom row, from left) Thai green chilis and dried chipotle chilis.*

dishes could be replaced with a less-heavy coating composed of extra-virgin olive oil, garlic, and fresh herbs.

Each menu category can be given added, healthy options. Appetizers frequently are overlooked; smaller portions of pastas served with vegetable-based sauces or lightly coated with oil and herbs are a good choice. Terrine recipes that break with tradition by reducing the total fat and sodium content could be showcased as a delicious alternative to pâtés swathed in fat. A good selection of salads that introduce some grilled or marinated vegetables (and the use of a marinade that greatly reduces or eliminates fat) are other wonderful opportunities to keep seasonality a part of the menu. Soups that feature a variety of beans and vegetables are usually easy to fit into the guidelines for nutritional cooking. Grilled, steamed, poached, baked, and roasted items prepared without any added fats are popular on any menu.

Before putting new items on the menu, the chef may decide to do a thorough analysis of the recipe, using computer software or nutrient analysis tables. An alternative that might be more convenient is to use established standards that give the suggested ranges for portion sizes, ingredient selection, and preparation practices. An example of one of the services available to a chef who is looking for some help in developing nutritional items is discussed in Focus 10-1.

FOCUS 10-1   Creative Cuisine in Vermont

The restaurateurs of Vermont have access to a special program that helps them introduce nutrition into their menus. Creative Cuisine is based on the program of the same name originally developed by the American Heart Association. According to Alison Gardener of the Vermont Department of Health, it is doing quite well.

Interested restaurant owners must send a letter of intent to the department of health and then sign a contract, agreeing to participate in the program for a year. They must offer at least one "heart-healthy" menu item. Dietitians will make two on-site visits during the year to evaluate the program through the use of a prepared checklist. Printed on the menu is a participatory statement, which says that foods marked with the Creative Cuisine symbol have been reviewed by a registered dietitian and are lower in fat, cholesterol, and sodium than other menu items.

The program is designed to help restaurants evaluate and identify menu items that meet the specific guidelines prepared by the department. This appraisal can be done in one of two ways: The restaurant can submit specific recipes for computer analysis, or they can be reviewed to determine if they meet suggested preparation and portion standards outlined in a handbook prepared for participants in the Creative Cuisine program. To get an idea of how these guidelines work, look at the recommendations for an entrée that includes a red meat:

- On the entire plated entrée, calories derived from fat should not exceed 35%.
- The portion size of the meat should be 5 ounces or less after cooking.
- All visible fat should be removed.
- No more than 1 teaspoon of an acceptable oil may be added during the cooking process.
- There should be less than 150 milligrams of cholesterol on the entire plate.

SPAS AND HEALTH RESORTS

Spas have been around for many years. Recently, however, they have taken on a special importance for more people. Instead of being a place where the rich go to shed a few pounds and have a facial, today's spa often offers an intensive program aimed at re-education. Nutrition is usually an important part of the total package, given equal status alongside exercise, stress management, and other services. In a typical program, the day's total calories are kept under a minimum amount and then divided between the meals and snacks that are served throughout the day.

An image problem that has traditionally afflicted spas is the belief that they serve unappealing "rabbit food" that leaves the client hungry. On a restricted regimen that might include only 800 calories, it is not an easy task to fill up the plate and make it look bountiful and taste good. However, the dinner plate that is composed only of a few slices of carrot, a leaf of lettuce, and a string bean is giving way as chefs have provided a whole new look to spa cuisine.

A significant change has occurred in the variety of foods served, due in large part to the fact that many spas have revised their standards in response to revised nutritional guidelines, and now allow their clients to consume more calories in the interest of good health. In addition, the growing interest in health and nutrition in all parts of our society has spurred a great deal of creative responses in developing foods that meet dietary guidelines without looking skimpy and tasting bland. An example of a typical meal pattern at a modern spa can be seen in Focus 10-2: Canyon Ranch.

Many of the same principles used in upscale restaurants apply to the development of spa menu selections. A variety of foods, selected for seasonality and quality, carefully prepared, and properly proportioned, is usually the key to a successful spa menu. Flavors should be big and bold. Appropriate techniques such as grilling, steaming en papillote, and roasting are very popular. Inspiration for new flavors and combinations can come from other cuisines, other restaurants, and very often from the food itself.

Pizzas, pasta, grains, breads, and potatoes were once forbidden on spa menus. Today, clients are surprised, and usually pleased, to find these hearty, filling foods on their plates. Alternatives to heavy cream sauces, cheeses, and sour cream make these foods fit well within a spa's dietary parameters.

HOSPITALS AND OTHER INSTITUTIONS

Some hospitals are trying to escape their image as a place to avoid the meal cart. It isn't always an easy task to change institutional menus, especially because of special problems that face a hospital's kitchen staff. These include maintaining several menu cycles to meet the dietary needs of a variety of patients—children, older people, diabetics, or heart patients—and preparing large volumes of food so that everyone can be served promptly.

FOCUS 10-2 CANYON RANCH

The clients who come to Canyon Ranch today are looking for an experience quite different from what a typical visitor might have had in the past, even as recently as a few years ago. Nowhere is the difference more apparent than in the foods that are served. The philosophy behind Canyon Ranch's cuisine is that the food not only has to be nutritious, but also good enough that a client will take the cooking styles and selected foods home to become a part of everyday eating habits.

There are two daily calorie levels, 1,200 or 1,800 calories, and the guests select foods from the daily menu to meet their own personal goals. The dietary goals for both plans are similar: 60% of the day's calories come from carbohydrates, 20% from protein, and 20% from fats. Breakfast is usually kept at 200 calories for the 1,200-calorie program and 400 for the 1,800-calorie one. Lunch and dinner are 500 and 700 calories, respectively. This eating plan is intended as a pattern that can transfer back into the real world.

A typical breakfast is usually high in carbohydrates, and includes such items as sweet-potato waffles with a fruit compote or breakfast bread pudding. Guests who are eating 1,800 calories can have a double portion of these items. An omelet bar is available also. The omelets are prepared with egg whites and filled with a generous portion of cooked vegetables. Low-fat cheese is available, at the guest's request.

Lunches normally consist of a 6-ounce portion of soup, with a slice of bread for those eating more calories, and a luncheon item: sandwiches, chicken burgers, and so forth. Dinner selections include a 2-cup portion of pasta with a marinara sauce or the special sauce of the day. Half portions of pasta are available as well, and the guest who wants to consume 1,800 calories will normally order a half portion of pasta along with an entrée such as duck breast or beef tenderloin with special sauces and other accompaniments.

Vegetarian dishes used to be a special problem because they often contained cheese in order to supplement the protein content of the dish. That had a tendency to increase not only saturated fat and cholesterol, but also sodium. Tempeh, a product made of fermented soy, is now used in many dishes to provide protein, including one called French Country Stew with Aioli.

The guests at Canyon Ranch are not served alcoholic beverages, but wine and beer are used in the kitchen. For instance, the fajitas are marinated in a combination of fruit juice and beer before they are grilled. These items are identified on the menu so that guests who do not wish to have any alcohol can avoid it.

School cafeterias have similar difficulties, as they try to feed a clientele that may range in age from 6 to 18. The needs of a 15-year-old boy are very different from those of a 10-year-old girl. And the challenge of preparing foods that teenagers will actually eat can be enormous.

Airlines must overcome a number of obstacles. Meals must be prepared in advance, portioned, packaged, and then held until the flight is actually under way. In addition, meals must be packaged so that they will fit into the limited space allowed in airplane galleys. There are always changes and unforeseen upsets to schedules. Different companies have adopted a policy of making special meals—vegetarian, kosher, and low-sodium meals, for example—available to passengers who make arrangements in advance.

Some of the same approaches used in a family-style restaurant can be implemented in these institutional feeding situations. Using low-fat and nonfat milks, yogurts, and cheeses is one possibility. Another is to offer as great a variety of fresh fruits, vegetables, whole juices, and whole-grain breads as can be managed. Usually, dishes that include pasta or noodles will be popular with all age groups, and they often are quite easy to modify in order to reduce or eliminate added fats and sodium and to trim away unnecessary calories. Fresh fruits, fruit ices, and even modified puddings such as rice, semolina, or bread puddings, can be offered as healthy desserts.

An important change for institutional foodservice operations to implement is a training program to help the kitchen staff learn new cooking skills and eliminate some ingrained habits. This may require an initial expenditure for videos, instructors, or off-site classes. As the quality of the food improves, with better taste, color, texture, and of course, nutritive value, this expense will usually pay off.

Introducing some innovations in the dining hall, such as a salad bar or special events like those described in Focus 10-3: Valley Central Schools, can do a lot to improve the nutritional quality of school lunches. At the same time, these changes can also have a positive and lasting influence on the way that the students think about food and nutrition for the rest of their lives.

FAST-FOOD RESTAURANTS

Fast-food restaurants do not always have a homogenous clientele. Without a typical customer to use as a guide for developing a total menu, the chef must devise plans to meet the needs of a mixed audience. The nutritional changes that are most likely to take are those that fit into the basic philosophy of the restaurant: dishes that are quick to prepare and quick to serve.

Nutritious selections in fast-food restaurants are received with more alacrity today than they might have been in the past. Changes in many of these operations clearly show that there are enough people interested in eating more nutritious foods to justify their place on the menu. These include fresh salads, low-fat milk, whole-wheat buns, grilled chicken instead of fried, and reduced-calorie dips and sauces.

FOCUS 10-3   VALLEY CENTRAL SCHOOLS

School lunches are common threads of the American culture. No matter in what state you grew up, it seems that the vegetables were the same drab green, floating in the same pool of butter. There were the same mysterious ingredients put together into the same combinations. Of course, there were, and are, exceptions. A school district in New York went to rather extraordinary lengths to make sure that its lunches did not get failing grades from nutritionists.

Developing a training program for the kitchen staff was one of the first steps. For example, they learned new ways to prepare vegetables. No longer were the green beans cooked first thing in the morning and left to decompose in the steam table until the lunch bell rang. Now, they are cooked just before they are served. Giving some attention to the kitchen staff had special consequences in addition to better preparation techniques for the success of this new lunch program. Treating them as valuable employees and as professionals gave kitchen staff members the desire to turn out foods that looked and tasted better.

Developing menus is not always easy. Instead of coming up with a calorie limit or percentages to govern the amount of various nutrients, attention was paid to the overall amount of fats, cholesterol, and salt in the foods the schools were using and in the dishes being prepared. Some innovations, including salad bars, and "build your own taco" and "build your own burger" days, gave students the chance to create their own meals. The selections are as varied, fresh, and nutritious as possible. School lunches for students at Valley Central are now a learning experience. Vegetables, fruits, and other foods that might not be familiar are introduced in a setting that encourages sampling. Turkey meat replaces the more fatty beef in spaghetti and lasagna.

"Purchasing either fresh or frozen fruits and vegetables as much as possible and working with the commodities agency to start to change the standards for purchased items and those supplied as government surplus has had a positive impact," says Clare Ciardullo, director of foodservice for the district. "The time and energy we have put into this project will reap its ultimate reward in the years to come, when our students have learned to make healthy choices naturally, without even really thinking about it."

Reasonable changes for a fast-food restaurant will depend upon the style of food that it serves. A Tex/Mex-style restaurant could offer an enchilada filled with fresh vegetables. A Chinese-style restaurant can offer the option of dishes prepared without added salt, soy sauce, or monosodium glutamate (MSG). Pizza parlors might promote pizzas with vegetable toppings.

SETTING STANDARDS FOR MENU ITEMS

On an individual level, the basic goal is balancing the entire day's nutrients, rather than focusing exclusively on a single meal or dish. The chef needs to keep this same principle in mind when developing a new menu item. The different approaches to developing either a whole menu or a single option have all been built upon the premise that the suggestions and standards should be used as ranges meant to accommodate a variety of situations.

For instance, entrée selections at the main meal of the day typically include more protein than for a lighter meal. Adding an extra ounce or two to the meat portion of the dish might mean a slight increase in fat, as well. It also would probably mean that the percentages of carbohydrates, proteins, and fats for the entire meal will not be the same as the recommended goals. This is fine, as long as the goal of keeping all menu selections within acceptable parameters is kept in mind.

Restaurant chefs who want to develop one or two nutritional selections can use a variety of resources to help them devise some parameters for the different menu categories. It is important to remember that none of these suggested limits is meant as a strict rule. Flexibility is important. For most operations it is best to begin by offering alternatives that are a nutritional improvement over current selections, rather than a drastic change.

As the customers begin to ask for more information about the nutritional content of foods or to have healthy foods highlighted on the menu, it may be a good idea to adopt a prepared system of standards such as those available from the American Heart Association. Under this system, the appropriate foods (USDA choice meats from specific cuts, fish, grains, and pastas, for instance) and the correct portion sizes should be identified. The chef then has specific guidelines to follow.

Developing a total menu, menu cycle, or meal plan can be a more complicated procedure. One of the best ways to streamline the process is to use a computer software program that can perform nutrient analysis. If a computer is not available, the same effect can be achieved by performing an analysis using nutrition tables and handbooks. The process will take longer, but it will yield the same basic information.

The kitchen and dining room staffs should be informed about the changes. Training sessions to educate them about basic nutrition principles, foods, and cooking techniques are a good way to start familiarizing everyone with the new program.

The kitchen staff may need some special hands-on training to learn preparation practices, or to handle foods that might be unfamiliar. Old habits die hard, but it is important to reinforce the idea that foods can be prepared without adding butter or cream, and that there are alternatives to techniques such as pan-frying or deep-frying. Portion sizes need to be weighed out until the staff knows them well enough to consistently portion foods to meet the

10-3. *Careful control of ingredients used in recipes as well as portion sizes is crucial to nutritional cooking. The kitchen should be equipped with properly functioning scales of various types to meet all its needs. Shown here, a portion scale (spring type), a balance scale, and in the foreground, an electronic scale with a digital readout that converts instantly from ounces and pounds to grams and kilograms.*

established standards. Vegetables should be prepared close to service time, and never left to stand in water. These and other preparation practices will eventually become a normal and comfortable procedure, rather than an unfamiliar chore. It will take time, and everyone needs to give the new habits a chance to take hold.

The dining room staff should be given enough information about the new menu items to allow them to explain these dishes to the guests. Typical customer questions include: What foods go into the dish? How is it prepared? What kind of sauce accompanies the dish? The staff will also need to be able to clearly communicate special requests to the kitchen. Knowing what is possible can be an invaluable help.

RECIPE DEVELOPMENT

It is important for the chef to establish parameters for each menu category and each meal period so that the staff can more easily meet the expectations of the guest. Dinner is usually the meal at which the largest portion of meat or animal protein is eaten. Calories are usually lowest at breakfast, higher at lunch, and highest at dinner. Keeping all of this information in mind may sound like a daunting task. Once the standards for each category are established, it becomes easier. A look at the way that one restaurant has elected to budget calories and nutrients is found in Focus 10-4: St. Andrew's Cafe.

There are many resources available to the chef looking for nutrition-oriented ideas. Cookbooks, magazines, newspapers, and television programs are good sources. Most chefs will find it relatively easy to develop a repertoire of dishes that meet the nutritional cooking guidelines.

USING EXISTING RECIPES

The first step in introducing nutrition is to evaluate recipes as they currently exist. If it appears to fall within the guidelines, then a recipe doesn't need any further work. The first thing to look at is the technique. Certain cooking techniques have already been identified as good choices. Grilling, broiling, roasting, poaching, steaming, stewing, and baking are all acceptable

FOCUS 10-4   ST. ANDREW'S CAFE

The best nutritional theory urges us to eat most of the day's calories at the first meal of the day, less at midday, and the fewest in the evening. But for most Americans the sequence is reversed. Ingrained eating patterns aren't easily changed. And the intention isn't to make developing menu items a difficult and disagreeable chore. The standards for portion sizes, calorie allotment, and nutrient distribution used at St. Andrew's Cafe at The Culinary Institute of America have been developed with a definite nod toward the way that the "average person" actually eats breakfast, lunch, dinner, and, yes, snacks.

The following parameters for menu categories are based on a range of 1,800 to 2,500 total calories for the day. Breakfast is allotted about 300 to 400 calories. Lunch has a budget of 500 to 600 calories, and a snack of around 100 to 200 calories is allowed. Dinner is considered the main meal, and nearly half of the day's calories—about 800 to 1,000—are reserved for it.

Table 10-1 shows parameters for dinner menu selections, with suggested maximums for calories, fat, protein, sodium, and cholesterol. These are general recommendations, not holy writ. The chef will need to keep in mind that the responsibility for selecting a healthy meal rests solely upon the individual guest. There are no suggested maximums for carbohydrates. Applying the guidelines for calorie, protein, and fat limits will tend to keep the carbohydrate calories at an appropriate level.

TABLE 10-1.
DINNER MENU SELECTION PARAMETERS

COURSE	CALORIES	PROTEIN (GM)	FAT (GM)	CARB. (GM)	NA (MG)	CHOL (MG)
Appetizer	150	10	5	5–10	300	50
Soup	100	—	2	5–10	300	—
Entrée/sauce	225	30	12	—	500	100
Starch	100	—	—	15–20	—	—
Vegetable	50	—	—	5–10	—	—
Dessert	200	—	4	30–40	100	—
Bread	100	—	—	15–20	200	—
TOTALS	925	40	33	75–110	1400	150

because they do not necessarily require any added fats during cooking. Recipes for clear soups, consommés, pilafs, and steamed or stir-fried vegetable dishes are also normally appropriate. The methods normally require little if any modification.

10-4. *Replacing puff pastry with phyllo dough is one way to achieve a desired result without adding unwanted fat and calories to a dish. Other ingredients suitable for coating a food when the desired finished texture should be crunchy include (row immediately below sheets of phyllo, from left) cornmeal and fresh bread crumbs and (bottom row, from left) whole-wheat flour and crushed cornflakes.*

Next, the chef should review the types of foods in the recipe, and their measurements. Fish, grains, fruits, vegetables, pasta, lean meats, and poultry with the skin removed before it is served all fit the parameters of a nutritional recipe. Sauces that are used should not introduce a great deal of added fat or salt. Garnishes, flavoring ingredients, and other potentially high-fat, high-sodium ingredients should be carefully measured to keep them from upsetting the dish's balance. The only change that may be necessary for some recipes would be an adjustment to the portion size.

MODIFYING RECIPES

A traditional or classic recipe can often be modified to reduce calories, sodium, sugar, fats, and cholesterol. This is a less painful process than might be thought at first. Two areas can be adjusted, the techniques and the ingredients.

Modifications of technique are often quite easy. For example, putting far less fat in the pan, using a nonstick pan, or relying on the fat naturally present in the food are ways to modify a sauté. The chef may also simply substitute one technique for another. Instead of roasting a bird and basting it with an oil-based sauce, he or she could grill it with a light glaze. Special coatings, such as those shown in the accompanying photograph, can produce the crisp flaky textures usually associated with high-fat pastry or with pan-fried items. A game bird might be poached instead of poêléd in a bath of butter. When reheating vegetables for service, the chef could steam them instead of tossing them in butter.

Ingredient substitution is another area where a favorite recipe could be "renovated." Instead of using heavy cream, the chef can substitute evaporated skimmed milk. A mixture of nonfat yogurt and ricotta cheese can fill in for a traditional Bavarian cream base. Replacing a béarnaise sauce with a velouté-style sauce seasoned with plenty of fresh herbs and flavored with a puree of peppers can rescue a dish that would otherwise be unacceptable.

Portion sizes should also be adjusted to meet guidelines suggested in this book. For example, a 4-ounce portion of scallops will make it easier to meet dietary goals. Putting a generous amount of steamed vegetables on the plate also tips the scales in favor of good nutrition. High-calorie, high-fat, or high-sodium ingredients such as sour cream, cream cheese, whipped cream, or guacamole can still be retained in a modified version, if the chef uses moderate amounts instead of totally eliminating them.

Be sure that the new version won't invite negative comparisons. A chocolate mousse should taste "chocolaty." It can be done, as the recipe for a modified version of this mousse found in Chapter 20 clearly shows. The basic elements that made the traditional dish successful can usually be retained, even after the dish is modified, if the chef takes an open-minded approach to solving the puzzle. Heavy cream sauces or cream-style soups can be made using a velouté thickened with a modified starch instead of a roux, and "creamed" with

FOCUS 10-5 MODIFYING A CLASSIC RECIPE: SEAFOOD NEWBURG

A classic dish that has appeared on the menu at St. Andrew's Cafe is Seafood Newburg. Looking at the process this recipe underwent to meet the nutritional guidelines of the restaurant's kitchen is very useful: It provides an excellent insight into some of the ways that recipes traditionally prepared with lots of butter and cream can be successfully adapted to a healthful cooking style.

The first step in any change to a recipe is to analyze the components of the dish and determine what role they are expected to play. The main items in classic Seafood Newburg are shrimp, lobster, and scallops, cooked in butter. They are served in a cream sauce that is finished with dry sherry and a quantity of paprika. Both ingredients add flavor, and the paprika also provides color. A typical portion size, along with the sauce, is about 9 to 10 ounces.

The first place to make some adjustments is in the portion size of the main items. The usual portion for each is slightly more than 1 ounce, cooked weight. In the modified version, the portion size will be cut back to a little less than 1 ounce.

Next, the amount of fat is reduced by using a richly flavored fish stock to poach the seafood items. This stock is also used in the sauce, thereby obtaining the full benefit of the seafoods' flavors. A significant quantity of butter is "lost" from the original recipe. Even more can be saved by modifying the procedure for making the sauce.

Cream sauces are normally prepared by cooking together butter and flour for a roux, adding whole milk to make a béchamel, and finishing with heavy cream. In the modified version of this recipe the sauce is prepared by sautéing the shrimp and lobster shells in a small amount of oil to start the release of their flavor and color. Tomato paste is sautéed until the flavor mellows; it will furnish some color for the sauce. Also added to bolster the taste are other aromatic ingredients such as shallots and brandy. Next the shells and aromatics are simmered in the poaching stock. This sauce is then thickened with arrowroot, a modified starch, instead of a roux. Evaporated skimmed milk is used to finish the sauce, giving the appearance, flavor, and texture of heavy cream without the fat. A dash of sherry is added to complete the dish.

The final adjustment is made at the time of service. In the classic presentation, the dish is nestled in a shell of puff pastry. The new version replaces this with a bed of rice.

The high-fat components of the dish have been either moderated or replaced, all without sacrificing flavor, color, or texture. The guest will probably notice only that the sauce is more flavorful and the entire dish less heavy.

10-5. *It is a good idea to make it as easy as possible to portion foods accurately and consistently. The small hand tools shown here are perfect for that use. Graduated measuring pitchers (top row), measuring cups and scoops of various sizes (middle row), and ladles (bottom row) should all be readily available throughout the kitchen for use during both preparation and service.*

a low- or nonfat yogurt or evaporated milk. Often, the same flavor can be produced using less of an ingredient than is specified in the classic version. A sprinkle of Parmesan cheese on top of a potato casserole gives the dish the taste a guest expects, without all the fat and sodium in the original.

For a more detailed look at the steps used to modify one recipe, read Focus 10-5: Modifying a Classic Recipe: Seafood Newburg.

CREATING ORIGINAL RECIPES

The inspiration for a new dish can come from many sources. Perhaps a particular delivery brings in a brilliantly colored, fragrant box of fruits that leads to a new dessert item. Or maybe the memory of a dish enjoyed in another country returns at the sight of a bouquet of pungent herbs. A new cookbook, a magazine article, or a clipping saved from years ago might be the impetus.

Inventing a new recipe is a great way to take an idea and develop it into a wonderful addition to the menu. Once the basic strokes of the recipe are laid down—a dish of steamed fish with an Asian-inspired sauce, for example—it is time to start putting it down on paper or plugging it into a computer. This is where portion sizes and ingredient measurements come under their first scrutiny.

Perhaps when the chef first imagined the dish, the fish was supposed to be a 6-ounce portion of mako shark. The analysis of this version shows that the calories are too high, and that the dish was over 38% protein. When the portion size is reduced to 4 ounces, the dish begins to come within the suggested parameters.

The tamari sauce originally selected is replaced with a low-sodium version, and all of the added salt in the marinade is deleted to keep the sodium level appropriate for the menu category. When as many adjustments to the dish as possible are completed at this stage, the chef makes a few trial runs.

As each test recipe is prepared, it is evaluated to be certain that not only nutrition, but also eye appeal, flavor, texture, and color interest are kept in mind. The consensus might be that 4 ounces of fish is simply not enough to fill the plate, so it is increased to 5 ounces. To keep the calories in line, as well as to increase the visual appeal of the dish, rice pilaf is replaced with a bed of spinach and baby bok choy that is quickly wilted over high heat in a dash of stock.

There are no strict rules that govern how to go about creating a new recipe. Just as the inspiration for the dish might have come from one of a thousand different sources, so the evolution might follow a number of different paths. Perhaps the ingredients that normally went into the pasta dish prepared for a midnight supper weren't on hand. Rather than the minced bacon used to infuse a deep, smoky taste to the dish, a few spoonfuls of chopped sundried tomatoes could have been substituted. And instead of the usually liberal dousing with heavy cream and parmesan cheese, the refrigerator yielded only Gorgonzola cheese to crumble lightly over the top of each serving and no cream at all. The heavy cream gave way to chopped fresh vegetables and herbs and a light coating of a walnut oil vinaigrette.

Even though the intention may not necessarily have been to create a low-fat, high-carbohydrate entree, the end result might be a brand new item for the lunch or brunch menu. A open-minded approach to using the items at hand is a good way to pratice some creative problem-solving approaches to putting a whole new, lighter face on the foods that are prepared in any kitchen, for virtually any part of the menu.

III

Recipes

Early cookery books included recipes, or "receipts," for many preparations, but a modern cook might have a difficult time deciphering them. There is no way to recreate the expected flavor and texture sensations that a medieval or Renaissance chef knew by heart because tastes in food have changed over time.

Today, recipes are usually carefully written formulas that specify each ingredient and its required quantity. The method carefully explains each step along the way. Still, people may have difficulty producing the desired result until they accumulate enough practical cooking knowledge to learn how to "read between the lines."

For many trained chefs, a recipe is more a suggestion or an inspiration than a literal "start to finish" guide. The chef's familiarity with basic cooking methods and principles and general ratios makes it easier for him or her to experiment. If the sauce is not appropriate, or an ingredient is unavailable or out of season, the chef can usually improvise.

Learning to cook foods nutritionally will usually require some meticulous attention at the beginning, which may be frustrating. For example, long years spent adding butter by eye to finish a sauce have probably dulled any innate sense of what a single teaspoon (or less!) actually looks like in a sauté pan.

MEASURING CUPS, TABLESPOONS, AND SCALES

Recipes are not meant to replace or stifle the chef's creativity. Instead, they should be thought of as a way to channel that creativity into a new style of cooking. A thorough mastering of the basic principles and the reasoning behind them allows the practitioner to make an enlightened, creative use of the tools of the trade.

The recipes included in this book have been written to help the chef learn, or relearn, what portion sizes and ingredient measurements will look like when using nutritional cooking guidelines. This will take some extra time at first, and it may seem cumbersome to measure out certain ingredients. The extra time will pay off.

Once the chef is familiar with the correct measures and portions, using them consistently becomes easier. As this retraining continues, the chef will also discover that it will probably always be best to weigh or measure ingredients that could add extra calories, cholesterol, sodium, and fats not intended to be part of the dish. The analysis provided at the end of each recipe is based on the exact measurements supplied in the ingredient list. Adding a few teaspoons more of butter, an extra ounce of heavy cream, or another slice of bacon is likely to have a bad effect on the dish's composition.

Not every component needs the same careful monitoring as certain ingredients such as cream, butter, bacon, cheese, or oil. For example, adding more basil to the pasta, substituting a pepper salad for a tomato salsa, or increasing the amount of vegetable garnish in a soup will probably not have a negative impact on the dish's nutritional composition. These changes actually might be beneficial.

BALANCE

The nutrient analyses included with these recipes might surprise some people. Some recipes do not reflect the exact ratios and percentages for the suggested diet. For instance, an appetizer might include more than 20% fat. Is this recipe a mistake? Not at all.

A single food, a single dish, and a single meal do not constitute the day's total nutritional intake. It cannot be repeated often enough that balance in one's *overall* diet is the key. This means achieving balance at the end of the day, after every meal and every snack has been consumed. There are even some nutritionists who say the balance should be struck on a weekly basis.

This more forgiving approach enables the chef to include some "forbidden" foods. However, when dishes and ingredients high in calories, fat, sodium, and cholesterol are part of the menu, portion sizes must be kept under control.

GENERAL NOTES

In these recipes, the ingredient list will often indicate the way a food should be cut, if it should be peeled, and if any parts are removed. The measurement should be made after the completion of all of this advance preparation. For example, if a recipe calls for 2 pounds of sliced Granny Smith apples, they should be weighed after the peel and core have been removed and after the apples have been sliced. Similarly, 3 ounces of minced garlic is weighed out after the garlic is peeled and chopped.

Volume and weight measurements are different. A volume measure, when preferred, is indicated by the following terms: teaspoon, tablespoon, fluid ounce, cup, pint, quart, gallon, milliliter, or liter. Otherwise, the ingredient should be weighed using a scale.

When selecting meats, choose lean cuts and trim as much of the visible fat away as possible. The skin may be left on poultry during cooking, but it should usually be removed before service.

Except where the dried version is indicated, fresh herbs have been used because of their lively flavors. If necessary, dry herbs may be substituted for fresh ones. Use about one-third the measure for fresh herbs, and then continue to add more to taste. Dried herbs also should be added earlier in the cooking process.

Each recipe is accompanied by a nutrient analysis that provides the following information: total calories by single serving; grams of carbohydrate, fat, and protein; milligrams of sodium and cholesterol. Basic sauces and marinades were analyzed according to the specific measures in the recipes. As the chef increases or decreases the amount of a sauce used as an ingredient in another recipe, it will be necessary to adjust the analysis as well.

11

Basic Hot Sauces

A sauce has many uses, from adding a glossy sheen to medallions of pork to providing the extra flavor boost of a tomato coulis finished with fresh herbs and capers. The chef should choose the sauce to fulfill the intended purpose. Some sauces may help increase a dish's nutritional value; Black Bean Sauce and Lentil Ragout, which contain complex carbohydrates and fiber, are two excellent examples. Other sauces may provide a vibrant pool of color to act as a foil for a simply prepared main item.

In all cases, the fundamentals of proper sauce-making apply. All ingredients should be the freshest and most flavorful available. Any base ingredients, such as stocks or purees, should be properly prepared. Recipes for both meat- and vegetable-based stocks are included here. Preparing stocks from scratch is the best way for the chef to ensure that sauces and other dishes made with stock are low in sodium.

Each sauce will reach its peak flavor at a particular time. The chef should taste the sauce as it develops so that cooking is stopped just at the point that the most desirable flavor is reached. Seasoning and flavoring ingredients used as adjustments—minced, fresh herbs, a dash of fortified wine or flavored vinegar, a touch of freshly ground pepper—should be made just before the dish is served.

Sauces that can be prepared in bulk in advance should be cooled in a cold-water bath to get them quickly out of the danger zone. They should be placed in clean storage containers, carefully wrapped, and labeled with their name and the preparation date. A similar degree of care should be employed when reheating sauces. The amount needed for service should be measured out and very quickly brought over direct heat to a safe temperature.

FOCUS FOND DE VEAU LIÉ

A flavorful brown sauce, fond de veau lié, can be used as the basis for a number of sauces, such as those featured throughout this book. For example, it can be infused with fresh sage and then paired with a wild mushroom strudel. Both the sauce and the strudel filling have strong flavors, but rather than one drowning out the other, both are enhanced. Another intriguing sauce mixes an ancho chili–flavored base with an equal amount of fond de veau lié.

The amount of oil may seem rather exorbitant, but this lavish use helps obtain the best color and flavor when browning the ingredients. While the sauce is simmering, impurities are thrown to the surface and are continually skimmed away. This will remove the majority of the oil. Any that remains can easily be lifted away once the sauce has cooled and the fat has risen to the surface.

Using a modified starch such as arrowroot thickens the sauce without resorting to a traditional roux. The end result is an extremely translucent sauce. However, arrowroot does have a tendency to break down, so the chef should thicken only as much fond de veau as is needed for one meal period. Using arrowroot also considerably shortens the simmering time as compared to that needed with a flour-and-butter roux. To give the sauce a special flavor, a fortified wine or flavored vinegar can replace the water for diluting the arrowroot.

FOND DE VEAU LIÉ

Yield: approximately 1½ gallons/5.75 liters*

MIREPOIX

6 ounces	Onions, rough cut	170 grams
6 ounces	Carrots, rough cut	170 grams
6 ounces	Leeks, rough cut	170 grams
6 ounces	Celery, rough cut	170 grams
5 fluid ounces	Vegetable oil	150 milliliters
10 ounces	Tomato paste	285 grams
3 pints	Red wine, dry	1.4 liters
2	Garlic cloves, whole	2
4	Bay leaves	4
½ teaspoon	Thyme, dried leaves	500 milligrams
6 gallons	Brown veal stock	22.5 liters
25 pounds	Veal bones, roasted	11.35 kilograms
9 ounces	Arrowroot, diluted in cold water	255 grams

a *Adding a cool liquid (Madeira wine) to the arrowroot so that it can be added to the hot base sauce.*

b *The correct consistency of diluted arrowroot.*

1. Sauté the onions, carrots, leeks, and celery in hot oil until the onions and carrots are well browned.

2. Add the tomato paste and sauté until it takes on a rusty color and has a sweet aroma.

3. Deglaze the pan by adding the red wine in thirds. Allow the wine to reduce after each addition.

4. Add the garlic, herbs, stock, and roasted bones. Bring this mixture slowly to a simmer, skimming the surface as necessary throughout cooking time (approximately 6 hours).

5. Strain the sauce, pressing the solids to release all juices.

6. Reduce the strained sauce until it has a volume of 6 quarts.

7. Thicken it by gradually whipping in the diluted arrowroot.

Roast Loin of Lamb.

8. Check for seasoning, and add salt and pepper to taste, if needed. Strain the sauce through cheesecloth.

9. The sauce may be used or properly cooled and stored.

---

* The final volume of the sauce may vary, depending upon the amount of reduction. Taste, texture, and appearance should be the guides.

A typical single serving portion of this sauce is about 2 fluid ounces or 45 milliliters. If desired, the unthickened sauce can be further reduced to a thick syrup, referred to as "glace de viande," or meat glaze.

Although this recipe does indicate the use of oil, it will be removed as the sauce is skimmed. Any remaining fat or oil can easily be removed once the sauce has been refrigerated for several hours.

Veal bones may be replaced with other bones (chicken, lamb, venison, pheasant, etc.) and an appropriate stock used to make different flavored fonds.

PORTION	KCAL	PROTEIN	FAT	CARB	SODIUM	CHOL
2 oz	20	2 gm	trace	2 gm	10 mg	5 mg

VEGETARIAN DEMI-GLACE

Yield: 1 quart/1 liter

2 teaspoons	Olive oil	10 milliliters
4 ounces	Carrots, roughly chopped	115 grams
4 ounces	Celery, roughly chopped	115 grams
4 ounces	Leeks, diced	115 grams
7 ounces	Onions, roughly chopped	200 grams
2½ ounces	Tomato paste	70 grams
1 teaspoon	Shallots, minced	5 grams
1 teaspoon	Garlic, minced	5 grams
10 fluid ounces	Red wine, dry	300 milliliters
1	Bay leaf	1
1	Thyme sprig	1
2 quarts	Water or vegetable stock	2 liters
1¾ ounces	Arrowroot	50 grams

1. Heat the olive oil over medium heat. Add the carrots and celery and cook until the carrots take on a little color. Add the leeks and onions. Continue to sauté gently until the onions are a deep golden-brown (about 8 minutes).

2. Add the tomato paste, shallots, and garlic. Sauté until the tomato paste takes on a rusty color and has a sweet aroma.

3. Add the red wine in thirds; allow it to reduce completely between each addition.

4. Add the bay leaf, thyme, and cold water. Bring this to a simmer, and allow it to reduce by nearly half, skimming the surface throughout cooking time.

5. Dilute the arrowroot in a little cold water and add enough of it to thicken the sauce so that it will coat the back of a spoon.

6. Strain the sauce. It may be used, or properly cooled and stored.

———

Although this sauce will not have the same body and depth of flavor as fond de veau lié, it is an excellent alternative for use in vegetarian entrées; giving them a noticeable flavor boost.

It is appropriate to add other herbs and spices, depending upon the intended use for this sauce. For example, fines herbes (chives, chervil, tarragon, and parsley) may be selected for dishes that have a "classical" flavor. A combination of lemon grass, tamarind, and ginger would vary the flavor, making the sauce appropriate to a variety of dishes from Asian cuisines such as Vietnamese or Thai.

PORTION 2 oz	KCAL 30	PROTEIN 1 gm	FAT 1 gm	CARB 6 gm	SODIUM 45 mg	CHOL 0 mg

CIDER SAUCE

Yield: 2 quarts/2liters

2 fluid ounces	Cider vinegar	60 milliliters
2 quarts	Apple cider, fresh, unfiltered	2 liters
1 quart	Fond de veau lié	1 liter
¼ teaspoon	Salt	2 grams
¼ teaspoon	Black pepper, freshly ground	500 milligrams
4½ pounds	Granny Smith apples, peeled, diced	2 kilograms

1. Combine the vinegar and cider and reduce to a heavy syrup.

2. Add the fond de veau lié and bring to a simmer.

3. Taste the sauce and adjust with salt and pepper.

4. The sauce is ready to finish, or it may be properly cooled and stored. Before service, return the sauce to a full boil and add the apples.

This sauce is a good accompaniment to roasted, grilled, or sautéed pork or chicken.

Because of the addition of diced apples, the portion size should be slightly greater—about ⅓ cup, by volume measure—than usual.

PORTION 2 oz	KCAL 65	PROTEIN trace	FAT trace	CARB 17 gm	SODIUM 45 mg	CHOL 0 mg

BASE FOR ANCHO CHILI SAUCE

Yield: 2 quarts/2 liters*

3½ fluid ounces	Olive oil	100 milliliters
1 large bulb	Garlic, roasted, pureed	60 grams
1 pound	Onion, medium diced	450 grams
12 ounces	Ancho chilies, rehydrated**, diced	340 grams
6 ounces	Tomato paste	170 grams
2¼ pounds	Red peppers, roasted, diced, or julienned	1 kilogram
1 pint	White stock, heated	480 milliliters
1 tablespoon	Cumin, ground	6 grams
2 teaspoons	Oregano leaves, dried	1 gram
1 teaspoon	Cinnamon, ground	2 grams
¼ teaspoon	Cayenne pepper	500 milligrams

1. Heat the olive oil, then add the onions, garlic, and the chilies. Sauté until they are heated through.

2. Add the tomato paste and sauté until it has a sweet aroma and a rusty color.

3. Add the peppers; sweat briefly. Add the stock; bring the sauce to a simmer.

4. Add the cumin, oregano, cinnamon, and cayenne pepper. Simmer for about 30 minutes.

5. Puree this mixture until smooth. It can be used to prepare Ancho Chili Sauce at this point, or properly cooled and stored for later use.

6. To finish sauce, combine equal parts of the base and fond de veau lié. Bring sauce to a simmer.

---

* Ancho Chili Sauce can easily be finished one portion at a time, or in larger batches, depending on the needs of the kitchen. Chefs preparing for banquets or large-volume operations will want to make a few quarts or more at a time. Bistros and other restaurants with à la carte menus should finish the sauce portion by portion, as needed. The base will keep well if properly refrigerated at all times.

** To rehydrate dried chilies, pour boiling water over them in a small bowl and allow them to steep until softened. The liquid should be added to the sauce along with the chilies for the best flavor retention.

Ancho Chili Sauce can be used to bolster the flavor of stews or braises, or as an accompaniment to roasted, smoke-roasted, grilled, or sautéed chicken, tuna, shark, swordfish, veal, pork, or beef.

PORTION	KCAL	PROTEIN	FAT	CARB	SODIUM	CHOL
1 oz	40	1 gm	2 gm	6 gm	45 gm	trace

CHICKEN STOCK

Yield: 1 gallon/3.75 liters

8 pounds	Chicken bones, cut into 3-inch lengths*	3.6 kilograms
6 quarts	Cold water or remouillage	5.75 liters
1 pound	Mirepoix	450 grams
1	Standard sachet d'épices**	1

1. Rinse the bones; blanch if they are frozen.
2. Combine the bones and water.
3. Bring them slowly to a boil.
4. Skim the surface, as necessary.
5. Simmer the stock for 5 hours.
6. Add mirepoix and sachet d'épices; simmer an additional 1 to 2 hours.
7. Strain, cool, and store.

---

* This recipe includes the basic ratio for chicken, veal, game, and beef stock. Use the same amount of the desired bones, and apply the appropriate cooking times. Chicken and game bird stocks require a total of 5 to 6 hours simmering time; veal, beef, and venison stocks require 7 to 8 hours. Using stock produces a "double-rich" broth or stock.

To make brown stocks, roast the bones in a hot oven until they are evenly browned before beginning simmering. Brown the mirepoix and 6 ounces of tomato puree or paste together. Proceed with the recipe.

** A standard sachet d'épices is explained in the Cooking Glossary.

PORTION 16 oz	KCAL 56	PROTEIN 8 gm	FAT 2 gm	CARB 2 gm	SODIUM 20 mg	CHOL 2 mg

a Straining the stock. Cheesecloth should be well-rinsed and then wrung out.

b Cooling chicken stock.

c Once cooled, the stock is placed in suitable storage containers, covered tightly, labeled and dated.

FOCUS   HANDLING STOCKS, SOUPS, AND SAUCES SAFELY

Certain preparations, especially stocks, soups, and sauces, may be prepared in single large batches. This is the most efficient way to handle operations that might require several hours of cooking time. In order to be certain that these items remain wholesome and flavorful over the course of several days, it is critical that the chef understand how to handle hot liquids in a way that will avoid any contamination with harmful bacteria.

There is a specific temperature range from 45 degrees F to 140 degrees F (7 degrees C to 74 degrees C), often referred to as the "danger zone," which is particularly hospitable to a variety of pathogens such as bacteria. In order to lessen the amount of time a liquid food spends in the danger zone, the following procedures should be followed.

First, place the hot liquid in a clean container. The chicken stock shown here is being strained through rinsed cheesecloth. The container selected should be metal, since metal is a good conductor of heat. Plastic is fine for storage but is a poor choice for actually cooling the stock. Now, the entire container is placed in a cold water bath, with enough water to come up to the level of the hot liquid in the container. If a drain pipe is available, a constant stream of cold water can run into the sink. Adding ice to the water will also help to reduce the length of time it takes to cool a pot of a hot liquid.

Bricks or a rack should be used to elevate the container so that cold water comes in contact with all surfaces. Stirring the liquid as it cools helps to speed the process, as well as to prevent anaerobic bacteria (which thrive in the absence of oxygen) from growing in the center of the pot. The larger the container, the more time it will take to cool down, and the more important it is to take every possible step to accelerate the cooling.

Once the entire contents of the pot have been cooled to around 45 degrees F/7 degrees C, the stock, soup, or sauce is ready to be refrigerated. While it is fine to store foods in stainless steel bain maries, plastic containers are often used because they are frequently in greater supply than metal containers. Clearly writing the name of the contents and the date that it was prepared makes it easier for everyone to find the item they need, and to use it in the correct sequence (oldest first, freshest last).

VEGETABLE STOCK

Yield: 7 quarts/6.65 liters

2 teaspoons	Olive oil	10 milliliters
½ ounce	Garlic, chopped	15 grams
1 ounce	Shallots, chopped	30 grams
7 quarts	Water	6.65 liters
8 fluid ounces	Dry vermouth	240 milliliters
7 ounces	Carrots, thinly sliced	200 grams
6 ounces	Wild mushrooms	170 grams
5 ounces	Button mushrooms	140 grams
6 ounces	Celery, thinly sliced	170 grams
3½ ounces	Fennel, sliced	100 grams
3 ounces	Leeks, sliced	85 grams
1	Bouquet garni*	1
1 tablespoon	Juniper berries, toasted	5 grams
1 teaspoon	Black peppercorns, cracked	2 grams
2	Bay leaves	2

1. In a stock pot, heat the olive oil, then add the garlic and shallots. Cook gently over moderate heat until they are tender and translucent and the aroma is released.

2. Add the rest of the ingredients.

3. Bring the stock to a boil, then reduce the heat and simmer slowly for about 45 minutes.

4. Strain the stock, and properly cool and store it under refrigeration.

———

* For ingredients and a definition of bouquet garni, refer to the Cooking Glossary.

This stock can be prepared with a variety of vegetables, including parsnips, celeriac, onions, scallions, and green beans. Certain vegetables, such as beets and leafy greens, might give the stock a deep color that may be inappropriate for some uses. Starchy vegetables, including squashes, potatoes, and yams, will thicken the stock slightly and give it a cloudy appearance.

In some cases, it may be appropriate to save the steaming or boiling liquid from vegetable preparation to use as a base for the stock, replacing some or all of the water. Be certain that the cooking liquid is cooled properly and stored carefully until needed.

Vegetable stock may be used for vegetarian-style soups, stews, and rice and bean dishes, and as the base for a velouté.

PORTION	KCAL	PROTEIN	FAT	CARB	SODIUM	CHOL
16 oz	30	2 gm	1 gm	3 gm	20 mg	0 mg

FISH FUMET

Yield: 1 gallon/3.75 liters

2 fluid ounces	Oil	60 milliliters
11 pounds	Fish bones or crustacean shells	5 kilograms
1 pound	Mirepoix*	450 grams
10 ounces	Mushroom trimmings or stems	285 grams
5 quarts	Cold water	4.75 liters
1 quart	Dry white wine	1 liter
1	Standard sachet d'épices	1

1. Heat the oil; add the bones and mirepoix.

2. Sweat the bones and mirepoix.

3. Add the rest of the ingredients; bring to a simmer.

4. Simmer for 35 to 40 minutes, skimming the surface as necessary.

5. Strain, cool, and store properly.

---

* Mirepoix is explained in the Cooking Glossary.

White mirepoix may be used, if desired. Correct ratios for white mirepoix may also be found in the Cooking Glossary.

PORTION	KCAL	PROTEIN	FAT	CARB	SODIUM	CHOL
16 oz	40	5 gm	1 gm	2 gm	20 mg	2 mg

VELOUTÉ-STYLE SAUCE/WHITE SAUCE

Yield: 1 quart/1 liter

1 quart	White stock or fish fumet	1 liter
1½ ounces	Arrowroot	40 grams
8 fluid ounces	Evaporated skimmed milk	240 milliliters
¼ teaspoon	Salt	2 grams
¼ teaspoon	White pepper, ground	500 milligrams

1. Bring the stock to a boil.

2. Dilute the arrowroot in a little cold stock or milk. (It should have the consistency of heavy cream.)

3. Add the diluted arrowroot and the evaporated skimmed milk. Return the sauce to a boil, stirring constantly. (The sauce should be thick enough to lightly coat the back of a wooden spoon.)

4. Taste the sauce and adjust the seasoning with salt and pepper.

4. Strain, if necessary.

5. Sauce may be used or properly cooled and stored.

———

This sauce may be prepared with any good-quality white stock or fumet, including fish, chicken, beef, or vegetable. All traces of fat must be removed from the surface of the stock before using it.

For a béchamel-style sauce, replace the white stock with an equivalent measure of skimmed milk. Cook the sauce at a simmer; do not allow the milk to come to a full boil in Steps 1 and 3.

Using arrowroot produces a sauce that has good body, but it will not stand up to long holding periods in a steam table. Because the sauce can be prepared quickly, it is not essential to make batches large enough to last several days.

PORTION	KCAL	PROTEIN	FAT	CARB	SODIUM	CHOL
2 oz	25	2 gm	trace	3 gm	70 mg	trace

CHIVE SAUCE

Yield: 24 fluid ounces/720 milliliters

2 ounces	Shallots, minced	60 grams
½ ounce	Garlic, minced	15 grams
2 teaspoons	Butter, unsalted	10 grams
3 fluid ounces	Dry vermouth	90 milliliters
1	Bay leaf	1
1 pint	Fish velouté*	480 milliliters
1 bunch	Chives, fresh, snipped	18 grams
2 fluid ounces	Heavy cream, boiling	60 milliliters
¼ teaspoon	Salt	2 grams
¼ teaspoon	White pepper, freshly ground	500 milligrams

1. Sauté the shallots and garlic in the butter over low heat.

2. Deglaze the pan with the vermouth. Reduce to a heavy syrup.

3. Add the bay leaf, fish velouté, and chives. Simmer until the flavor is fully developed, approximately 15 minutes.

4. Finish the sauce with the heavy cream. Strain the sauce through cheesecloth or a fine strainer.

5. Taste and adjust with salt and pepper as needed.

6. The sauce may be used or properly cooled and stored.**

––––––

* Fish velouté should be prepared following the recipe for Velouté-Style Sauce, using fish stock or fumet.

** Before serving this sauce, return it to a simmer and add a garnish of minced fresh chives.

This Chive Sauce is an excellent replacement for the beurre blanc typically paired with shallow-poached fish entrées. If desired, it may be used with poultry dishes as well. Simply replace the fish velouté with one prepared with chicken stock.

Chive Sauce could also be used to replace an Alfredo sauce in pasta dishes, especially those using fresh pastas. A sauce garnished with a small amount of shrimp, diced poached monkfish, or a julienne of smoked salmon and served over fettuccine or linguine would make an excellent appetizer or entrée. If desired, dust the top of the dish with a sprinkling of Parmesan cheese and lightly gratiné before serving.

PORTION	KCAL	PROTEIN	FAT	CARB	SODIUM	CHOL
2 oz	90	2 gm	6 gm	5 gm	322 mg	20 mg

MUSTARD AND HORSERADISH SAUCE

Yield: 3 pints/1.35 liters

40 fluid ounces	Fish velouté*	1.2 liters
1¾ ounces	Golden mustard	50 grams
1¾ ounces	Pommery mustard	50 grams
1½ ounces	Horseradish, drained, rinsed	40 grams
7 fluid ounces	Heavy cream	200 milliliters

1. Heat the velouté and bring it to a simmer.
2. Blend the mustards with the horseradish and add them to the simmering velouté. Blend well.
3. Heat the heavy cream and add to the sauce.
4. The sauce may be served at this point.

---

* See the first note in the recipe for Chive Sauce regarding preparing a fish velouté.

This sauce would be a good accompaniment to poached, grilled, or baked salmon, or for pan-smoked fish and shellfish.

Other mustards may be substituted for those suggested in the ingredient list, such as a grainy mustard, Dijon-style mustard, or specially flavored mustards.

PORTION	KCAL	PROTEIN	FAT	CARB	SODIUM	CHOL
2 oz	60	2 gm	4 gm	4 gm	145 mg	15 mg

BASIL SAUCE

Yield: 24 fluid ounces/720 milliliters

2 ounces	Shallots, minced	60 grams
⅓ ounce	Garlic, minced	10 grams
½ fluid ounce	Olive oil	15 milliliters
3 fluid ounces	White wine, dry	90 milliliters
1 ounce	Basil stems, chopped	30 grams
1 pint	Velouté-style Sauce*	480 milliliters
2 fluid ounces	Heavy cream	60 milliliters
½ ounce	Basil leaves, chopped	15 grams
½ teaspoon	Salt	3 grams
¼ teaspoon	White pepper, freshly ground	500 milligrams

1. Sweat the shallots and garlic in the olive oil over low heat. Add the white wine and basil stems; reduce to form a syrup. Strain this reduction and add it to the velouté.

2. Slowly bring the velouté to a simmer.

3. Puree the basil leaves with the heavy cream, and add it to the velouté. Add the salt and pepper.

4. The sauce may be used at this point or properly cooled and stored.

———

* The recipe for Velouté-Style sauce is in this chapter. To make any herb sauce variation on this recipe, replace the basil with other herbs or combinations of them. Use the stems in the reduction, and enough chopped, fresh leaves to flavor the sauce and give it an intense, green color. The sauce will not hold for very long, however. It is best to prepare small batches as they are needed.

PORTION	KCAL	PROTEIN	FAT	CARB	SODIUM	CHOL
2 oz	85	2 gm	5 gm	5 gm	300 mg	20 mg

SHRIMP SAUCE

Yield: 24 fluid ounces/720 milliliters

½ ounce	Garlic cloves, minced (about 4)	12 grams
¾ ounce	Shallots, minced	20 grams
½ fluid ounce	Olive oil	15 milliliters
3 ounces	Tomato paste	85 grams
8 ounces	Shrimp shells	225 grams
2 fluid ounces	Brandy	60 milliliters
8 fluid ounces	Chicken stock, boiling	250 milliliters
1 pint	Fish velouté	500 milliliters
4 fluid ounces	Heavy cream	125 milliliters
½ teaspoon	Salt	2.5 grams
¼ teaspoon	White pepper, freshly ground	500 milligrams

1. Sauté the garlic and shallots in the olive oil until translucent, about 5 minutes.
2. Add the tomato paste; sauté until it takes on a rusty color and has a sweet aroma.
3. Add the shrimp shells and sauté them until a deep-pink color develops, about 4 minutes.
4. Deglaze the pan with brandy; allow it to reduce. (It may be flamed if desired.)
5. Add the stock and bring to a boil; simmer until reduced by approximately half.
6. Puree this mixture in a blender, or with an immersion blender, until very smooth.
7. Combine the puree with the velouté and cream. Bring the sauce up to a simmer, but do not allow it to come to a full boil.
8. Taste the sauce and adjust seasoning with salt and pepper.
9. Strain through cheesecloth.
10. The sauce may be used or properly cooled and stored.

PORTION	KCAL	PROTEIN	FAT	CARB	SODIUM	CHOL
2 oz	70	2 gm	5 gm	5 gm	145 mg	15 mg

TOMATO COULIS

Yield: 3 quarts/2.8 liters

1 ounce	Garlic cloves (about 8), minced	30 grams
8 ounces	Onion, minced	225 grams
1 fluid ounce	Olive oil	30 milliliters
1 pound	Tomato paste	450 grams
6 pounds	Tomato concassé	2.75 kilograms
2 quarts	Chicken stock, boiling	2 liters
1	Bouquet garni*	1
1 teaspoon	Salt	5 grams
½ teaspoon	Black pepper, freshly ground	1 gram

1. Sauté the garlic and onions in olive oil; cook until the onions are translucent.

2. Add the tomato paste; sauté until it takes on a rusty color and has a sweet aroma.

3. Add the tomatoes, stock, and bouquet garni; simmer for about 2 hours.

4. Remove and discard the bouquet garni.

5. Puree the sauce in a food processor and adjust the consistency. To thin the sauce add a little boiling stock; to thicken, continue reducing it over moderate heat.

6. Taste the sauce and adjust with salt and pepper.

7. The sauce may be used, or properly cooled and stored.

———

* For ingredients and a definition of bouquet garni, refer to the Cooking Glossary.

The addition of different herbs and flavoring ingredients can make this sauce one of the most versatile in the kitchen. Some suggestions include adding diced and steamed vegetables such as fennel, leeks, and celery. The sauce can be "creamed" by adding a little evaporated skimmed milk. If fresh plum tomatoes are unavailable to prepare concassé, substitute a No. 10 can of whole plum tomatoes and omit the salt adjustment. This sauce holds well, and the recipe can be multiplied.

PORTION	KCAL	PROTEIN	FAT	CARB	SODIUM	CHOL
2 oz	40	1 gm	2 gm	4 gm	15 mg	trace

RED PEPPER COULIS

Yield: 2 quarts/2 liters

6 pounds	Sweet red peppers, coarsely chopped*	2.75 kilograms
1	Jalapeño pepper, minced	1
8 ounces	Onions, coarsely chopped	225 grams
1 tablespoon	Garlic cloves (about 4), minced	12 grams
2 fluid ounces	Olive oil	60 milliliters
1 quart	Chicken stock, boiling	1 liter
2 fluid ounces	Balsamic vinegar	60 milliliters
1 teaspoon	Salt	5 grams

1. Sauté the peppers, onion, and garlic in the olive oil until they are heated through.

2. Cover the pot and sweat until the vegetables are softened.

3. Add the stock; simmer until the sauce is reduced to the point at which there is no free liquid visible on the bottom of the pan (about 12 minutes).

4. Puree the sauce in a blender and strain it through a coarse sieve. Adjust the consistency as needed: to thin the sauce add a little boiling stock; to thicken, continue reducing it over moderate heat.

5. Taste the sauce and finish by adding balsamic vinegar and salt to taste.

6. Sauce may be used, or properly cooled and stored.

———

* To give a more intense flavor, roast and peel the red peppers before preparing this sauce. Peppers roasted in a hot oven have a better flavor, but it will be necessary to use about 30 average-sized peppers to get the same yield as fresh peppers. If the peppers are roasted in a flame, the flavor is less fully developed, but the yield is about the same as in the original recipe.

PORTION	KCAL	PROTEIN	FAT	CARB	SODIUM	CHOL
2 oz	60	1 gm	4 gm	6 gm	140 mg	trace

TOMATO-HORSERADISH SAUCE

Yield: 3 pints/1.35 liters

1 fluid ounce	Olive oil	30 milliliters
1 ounce	Garlic, minced	30 grams
2 ounces	Shallots, minced	60 grams
4 ounces	Tomato paste	115 grams
2 fluid ounces	Lemon juice, fresh-squeezed	60 milliliters
2 fluid ounces	White wine vinegar	60 milliliters
2¼ pounds	Plum tomato concassé	1 kilogram
1 sprig	Thyme	1 sprig
1	Bay leaf	1
2½ ounces	Horseradish, drained	70 grams
28 fluid ounces	Chicken stock*	840 milliliters

1. Heat the olive oil over medium heat; add the garlic and shallots. Sweat until they are tender and translucent.

2. Add the tomato paste and sauté until it has a rusty color and a sweet aroma.

3. Add the lemon juice, vinegar, tomato concassé, thyme, bay leaf, horseradish, and stock (reserve about 8 fluid ounces/240 milliliters for a final adjustment after the sauce is pureed).

4. Bring the sauce to a simmer and allow it to reduce over moderate heat for about 15 minutes. Remove and discard the thyme and bay leaf.

5. Puree the sauce by putting it through a food mill or a sieve. If necessary, add enough stock to thin it to the desired consistency. The sauce should pour easily from a spoon.

---

* See the recipe in this chapter.

   This sauce is an excellent accompaniment to grilled, roasted, or smoke-roasted items.

PORTION	KCAL	PROTEIN	FAT	CARB	SODIUM	CHOL
2 oz	70	3 gm	3 gm	9 gm	25 mg	trace

TOMATO SAUCE WITH JALAPEÑOS AND BALSAMIC VINEGAR

Yield: 3 pints/1.35 liters

1 fluid ounce	Olive oil	30 milliliters
1 ounce	Jalapeño peppers, minced	30 grams
2 ounces	Garlic, minced	60 grams
4 ounces	Shallots, minced	115 grams
2 ounces	Tomato paste	60 grams
1¾ fluid ounces	Lemon juice	50 milliliters
7 fluid ounces	Balsamic vinegar	200 milliliters
2¼ pounds	Plum tomato concassé	1 kilogram
3	Rosemary sprigs	3
3	Tarragon sprigs	3
28 fluid ounces	Chicken stock	840 milliliters

1. Heat the olive oil over medium heat; add the jalapeños, garlic, and shallots. Sweat until they are tender and translucent.

2. Add the tomato paste and sauté until it has a rusty color and a sweet aroma.

3. Add the lemon juice, vinegar, tomatoes, rosemary, tarragon, and the chicken stock, reserving about 8 fluid ounces/240 milliliters for a final adjustment to the sauce after it is pureed.

4. Bring the sauce to a simmer. Reduce over moderate heat for about 15 minutes; then remove the rosemary and tarragon.

5. Puree the sauce by putting it through a food mill or a sieve. Add enough stock to thin it to the desired consistency, if necessary. The sauce should pour easily from a spoon.

This sauce can be stored for several days in a well-covered container. It may thicken during storage, and will require an additional adjustment to regain a pourable consistency. Be sure to check the flavor, and add another dash of lemon juice or a grinding of black pepper. If desired, some chopped fresh tarragon leaves may be added just before service.

The sauce's robust flavor makes it a good foil for a variety of meats, including broiled or grilled poultry and game birds; roasted meats; and grilled fish such as shark, tuna, or swordfish. It would also marry well with a variety of pasta dishes, such as a lasagna, ravioli or tortellini filled with a reduced-fat sausage or forcemeat.

To vary the flavor, add some drained and rinsed horseradish (enough to flavor the sauce but not to overwhelm the other tastes), and/or prepared mustard. Another option: add a small amount of evaporated skimmed milk to "cream" the sauce.

PORTION	KCAL	PROTEIN	FAT	CARB	SODIUM	CHOL
2 oz	75	1 gm	2 gm	15 gm	200 mg	trace

LENTIL RAGOÛT

Yield: 3 quarts/3 liters

1 ounce	Bacon, chopped	30 grams
8 ounces	Onions, minced	225 grams
8 ounces	Leeks, finely diced	225 grams
8 ounces	Carrots, finely diced	225 grams
8 ounces	Celery, finely diced	225 grams
2	Garlic cloves, minced	8 grams
3 ounces	Tomato paste	85 grams
12 ounces	Lentils*	340 grams
3 pints	Chicken stock, boiling	1.4 liters
½ teaspoon	Salt	3 grams
⅛ teaspoon	White pepper, ground	250 milligrams
1	Sachet d'épices**	1

2 fluid ounces	Sherry wine vinegar	60 milliliters
4 fluid ounces	Riesling wine	120 milliliters
6 fluid ounces	Fond de Veau Lié or Vegetarian Demi-glace***	180 milliliters

1. Render the bacon. Add the onions, leeks, carrots, celery, and garlic. Cover the pot and sweat until ingredients are tender and translucent.

2. Add the tomato paste; sauté until it takes on a rusty color and has a sweet aroma.

3. Add the lentils, stock, salt, pepper, and sachet. Simmer until the lentils are tender (approximately 45 minutes).

4. Remove and discard the sachet.

5. Taste the sauce and adjust with the vinegar, wine, and fond de veau lié or demi-glace.

6. The sauce may be used or properly cooled and stored for up to 1 week under refrigeration. Return refrigerated sauce to a full boil before using.

---

* French lentils are recommended because they tend to hold their shape better than other kinds, preventing the sauce from becoming too thick. Other lentils may be used, however. Red lentils cook very rapidly and should be carefully watched to avoid overcooking.

** For ingredients and a definition of sachet d'épices, refer to the Cooking Glossary. If desired, add caraway seeds and lemon zest to the standard sachet.

*** The recipes for Fond de Veau Lié and Vegetarian Demi-glace are both found in this chapter.

If a vegetarian version of this recipe is desired, replace the bacon with ½ ounce of olive oil, use vegetable stock instead of chicken stock, and use the Vegetarian Demi-glace.

PORTION	KCAL	PROTEIN	FAT	CARB	SODIUM	CHOL
2 oz	60	4 gm	1 gm	8 gm	85 mg	trace

BLACK BEAN SAUCE

Yield: 3 quarts/2.8 liters

¾ ounce	Bacon, minced	20 grams
1 pound	Onions, minced	450 grams
½ ounce	Garlic, minced	15 grams
1½ ounces	Ancho chili (dried), finely chopped	40 grams
5 quarts	Chicken stock, boiling	4.75 liters
2 pounds	Black beans, sorted, rinsed	900 grams
3 ounces	Sun-dried tomatoes, chopped	85 grams
1 teaspoon	Oregano, dried leaves	1 gram
2 teaspoons	Cumin seeds, ground	4 grams
1	Lemon, thickly sliced	1
1 teaspoon	Salt	5 grams
4 fluid ounces	Sherry wine vinegar	120 milliliters

1. Render the bacon by sautéing over low heat for a minute or two. Add the onions, garlic, chili, and a ladleful of stock. Cover the pot and sweat until the onions are translucent.

2. Add the remaining stock, and the beans, tomatoes, oregano, cumin, and lemon. Simmer for about 2 hours, until the beans are tender to the bite.

3. Remove and discard the lemon slices. Add salt, if necessary.

4. Puree approximately half of the sauce in a food processor until smooth.

5. Return the bean puree to the sauce and blend thoroughly.

6. Taste the sauce and adjust the seasoning with the vinegar and salt.

7. The sauce may be used or properly cooled and stored.

Soaking the beans overnight in cold water to cover by 3 inches will reduce the overall cooking time. Use cool water, and drain it away before beginning cooking.

The black beans may be replaced by other kinds, such as cannellini, navy, Great Northern, pink, or kidney beans. The cooking times will be similar, but be sure to check them periodically. The speeds at which different types of beans cook depend upon how fresh they are.

This sauce can be thinned with additional stock and used as a soup. Or, the beans can all be left whole, and then used in a variety of salads or served as a side dish. Or, all of the beans may be pureed, and then used as a filling for enchiladas.

PORTION	KCAL	PROTEIN	FAT	CARB	SODIUM	CHOL
2 oz	60	4 gm	1 gm	9 gm	75 mg	trace

BARBECUE SAUCE

Yield: approximately 2 quarts/2 liters

8 ounces	Onions, minced	225 grams
1 ounce	Garlic, minced	30 grams
1 ounce	Jalapeño pepper, minced	30 grams
2 fluid ounces	Vegetable oil	60 milliliters
1 pound	Tomato paste	450 grams
1 ounce	Chili powder	30 grams
1 pint	Brewed coffee, strong	480 milliliters
6 fluid ounces	Worcestershire sauce	180 milliliters
12 fluid ounces	Cider vinegar	360 milliliters
12 ounces	Brown sugar	340 grams
12 fluid ounces	Apple cider	360 milliliters

1. Sauté the onions, garlic, and jalapeños in the oil until they glisten. Cover the pot and sweat until the onions are translucent.

2. Add the tomato paste; sauté until it takes on a rusty color and has a sweet aroma.

3. Add the remaining ingredients, mix well, and bring to a full boil. Reduce to a simmer and continue to cook for another 4 to 5 minutes.

4. The sauce may be used or properly cooled and stored for up to 2 weeks under refrigeration.

PORTION	KCAL	PROTEIN	FAT	CARB	SODIUM	CHOL
1 oz	75	1 gm	2 gm	15 gm	190 mg	15 mg

HONEY-MUSTARD GLAZE

Yield: 28 fluid ounces/840 milliliters

2 ounces	Shallots, minced	60 grams
1½ ounces	Garlic cloves, minced	40 grams
1 fluid ounce	Chicken stock	30 milliliters
8 ounces	Tomato paste	225 grams
2 tablespoons	Thyme leaves, fresh	4 grams
8 ounces	Dijon mustard	225 grams
1 pound	Honey	450 grams
4 fluid ounces	Red wine vinegar	120 milliliters
1 tablespoon	Black pepper, ground	5 grams

1. Smother the shallots and garlic in the stock until they are tender.

2. Add the tomato paste; sauté until it takes on a rusty color and has a sweet aroma.

3. Add the remainder of the ingredients and simmer until the glaze reduces by about a third.

4. The sauce may be used or properly cooled and stored for up to 2 weeks under refrigeration. Warm the glaze gently before using so that it will spread easily.

This glaze does contain a large percentage of honey, but because only a small amount is required to coat items that will be grilled or roasted, it will not add a great many calories to the finished item.

This glaze will thicken as it is stored under refrigeration. If necessary, it may be thinned by adding a small amount of hot water or stock.

PORTION	KCAL	PROTEIN	FAT	CARB	SODIUM	CHOL
1 oz	70	1 gm	1 gm	16 gm	120 mg	trace

CHAPTER

12

Cold Sauces and Relishes

The addition of a tangy relish or herb-flavored vinaigrette to a dish can lift it out of the ordinary. The collection of recipes in this chapter provides the chef with a wide array of options for adding special flavors, textures, and colors to the finished plate. Recipes for classic cold sauces, such as vinaigrettes and mayonnaise, have been modified to reduce total fat and calories, while retaining the integrity of the original's texture, taste, color, and coating capabilities.

Most of these recipes can be completed in advance, and will maintain their quality over the course of several days, when properly covered and held under refrigeration. High-fat ingredients such as tahini, oil, and crème fraîche must be measured carefully to avoid adding too many fat calories. The same precaution must be taken with ingredients such as capers, anchovies, and salt to avoid introducing too much sodium. Most other ingredients, such as herbs, spices, fresh vegetables, citrus juices, vinegar, and stock, can generally be used with less rigid concern for absolute accuracy in measuring, as long as the end product has a pleasing balance of flavors and a good consistency.

Some of the recipes included in this chapter may appear to be alarmingly high in sodium and fats. They are meant to be used as a "grace note" garnish, applied with a very frugal hand in such a way that they deliver the maximum flavor and color impact without using more than a few grams. Tapenade, for instance, prepared with olives and capers, is used as the thinnest coating on croutons. Saffron aioli is drizzled onto the tops of soups or stews to add flavor and a rich golden color.

FOCUS   Vinaigrette-Style Dressing

The traditional oil to vinegar ratio for a classic vinaigrette is three parts to one part, respectively. In this recipe, two-thirds of the oil is replaced by thickened stock. The difference in both calories and fats between the two versions is quite dramatic. A comparison of a 1-ounce portion of each is given below.

Using a thickened stock gives the new version excellent coating abilities. The texture is similar enough to that of a classic vinaigrette to effectively "fool" the mouth. Mixing the salad dressing by using a regular or immersion blender not only adds to the dressing's body, it also thoroughly distributes the oil.

Apart from its use as a salad dressing, vinaigrette can be a part of the mise en place for the grill station, where it serves as a marinade for vegetables, meats, poultry, and fish. A light drizzle of some vinaigrette gives special zest to pan-steamed vegetables, which could be served on their own, as a part of an hors d'oeuvre plate, or as a salad garnish.

Vinaigrette	KCAL	PROTEIN	FAT	CARB	SODIUM	CHOL
Classic	175	trace	20 gm	trace	170 mg	0 mg
Modified	50	trace	5 gm	trace	50 mg	trace

VINAIGRETTE-STYLE DRESSING

Yield: 1 gallon/4 liters

2 quarts	Stock	2 liters
1½ ounces	Arrowroot	40 grams
1 quart	Red wine vinegar	1 liter
1 quart	Extra-virgin olive oil	1 liter
1 tablespoon	Salt	15 grams
As needed	Seasonings*	as needed

a *A small mix stick is used to properly emulsify the vinaigrette.*

1. Bring the stock to a boil. Dilute the arrowroot in a little cold water or stock. Gradually incorporate the diluted arrowroot, just until the stock is thick enough to lightly coat a spoon.

2. Allow the stock to cool. Whip the vinegar and oil into it.

3. Add the salt and seasonings, to taste. It may be used at this point or stored under refrigeration.

---

* The choice of seasonings includes prepared mustards, chopped fresh herbs, drained and chopped capers, minced vegetables, onions, garlic, or citrus zest.

This dressing will thicken as it cools during storage under refrigeration. It can be stored under refrigeration for up to 1 week without losing quality.

Juices such as orange or tomato juice, apple or pear ciders, and fruit nectars may be used to replace the stock. Thick juices will require very little, if any, thickening.

The use of special vinegars, including balsamic, sherry wine, or red wine, will provide a different flavor, as will the use of lemon, lime, or grapefruit juice in place of the vinegar.

Oils other than olive may be used, including various nut oils (peanut, sesame, walnut), canola oil, or other mono- or polyunsaturated oils.

b *The modified vinaigrette coats as well as a traditional one.*

c *A plain vinaigrette without herbs or other flavoring ingredients can be "sprayed" onto salads for easier banquet or à la carte service.*

PORTION	KCAL	PROTEIN	FAT	CARB	SODIUM	CHOL
1 oz	50	trace	5 gm	trace	50 mg	trace

RATATOUILLE VINAIGRETTE

Yield: 3 pints/1.4 liters

14 fluid ounces	Chicken stock	415 milliliters
½ ounce	Arrowroot	15 grams
1 tablespoon	Dijon mustard	15 grams
7 fluid ounces	Sherry vinegar	200 milliliters
7 fluid ounces	Extra-virgin olive oil	200 milliliters
¾ ounce	Garlic, minced	20 grams
⅓ ounce	Shallots, minced	10 grams
6 ounces	Zucchini, small dice, blanched	170 grams
6 ounces	Red pepper, brunoise	170 grams
6 ounces	Yellow pepper, brunoise	170 grams
2 tablespoons	Basil, fresh, chopped fine	6 grams
2 tablespoons	Oregano, fresh, chopped fine	6 grams
2 tablespoons	Chervil, fresh, chopped fine	6 grams
1 teaspoon	Salt	5 grams

1. Heat the stock to a simmer. Add the arrowroot to thicken. Return to a simmer, then remove from the heat and cool.

2. Add the mustard and vinegar to the chicken stock.

3. Gradually incorporate the oil, whipping constantly.

4. Add all remaining ingredients. Refrigerate until needed.

PORTION	KCAL	PROTEIN	FAT	CARB	SODIUM	CHOL
¾ oz	55	trace	5 gm	2 gm	50 mg	trace

FIVE-MUSTARD VINAIGRETTE

Yield: 2¾ quarts/2.6 liters

2½ ounces	Arrowroot	70 grams
2½ pints	Vegetable Stock*	1.2 liters
2 fluid ounces	White wine	60 milliliters
2 ounces	Whole yellow mustard seed, dry	60 grams
1 tablespoon	Coleman's dry mustard	7 grams
4 ounces	Dijon mustard	115 grams
2 ounces	Pommery whole-grain mustard	60 grams
1 tablespoon	Chinese mustard	15 grams
4 fluid ounces	Red wine vinegar	120 milliliters
4 fluid ounces	Sherry wine vinegar	120 milliliters
4 fluid ounces	Cider vinegar	120 milliliters
4 fluid ounces	Balsamic vinegar	120 milliliters
4 fluid ounces	Malt vinegar	120 milliliters
7 fluid ounces	Olive oil, extra-virgin	200 milliliters
7 fluid ounces	Walnut oil	200 milliliters
7 fluid ounces	Safflower oil	200 milliliters
4 tablespoons	Chives, chopped	12 grams
4 tablespoons	Tarragon, chopped	12 grams
1 tablespoon	Salt, kosher	15 grams
1 tablespoon	Black peppercorns, cracked	7 grams

1. Combine arrowroot with enough cold vegetable stock to form a smooth, liquid paste.

2. Bring the remaining stock to a boil, add the diluted arrowroot, and simmer for about 2 minutes, until stock is thickened. Remove it from the heat and allow to cool completely.

3. Combine the mustard seeds with the white wine and bring to a boil. Remove it from the heat and stir in the Coleman's mustard; blend thoroughly. Add the remaining mustards and stir until smooth.

4. Combine the thickened stock, mustards, vinegars, oils, herbs, and salt and pepper. Blend well with a whip or an immersion blender.

5. Refrigerate until needed.

---

* See the recipe in Chapter 11.

This is especially good with wild, bitter greens that have assertive flavors. It will keep relatively well under refrigeration. In case of separation, be sure to recombine before using.

PORTION	KCAL	PROTEIN	FAT	CARB	SODIUM	CHOL
¾ oz	45	trace	5 gm	1 gm	75 mg	0 mg

PORT WINE VINAIGRETTE

Yield: 20 fluid ounces/600 milliliters

2½ teaspoons	Arrowroot	7.5 grams
5 fluid ounces	Vegetable Stock	150 milliliters
5 fluid ounces	Port wine, red	150 milliliters
5 fluid ounces	Red wine vinegar	150 milliliters
5 fluid ounces	Olive oil, extra-virgin	150 milliliters

1. Combine the arrowroot with enough cold vegetable stock to form a smooth, liquid paste.

2.. Bring the remaining stock and the wine to a boil and add the diluted arrowroot; simmer for about 2 minutes, until stock is thickened. Remove it from the heat and allow to cool completely.

3. Add the vinegar to the stock mixture, and gradually incorporate the oil, whipping constantly, or use an immersion blender.

PORTION	KCAL	PROTEIN	FAT	CARB	SODIUM	CHOL
1 oz	53	trace	5 gm	1 gm	trace	0 mg

TOMATO VINAIGRETTE

Yield: 3 pints/1.4 liters

1½ fluid ounces	Olive oil	45 milliliters
¾ ounce	Shallots, minced	20 grams
⅓ ounce	Garlic, minced	10 grams
4 ounces	Tomato paste	115 grams
2¼ pounds	Tomato concassé	1 kilogram
½ teaspoon	White pepper, ground	1 gram
1 tablespoon	Basil, chiffonade	3 grams
1 tablespoon	Dill, chopped	3 grams
1 teaspoon	Tarragon, chopped	1 gram
1½ fluid ounces	Balsamic vinegar	45 milliliters

1. Sauté the garlic and shallots in the olive oil until the aroma is apparent.

2. Add the tomato paste and sauté briefly, but do not allow it to brown.

3. Add the tomato concassé and simmer for 20 minutes, or until the mixture is reduced by about one-quarter. Puree this mixture until smooth and allow it to cool.

4. Add the pepper, fresh herbs, and vinegar. Refrigerate until needed.

PORTION	KCAL	PROTEIN	FAT	CARB	SODIUM	CHOL
¾ oz	20	trace	1 gm	2 gm	30 mg	0 mg

CREAMY-STYLE DRESSING

Yield: approximately 1 quart/1 liter

10 ounces	Ricotta cheese, part-skim	285 grams
20 fluid ounces	Nonfat yogurt	600 milliliters
5 fluid ounces	Red wine vinegar	150 milliliters
as needed	Seasonings*	as needed

1. Puree ricotta in a food processor or blender until very smooth.
2. Add the yogurt and vinegar. Process until fully incorporated.
3. Remove from the processor.
4. Add seasonings, as desired.

---

* Add a variety of chopped herbs to this basic dressing to vary the flavor. Chives, tarragon, chervil, and basil are all good choices when the dressing will be used as a dipping sauce, an accompaniment to hors d'oeuvre and terrines, or a salad dressing.

Prepared mustards may be added to this base, in addition to herbs, pepper, chopped onions, scallions, or chives. Onions, garlic, and other raw members of the onion family may be smothered in oil before being added. This will extend the dressing's shelf life.

If during storage the dressing becomes too thick, it may be thinned with a small amount of buttermilk.

PORTION	KCAL	PROTEIN	FAT	CARB	SODIUM	CHOL
¾ oz	20	2 gm	1 gm	2 gm	20 mg	2 mg

ANCHOVY-CAPER DRESSING

Yield: approximately 1 quart/1liter

10 ounces	Ricotta cheese, part-skim	285 grams
20 fluid ounces	Nonfat yogurt	600 milliliters
5 fluid ounces	Red wine vinegar	150 milliliters
4 ounces	Capers, drained, rinsed	115 grams
2	Anchovy fillets, mashed	2
2 ounces	Shallots, minced	60 grams
½ ounce	Garlic, cloves (about 4), minced	15 grams
½ ounce	Chives, fresh, chopped	15 grams
½ ounce	Parsley leaves, fresh, chopped	15 grams
½ ounce	Basil leaves, fresh, chopped	15 grams

1. Puree ricotta in a food processor or blender until very smooth.
2. Add the yogurt and vinegar. Process until fully incorporated.
3. Add the remaining ingredients and puree until the dressing is evenly mixed.
4. The sauce may be used at this point or stored under refrigeration.

This sauce is suggested as an accompaniment to the Carpaccio of Beef with Fresh Artichokes and Tomato Salad and the Carpaccio of Tuna with Shiitake Salad, both found in Chapter 13. It is also a good salad dressing. Adding a small amount of Parmesan cheese will approximate a Caesar-style dressing.

PORTION	KCAL	PROTEIN	FAT	CARB	SODIUM	CHOL
¾ oz	20	2 gm	1 gm	2 gm	90 mg	2 mg

BLUE CHEESE DRESSING

Yield: 1½ pints/750 milliliters

10 ounces	Ricotta cheese, part-skim	285 grams
7 fluid ounces	Buttermilk	200 milliliters
3½ ounces	Blue cheese, crumbled	100 grams
2 teaspoons	Ketchup	10 grams
2 teaspoons	Worcestershire sauce	10 grams
2 fluid ounces	Cider vinegar	60 milliliters
1 teaspoon	Garlic puree, roasted*	3 grams
2 tablespoons	Chives, chopped	6 grams
½ teaspoon	Black peppercorns, cracked	1 gram

1. Using a food processor, blender, or an immersion blender, combine all ingredients except the chives and pepper. Blend until very smooth.

2. Fold in the chives and pepper by hand. Refrigerate until needed.

---

* See Chapter 16 for directions on roasting garlic.

Any quality blue cheese could be used for this dressing. Domestically produced cheeses such as Maytag, or an Italian blue-veined cheese such as Gorgonzola, are likely to produce the smoothest, creamiest results and the fullest flavor.

PORTION	KCAL	PROTEIN	FAT	CARB	SODIUM	CHOL
¾ oz	25	2 gm	2 gm	1 gm	65 mg	5 mg

SOUR CREAM REPLACEMENT

Yield: 1 pint/480 milliliters

8 fluid ounces	Crème fraîche or sour cream	240 milliliters
8 fluid ounces	Yogurt, drained	240 milliliters
as needed	Seasonings*	as needed

1. Whip the crème fraîche to a firm peak. Fold in the drained yogurt.

2. Add the seasonings, to taste. The sauce may be used at this point or stored under refrigeration for 3 to 4 days.

---

* Prepared mustards, chopped fresh herbs, drained and chopped capers, minced vegetables, onions, garlic, citrus zest, according to the desired flavor.

PORTION	KCAL	PROTEIN	FAT	CARB	SODIUM	CHOL
¾ oz	50	1 gm	4 gm	1 gm	15 mg	20 mg

HORSERADISH AND APPLE CREAM SAUCE

Yield: 1 pound/450 grams

1 pound	Creamy-style Dressing, unflavored	450 grams
1½ tablespoons	Prepared horseradish, drained, squeezed	45 grams
2 ounces	Granny Smith apple, peeled, grated	60 grams

1. Fold together all ingredients.

2. Taste, and adjust the seasoning, if necessary, with lemon juice or pepper.

PORTION	KCAL	PROTEIN	FAT	CARB	SODIUM	CHOL
¾ oz	50	3 gm	1 gm	6 gm	45 mg	5 mg

SAFFRON AÏOLI

Yield: 1½ pints/750 milliliters

6 bulbs	Garlic, roasted*	6 bulbs
1½ tablespoons	Arrowroot	15 grams
1 pint	Vegetable Stock**	480 milliliters
1 tablespoon	Saffron	3 grams
2 teaspoons	Yogurt, nonfat, drained	10 grams
2 teaspoons	Sour cream	10 grams

1. Squeeze garlic from the skins and place the meat in a blender.

2. Dilute the arrowroot in enough of the stock to make a thin paste. Bring the remaining stock to a simmer and add the diluted arrowroot. Simmer for another 2 minutes, or until thickened. Remove from the heat and add the saffron. Allow it to steep until cool.

3. Puree the garlic, then add the thickened stock in a gradual, thin stream. Continue to puree until smooth and creamy.

4. Remove the mixture to a bowl and stir in the drained yogurt and sour cream. Keep refrigerated until needed.

---

* See Chapter 16 for directions on roasting garlic.

** See the recipe in Chapter 11.

Because this sauce is used in small amounts, place it in a squeeze bottle with a narrow tip. To give special visual appeal, use a free-form design, or if preferred, apply it in streams or dots, and then feather by passing a skewer or the thin blade of a knife through it to create a regular or uneven pattern.

PORTION	KCAL	PROTEIN	FAT	CARB	SODIUM	CHOL
1 tsp	15	1 gm	trace	3 gm	2 mg	trace

PESTO

Yield: 10 ounces/285 grams

3½ ounces	Basil leaves, rinsed, dried	100 grams
2½ ounces	Pine nuts, toasted	70 grams
1 fluid ounce	Olive oil	30 milliliters
2 ounces	Parmesan cheese, freshly grated	60 grams
2 teaspoons	Garlic, minced	10 grams
as needed	Water	as needed

1. Combine all ingredients in a blender or food processor and puree to form a coarse paste.
2. While the machine is still running, add water, a little at a time, until a smooth paste forms.

The nutrient analysis of this recipe shows that it is high in fat. Therefore, use it in small amounts that should be carefully measured to avoid adding too much fat to a dish.

PORTION	KCAL	PROTEIN	FAT	CARB	SODIUM	CHOL
½ oz	70	3 gm	6 gm	2 gm	90 mg	5 mg

LEMON GLAZE FOR VEGETABLES

Yield: 10 fluid ounces/300 milliliters

28 fluid ounces	Chicken Stock*	800 milliliters
2 fluid ounces	Lemon juice, fresh-squeezed	60 milliliters
1 tablespoon	Ginger, fresh, grated	12 grams
1 tablespoon	Lemon zest	10 grams
½ teaspoon	Black pepper, cracked	1 gram
½ teaspoon	Salt	3 grams
as needed	Sesame seeds, toasted**	as needed

1. Combine the stock, lemon juice, ginger, and zest. Bring to a boil and reduce to about 10 fluid ounces/300 milliliters.

2. Add the salt and pepper, cool the glaze, and store it properly.

----

* See the recipe in Chapter 11.

**Use about ½ teaspoon/1 gram of sesame seeds to sprinkle over each portion.

To use the glaze, gently reheat it before service over a hot water bath or in a microwave on half power. Use a pastry brush to lightly coat steamed vegetables with the glaze, and top with toasted sesame seeds.

Replace the lemon juice with lime juice, and add chopped, fresh cilantro.

PORTION	KCAL	PROTEIN	FAT	CARB	SODIUM	CHOL
1 tbsp	5	1 gm	trace	trace	60 mg	trace

FRESH TOMATO SALSA

Yield: 1¼ pounds/565 grams

1 pound	Tomato concassé*	**450 grams**
1 ounce	Jalapeño pepper, minced	**30 grams**
3 ounces	Red onion, minced	**85 grams**
½ ounce	Cilantro, fresh, chopped	**15 grams**
½ ounce	Lime juice, fresh	**15 milliliters**

1. Combine all ingredients and mix well.
2. Refrigerate for several hours to let the flavors combine.
3. Check seasoning again before serving.

———

* Good-quality canned tomatoes may be used if fresh tomatoes do not have a good flavor, color, and texture. Whole plum tomatoes are the best choice, and the seeds and excess juice should be removed before chopping. Reserve the liquid for some other use (such as adding to braised dishes, vegetable stock, or vegetarian demi-glace).

You may add additional chopped fresh jalapeños or Tabasco sauce to give this sauce more fire.

Other ingredients that may be added, if desired, include parsley, chopped celery, jicama, celeriac, and sweet bell peppers. The ultimate yield will vary, depending on what additions are made and how many. If desired, a small amount of red wine or sherry vinegar, as well as some cayenne pepper, may be added to adjust the flavor.

This salsa would make a good accompaniment to a variety of Southwestern or Tex/Mex dishes such as fajitas, burritos, or enchiladas. It is also excellent when served with grilled fish, meats, or poultry. A typical portion is about 3 tablespoons/45 grams.

PORTION	KCAL	PROTEIN	FAT	CARB	SODIUM	CHOL
1 oz	10	trace	trace	2 gm	25 mg	0 mg

MOUTABEL

Yield: 24 ounces/700 grams

1 pound	Eggplant, roasted, flesh only	450 grams
8 fluid ounces	Chicken stock	240 milliliters
½ fluid ounce	Extra-virgin olive oil	15 milliliters
½ fluid ounce	Lemon juice, fresh	15 milliliters
1 tablespoon	Tahini paste	20 grams
2 cloves	Garlic, minced	10 grams
¼ teaspoon	Salt	2 grams

1. Combine all ingredients in a food processor. Puree until very smooth.

2. The moutabel may be used at this point or stored under refrigeration for 2 to 3 days. Taste for seasoning before serving.

PORTION	KCAL	PROTEIN	FAT	CARB	SODIUM	CHOL
1 oz	15	1 gm	1 gm	1 gm	30 mg	trace

RED ONION CONFIT

Yield: 20 ounces/570 grams

2 pounds	Red onion, julienned	900 grams
4 fluid ounces	Honey	120 milliliters
4 fluid ounces	Red wine vinegar	120 milliliters
4 fluid ounces	Red wine, dry	120 milliliters
to taste	White pepper, ground	to taste

1. Cook all ingredients, except pepper, over low to moderate heat until the mixture has the same consistency as marmalade (about 30 minutes).

2. Adjust seasoning, to taste, with pepper. The confit is ready to use at this point. It may be made in advance and stored for up to 4 days.

A typical portion of this confit would be about 1 ounce/30 grams.

If desired, additional red wine vinegar may be added to adjust a too-sweet flavor. (As the onions cook, they will take on a sweet flavor.) A small amount of drained, prepared horseradish may be added to give the sauce some additional heat.

PORTION	KCAL	PROTEIN	FAT	CARB	SODIUM	CHOL
2 oz	100	1 gm	trace	30 gm	1 mg	0 mg

TAPENADE

Yield: 4 ounces/120 grams

1¾ ounces	Niçoise olives, pitted	50 grams
1 ounce	Anchovy fillets, rinsed, dried	30 grams
½ ounce	Capers, rinsed	15 grams
1 teaspoon	Garlic, minced	5 grams
1 teaspoon	Olive oil, extra-virgin	5 milliliters
1 tablespoon	Lemon juice, fresh-squeezed	15 milliliters

1. Using a mortar and pestle, combine the olives, anchovies, capers, and garlic, pounding to form a coarse paste.

2. Add the oil and lemon juice; blend until an even mixture is formed. (It should retain a fair amount of texture.)

This recipe is exceptionally high in sodium, so it is important to measure it carefully. A small "dot" weighing about 1 gram should be dispensed by using a pastry bag fitted with a straight (#5) tip.

PORTION	KCAL	PROTEIN	FAT	CARB	SODIUM	CHOL
¼ oz	16	1 gm	2 gm	trace	60 mg	2 mg

FRESH MANGO CHUTNEY

Yield: 2¼ pounds/1 kilogram

2 pounds	Mango, fresh, diced	900 grams
4 ounces	Yogurt, drained	115 grams
1 ounce	Basil or cilantro, fresh, chopped	15 grams

1. Combine all ingredients.
2. Let the mixture macerate under refrigeration for several hours before serving.

———

This chutney will keep for about 7 days. For the best flavor, allow it to return to room temperature before serving.

If desired, the basil may be replaced with fresh mint. Replace half of the mango with cucumber flesh (peeled, seeded, and diced) for a different flavor.

PORTION	KCAL	PROTEIN	FAT	CARB	SODIUM	CHOL
1½ oz	50	1 gm	trace	12 gm	10 mg	trace

PRESERVED MANGO CHUTNEY

Yield: 3 pounds/1.3 kilograms

2½ pounds	Mango, fresh, diced	1 kilogram
7 ounces	Brown sugar	200 grams
6 ounces	Onion, diced	170 grams
5 ounces	Raisins	140 grams
1 ounce	Walnuts, chopped	30 grams
2 cloves	Garlic, minced	10 grams
1 fluid ounce	Cider vinegar	30 milliliters
1	Lemon, juice and zest	1
½ ounce	Ginger, fresh, minced	15 grams
½ ounce	Jalapeño pepper, minced	15 grams
½ teaspoon	Mace, ground	750 milligrams
¼ teaspoon	Cloves, ground	500 milligrams

1. Combine all ingredients and simmer until reduced and thickened (about 30 minutes).

2. Cool the chutney and taste. Adjust seasoning with additional lemon juice, if necessary. Chutney may be used at this point or stored under refrigeration for 7 to 10 days, or longer.

This chutney may be prepared using a variety of fruits. Replace the mango with tart cooking apples (they should be peeled, cored, and diced), pineapple (peeled and diced), plums (pitted and diced), or a combination of fruits.

A typical serving is about ½ ounce/15 grams. It may be used as an accompaniment to a variety of roasted and grilled foods or as a condiment for curries and other spicy dishes.

PORTION	KCAL	PROTEIN	FAT	CARB	SODIUM	CHOL
1½ oz	65	1 gm	1 gm	17 gm	10 mg	0 mg

TANDOORI MARINADE

Yield: 1 pint/450 milliliters

8 fluid ounces	Nonfat yogurt	240 milliliters
4 fluid ounces	Lemon juice, fresh	120 milliliters
1 ounce	Gingerroot, fresh, grated	30 milliliters
2 cloves	Garlic, minced	10 grams
¼ teaspoon	Cayenne pepper, ground	500 milligrams
1 tablespoon	Cumin seeds, toasted, crushed	10 grams
½ ounce	Cilantro leaves, fresh, chopped	15 grams
1 teaspoon	Salt	5 grams

1. Combine all ingredients, mix well, and spread thickly on the item to be cooked. Marinate several hours under refrigeration. A whole chicken would require 2 to 3 fluid ounces/60 to 85 milliliters.

PORTION	KCAL	PROTEIN	FAT	CARB	SODIUM	CHOL
1 oz	10	1 gm	trace	2 gm	145 mg	0 mg

GUACAMOLE

Yield: 30 ounces/850 grams

24 ounces	Avocados (4 average), very ripe	680 grams
1 ounce	Scallion, minced	30 grams
1 ounce	Garlic, minced	30 grams
2 fluid ounces	Lime juice, fresh	60 milliliters
½ ounce	Jalapeño pepper, seeded, minced	15 grams
1 ounce	Cilantro, chopped	30 grams
1 teaspoon	Salt	5 grams

1. Using a fork, mash the avocados to a paste. There should still be a little texture. (Food processors and blenders will make the mixture too smooth.)

2. Add the remaining ingredients and stir to blend. Press plastic wrap directly against the surface of the guacamole to prevent discoloring and let the flavors blend for 1 hour.

3. Serve at once.

———

Guacamole is a rich condiment, because of the high fat content of the avocados. The fat is monounsaturated, but the amount of guacamole used in a dish should be monitored to be sure that the entire dish does not exceed recommended limits for both fat and calories.

Guacamole does not keep well, and it should not be prepared far in advance. It could discolor and lose flavor.

PORTION	KCAL	PROTEIN	FAT	CARB	SODIUM	CHOL
1 oz	45	1 gm	4 gm	3 gm	75 mg	0 mg

CRANBERRY SALSA

Yield: 1 pound/450 grams

12 ounces	Cranberries, whole, raw	340 grams
1 fluid ounce	Lime juice, fresh-squeezed	30 milliliters
1 fluid ounce	Orange juice, fresh-squeezed	30 milliliters
2 tablespoons	Honey	40 grams
2 ounces	Green onion, finely chopped	60 grams
2 teaspoons	Jalapeño, seeded, minced	12 grams
2 tablespoons	Cilantro leaves, chopped	6 grams
1 tablespoon	Parsley leaves, chopped	3 grams
½ teaspoon	Black peppercorns, cracked	1 gram
½ fluid ounce	Tequila or dark rum (optional)	15 milliliters

1. In a food processor, combine all ingredients and process just until mixed to a chunky consistency. (The salsa should not be too smooth.)

2. Refrigerate until needed.

PORTION	KCAL	PROTEIN	FAT	CARB	SODIUM	CHOL
1 oz	22	trace	trace	5 gm	11 mg	0 mg

CHAPTER

13

Appetizers and Salads

These recipes offer some exciting new starts for a meal. In addition, using a selection of appetizers as an entire meal has become an intriguing alternative to traditional entrées. This unorthodox approach makes it easier for the diner to sample a number of different house specialties and at the same time meet personal nutritional goals.

This presents interesting challenges for the chef because appetizers, salads, and other "starters" have often relied upon ingredients that are high in fat, sodium, and calories. In the following recipes, certain preparations, such as terrines, have been modified to eliminate or reduce the amount of high-fat meats, heavy cream, or added fat.

The puff pastry that is often found in many appetizers has been replaced with a flaky phyllo dough, such as in the Wild Mushroom and Goat Cheese Strudel. A light coating of butter is spritzed through a spray bottle onto the dough, giving the desired taste and color without adding too many calories or too much fat.

In other recipes, high-calorie ingredients have been modified. The Ceviche of Scallops, for example, is served with Guacamole, but the amount is carefully monitored, because of the high fat content of avocados. The traditional oil-based marinade used for dishes such as Marinated Grilled Peppers is replaced with a reduced-oil vinaigrette. Marinated Chanterelles are simmered in a flavorful broth of stock, wine, vinegar, and herbs.

FOCUS MOUSSELINE-STYLE FORCEMEAT

St. Andrew's Garden Terrine, a beautiful dish that is included in this chapter, is made from a light mousseline-style forcemeat based on lean white chicken meat that has been combined with a variety of colorful, seasonal vegetables. A Mediterranean Seafood Terrine uses one of the world's most exotic spices, saffron, to give this recipe a rich color and a perfect foil to the succulence of a shrimp- and scallop-based terrine. These modern versions of classic garde-manger specialties are as delicious and appealing as their higher-fat ancestors.

Apart from its use as the base for a variety of terrines, galantines, and sausages, mousseline-style forcemeats can be used in other dishes. The modifications made to the traditional formulas for forcemeats have enabled the nutrition-conscious restaurant to feature items such as ravioli filled with a lobster mousseline or zucchini "tulips" filled with a salmon mousseline.

There are times when the chef may prefer to replace some or all of the evaporated skimmed milk called for in the recipe with heavy cream. This is certainly acceptable, as long as the overall nutritional analysis of the recipe shows that there is room for such enrichment. Remember that heavy cream is high in saturated fats, and will tend to increase the amount of cholesterol in the dish slightly. This may be a concern, especially when high-cholesterol seafood items have been selected as the base and garnish ingredients.

MOUSSELINE-STYLE FORCEMEAT

Yield: 3½ pounds/1.6 kilograms

4 ounces	Carolina rice, uncooked	115 grams
12 fluid ounces	Stock	360 milliliters
2 pounds	Meat, lean, trimmed	900 grams
8 fluid ounces	Evaporated skimmed milk, chilled	240 milliliters
as needed	Garnish ingredients*	as needed
as needed	Flavorings and seasonings**	as needed
1 teaspoon	Salt	5 grams
½ teaspoon	White pepper, ground	1 gram

a *A modified mousseline forcemeat is used to replace a traditionally high-fat farci. This recipe is for Chicken Roulade, found in this chapter.*

1. Cook the rice in the stock, using the pilaf method, until dry.

2. Spread the rice on a sheet pan to cool. Refrigerate until thoroughly chilled.

3. Cut the trimmed meat or fish into cubes. Marinate in combination with fresh herbs, spices, or liquors under refrigeration (see note).

4. Combine the meat and the rice and grind, using a coarse die.

5. Put the ground mixture into a food processor (chill the bowl and blade first). Add half of the milk and puree to a fine paste, scraping the sides of the bowl once or twice. (Do not allow the mixture to become warm.)

6. Add the remaining milk and pulse the machine on and off until just incorporated. For the finest texture, push the forcemeat through a drum sieve at this point.

7. Fold in desired garnish and seasonings. Make a test quenelle and poach it in a court bouillon, stock, or water. Check the quenelle for seasoning and consistency. Make any necessary adjustments. If the forcemeat is too tight, add additional stock or evaporated skimmed milk. Forcemeat can be used for a variety of applications. Keep refrigerated.

b *Another suggestion is to use this modified forcemeat to prepare filled fresh pastas such as the spinach agnolotti shown here.*

---

* See the recipe for St. Andrew's Terrine for vegetable garnishes. Use fresh herbs and/or spices as desired.

PORTION	KCAL	PROTEIN	FAT	CARB	SODIUM	CHOL
2 oz	55	8 gm	1 gm	4 gm	100 mg	20 mg

SAUSAGE-STYLE FORCEMEAT

Yield: 3½ pounds/1.6 kilograms

4 ounces	Carolina rice, uncooked	115 grams
20 fluid ounces	Stock (total)	600 milliliters
2 pounds	Meat (veal, poultry, game, shellfish, fish, etc.), lean, trimmed	900 grams
as needed	Garnish ingredients*	as needed
as needed	Flavorings and seasonings**	as needed
2 teaspoons	Salt	10 grams
1 teaspoon	Black pepper, freshly ground	2 grams

1. Cook the rice in 12 fluid ounces/360 milliliters of stock, using the pilaf method, until dry.

2. Spread the rice on a sheet pan to cool. Refrigerate until thoroughly chilled.

3. Cut the trimmed meat or fish into cubes. Marinate in combination with fresh herbs, spices, or liquors under refrigeration (see note).

4. Combine the meat and the rice and grind, using a coarse die, into a bowl set in an ice bath. With a wooden spoon, slowly stir in the remaining cold stock, working over ice.

5. Fold in desired garnish and seasonings. Make a test patty and bake or dry-sauté. Check the patty for seasoning and consistency. Make any necessary adjustments. The forcemeat may be used for sausages at this point or stored under refrigeration for 1 or 2 days.

---

* Most breakfast sausage formulas call for a heavy dose of herbs, spices, and aromatics to produce a full, robust flavor. Fennel seeds, oregano, basil, marjoram, sage, rosemary, chives, garlic, shallots, pepper, cayenne, and spice blends such as chili powder or pâté spice are often used.

** Additional garnish ingredients, such as chopped cooked vegetables, olives, capers, and pickles could also be included. If a high sodium ingredient is used as a garnish, reduce the amount of salt added to the recipe.

PORTION	KCAL	PROTEIN	FAT	CARB	SODIUM	CHOL
2 oz	60	9 gm	1 gm	3 gm	180 mg	20 mg

SHRIMP SAUSAGE

Yield: approximately 30 links

½ ounce	Garlic, minced	15 grams
½ ounce	Shallots, minced	15 grams
¾ fluid ounce	Stock	20 milliliters
2¼ pounds	Shrimp, peeled, de-veined, diced	1 kilogram
8 fluid ounces	Heavy cream, chilled	240 milliliters
¾ ounce	Herbs, chopped*	20 grams
¾ fluid ounce	Lemon juice, fresh, strained	20 milliliters
1 teaspoon	Salt	5 grams
10 drops	Tabasco sauce	10 drops
as needed	Lamb casings	as needed

1. Prepare the forcemeat: Sweat the garlic and shallots in the stock until they are tender. Let them cool completely.

2. Combine the shrimp and the cream in a food processor, pulsing it on and off, to form a coarse paste.

3. Remove the shrimp paste to a bowl set over ice; fold in the shallot/garlic mixture, herbs, lemon juice, salt, and Tabasco.

4. Pipe the forcemeat into the casings, and twist into links that weigh 1¼ ounces/35 grams each.

5. To serve, shallow-poach sausages, as ordered, in fish fumet.

---

* Fresh herbs that might be appropriate for this preparation include chives, tarragon, parsley, and chervil. Additional flavoring options include curry powder and dried mustard.

PORTION	KCAL	PROTEIN	FAT	CARB	SODIUM	CHOL
1 link	60	7 gm	3 gm	1 gm	130 mg	60 mg

MEDITERRANEAN SEAFOOD TERRINE

Yield: 30 portions

½ teaspoon	Saffron threads, crushed	500 milligrams
5 fluid ounces	Heavy cream, heated	150 milliliters
20 ounces	Scallops, quartered	570 grams
2	Egg whites	2
½ teaspoon	Salt	3 grams
to taste	Pepper, ground	to taste
1 pound	Shrimp, cleaned, de-veined, diced	450 grams
1 tablespoon	Parsley, chopped	3 grams
½ tablespoon	Basil, chopped	2 grams

1. Steep the saffron in the heated cream; cool completely.

2. Prepare a forcemeat: Combine half of the scallops, the chilled saffron cream, egg whites, salt, and pepper in a food processor and process to a smooth paste.

3. Remove to a bowl set over ice and fold in the remaining scallops, the shrimp, parsley, and basil.

4. Line terrine molds with plastic wrap and fill with the forcemeat mixture. Press out all air pockets.

5. Cook in a bain-marie (maintain at 170 degrees F/75 degrees C) to an internal temperature of 145 degrees F/62 degrees C.

6. Allow the terrine to cool to room temperature and then rewrap tightly in new plastic wrap. Refrigerate until ready to serve, at least 2 to 3 hours.

Serve slices of this terrine on a bed of Red Pepper Coulis (Chapter 11), Tomato Vinaigrette (Chapter 12), or mache with steamed snow peas or sugar snap peas.

This could also be served with Marinated Grilled Peppers or a small salad of mixed greens dressed with basil vinaigrette or Anchovy-Caper Dressing (see Chapter 12).

PORTION	KCAL	PROTEIN	FAT	CARB	SODIUM	CHOL
1 portion	105	9 gm	5 gm	6 gm	250 mg	45 mg

ST. ANDREW'S GARDEN TERRINE

Yield: 25 portions

St. Andrew's Garden Terrine (foreground) and Mediterranean Seafood Terrine.

1 pound	Ground chicken breast, skinless, ground	450 grams
2	Egg whites	2
8 fluid ounces	Heavy cream	240 milliliters
1 teaspoon	Salt	5 grams
1 tablespoon	Dill, chopped	3 grams
1 tablespoon	Tarragon, chopped	3 grams
1 tablespoon	Basil, chopped	3 grams
¼ teaspoon	White pepper, ground	500 milligrams
1 pound	Carrots, medium dice	450 grams
8 ounces	Zucchini, seeded, medium dice	225 grams
8 ounces	Artichoke bottoms, small pie cuts	225 grams

8 ounces	Shiitake mushrooms, bâtonnet	**225 grams**
1 pound	Spinach, deribbed	**450 grams**
1 pound	Red peppers, julienne	**450 grams**

1. Place the ground chicken meat and the egg whites in a well-chilled bowl of a food processor. Process to a fine paste.

2. Add the heavy cream, salt, dill, tarragon, basil, pepper. Process using quick on-off pulses until the ingredients are *just* incorporated; do not overprocess. Place in a bowl and hold under refrigeration until the vegetables are prepared.

3. Steam the carrots, zucchini, artichokes, mushrooms, spinach and peppers separately until tender. Drain and dry on baking sheets lined with several layers of absorbent toweling.

4. Coarsely chop the cooled and dried spinach leaves. Fold all vegetables gently into the chicken mousseline.

5. Line two 12-inch (30-centimeter) enameled loaf pans or molds with plastic wrap. Divide terrine mixture evenly between the molds. Cover with additional plastic wrap and place in a prepared bain-marie.

6. Place in preheated 350 degree F/175 degree C oven. Immediately reduce heat to 275 degrees F/135 degrees C.

7. Check bain-marie during cooking and maintain a fairly steady temperature of 170 degrees F/75 degrees C in the water bath.

8. Terrines are done when an internal temperature of 140 degrees F/60 degrees C is reached. Take out of the bain-marie and remove the plastic wrap. Cool to room temperature, then refrigerate overnight before serving.

Be sure that all of the steamed vegetables are allowed plenty of time to dry before folding them into the mousseline mixture. This will prevent them from "falling out" of the terrine slices, and from bleeding their individual colors into the mousseline.

This terrine could be varied by changing the types of vegetables, according to what is in season: peas, green beans, different mushrooms, celery, and cucumbers are all appropriate in addition to, or in place of, those suggested here.

Serve this terrine in slices, with a dollop of Fresh Tomato Salsa and Sour Cream Replacement (see Chapter 12 for the recipes).

PORTION	KCAL	PROTEIN	FAT	CARB	SODIUM	CHOL
1 portion	120	13 gm	5 gm	5 gm	125 mg	30 mg

RABBIT TERRINE

Yield: 30 portions

2¼ pounds	Rabbit, disjointed	1 kilogram
3 quarts	Chicken stock	3 liters
1	Sachet d'épices*	1
2½ ounces	Carrots, brunoise, blanched	75 grams
2½ ounces	Parsnip, brunoise, blanched	75 grams
2½ ounces	Turnip, brunoise, blanched	75 grams
½ fluid ounce	Vinegar, red wine	15 milliliters
2 tablespoons	Sage, chopped	6 grams

1. Simmer the rabbit in the chicken stock with the sachet until very tender. Remove the rabbit and let it cool.

2. Remove the sachet and discard it. Reduce the stock until it is very gelatinous. (There should be about 1 pint/480 milliliters.)

3. Remove the rabbit meat from the bones as soon as it is cool enough to handle. Cut it into bâtonnet.

4. Combine the meat with the reduced stock, blanched vegetables, vinegar, and fresh sage.

5. Place the mixture in a plastic-lined terrine mold. Chill, weighted so it will produce the best texture, until completely set.

---

* Combine the following herbs and spices in a cheesecloth bag: 2 bay leaves, 1 sprig of thyme, 3 tablespoons/45 grams of juniper berries, 5 black peppercorns, 1 sage leaf, and 5 unpeeled garlic cloves.

The loin will cook more quickly than the legs, so be sure to remove the loin pieces as soon as they are properly cooked. This will keep them from becoming dry.

Once the terrine is chilled, slice it using a knife dipped in hot water. Serve with chilled Marinated Chanterelles (see this chapter for recipe) and Red Onion Confit (see Chapter 12) or a Winter Fruit Compote (see Chapter 21).

PORTION	KCAL	PROTEIN	FAT	CARB	SODIUM	CHOL
1 portion	145	13 gm	5 gm	4 gm	120 mg	50 mg

ROASTED PEPPER AND EGGPLANT TERRINE

Yield: 20 portions

6 fluid ounces	Vinaigrette-style Dressing*	180 milliliters
1 tablespoon	Gelatin, granulated	8 grams
1¼ pounds	Eggplant, sliced thin, grilled	570 grams
1¼ pounds	Bell peppers, roasted, cut into strips	570 grams
as needed	Garnish**	as needed

1. Line a terrine mold with plastic wrap.

2. Sprinkle the gelatin over the surface of the vinaigrette and allow it to soften. Warm the vinaigrette gently to melt the gelatin crystals.

3. Fill the mold by alternating layers of eggplant, roasted peppers, and the vinaigrette/gelatin mixture.

4. Cover the terrine with additional plastic and weight the terrine. Refrigerate overnight until completely firmed.

---

* The vinaigrette recipe is found in Chapter 12. Use balsamic vinegar and olive oil, and add plenty of fresh basil.

**If desired, croutons may accompany slices of this terrine. Prepare them as follows: Slice a whole-wheat baguette thinly. Spray or brush each slice lightly with olive oil. Rub them with a halved garlic clove and dust lightly with grated Parmesan cheese. Brown under a salamander or broiler. Serve two per order.

A small portion of a mixed green salad could also be served, if desired. Toss the greens with a small amount of the same vinaigrette as was used in the terrine.

PORTION	KCAL	PROTEIN	FAT	CARB	SODIUM	CHOL
1 portion	90	4 gm	3 gm	12 gm	125 mg	5 mg

SEARED VENISON TERRINE

Yield: 20 portions

1¼ pounds	Venison loin, cut in ¾-inch strips	570 grams
1 pound	Wild mushrooms, sliced	450 grams
1 ounce	Shallots, minced	30 grams
4 fluid ounces	White wine	120 milliliters
3 pints	Venison consommé	1.5 liters
1 tablespoon	Basil leaves, chopped	4 grams
1 teaspoon	Thyme leaves, chopped	1 gram
1 ounce	Gelatin	30 grams
6 to 8	Artichoke bottoms, cooked until tender*	6 to 8

1. Sear the venison strips on all sides in a dry cast-iron skillet until browned. Cut the strips so that they will fit lengthwise into a terrine mold.

2. In a sauté pan, sweat the shallots and mushrooms with the white wine. Continue to cook until the wine is cooked away. Add the venison consommé and simmer briefly. Remove from the heat and stir in the herbs.

3. Dissolve the gelatin in 2 to 3 tablespoons of cold water, then add to the warm consommé and mushroom mixture. Place it in a bowl set over ice. Cool until the mixture has begun to set (it will mound slightly when dropped from a spoon).

4. Line a terrine mold with plastic. Place a layer of the fortified consommé and mushrooms in the terrine, and lay in some of the venison strips.

5. Trim the artichoke bottoms so that they will lie neatly, touching edges, in the terrine.

6. Lay in the remaining strips of venison, and fill the mold with the remaining consommé and mushroom mixture. Fold the plastic wrap back over the top of the terrine.

7. Refrigerate the terrine until it is completely set, which will take several hours or overnight.

8. To serve, unmold the terrine, remove the plastic, and slice with a knife that has been dipped into hot water.

———

* The number of artichoke bottoms required will vary, depending upon the size of the artichoke. They should be cooked until tender in water that has had the juice of 1 lemon added to it. To check for doneness, pierce them with a paring knife. There should be no resistance.

The sliced terrine is shown in the photograph at the opening of this chapter. It is served with steamed or boiled brussels sprouts and a steamed julienne of carrots flavored with a vinaigrette.

PORTION	KCAL	PROTEIN	FAT	CARB	SODIUM	CHOL
1 portion	80	11 gm	1 gm	6 gm	125 mg	25 mg

CHICKEN ROULADE

Yield: 20 portions

1 pound	Chicken breast, skinned, trimmed	450 grams
2	Egg whites, lightly beaten	2
2 fluid ounces	Heavy cream, chilled	60 milliliters
½ teaspoon	Shallots, minced	2 grams
½ teaspoon	Garlic, minced	2 grams
2 teaspoons	Herbs, chopped*	2 grams
7 ounces	Peppers, roasted, diced	200 grams
¾ ounce	Gelatin	20 grams

1. Grind 6 ounces/170 grams of the chicken meat, and reserve under refrigeration until needed. Pound the remainder of the chicken to flatten and reserve under refrigeration until needed.

2. Combine the ground chicken, egg whites, and cream in a food processor; process just until a paste forms.

3. Remove the mixture to a bowl set over ice and fold in the shallots, garlic, herbs, and peppers.

4. Sprinkle the pounded chicken breast with gelatin and fill with the forcemeat mixture. Roll up in plastic wrap as for a galantine.

5. Poach the roulade in 165 degrees F/73 degrees C water to an internal temperature of 145 degrees F/62 degrees C. Remove the roulades from the water, rewrap tightly in fresh plastic, and chill until service. Remove plastic before slicing and serving.

———

* Appropriate herbs include thyme, basil, tarragon, or sage.

Serve the sliced roulade on a pool of Red Pepper Coulis or Tomato Coulis (see Chapter 11) and garnish with Pan-steamed Zucchini and Yellow Squash Noodles (see Chapter 17).

PORTION	KCAL	PROTEIN	FAT	CARB	SODIUM	CHOL
1 portion	90	11 gm	5 gm	2 gm	170 mg	25 mg

ASPARAGUS WITH LUMP CRABMEAT AND VINAIGRETTE

Yield: 10 portions

40 pieces	Asparagus, peeled, blanched	40 pieces
8 fluid ounces	Sherry wine vinaigrette*	240 milliliters
7 ounces	Lump crabmeat, picked	200 grams
9 ounces	Plum tomatoes, julienned	250 grams

1. Brush the asparagus lightly with the vinaigrette and arrange on a plate.

2. Top with the crabmeat and julienned tomato and drizzle with additional vinaigrette. Serve.

* Sherry wine vinaigrette is a variation on the Vinaigrette-style Dressing recipe in Chapter 12.

Drain asparagus as soon as it has cooled, and place it flat on a tray. Cover well and refrigerate until needed.

PORTION	KCAL	PROTEIN	FAT	CARB	SODIUM	CHOL
1 portion	80	6 gm	5 gm	4 gm	250 mg	20 mg

MARINATED GRILLED PEPPERS

Yield: 12 portions

4	Red bell peppers, halved, seeded	4
4	Green bell peppers, halved, seeded	4
4	Yellow bell peppers, halved, seeded	4
7 fluid ounces	Balsamic vinaigrette*	200 milliliters
7 ounces	Tomato concassé	200 grams
¾ ounce	Shallots, minced	20 grams
2 cloves	Garlic, minced	10 grams
1¾ ounces	Niçoise olives, pitted, sliced	50 grams
1 ounce	Capers, drained, rinsed	30 grams

1. Place the peppers, cut-side down, on a baking sheet and broil or bake in a very hot (500 to 525 degree F/260 to 275 degree C) oven until the peppers turn black and blister.

2. Remove from the oven, cover with an inverted sheet pan, and allow the peppers to sweat briefly to loosen their skins. Peel peppers and place in a bowl.

3. Add the remaining ingredients to the peppers. Turn to coat evenly; allow to marinate for at least 30 minutes.

4. Remove the peppers from the marinade and grill until marked on both sides. Remove from the grill, cut into wide strips, and place in a bowl.

5. Heat the marinade, and pour it over the pepper strips.

---

* Use the recipe for Vinaigrette-style Dressing found in Chapter 12. Include balsamic vinegar and extra-virgin olive oil. Add additional herbs as desired.

The following is one serving suggestion: Grill slices of eggplant and of French bread. Mound the warm pepper salad on the plate, then arrange the grilled eggplant and bread. Place one or two Parmesan "curls" (made by using a swivel-bladed peeler) on top of the peppers.

The peppers may also be served as an accompaniment to meat or poultry entrées that have been grilled or roasted.

PORTION	KCAL	PROTEIN	FAT	CARB	SODIUM	CHOL
1 portion	105	2 gm	6 gm	14 gm	150 mg	0 mg

CEVICHE OF SCALLOPS

Yield: 10 portions

1¼ pounds	Sea scallops, cleaned, sliced	570 grams
6 fluid ounces	Lime juice, fresh	180 milliliters
9 ounces	Tomato concassé	255 grams
2½ ounces	Red onion, sliced very thin	70 grams
1½ ounces	Jalapeño peppers, seeded, minced	40 grams
2 ounces	Scallions, split, bias-cut	60 grams
2 teaspoons	Garlic, minced	10 grams
1 fluid ounce	Extra-virgin olive oil	30 milliliters
1 tablespoon	Cilantro, chopped	3 grams
1	Avocado, ripe, peeled	1

1. Slice the scallops into ⅛-inch-thick rounds.
2. Combine the scallops with 5 ounces/150 milliliters of the lime juice, and the tomato concassé, jalapeños, scallions (reserve 1 tablespoon for the guacamole), garlic, oil, and cilantro. (Allow the ceviche to marinate for at least 1 hour before serving.)
3. Mash the avocado flesh with the remaining lime juice to a coarse paste. Add the remaining scallions.
4. Serve the ceviche with the guacamole on chilled plates.

———

Other fish may be used, including snapper, grouper, roughy, tuna, or sword-fish. The fish should become opaque and firm as it "cooks" in the lime juice.

If desired, a julienne, dice, or chiffonade of additional vegetables—tomatoes, radicchio, cucumber, celery, red cabbage, and/or romaine—may be used to give the plate some extra appeal.

PORTION	KCAL	PROTEIN	FAT	CARB	SODIUM	CHOL
1 portion	130	11 gm	6 gm	9 gm	175 mg	25 mg

SMOKED CHICKEN WITH TABBOULEH
AND TOMATO HERB SAUCE

Yield: 10 portions

4 fluid ounces	Water, tepid	120 milliliters
3½ ounces	Bulgur wheat	100 grams
1½ ounces	Scallions, finely diced	45 grams
1¾ ounces	Parsley, flat leaf, minced	50 grams
3 tablespoons	Mint, minced	10 grams
½ fluid ounce	Extra-virgin olive oil	15 milliliters
1 fluid ounce	Lemon juice, fresh	30 milliliters
½ lemon	Lemon zest	½ lemon
5 drops	Tabasco sauce	5 drops
1 pound	Chicken breast, smoke-roasted	450 grams
10 fluid ounces	Tomato herb sauce*	300 milliliters
as needed	Plum tomatoes, julienned	as needed

1. Combine the water and bulgur to hydrate the grains.

2. Drain away any excess water, if necessary, and then stir in the scallions, parsley, mint, oil, lemon juice and zest, and Tabasco sauce. Refrigerate overnight.

3. Portion the salad and place on chilled plates (1½ ounces/40 grams per portion).

4. Slice the chicken breast very thinly on the diagonal. Shingle the slices (1½ ounces/ 40 grams per order) around the salad.

5. Serve with tomato herb sauce and garnish with julienned tomato.

---

* To prepare the Tomato herb sauce for this recipe, refer to the recipe for Tomato Coulis found in Chapter 11. Add chopped fresh herbs such as basil, oregano, and thyme to taste.

The smoked chicken may be replaced with pan-smoked shrimp, scallops, or trout to vary this dish. Another garnish idea would be to very briefly pan-smoke tomato concassé and sprinkle it on top of the appetizer.

The tabbouleh salad may be served by itself or as an accompaniment to grilled fish or poultry, especially those treated with the Tandoori Marinade found in Chapter 12. It would also be good as part of a salad sampler plate featuring a selection of vegetable, grain, and fruit salads.

PORTION	KCAL	PROTEIN	FAT	CARB	SODIUM	CHOL
1 portion	140	16 gm	3 gm	13 gm	225 mg	40 mg

ASPARAGUS SALAD WITH ORANGE-BASIL VINAIGRETTE

Yield: 10 portions

20 fluid ounces	Orange juice, fresh-squeezed	600 milliliters
40 pieces	Asparagus spears, peeled, blanched	40 pieces
1 ounce	Belgium endive, chiffonade	30 grams
10 ounces	Orange sections	300 grams
1¾ fluid ounces	Basil oil*	50 milliliters
2 teaspoons	Pine nuts, toasted	10 grams

1. Reduce the orange juice by half and let it cool completely.

2. Combine the juice with the basil oil to make a vinaigrette.

3. Arrange the asparagus on chilled plates and brush lightly with the vinaigrette.

4. Garnish with the endive, orange sections, and pine nuts.

---

* Basil oil is prepared by pureeing fresh basil leaves with a small amount of olive oil in the blender or with a small mix stick. It will keep fairly well for a few days under refrigeration.

PORTION	KCAL	PROTEIN	FAT	CARB	SODIUM	CHOL
1 portion	110	3 gm	6 gm	13 gm	5 mg	0 mg

WILD MUSHROOM AND GOAT CHEESE STRUDEL

Yield: 10 portions

1 ounce	Butter, unsalted	30 grams
2 ounces	Shallots, minced	60 grams
¾ ounce	Garlic cloves (about 5), minced	20 grams
1 pound	Wild mushrooms, diced*	450 grams
3½ fluid ounces	White wine	100 milliliters
2 ounces	Goat cheese	60 grams
2 tablespoons	Mixed herbs, fresh, chopped	6 grams
6	Phyllo sheets	6
14 fluid ounces	Sauce, heated**	400 milliliters

1. Heat half of the butter; add the shallots and garlic and sweat until they are translucent.

2. Add the mushrooms and continue to sweat until the liquor released by the mushrooms has cooked away.

3. Add the white wine; continue to cook until the mixture is fairly dry. Remove from the heat and cool completely over an ice bath or by spreading out on a sheet pan.

4. Add the goat cheese and mixed herbs to the mushroom filling once it is thoroughly chilled.

5. Prepare the strudel: stack three sheets of phyllo dough and brush or spray them with half of the remaining butter. Mound half of the mushroom filling along the long edge of the dough. Roll the strudel up tightly. Repeat the sequence to prepare the second strudel.

6. Score the tops of each strudel to indicate cutting lines for portions.

7. Bake the strudel at 350 degrees F/175 degrees C until golden brown (about 10 minutes). Slice carefully.

8. Pool the heated sauce on a heated plate, slice the strudel, and garnish as desired (see suggestions in the notes).

---

* Wild mushrooms will vary in availability, according to the season. If none are to be found in your area, prepare the recipe with domestic mushrooms. If desired, add some reconstituted dried mushrooms (such as cèpes, porcini, or shiitake), along with the liquid used to reconstitute them, while preparing the filling.

** Heat fond de veau lié (about 1½ fluid ounces/40 milliliters per order) and add chopped fresh herbs (sage, tarragon, chives, marjoram) as available, and/or a small amount (1 teaspoon/5 milliliters) of fortified wine (madeira, port, marsala, or sherry).

This appetizer may be garnished with fluted mushroom caps that have been lightly sautéed and a teaspoon (5 grams) of sour cream or fromage blanc.

PORTION	KCAL	PROTEIN	FAT	CARB	SODIUM	CHOL
1 portion	115	4 gm	7 gm	11 gm	140 mg	20 mg

CARPACCIO OF BEEF WITH FRESH ARTICHOKES AND TOMATO SALAD

Yield: 10 portions

12 ounces	Beef tenderloin, trimmed	340 grams
as needed	Black peppercorns, cracked	as needed
1¾ pounds	Artichoke hearts, cooked, quartered	800 grams
10 ounces	Plum tomatoes, small diced	285 grams
1¾ ounces	Shallots, minced	50 grams
½ ounce	Basil, chopped	15 grams
5 fluid ounces	Anchovy-Caper Dressing*	150 milliliters
3½ fluid ounces	Basil vinaigrette	100 milliliters
as needed	Mixed salad greens	as needed

1. Chill the beef thoroughly so that it becomes firm enough to slice easily. Slice it very thinly on a slicing machine or with a sharp slicing knife. Lay the slices out on parchment paper as they come off the blade. Do not stack them one on top of the other.

2. Place the quartered artichokes, tomatoes, shallots, and basil in a bowl. Add the vinaigrette and toss to coat evenly. Remove these ingredients with a slotted spoon, allowing the excess vinaigrette to drain back into the bowl.

3. Add the mixed greens (one handful per portion) to the vinaigrette remaining in the bowl and toss to coat the leaves lightly.

4. Place the sliced beef on chilled plates and season with a generous amount of cracked black pepper.

5. Drizzle the Anchovy-Caper Sauce and the vinaigrette on each portion and serve at once.

———

* The recipes for Anchovy-Caper Dressing and basil vinaigrette are found in Chapter 12. (Basil vinaigrette is a Vinaigrette-style Dressing prepared with the addition of chopped basil leaves.)

As an alternative garnish for the carpaccio of beef, marinate thinly sliced fennel and red onion in a basil vinaigrette. Garnish with shaved Parmesan and a drizzle of lemon and an olive oil vinaigrette (see Chapter 12). Or, serve it with a portion of Roasted Eggplant (see Chapter 16), as shown in the accompanying photograph.

PORTION	KCAL	PROTEIN	FAT	CARB	SODIUM	CHOL
1 portion	160	12 gm	8 gm	12 gm	150 mg	30 mg

CARPACCIO OF TUNA WITH SHIITAKE SALAD

Yield: 10 portions

1 pound	Tuna fillet, trimmed, uncooked	450 grams
1 fluid ounce	Sake	30 milliliters
7 ounces	Shiitakes, stems removed, julienned	200 grams
3½ ounces	Carrot, julienned, blanched	100 grams
3½ ounces	Red onion, julienned	100 grams
2 ounces	Bok choy, chiffonade	60 grams
4 fluid ounces	Rice wine vinegar	120 milliliters
2 fluid ounces	Soy sauce, low-sodium	60 milliliters
2 ounces	Yogurt, plain, nonfat	60 grams
2 teaspoons	Wasabi powder	4 grams

1. Slice and flatten the tuna until it is paper-thin. Marinate briefly in the sake.

2. Combine the shiitakes, carrots, onion, and bok choy with the rice wine vinegar and 2 tablespoons/30 milliliters of soy sauce. Let marinate under refrigeration until needed.

3. Place the tuna on well-chilled plates, add the shiitake salad.

4. Combine the yogurt with the remaining soy sauce and wasabi powder to make a wasabi sauce.

5. Top the tuna with 1 teaspoon/5 grams of the wasabi sauce. Serve immediately.

––––––

The tuna should be spread into a thin, even layer on the plates so that it appears almost translucent.

If a richer sauce is desired, replace the yogurt with sour cream. Be sure to taste the wasabi sauce for heat and adjust, if necessary, by adding a little more powder.

Additional vegetables such as fennel, celery, or jicama may be added, if available.

PORTION	KCAL	PROTEIN	FAT	CARB	SODIUM	CHOL
1 portion	75	12 gm	1 gm	5 gm	240 mg	20 mg

SMOKED DUCK SALAD WITH BITTER GREENS

Yield: 10 portions

14 ounces	Duck breast, skinless, trimmed	400 grams
1½ pounds	Frissé lettuce	680 grams
7 fluid ounces	Lime-cilantro vinaigrette*	200 milliliters
7 ounces	Assorted bell peppers, large dice	200 grams
3½ ounces	Corn kernels (roasted or steamed)	100 grams
3½ ounces	Cucumber, small dice	100 grams
2 ounces	Plum tomato, concassé	60 grams
1	Corn tortilla, julienned, toasted	1

1. Scatter hardwood chips (hickory, grapevine, apple, mesquite, etc.) in the bottom of a roasting pan, and add the duck, on a rack. Cover tightly, and place over direct heat until the smoke is easy to smell.

2. Roast the duck in a moderate (350 degree F/175 degree C) oven for another 2 to 3 minutes, then remove the duck from the pan. Finish the duck in a second roasting pan, uncovered, another 10 to 12 minutes. The meat should still be a little pink. Allow the duck to cool.

3. Slice the duck into medallions, julienne, or dice.

4. Place the lettuce in a salad bowl and add the vinaigrette; toss until the leaves are evenly and lightly coated. Remove to chilled salad plates, allowing the dressing to drain back into the bowl.

5. Add the duck, peppers, corn, cucumbers, and tomatoes to the bowl and toss to coat with the remaining dressing. Place on top of the greens.

6. Scatter a little of the toasted tortilla on each salad.

---

* See the notes under the recipe for Black Bean Salad in this chapter.

PORTION	KCAL	PROTEIN	FAT	CARB	SODIUM	CHOL
1 portion	100	10 gm	4 gm	6 gm	50 mg	40 mg

BLACK BEAN SALAD

Yield: 10 portions

1½ pounds	Black beans, cooked, drained	680 grams
14 ounces	Assorted bell peppers, diced	400 grams
3 ounces	Red onion, small dice	85 grams
1½ ounces	Jalapeños, small dice	40 grams
¾ ounce	Garlic, minced	20 grams
as needed	Cilantro leaves, whole	as needed
7 fluid ounces	Lime-cilantro vinaigrette*	200 milliliters

1. Combine the ingredients for the salad, tossing to coat evenly with the vinaigrette.
2. The salad should marinate for a few hours, allowing the flavors to develop.

———

* Use the recipe for Basic Vinaigrette found in Chapter 12. Replace the vinegar with lime juice, and use peanut or sesame oil. Add chopped, fresh cilantro leaves.

If desired, other beans—such as lentils, navy beans, or other "specialty" beans—may be used instead of the black beans. Or, a combination of beans may be used.

This salad may be served as an accompaniment to grilled fish, shellfish, poultry, game, or other meats, or as a component of a salad sampler.

Another suggestion is to smoke-roast chicken, duck, or pheasant breast, as described in the recipe for Smoked Duck Salad with Bitter Greens (see recipe in this chapter). Then, arrange sliced duck breast and beans on a toasted tortilla and top with Fresh Tomato Salsa and a small portion of Guacamole (both recipes may be found in Chapter 12).

PORTION	KCAL	PROTEIN	FAT	CARB	SODIUM	CHOL
1 portion	120	7 gm	2 gm	21 gm	6 mg	0 mg

WILD RICE SALAD

Yield: 3¼ pounds/1.5 kilograms

1 pound	Wild rice	450 grams
as needed	Stock or water	as needed
5 fluid ounces	Vinaigrette*	150 milliliters
5 ounces	Granny Smith apple, cored, julienne	140 grams
5 ounces	Red pepper, julienne	140 grams
2 ounces	Walnuts, toasted	60 grams
1¾ fluid ounces	Apple cider	45 milliliters
½ ounce	Shallots, minced**	15 grams
½ ounce	Garlic, minced**	15 grams
1 teaspoon	Sage leaves, chopped	1 gram

1. Cook the rice in boiling stock or water until the grains just start to burst. Drain in a colander, separating the grains with a fork to release the moisture.

2. While the rice is still hot, add the vinaigrette and toss well.

3. Gently fold in the remaining ingredients. Serve at room temperature.

———

* The most agreeable vinaigrette for this salad is made according to the basic recipe in Chapter 11, using walnut oil and apple cider vinegar.

** For the best flavor, the garlic and shallots should be smothered in a small amount of stock to cook away the raw, "sulphur"-like odor. They should cool to room temperature, and should be measured after they have been smothered.

This salad's flavor is at its best when the salad is served at room temperature. If it is made in advance, however, it must be stored under refrigeration. The amount required for service can be allowed to warm at room temperature, as needed.

If the salad is made in advance, sprinkle toasted walnuts on top of the salad just before it is served.

PORTION	KCAL	PROTEIN	FAT	CARB	SODIUM	CHOL
2 oz	90	3 gm	3 gm	11 gm	20 mg	trace

SALAD OF OAK LEAF LETTUCE WITH PEARS, WALNUTS, AND BLUE CHEESE

Yield: 10 portions

7 ounces	Red oak leaf lettuce, rinsed, well-drained, and dried	200 grams
14 ounces	Seckel pears*	400 grams
5 fluid ounces	Port Wine Vinaigrette**	150 milliliters
1½ ounces	Walnuts, whole, toasted	40 grams
1½ ounces	Blue cheese, crumbled	40 grams

1. Chill the lettuce until it is needed.

2. Quarter the pears and remove the seeds.

3. Combine the lettuce and vinaigrette in a salad bowl; toss to coat evenly and then place on chilled salad plates.

4. Top salad with pears (1½ ounces/40 grams each), walnuts (1 teaspoon/4 grams each), and blue cheese (1 teaspoon/4 grams each).

———

* Other pears may be used, depending upon seasonal availability. Be sure that the pear is quite ripe. If possible, leave the skin on.

** The recipe for Port Wine Vinaigrette may be found in Chapter 12.

PORTION	KCAL	PROTEIN	FAT	CARB	SODIUM	CHOL
1 portion	120	2 gm	9 gm	9 gm	60 mg	3 mg

GREEN BEAN SALAD

Yield: 10 portions

1 pound, 9 ounces	Green beans	700 grams
3½ ounces	Red pepper, roasted, julienned	100 grams
3½ ounces	Yellow pepper, roasted, julienned	100 grams
1 tablespoon	Basil, chiffonade	3 grams
1 tablespoon	Oregano leaves, chopped	3 grams
1 tablespoon	Chives, chopped*	3 grams
7 fluid ounces	Sherry vinaigrette**	200 milliliters

1. Cut the beans into a julienne, cutting along the bias (frenched). Steam the beans until they are bright green and still a little crisp to the bite. Refresh them in cold water to stop the cooking; then drain well.

2. While the beans are draining, combine all of the remaining ingredients in a bowl.

3. Add the drained beans and toss to coat well. Serve at room temperature.

---

* If desired, the chives may be cut on the bias into ½-inch-long pieces.

** Use the recipe for Basic Vinaigrette found in Chapter 12. Include sherry wine vinegar, extra-virgin olive oil, and a combination of basil, oregano, and chives.

This recipe may be served as part of a salad sampler; to accompany grilled meats, fish, or poultry; or on its own as an appetizer.

PORTION	KCAL	PROTEIN	FAT	CARB	SODIUM	CHOL
1 portion	95	1 gm	7 gm	7 gm	4 mg	0 mg

SEARED SCALLOPS WITH BEET VINAIGRETTE

Yield: 10 portions

8 ounces	Beets, whole	225 grams
3 fluid ounces	Cider vinegar	90 milliliters
1½ fluid ounces	Olive oil, extra-virgin	45 milliliters
5 fluid ounces	Chicken Stock*	150 milliliters
2 ounces	Dill leaves, chopped	12 grams
½ teaspoon	Salt	3 grams
¼ teaspoon	Black pepper, ground	2 grams
18 ounces	Scallops, cleaned	500 grams
3 ounces	Carrots, shredded	85 grams
3 ounces	Daikon radish, shredded	85 grams
10 leaves	Wild greens, assorted	10 leaves

1. Cook the beets in their skins until tender enough to be pierced easily with a kitchen fork. Peel them and grate. Using an immersion blender, food processor, or blender, puree them. Gradually incorporate the vinegar, olive oil, and stock to make a vinaigrette. Add dill, salt, and pepper by hand.

2. Pat the scallops as dry as possible and then pan-sear in a nonstick or seasoned cast-iron skillet until browned on both sides.

3. Serve the scallops with the beet vinaigrette, carrots, daikon, and greens.

———

* See the recipe in Chapter 11.

The following is one presentation suggestion: Pool about 1½ fluid ounces/45 milliliters of vinaigrette on a plate, and place a lettuce leaf in the center. Mound the carrots and daikon on top of the lettuce, and arrange the scallops around the salad.

PORTION	KCAL	PROTEIN	FAT	CARB	SODIUM	CHOL
1 portion	100	9 gm	5 gm	5 gm	160 mg	25 mg

ROASTED PEPPER SALAD

Yield: 10 portions

12 ounces	Bell peppers, assorted colors, halved	360 grams
2 ounces	Golden raisins	60 grams
10 fluid ounces	Balsamic vinaigrette*	300 milliliters
7 ounces	Plum tomato concassé	200 grams
2 ounces	Red onion, julienned	60 grams
2 ounces	Black olives, pitted, quartered	60 grams
¾ ounce	Garlic, minced	20 grams
¾ ounce	Jalapeños, finely diced	20 grams
¾ ounce	Pine nuts, toasted	20 grams
⅛ teaspoon	Cayenne pepper	250 milligrams

1. Place the peppers, cut-side down, on a roasting sheet, and broil or bake in a very hot (500 to 525 degree F/260 to 275 degree C) oven until the peppers turn black and blister.

2. Remove from the oven, cover with an inverted sheet pan, and allow the peppers to sweat briefly to loosen their skins. Peel peppers, cut them into strips, and place in a bowl.

3. Combine the raisins with enough warm water or stock to cover, and let them plump for about 15 minutes. Drain and add to the peppers.

4. Add all of the remaining ingredients to the pepper and raisin mixture; marinate under refrigeration for at least 2 hours, or overnight, before serving.

---

* See the notes under the recipe for Marinated Grilled Peppers in this chapter.

If desired, this salad may be lightly warmed by sautéing it over moderate heat for a few minutes or heating it in a microwaved before serving.

This serves as an excellent "relish" to accompany a variety of grilled and roasted meats and fish.

PORTION	KCAL	PROTEIN	FAT	CARB	SODIUM	CHOL
1 portion	85	2 gm	6 gm	8 gm	trace	0 mg

MARINATED ASIAN VEGETABLE SALAD

Yield: 10 portions

½ fluid ounce	Soy sauce, low-sodium	15 milliliters
2 cloves	Garlic, minced	10 grams
1 tablespoon	Shallots, minced	10 grams
1 tablespoon	Whole-grain mustard	15 grams
2 fluid ounces	Rice wine vinegar	60 milliliters
4 fluid ounces	Safflower oil	120 milliliters
4 fluid ounces	Sparkling mineral water	120 milliliters
1 tablespoon	Chives, minced	4 grams
1 pound	Carrots, cut into curls or allumette	450 grams
1 pound	Daikon, cut into curls or allumette	450 grams
1 ounce	Pickled gingerroot, minced	30 grams
¼ sheet	Nori, cut into strips, toasted	¼ sheet
2 teaspoons	Sesame seeds, natural and black	7 grams

1. Combine the soy sauce, garlic, shallots, mustard, vinegar, oil, water, and chives; mix well into a vinaigrette. Refrigerate.

2. Place the carrots, daikon, and gingerroot in a bowl, and toss with 5 ounces/150 milliliters of the prepared vinaigrette.

3. Portion the salad (approximately 3 ounces/85 grams per portion) and top each portion at service with a few strips of nori and a sprinkling of sesame seeds.

The vinaigrette made as a part of this recipe will produce more dressing than is needed. It can be stored under refrigeration and used for other purposes, such as marinade for cucumbers, carrots, and lightly steamed broccoli stems or for fish that will be grilled or broiled. It also would make an excellent dipping sauce for steamed halibut or other types of fish.

PORTION	KCAL	PROTEIN	FAT	CARB	SODIUM	CHOL
1 portion	75	2 gm	4 gm	7 gm	70 mg	trace

MARINATED CHANTERELLES

Yield: 10 portions

2 teaspoons	Olive oil	10 milliliters
3 cloves	Garlic, minced	15 grams
9 ounces	Chanterelles, small	255 grams
1 ounce	Fennel, julienned	30 grams
1 ounce	Pearl onions, parcooked	30 grams
1½ ounces	Carrot, julienned	40 grams
½ tablespoon	Basil, chopped	2 grams
½ tablespoon	Parsley, chopped	2 grams
½ teaspoon	Salt	2.5 grams
¼ teaspoon	White pepper, ground	500 milligrams
2 teaspoons	White wine	10 milliliters
1½ teaspoons	Sherry vinegar	8 milliliters
1½ teaspoons	White wine vinegar	8 milliliters
3 fluid ounces	Chicken stock	85 milliliters

1. Heat the olive oil, add the garlic, and sauté over moderate heat.
2. Add the chanterelles, fennel, onions, and carrots. Sauté until the mushrooms release their juices.
3. Add the herbs, salt, pepper, wine, vinegars, and chicken stock. Simmer until the mushrooms are completely cooked.
4. Cool the mushrooms in the liquid. They are ready to be served, or stored under refrigeration for up to one week. Drain before serving.

———

This dish would be a good accompaniment to a variety of salads, grilled items, or roasted foods. It would also be appropriate as a part of an hors d'oeuvre plate.

PORTION	KCAL	PROTEIN	FAT	CARB	SODIUM	CHOL
1 portion	20	1 gm	1 gm	2 gm	5 mg	trace

GAZPACHO GRANITÉ

Yield: 10 portions

8	Plum tomatoes, juiced, strained	8
½ cup	Onion, finely minced	60 grams
3 fluid ounces	White wine, dry	90 milliliters
3 tablespoons	Chervil, chopped	10 grams
1 fluid ounce	Simple syrup	30 milliliters
1 fluid ounce	Extra-virgin olive oil	30 milliliters
1	Lemon, juiced	1
1 teaspoon	Basil, minced	2 grams
1 clove	Garlic, finely minced	5 grams
to taste	Black peppercorns, ground	to taste

1. Combine all ingredients.

2. The granité may be frozen by the still method; pour it into a shallow pan and allow it to freeze without agitating it. When ready to serve, scrape a serving spoon across the surface to form large crystals. Or, it may be frozen in an ice cream machine according to the manufacturer's directions.

Serve two small scoops in a well-chilled champagne glass (coupe style) as a palate refresher between courses.

PORTION	KCAL	PROTEIN	FAT	CARB	SODIUM	CHOL
1 portion	70	1 gm	3 gm	9 gm	10 mg	0 mg

CUCUMBER GRANITÉ

Yield: 10 portions

2¼ pounds	Cucumber, peeled, seeded, chopped	1 kilogram
1½ fluid ounces	Champagne vinegar	45 milliliters
3 tablespoons	Sugar, granulated	45 grams
1	Egg white, lightly beaten	1

1. Puree the cucumber in a blender. Remove to a bowl.

2. Add the vinegar, sugar, and egg white; stir until combined.

3. Freeze by the still method (pour it into a shallow hotel pan, freeze, and then scrape to form large crystals) or use an ice cream freezer, following the manufacturer's directions.

If desired, some fresh chopped dill could be added to the mixture before it is frozen.

Serve two small scoops of this as a palate refresher.

PORTION	KCAL	PROTEIN	FAT	CARB	SODIUM	CHOL
1 portion	30	1 gm	trace	7 gm	0 mg	0 mg

Soups

Soups are familiar, comfortable foods. They offer the chef a chance to be creative by successfully introducing new ingredients and flavors, all without alarming the guest. Very few soup recipes fall outside nutritional parameters, and even those can usually be modified.

A well-balanced menu will usually offer at least one clear or clear-style soup, and one cream-style soup. The clear soups usually are nutritionally sound. Such standards as broths and consommés garnished with seasonal vegetables and small strips of meat, poultry, or fish are certainly within the nutritional guidelines. A quick look through the recipes included in this chapter shows that even some classic garnishes, such as quenelles and custards, can be made as tasty, smooth, and delicious as traditional versions, without relying upon large quantities of such high-fat ingredients as heavy cream and egg yolks.

Cream soups and purees are also included here. Substituting evaporated skimmed milk for heavy cream makes it easy to produce a high-quality soup that is low in fat and calories. Soups with a creamy texture based on purees of ingredients such as grains, legumes, and starchy vegetables usually require very little, if any, modification. The only ingredients that possibly might require attention are butter, oil, and pork products used in the initial sautéing of aromatics such as garlic and onions. Careful measuring of these ingredients may be all that is necessary. A small amount of bacon or sausage is still acceptable, and gives the delicious smoky taste and aroma that are expected in chowders and minestrones.

The basic guidelines for preparing and serving soups are these:

Use fresh, full-bodied stocks free of all traces of fat as the base for soups.

Thicken soups with purees of vegetables or starchy ingredients instead of roux.

Reduce the amount of salt to less than ⅓ teaspoon (400 milligrams) per portion by using fresh herbs, spices, citrus juices, and vinegar.

Emphasize soups based on vegetables.

Keep portion sizes appropriate (about 6 fluid ounces/180 milliliters), and aim for a calorie count per portion of around 100.

FOCUS   BASIC CONSOMMÉ

A crystal-clear consommé with a deep, rich flavor is one of the most satisfying dishes on a menu. It is essential to allow sufficient time for the consommé to clarify properly and to keep good control over the speed at which it cooks.

Selecting mature cuts of meat and poultry or extremely fresh and flavorful fish is the first step in preparing the best consommés. These ingredients are combined with vegetables, aromatics, spices, and herbs, then gently simmered to make a full-bodied stock or broth.

The clarification is a mixture of lean ground meat, poultry, or fish that is blended with mirepoix, herb stems, tomato paste or puree, egg whites, and a charred onion. Cold stock is incorporated, and the whole mixture is brought very slowly to a simmer. It is hard to believe that from such an unappetizing appearing combination of ingredients, one of the masterpieces of cooking will evolve. As the clarification mixture begins to adhere and rise to the surface, it draws out all of the fine sediment in the broth. The meat, vegetables, and onion impart additional flavors and a depth of color.

Garnish choices are limitless. For example, a lobster-filled tortellini or a ravioli stuffed with chorizo or goat cheese are excellent accompaniments (see Chapter 19 for recipes). A light custard timbale, prepared from skim milk and a combination of egg whites and a few egg yolks, is flavored with roasted garlic. Diced tomatoes, wild rice, and cilantro are also added for both flavor and visual appeal.

BASIC CONSOMMÉ

Yield: 1 gallon/3.75 liters

CLARIFICATION MIX

2	Onion brûlée*	2
1 pound	Mirepoix*	450 grams
3 pounds	Ground meat, lean**	1.35 kilograms
10 ounces	Egg whites, lightly beaten	285 grams
12 ounces	Tomato concassé	340 grams
1	Sachet d'épices*	1
5 quarts	Stock or broth	4.75 liters

a *The stock and clarification are thoroughly blended.*

1. Combine all clarification mix ingredients in a stock pot until blended.

2. Add cold stock to the mixture and blend well.

3. Place the pot over low to moderate heat and bring it very slowly to a simmer. Stir as it comes to a simmer.

4. Once a simmer is reached and the clarification mixture begins to adhere into a solid mass (called the raft), stop stirring. Break a small hole in the raft so that the cooking speed can be monitored.

5. Adjust the temperature so that a very lazy simmer is established. Simmer until it is very clear and the raft has just started to sink (about 45 minutes to 1 hour).

b *The consomme is breaking through the raft. An onion brulé gives additional color and flavor.*

6. Drain the consommé through the spigot into a cheesecloth-lined strainer. If the pot has no spigot, carefully enlarge the opening in the raft and ladle the consommé out, disturbing the raft as little as possible.

7. Properly cool and refrigerate the consommé so that any remaining traces of fat will solidify on the top. Remove this layer before reheating, garnishing, and serving.

---

* For ingredients and definitions see the Cooking Glossary.

    ** The choice of meat should be one that will complement the flavor of the stock or broth. Use a lean cut of meat, poultry or fish.

PORTION	KCAL	PROTEIN	FAT	CARB	SODIUM	CHOL
1 portion	30	7 gm	trace	0 gm	30 mg	0 mg

c *The raft has risen to the top.*

TURKEY BROTH WITH MUSHROOMS AND SAGE TORTELLINI

Yield: 10 portions

TORTELLINI

¼ ounce	Butter	7 grams
3 cloves	Garlic, minced	15 grams
1½ tablespoons	Shallots, minced	20 grams
9 ounces	Wild mushrooms, roughly chopped	255 grams
1 fluid ounce	Sherry, dry	30 milliliters
1 tablespoon	Sage, fresh, chopped	3 grams
1 teaspoon	Parsley, fresh, chopped	1 gram
½ teaspoon	Salt	3 grams
12 ounces	Lemon pasta*, cut into 1-inch circles	340 grams
2 quarts	Turkey broth	2 liters
7 ounces	Turkey breast, cooked, allumette	200 grams
10 tablespoons	Escarole, chiffonade	20 grams

1. Sweat the garlic and shallots in the butter until barely translucent. Add the remaining ingredients for the filling and cook until a dry duxelle is formed. Remove from the heat and let cool.

2. Place a small amount of the duxelle in the center of each pasta circle. Brush the edges with water and fold and seal to form tortellini. Cook the tortellini in boiling water; remove and reserve under refrigeration until needed.

3. At service, heat the broth, tortellini, turkey meat, and escarole in a microwave.

---

* Add lemon juice and zest to Basic Pasta (see Chapter 19.)

PORTION	KCAL	PROTEIN	FAT	CARB	SODIUM	CHOL
1 portion	100	12 gm	1 gm	10 gm	40 mg	10 mg

GAME HEN CONSOMMÉ WITH ROASTED GARLIC CUSTARDS

Yield: 10 portions

2 quarts	Game hen consommé*	2 liters
10 fluid ounces	Skim milk	300 milliliters
3½ fluid ounces	Evaporated skimmed milk	100 milliliters
2	Whole eggs	2
2	Egg whites	2
1 head	Garlic, roasted	1 head
dash	Pepper, white, ground	dash
1¾ ounces	Game hen breast meat, poached, brunoise	50 grams
1¾ ounces	Prosciutto, brunoise	50 grams
3½ ounces	Wild rice, cooked	100 grams

1. Heat the consommé to a boil just before serving.

2. To prepare the custard, combine all of the ingredients in a blender and puree until very smooth. Strain through a fine sieve.

3. Lightly butter 2-ounces timbales and add enough of the custard mixture to fill. Poach in a 170 degree F/76 degree C water bath until barely set. Remove from oven.

4. At the time of service, place the garnish ingredients in a heated soup cup or bowl (1 teaspoon/5 grams each of the game hen meat and prosciutto, 2 teaspoons/10 grams of wild rice, 1 garlic custard). Add boiling hot consommé and serve at once.

---

* Game hen consommé is prepared by first making a game hen stock, following the method for brown chicken stock (recipe is a variation on basic Chicken Stock recipe found in Chapter 11). Then, follow the recipe for Basic Consommé using ground chicken or game hen meat for the clarification. If desired, juniper berries may be added to the sachet d'épices.

PORTION	KCAL	PROTEIN	FAT	CARB	SODIUM	CHOL
1 portion	90	10 gm	3 gm	5 gm	150 mg	60 mg

LIGHT CHICKEN CONSOMMÉ WITH HERBED GOAT CHEESE RAVIOLI

Yield: 10 portions

2 quarts	Chicken consommé	2 liters
½ teaspoon	Olive oil	3 milliliters
1½ teaspoons	Shallots, minced	7 grams
1 clove	Garlic, minced	5 grams
1½ ounces	Spinach, wilted and chopped	40 grams
2½ ounces	Fresh goat cheese	70 grams
2½ ounces	Ricotta cheese, part-skim	70 grams
1¾ fluid ounces	Egg whites, beaten	50 milliliters
½ ounce	Parmesan cheese, grated	15 grams
1 teaspoon	Basil, chopped	1 gram
½ tablespoon	Oregano, chopped	2 grams
12 ounces	Pasta dough, cut into 2-inch circles	340 grams
5 ounces	Tomatoes, peeled, seeded, allumette	140 grams
2 tablespoons	Chives, fresh, sliced	6 grams

1. Heat the consommée to boiling just before serving. This may be done by the portion, with garnish added, in a microwave at the highest power setting.

2. To prepare the ravioli filling, sauté the shallots and garlic in olive oil until the aroma is apparent.

3. Add the sautéed shallots and garlic to the remaining ingredients and blend well.

4. Place a small amount of the filling on one of the pasta circles. Moisten the edges with water, top with a second circle, and press to close.

5. Cook the ravioli in boiling water. Drain and reserve.

PORTION	KCAL	PROTEIN	FAT	CARB	SODIUM	CHOL
1 portion	120	10 gm	4 gm	11 gm	140 mg	10 mg

DOUBLE CHICKEN BROTH WITH SPRING ROLLS

Yield: 10 portions

2 quarts	Double chicken stock, cold*	2 liters
18 ounces	Chicken meat, ground	500 grams
2½ ounces	Tomatoes, chopped	70 grams
1½ ounces	Onion, julienned or chopped	40 grams
1 ounce	Carrot, thinly sliced or chopped	30 grams
1 ounce	Celery, thinly sliced or chopped	30 grams
¾ ounce	Leeks, thinly sliced	20 grams
6 ounces	Egg whites, lightly beaten	180 grams
1	Thyme sprig	1
1	Bay leaf	1
2	Cloves, whole	2
10	Spring Rolls	10

1. Combine the stock with all of the remaining ingredients, except the spring rolls.

2. Gradually bring this mixture to a simmer over low to moderate heat, stirring frequently, until the solid ingredients begin to form a solid mass, known as a raft.

3. Once the raft is fully formed at the top of the pot, break a small hole so that the cooking speed can be monitored. Maintain a very gentle simmer for about 1 hour, or until the broth is very clear and fully flavored.

4. Carefully ladle the broth out of the pot, disturbing the raft as little as possible. Strain it through a conical sieve or a colander lined with doubled cheesecloth.

5. To serve, heat the spring rolls in a steamer or microwave and ladle broth into soup bowls over a spring roll. Add additional garnish as desired.

---

* To make double chicken stock, simmer chicken legs in a good chicken stock to bolster flavor, color, and body. Strain and store as for all stocks.

PORTION	KCAL	PROTEIN	FAT	CARB	SODIUM	CHOL
1 portion	80	16 gm	2 gm	9 gm	170 mg	10 mg

SPRING ROLLS

Yield: 10 rolls

7 ounces	Nappa cabbage, thinly sliced	200 grams
5 ounces	Converted white rice, cooked	150 grams
1¾ ounces	Chicken leg meat, trimmed, cooked	50 grams
¾ fluid ounce	Soy sauce, reduced-sodium	20 milliliters
⅓ ounce	Prosciutto, minced	10 grams
⅓ ounce	Scallions, minced	10 grams
⅓ ounce	Sesame seeds, toasted	10 grams
⅓ fluid ounce	Fish sauce (*nuouc mam*)	10 milliliters
1 clove	Garlic, minced	5 grams
1 teaspoon	Tabasco sauce	5 milliliters
1 teaspoon	Sesame oil	5 milliliters
½ teaspoon	Ginger, fresh, grated	2 grams
1 teaspoon	Basil, chopped	1 gram
1 teaspoon	Mint, chopped	1 gram
1 teaspoon	Cilantro, chopped	1 gram
10	Rice paper wrappers*	10

1. Pan-steam the cabbage very briefly in a covered pan with a little water (use only enough to dampen).

2. Combine the steamed cabbage with the remaining ingredients, except for the wrappers.

3. Moisten one or two wrappers at a time in warm water, and place on a clean, flat-weave cloth (such as a linen napkin). Place the filling in the center of the wrapper, and roll, tucking in edges so that the filling is completely encased. Refrigerate until needed.

PORTION 1 each	KCAL 50	PROTEIN 6 gm	FAT 2 gm	CARB 2 gm	SODIUM 30 mg	CHOL trace

CHICKEN AND CORN SOUP

Yield: 10 portions

2½ quarts	Chicken stock	2.5 liters
2	Stewing hen, breast	2
2 pieces	Lemon peel strips	2 pieces
1 tablespoon	Thyme leaves, chopped	1 gram
1 tablespoon	Sage leaves, chopped	1 gram
2 cloves	Garlic, chopped	10 grams
2 tablespoons	Shallots, chopped	24 grams
½ teaspoon	Saffron threads, crushed	300 milligrams
1 ounce	Leeks, brunoise	30 grams
1 ounce	Onion, brunoise	30 grams
1 ounce	Celery, brunoise	30 grams
7 ounces	Corn kernels, roasted	200 grams
6 ounces	Meat from stewing hen, julienned	170 grams
5 ounces	Spätzle*	140 grams
1 teaspoon	Salt	5 grams

1. Simmer the stewing hen in the chicken stock until it is nearly tender (about 35 to 40 minutes). Then add the lemon, thyme, sage, garlic, shallots and saffron. Simmer for an additional 20 to 30 minutes.

2. Strain the soup through a sieve and remove the surface fat.

3. Gently stew the leeks, onion, and celery in a small amount of the broth until they are tender. Add this mixture and the remaining ingredients to the broth. Return the soup to a simmer before serving.

---

* The recipe for Spätzle can be found in Chapter 19.

PORTION	KCAL	PROTEIN	FAT	CARB	SODIUM	CHOL
1 portion	85	10 gm	2 gm	8 gm	190 mg	10 mg

OXTAIL BROTH

Yield: 1 gallon/3.75 liters

8 pounds	Oxtail, cut into sections	3.5 kilograms
6 quarts	Beef stock	5.6 liters
1 pound	Onions, diced	340 grams
12 ounces	Carrots, diced	340 grams
12 ounces	Celery, diced	360 grams
8 ounces	Parsnips, diced	225 grams
1 each	Bouquet garni	1 each

1. Brown the oxtail in a 400 degree F/205 degree C oven. Remove it to a soup pot, and add the stock.

2. Bring the stock to a gentle simmer slowly over moderate heat.

3. Add the onions and carrots to the same pan used to brown the oxtail. Sauté the onions and carrots in the pan over direct heat until the onions are a light golden brown. Ladle a little of the stock into the pan and stir well to release any reduced drippings.

4. Add the onions, carrots, and released drippings to the pot, along with the celery and parsnips. Continue to simmer, skimming the surface as necessary during cooking time.

5. Simmer the broth until it has a rich flavor, about 2 to 3 hours. Carefully strain the broth through a fine sieve or cheesecloth-lined strainer.

6. Cool the broth quickly in a cold-water bath, and then refrigerate.

7. Lift away all remaining traces of fat once the broth has been completely chilled. Garnish as desired.

———

To prepare a beggar's purse garnish, make crêpes using the recipe in Chapter 21. Pick the lean meat from the oxtail, and shred it finely. Combine it with a little mustard to taste and fresh herbs such as thyme, oregano, or marjoram. Place a spoonful of this mixture in the center of the crêpe, then gather the edges of the crêpe to make a purse. Tie it closed with a ribbon of leek or scallion greens that has been lightly blanched.

Other garnishes for this soup include a variety of winter vegetables such as leeks, turnips, fennel, celery, carrots, parsnips, that have been cooked separately. (This is done to assure that the broth does not become cloudy). A springtime version might include tiny peas, asparagus tips, neatly diced tomato concassé, and fresh herbs. Use a variety of cuts, as desired, including parisienne, battonet, fine or regular julienne, dice, brunoise, paysanne, fermière, or lozenge cuts.

PORTION	KCAL	PROTEIN	FAT	CARB	SODIUM	CHOL
1 portion	95	15 gm	2 gm	10 gm	35 mg	10 mg

MUSHROOM CONSOMMÉ WITH SHIITAKE, BOK CHOY, AND CARROT CURLS

Yield: 10 portions

2 quarts	Mushroom-flavored stock*	2 liters
18 ounces	Chicken meat, ground	500 grams
2½ ounces	Tomatoes, chopped	70 grams
1½ ounces	Onion, julienned or chopped	40 grams
1 ounce	Carrot, thinly sliced or chopped	30 grams
1 ounce	Celery, thinly sliced or chopped	30 grams
¾ ounce	Leeks, thinly sliced	20 grams
6 ounces	Egg whites, lightly beaten	170 grams
1 each	Thyme sprig and bay leaf	1 each
2	Cloves, whole	2
3 ounces	Shiitake mushrooms, sliced	85 grams
3 ounces	Carrots, cut into curls or julienne	85 grams
20	Baby bok choy leaves	20

1. Combine the mushroom-flavored stock with all of the remaining ingredients in a soup pot, except the mushrooms, carrot curls, and bok choy leaves.

2. Gradually bring this mixture to a simmer over low to moderate heat, stirring frequently, until the solid ingredients begin to form a raft.

3. Once the raft is fully formed at the top of the pot, break a small hole so that the cooking speed can be monitored. Maintain a very gentle simmer for about 1 hour, or until the broth is very clear and fully flavored.

4. Carefully ladle the broth out of the pot, disturbing the raft as little as possible. Strain it through a conical sieve or colander lined with doubled cheesecloth.** It may be necessary to slightly enlarge the hole. Or, if the pot has a spigot, drain it directly through the spigot and through the lined sieve.

5. Warm the sliced shiitake, carrot, and bok choy in a small amount of the consommé until heated through.

6. Portion the mushroom, carrot, and bok choy garnish into heated soup plates and ladle in the hot consommé.

---

* To make mushroom-flavored stock, prepare a stock (chicken, vegetable, or beef) as directed in the basic recipes for stocks found in Chapter 11, adding about 1 pound or more of mushroom stems or trim, or whole mushrooms. Wild mushrooms will give the stock a more intense flavor. Dried mushrooms are often more effective than fresh ones, because their flavors have been concentrated in the aging process.

    ** Rinse the cheesecloth thoroughly in hot water to remove any loose fibers or lint that might cloud the finished consommé. Wetting the cloth also helps it adhere to the sides of the strainer more effectively.

PORTION	KCAL	PROTEIN	FAT	CARB	SODIUM	CHOL
1 portion	60	6 gm	1 gm	2 gm	25 mg	2 mg

SEAFOOD MINESTRONE

Yield: 10 portions

16	Mussels, scrubbed, debearded	16
2½ fluid ounces	White wine	70 milliliters
3 pints	Fish stock	1.4 liters
1 ounce	Bacon, julienned	30 grams
½ fluid ounce	Olive oil	15 milliliters
2½ ounces	Onion, finely diced	70 grams
5 ounces	Leeks, finely diced	140 grams
1 ounce	Celery, finely diced	30 grams
½ ounce	Garlic, minced	15 grams
1¾ ounces	Tomato paste	50 grams
10 ounces	Tomato concassé	280 grams
½ teaspoon	Salt	3 grams
¾ teaspoon	Rosemary, chopped	750 milligrams
¾ teaspoon	Thyme, chopped	750 milligrams
⅛ teaspoon	Black pepper, ground	125 milligrams
1	Bay leaf	1
1 piece	Lemon, sliced thick	1 piece
1¾ ounces	Red kidney beans, soaked	50 grams
2½ ounces	Arborio rice	70 grams
1¾ ounces	Shrimp, raw, chopped	50 grams

1. Steam the mussels in the wine. Remove the mussels and strain the steaming liquid; add it to the fish stock. Remove the mussels from the shells, chop the meat, and reserve.

2. Render the bacon in the oil.

3. Sweat the onions, leeks, and celery, in the olive oil/bacon mixture.

4. Add the garlic and sauté until an aroma is apparent.

5. Add the tomato paste; sauté until it has a sweet aroma and a rusty color.

6. Add the concassé, salt, herbs, lemon, and kidney beans. Simmer until the beans are nearly cooked.

7. Add the rice. Continue to simmer until all of the ingredients are tender. (See below.*)

5. Add the reserved mussels and the shrimp; serve the soup or properly cool and store it.

---

* To serve the soup after it has been stored, bring it back to a simmer, and add the chopped, steamed mussels and raw shrimp (if desired, by the portion, about 1 teaspoon or 5 grams of each). Or, add the garnish by the portion to a soup cup, cover with plastic, and reheat in the microwave at the highest power setting.

PORTION	KCAL	PROTEIN	FAT	CARB	SODIUM	CHOL
1 portion	105	7 gm	2 gm	10 gm	170 mg	15 mg

TORTILLA SOUP

Yield: 10 portions

2 quarts	Chicken stock	2 liters
1 ounce	Garlic, minced	30 grams
4	Corn tortillas, toasted and crushed	4
2 tablespoons	Cilantro, chopped	6 grams
9 ounces	Onion, pureed	255 grams
9 ounces	Tomato puree	255 grams
1 tablespoon	Cumin, ground	14 grams
2 teaspoons	Chili powder	7 grams
2	Bay leaves	2

GARNISH

1¾ ounces	Cheddar cheese, shredded	50 grams
3	Tortillas, julienned, dried	3
7 ounces	Chicken meat, grilled, allumette	200 grams
3½ ounces	Avocado, diced	100 grams

1. Heat a small amount of the chicken stock and smother the garlic in it.

2. Add the crushed tortillas, cilantro, and onion and tomato purees; bring to a simmer.

3. Add the remaining chicken stock, cumin, chili powder, and bay leaves. Simmer until the soup has a full flavor.

4. Strain through a medium strainer.

5. Garnish each portion of soup with cheese, tortilla strips, chicken, and avocado.

PORTION	KCAL	PROTEIN	FAT	CARB	SODIUM	CHOL
1 portion	120	11 gm	5 gm	9 gm	60 mg	20 mg

TOMATO-BASIL SOUP

Yield: 10 portions

1 fluid ounce	Olive oil	30 milliliters
3 cloves	Garlic, minced	15 grams
3 ounces	Onions, minced	85 grams
3 ounces	Tomato paste	85 grams
2¼ pounds	Tomato concassé	1 kilogram
2 quarts	Chicken or vegetable stock	2 liters
½ ounce	Basil, chopped	15 grams
1½ teaspoons	Jalapeños, minced	8 grams
1 sprig	Oregano, chopped	1 sprig
1 sprig	Thyme, chopped	1 sprig
4½ fluid ounces	White wine, dry	175 milliliters
1	Bay leaf	1

1. Sweat the garlic and onions in the olive oil.

2. Add the tomato paste and sauté until it has a sweet aroma and beings to take on a rusty color.

3. Add the tomato concassé, stock, basil, jalapeños, oregano, thyme, wine, and bay leaf.

4. Simmer for approximately 30 minutes.

5. Strain the soup through a medium chinois.

PORTION	KCAL	PROTEIN	FAT	CARB	SODIUM	CHOL
1 portion	100	5 gm	2 gm	10 gm	155 mg	trace

LOUISIANA CHICKEN AND SHRIMP GUMBO

Yield: 10 portions

2½ ounces	Bread flour	70 grams
1 ounce	Andouille sausage, chopped	30 grams
2½ ounces	Lean chicken meat, chopped	70 grams
2½ ounces	Bell pepper (red and/or green), diced	70 grams
2½ ounces	Celery, diced	70 grams
¼ ounce	Jalapeños, diced	7 grams
1¾ ounces	Scallions, split, sliced on the bias	50 grams
1 clove	Garlic, minced	5 grams
3 pints	Chicken stock	1.4 liters
2½ ounces	Long grain rice	70 grams
1⅓ teaspoon	Filé powder	3 grams
1 teaspoon	Oregano, chopped	1 gram
1	Bay leaf	1
1 teaspoon	Thyme, chopped	1 gram
1 teaspoon	Basil, chopped	1 gram
dash	Black pepper, ground	dash
½ teaspoon	Onion powder	1 gram
½ teaspoon	Salt	3 grams
2½ ounces	Okra, large dice	70 grams
3½ ounces	Tomato concassé (large dice)	100 grams
1¾ ounces	Shrimp, raw, chopped	50 grams

1. Make a dry roux by roasting the bread flour in a moderate oven until it is dark-brown.

2. Render the sausage. Add the chicken and sauté it in the rendered fat.

3. Sauté the peppers, celery, jalapeños, scallions, and garlic until the aroma is apparent.

4. Add the stock and the rice. Bring the soup to a boil.

5. Add the filé powder, oregano, bay leaf, thyme, basil, pepper, onion powder, and salt. Simmer until the rice is almost cooked (approximately 10 minutes).

6. Add the okra and the tomatoes.

7. Place a conical sieve in the pot of soup (to push aside the vegetables and rice). Add the dry roux into the clear liquid in the sieve and whip well to blend until the mixture is smooth.

8. Remove the sieve, add the shrimp, and stir to blend. The soup is ready to serve.

PORTION	KCAL	PROTEIN	FAT	CARB	SODIUM	CHOL
1 portion	103	7 gm	2 gm	13 gm	210 mg	15 mg

BUTTERNUT SQUASH SOUP

Yield: 10 portions

2½ teaspoons	Ginger, fresh, minced	8 grams
1 fluid ounce	White wine, heated	30 milliliters
1¾ ounces	Onions, medium dice	70 grams
1¾ ounces	Celery, medium dice	70 grams
1 clove	Garlic, minced	5 grams
1¼ pints	Chicken stock	20 milliliters
2¼ pounds	Butternut squash, peeled, cubed	1 kilogram
3 ounces	Yogurt, plain, low-fat or nonfat	85 grams
1½ fluid ounces	Heavy cream	45 milliliters
3 fluid ounces	Mineral water, sparkling	85 milliliters
½ teaspoon	Salt	3 grams
dash	White pepper, ground	dash

GARNISH

1 tablespoon	Chives, fresh, chopped	8 grams

1. Steep the ginger in the wine for 30 minutes and strain. Discard the ginger.

2. Sweat the onions, celery, and garlic in a small amount of the stock.

3. Add the squash and stock. Simmer until all of the vegetables are tender enough to purée easily. If necessary, add more stock or water.

4. Purée the soup and, if necessary, strain through a sieve.

5. Add the ginger/wine infusion to the soup, along with the yogurt, heavy cream, mineral water, salt, and pepper. The soup may be served at this point (reheat if necessary) or properly cooled and stored.

6. Garnish each portion with some of the chopped chives.

PORTION	KCAL	PROTEIN	FAT	CARB	SODIUM	CHOL
1 portion	100	4 gm	3 gm	15 gm	250 mg	10 mg

a *An excellent method for pureeing soups is to use an immersion blender, as shown here. In the background is an example of one presentation style for this soup.*

b *A serving of butternut squash soup, garnished with a small dollop of whipped cream and toasted pumpkin seeds.*

FOCUS   BUTTERNUT SQUASH SOUP

Puréed soups, chowders, and clear soups are all excellent choices for any menu, but especially for the nutritional one. Unlike heavy soups of the past, the puréed soups featured in this book rely upon the natural texture of their ingredients to produce the best texture in the soup. Butternut squash, for example, is quite starchy, which makes it ideal for a thick, creamy puree. In this recipe, the soup is lightened with some sparkling mineral water and then finished to a creamy smoothness through the addition of evaporated skimmed milk instead of cream.

The immersion blender is used to quickly purée the soup to an extremely fine consistency. This tool is gaining in popularity, as it eliminates the need to transfer hot soups or sauces from the pot into a food processor. The large model can handle big batches of food, but smaller versions are also available for lighter tasks.

There are important points to keep in mind when preparing puréed soups. The texture of the soup should be substantial, but it should never be thick or gluey. Use richly flavored stocks or broths to thin the soup if necessary, rather than adding more evaporated skimmed milk. The milk might tend to dull the flavor of the major ingredients. Seasonings and flavorings should be carefully tested before the soup is served. It may be necessary to add a few drops of vinegar, lemon juice, another spoonful of fresh herbs or other ingredients. Finally, remember to serve hot soups piping hot, and be sure that bowls or cups are properly preheated.

BASIC BLACK BEAN SOUP

Yield: 10 portions

12 ounces	Black beans	340 grams
2 quarts	Chicken or vegetable stock	2 liters
1	Lemon, sliced thick	1
½ ounce	Bacon, diced	15 grams
4 ounces	Onion, minced	115 grams
2 cloves	Garlic, minced	10 grams
⅛ teaspoon	Cumin seeds	250 milligrams
½ ounce	Chilies, dried, mild flavor	15 grams
1 teaspoon	Jalapeño, fresh, seeded, chopped	4 grams
1 ounce	Sun-dried tomatoes, chopped	30 grams
1 teaspoon	Oregano	1 gram
½ teaspoon	Salt	3 grams
¾ fluid ounces	Sherry wine vinegar	20 milliliters

1. Soak the beans overnight in enough cold water to cover by 3 inches.*

2. Drain the beans, and then simmer them in the stock, along with the sliced lemon, until the beans are tender.

3. Render the bacon and then add the onion, garlic, and cumin. Sauté until the mixture is translucent and has a good aroma.

4. Add the sautéed onion mixture, along with the dried chilies, jalapeño, tomatoes, oregano, and salt, to the beans and simmer for an additional 15 minutes.

5. Remove and discard the lemon slices. Puree about one-third of the beans and add the puree back to the soup.**

6. Finish the soup by adding the sherry wine vinegar. If necessary, reheat the soup by bringing it up to a simmer before serving, or reheat by the portion in a microwave at the highest power setting.

———

* It is permissible to "quick soak" the beans by bringing the beans and the stock to a boil. They should then be removed from the heat and allowed to sit for 1 hour. Continue with the recipe.

** The soup may be properly cooled and stored once the pureed beans have been added back into the rest of the soup.

PORTION	KCAL	PROTEIN	FAT	CARB	SODIUM	CHOL
1 portion	150	10 gm	2 gm	22 gm	135 mg	10 mg

MICHIGAN WHITE BEAN SOUP

Yield: 10 portions

3 pints	Chicken stock	1.4 liters
12 ounces	Northern white beans	320 grams
1½ ounces	Bacon, chopped fine	40 grams
2½ ounces	Leeks, cut into thin ribbons	70 grams
2½ ounces	Red onions, minced	70 grams
2 cloves	Garlic, minced	10 grams
1 sprig	Thyme	1 sprig
2	Bay leaves	2
¼ teaspoon	Salt	2 grams
dash	Black pepper, ground	dash

1. Soak the beans overnight in enough cold water to cover by 3 inches. Drain and then simmer the beans in chicken stock for about 30 minutes.

2. Render the bacon and sweat the leeks, onions, and garlic, in it until they are translucent and tender.

3. Add the leek and onion mixture to the beans, along with the thyme sprig and bay leaves. Simmer until the beans are tender.

4. Remove the thyme and bay leaf, season the soup with salt and pepper. The soup may be served at this point or properly cooled and stored.

PORTION	KCAL	PROTEIN	FAT	CARB	SODIUM	CHOL
1 portion	150	10 gm	2 gm	23 gm	140 mg	10 mg

CUBAN BLACK BEAN SOUP

Yield: 10 portions

7 ounces	Black beans	180 grams
3 pints	Chicken or vegetable stock	1.5 liters
2	Cloves	2
⅛ teaspoon	Allspice berries	250 milligrams
¼ teaspoon	Cumin seeds, toasted	250 milligrams
¼ teaspoon	Oregano, dried	250 milligrams
¼ teaspoon	Salt	2 grams
¼ teaspoon	Black peppercorns, cracked	500 milligrams
3½ ounces	Onions, medium dice	100 grams
2 ounces	Green pepper, seeded, medium dice	60 grams
½ tablespoon	Garlic cloves, chopped	7 grams
½ fluid ounce	Sherry wine	15 milliliters
¾ fluid ounce	Lemon juice, fresh	20 milliliters
⅔ ounce	Spinach, chiffonade	18 grams

GARNISH

1 fluid ounce	Vinaigrette-style Dressing	30 milliliters
3 ounces	White rice, cooked	85 grams
1 teaspoon	Garlic, chopped	4 grams
1 ounce	Scallions, minced	30 grams

1. Soak the beans overnight in cold water (or use the quick soak method described in the note for Basic Black Bean Soup). Drain, and then simmer them in the stock.

2. Add the cloves, allspice berries, cumin seeds, oregano, salt, and black peppercorns and simmer until the beans are nearly tender.

3. Stew the onions, peppers, and garlic in a small amount of stock or water until tender.

4. Add the stewed vegetables to the beans and continue to simmer until the beans are very tender.

5. Puree about one-third of the beans and return them to the soup.

6. Cool the soup and add the sherry, lemon juice, and spinach. (The soup may be stored at this point.)

7. To serve, reheat the soup by bringing it just up to a simmer (do not boil). Combine all of the ingredients for the garnish and divide it evenly between the 10 portions.

PORTION	KCAL	PROTEIN	FAT	CARB	SODIUM	CHOL
1 portion	165	10 gm	2 gm	28 gm	185 mg	5 mg

COLD CARROT BISQUE

Yield: 10 portions

1½ pounds	Carrots, sliced	680 grams
1 quart	Chicken or vegetable stock	1 liter
1 fluid ounce	Orange juice concentrate	30 milliliters
1 tablespoon	Shallots, chopped	12 grams
3 cloves	Garlic, minced	15 grams
1 tablespoon	Gingerroot, fresh, minced	12 grams
1 ounce	Onions, chopped	30 grams
½ fluid ounce	White wine	15 milliliters
2½ ounces	Yogurt, plain, low-fat or nonfat	70 grams
20 fluid ounces	Mineral water, sparkling	600 milliliters

1. Simmer the carrots in the stock, along with the concentrate, shallots, garlic, gingerroot, onions, and white wine, until the carrots are tender enough to puree easily.

2. Puree the soup and chill thoroughly.

3. Add the yogurt and mineral water just before serving.

PORTION	KCAL	PROTEIN	FAT	CARB	SODIUM	CHOL
1 portion	60	3 gm	1 gm	10 gm	65 mg	5 mg

SUMMER-STYLE LENTIL SOUP

Yield: 10 portions

1 ounce	Bacon, finely diced	30 grams
3 ounces	Onions, diced	85 grams
2 cloves	Garlic, minced	10 grams
2½ ounces	Leeks, brunoise	75 grams
2 ounces	Carrots, brunoise	60 grams
1¾ ounces	Celery, brunoise	50 grams
1 ounce	Tomato paste	30 grams
2 quarts	Chicken or vegetable stock	2 liters
10 ounces	French lentils	300 grams
1	Sachet d'épices*	1
3 pieces	Lemon peel, cut into strips	3 pieces
2 fluid ounces	Riesling wine	60 milliliters
½ fluid ounce	Sherry wine vinegar	15 milliliters
½ teaspoon	Salt	3 grams
¼ teaspoon	Black pepper, ground	500 milligrams

GARNISH

as needed	Chives, fresh, chopped	as needed
as needed	Parsley, fresh, chopped	as needed

1. Render the bacon and add the onions and garlic. Sauté until there is a pleasing aroma.

2. Add the leeks, carrots, and celery. Cover and sweat the vegetables until they are translucent and begin to release some moisture.

3. Add the tomato paste and sauté until it has a sweet aroma and a rusty color.

4. Add the stock and lentils. Simmer with the sachet until the lentils are tender.

5. Remove and discard the sachet. Add the Riesling, vinegar, salt, and pepper. The soup may be served at this point or properly cooled and stored.

6. At service, reheat the soup by bringing it up to a simmer (if necessary) or portion the cold soup into soup cups or plates, cover, and microwave at the highest power setting until thoroughly heated. Add chopped herbs to the hot soup and serve.

———

* Add ¼ teaspoon of caraway seeds to the usual ingredients for a standard sachet. (See Cooking Glossary for ingredients and a definition of sachet.)

To garnish this soup, scatter chopped fresh chives and parsley over each portion as it is served, and/or float a very thin slice of lemon in each portion.

PORTION	KCAL	PROTEIN	FAT	CARB	SODIUM	CHOL
1 portion	115	8 gm	3 gm	16 gm	175 mg	trace

CORN VELVET SOUP WITH CRABMEAT

Yield: 10 portions

7 ounces	Corn kernels*	200 grams
1 ounce	Butter, unsalted	30 grams
4½ ounces	Scallions, sliced thin	125 grams
4½ ounces	Onions, small dice	125 grams
1½ ounces	Gingerroot, minced	40 grams
½ ounce	Jalapeños, seeded, chopped fine	15 grams
1½ sprigs	Thyme leaves, fresh	1½ sprigs
2 quarts	Chicken stock	2 liters
12 fluid ounces	Evaporated skimmed milk	360 milliliters
2 fluid ounces	Soy sauce, low sodium	60 milliliters

GARNISH

6 ounces	Lump crabmeat, cleaned	170 grams
1¾ ounce	Red pepper puree	50 grams

1. Cut the kernels from the cob, scraping well to release the milk, and reserve.

2. Heat the butter and then sauté the scallions, onions, ginger, and jalapeños until tender and translucent.

3. Add the roasted corn kernels and allow them to sweat for a few minutes.

4. Add the thyme and the chicken stock; simmer until the vegetables are soft enough to puree easily.

5. Puree the soup (use a food processor, blender, or immersion blender) until smooth. If necessary, strain through a sieve. Adjust the consistency by adding more chicken stock, if necessary.

6. The soup may be served at this point (reheat if necessary) or properly cooled and stored.

7. Add the crabmeat to the hot soup just before serving.

PORTION	KCAL	PROTEIN	FAT	CARB	SODIUM	CHOL
1 portion	115	10 gm	3 gm	12 gm	300 mg	30 mg

POTATO AND WATERCRESS SOUP

Yield: 10 portions

1 quart	Chicken Stock*	1 liter
1 tablespoon	Garlic, chopped	12 grams
2½ ounces	Onion, large dice	70 grams
1 ounce	Celery, large dice	30 grams
1½ ounces	Leeks, large dice	40 grams
2¾ pounds	Chef's potatoes, peeled, quartered	1 kilogram
⅔ teaspoon	Salt	4 grams
¾ teaspoon	Black peppercorns, cracked	750 milligrams
3½ fluid ounces	Heavy cream	100 milliliters
2½ ounces	Watercress leaves	70 grams
1 ounce	Parsley leaves, flat-leaf	30 grams

1. Heat a few spoonfuls of stock in a pot, and add the garlic, onions, celery, and leeks. Cover and sweat until the onions are translucent.

2. Add the remaining stock and the potatoes, and simmer until the potatoes are tender enough to mash easily (30 to 40 minutes).

3. Puree the soup through the fine die of a food mill (do not use a blender or food processor). Add the salt, pepper, and heavy cream.

4. Add the watercress and parsley, and use an immersion blender to puree the soup.** Serve immediately.

---

* See the recipe in Chapter 11.

** In order to prepare soup in advance, complete through Step 3; then properly cool and store. Reheat portions as required (either in small batches over direct heat or as single portions in the microwave). Add a generous pinch of watercress and slightly less of parsley for each portion, and puree with a hand-held immersion blender.

PORTION	KCAL	PROTEIN	FAT	CARB	SODIUM	CHOL
1 portion	100	3 gm	3 gm	15 gm	100 mg	10 mg

ASPARAGUS SOUP

Yield: 10 portions

½ ounce	Butter, unsalted	15 grams
2 ounces	Onions, small dice	60 grams
2 cloves	Garlic, minced	10 grams
2 teaspoons	Shallots, minced	8 grams
1 ounce	Flour	30 grams
2¼ pounds	Asparagus stems, peeled, sliced	1 kilogram
24 fluid ounces	Chicken stock	670 milliliters
1 teaspoon	Lemon zest, grated	5 grams
½ teaspoon	Salt	3 grams
4 fluid ounces	Evaporated skimmed milk	120 milliliters

GARNISH

1 fluid ounce	Heavy cream	30 milliliters
20	Asparagus tips, blanched	20

1. Sauté the onions, garlic, and shallots in the butter until they are tender.

2. Add the flour and cook out to prepare a dry roux.

3. Add the asparagus stems, stock, and zest.

4. Simmer just until the asparagus is tender enough to puree easily.

5. Puree the soup (use a food processor, blender, or immersion blender) and then strain through a sieve to remove all strings. Add the salt and evaporated skimmed milk to the strained soup. The soup may be served at this point (reheat if necessary) or properly cooled and stored.

6. Whip the heavy cream to medium peaks. Garnish each portion of hot soup with 1 teaspoon of whipped cream and 2 asparagus tips.

PORTION	KCAL	PROTEIN	FAT	CARB	SODIUM	CHOL
1 portion	80	6 gm	2 gm	9 gm	180 mg	10 mg

SWEET POTATO SOUP

Yield: 10 portions

3 ounces	Onion, small dice	85 grams
2½ ounces	Celery, small dice	70 grams
1½ ounces	Leeks, small dice	40 grams
1 clove	Garlic, minced	5 grams
2 quarts	Chicken stock	2 liters
1½ pounds	Sweet potatoes, peeled, diced	680 grams
1	Cinnamon stick	1
¼ teaspoon	Nutmeg, ground	.25 gram
½ ounce	Maple syrup	15 grams
1 teaspoon	Salt	5 grams
4 fluid ounces	Evaporated skimmed milk	120 milliliters

GARNISH

1¾ ounces	Heavy cream, whipped	50 grams
¾ ounce	Almonds, sliced, toasted	20 grams
¾ ounce	Dry currants	20 grams

1. Sweat the onions, celery, leeks, and garlic in a small amount of stock.

2. Add the remainder of the stock, potatoes, cinnamon, and nutmeg. Simmer until the potatoes are tender enough to puree.

3. Puree the soup (use a food processor, blender, or immersion blender) and then chill thoroughly.

4. Before serving, add the syrup, salt, and evaporated skimmed milk. Garnish each portion with whipped cream, almonds, and currants.

PORTION	KCAL	PROTEIN	FAT	CARB	SODIUM	CHOL
1 portion	130	4 gm	3 gm	21 gm	280 mg	5 mg

RED RADISH SOUP

Yield: 10 portions

½ ounce	Butter, unsalted	15 grams
2 cloves	Garlic, minced	10 grams
3 ounces	Celery, diced	85 grams
2 ounces	Leeks, diced	60 grams
10½ ounces	Onions, diced	300 grams
1 quart	Chicken Stock*	1 liter
5 ounces	Chef's potatoes, peeled, diced	140 grams
1 pound, 5 ounces	Red radishes, grated	600 grams
2 fluid ounces	Heavy cream	60 milliliters
½ teaspoon	Salt	3 grams
¼ teaspoon	Pepper	500 milligrams
1 fluid ounce	Lemon juice, freshly squeezed	30 milliliters
½ ounce	Herbs, minced**	15 grams

1. In a soup pot, heat the butter and add the garlic, celery, leeks, and onions. Sweat over moderate heat until the onions are tender and translucent.

2. Add the stock and potatoes. Bring to a boil; then reduce the heat to establish a simmer. Simmer until the potatoes are tender.

3. Add the radishes and simmer an additional 5 minutes.

4. Puree the soup through a food mill or use an immersion blender.***

5. Bring the cream to a boil and add it to the soup. Add the salt, pepper, lemon juice, and herbs before serving.

---

* See the recipe in Chapter 11.

    ** A single herb or a combination of herbs may be used. Because the taste of radishes tends to be sharp and peppery, good choices for herbs are those with strong, lively flavors: chives, cilantro, mint, thyme, or basil.

    *** If the soup is being prepared in advance, then it can be cooled and stored at this point. Add the cream, seasonings and herbs just before serving. If desired, the soup may be served chilled. In that case, do not heat the cream as directed in Step 5. If desired, the cream may be whipped and then a 2-teaspoon portion may be piped onto the soup just before it is served.

    A garnish of thinly sliced red radishes may be floated on the top of the soup.

PORTION	KCAL	PROTEIN	FAT	CARB	SODIUM	CHOL
1 portion	90	3 gm	4 gm	10 gm	290 mg	15 mg

CARROT SOUP WITH GINGER CREAM

Yield: 10 portions

½ ounce	Butter, unsalted	15 grams
2 cloves	Garlic, minced	10 grams
¾ ounce	Gingerroot, fresh, minced	20 grams
1 teaspoon	Curry powder	2 grams
2 ounces	Celery, small dice	60 grams
3 ounces	Onions, small dice	85 grams
1½ ounces	Leeks, small dice	40 grams
1 quart	Chicken stock	1 liter
2 pounds	Carrots, peeled, sliced thin	900 grams
9 ounces	Sweet potatoes, peeled, diced	250 grams
½ fluid ounce	White wine	15 milliliters
1 teaspoon	Salt	10 grams
1 teaspoon	Lime juice, fresh-squeezed	5 milliliters
4 fluid ounces	Heavy cream	120 milliliters

GARNISH

1¾ ounces	Carrots, small dice, blanched	50 grams
1¾ ounces	Ginger cream*	50 grams

1. Melt the butter in a soup pot. Sweat the garlic, ginger, curry, celery, onions, and leeks in the butter until tender.

2. Add the stock, carrots, and potatoes. Simmer until the vegetables are soft enough to puree easily.

3. Puree the soup (use a food processor, blender, or immersion blender) until smooth. If necessary or desired, strain through a sieve. Add the salt, lime juice, and heavy cream. The soup may be served at this point (reheat if necessary) or properly cooled and stored.

4. To serve, garnish each portion with 1 tablespoon of diced carrots and 1 teaspoon gingered whipped cream.

* To make ginger cream, whip chilled heavy cream to firm peaks and fold in enough grated gingerroot to flavor the cream.

PORTION 1 portion	KCAL 130	PROTEIN 4 gm	FAT 4 gm	CARB 19 gm	SODIUM 165 mg	CHOL 10 mg

PAN-SMOKED TOMATO BISQUE

Yield: 10 portions

1½ pints	Vegetable Stock*	720 milliliters
2 ounces	Onions, small dice	60 grams
2 ounces	Celery, small dice	60 grams
2 ounces	Leeks, small dice	60 grams
1 ounce	Parsnips, small dice	30 grams
1¾ pounds	Plum tomatoes, canned, with juice	800 grams
8 ounces	Tomato puree, canned	225 grams
1 ounce	Sun-dried tomatoes	30 grams
2 tablespoons	Thyme leaves, chopped	6 grams
4 ounces	White rice, long-grain, cooked	115 grams
2 fluid ounces	Balsamic vinegar	60 milliliters
5 ounces	Tomatoes concassé, smoke-roasted**	140 grams
10	Rusks from French bread, toasted	10
⅓ ounce	Tapenade***	10 grams
as needed	Saffron Aioli***	as needed

1. Heat a few spoonfuls of stock in a pot, add the onions, celery, leeks, and parsnips. Cover the pot and sweat until the vegetables start to release their juices.

2. Add the remaining stock, tomatoes (with juice), tomato puree, sun-dried tomatoes, and thyme. Simmer for 30 minutes.

continued ►

3. Add the rice and simmer for another 15 minutes; use an immersion blender to puree, and then strain.

4. If necessary, heat the soup before serving and add ½ ounce/15 grams of smoked tomatoes concassé. Pipe out tapenade (a small "dot") on each rusk, and serve with Saffron Aioli.

---

* See the recipe in Chapter 11.

   ** To prepare smoke-roasted tomatoes concassé, peel, seed, and dice tomatoes and put on a plate. Prepare a smoke bath by scattering fine wood chips in a skillet. Place a rack in the skillet, set the plate of concassé on the rack, cover tightly, and place over the heat just long enough to catch a hint of smoke. Remove from the heat, and let the tomato "smoke" for a minute or two, until it takes on a pleasant, smoky taste.

   *** The recipes for both Tapenade and Saffron Aioli can be found in Chapter 12. To use the aioli, fill a squeeze bottle with a narrow top, and then squeeze out a thin line or two, creating patterns as desired, on top of the soup. The amount should be no more than ½ teaspoon/3 milliliters.

PORTION	KCAL	PROTEIN	FAT	CARB	SODIUM	CHOL
1 portion	110	4 gm	3 gm	18 gm	275 mg	2 mg

PUMPKIN SOUP WITH LOBSTER AND GINGER CREAM

Yield: 10 portions

½ ounce	Butter, unsalted	15 grams
6 ounces	Onions, small dice	170 grams
3 ounces	Leeks, small dice	85 grams
2½ ounces	Celery, small dice	70 grams
⅓ ounce	Gingerroot, minced	10 grams
2 cloves	Garlic, minced	10 grams
1¼ pounds	Pumpkin meat, diced	570 grams
6 ounces	Sweet potatoes, peeled, sliced	170 grams

2 quarts	Lobster stock	2 liters
1	Cinnamon stick	1
¼ teaspoon	Nutmeg, ground	500 milligrams
1 teaspoon	Salt	5 gram
½ fluid ounce	Lime juice, fresh	15 milliliters
1 fluid ounce	White wine	30 milliliters
20 fluid ounces	Evaporated skimmed milk	280 milliliters

GARNISH

3½ ounces	Lobster meat, cooked, medium dice	100 grams
1¾ ounces	Pumpkin, cooked, small dice	50 grams
1¾ ounces	Ginger cream*	50 grams

1. Melt the butter in a soup pot. Sweat the onions, leeks, celery, ginger, and garlic in the butter until they are tender and translucent.

2. Add the pumpkin, potatoes, stock, cinnamon stick, and nutmeg. Simmer until the pumpkin is tender enough to puree easily.

3. Puree the soup (use a food processor, blender, or immersion blender) and strain, if necessary. The soup may be served at this point (after adding finishing and garnish ingredients; reheat if necessary) or properly cooled and stored.

4. Finish the soup by adding salt, lime juice, wine, and evaporated skimmed milk. Garnish with lobster meat, diced pumpkin, and gingered whipped cream.

---

* To make ginger cream, whip chilled heavy cream to firm peaks and fold in enough grated gingerroot to flavor the cream.

PORTION	KCAL	PROTEIN	FAT	CARB	SODIUM	CHOL
1 portion	120	7 gm	4 gm	14 gm	300 mg	20 mg

LIGHTLY SMOKED CORN CHOWDER

Yield: 10 portions

½ ounce	Butter, unsalted	15 grams
4 ounces	Leeks, diced	115 grams
1¼ pints	Skim milk	600 milliliters
1¼ pints	Chicken stock, fortified	600 milliliters
10 ounces	Corn kernels, roasted and smoked	285 grams
8 ounces	Idaho potatoes, peeled, medium dice	225 grams
2 teaspoons	Worcestershire sauce	10 milliliters
½ teaspoon	Salt	3 grams
1	Sachet d'épices*	1

LIAISON

6 fluid ounces	Evaporated skimmed milk	180 milliliters
½ ounce	Arrowroot	10 grams
2 fluid ounces	Heavy cream	60 milliliters

GARNISH

as needed	Chives, fresh, sliced	as needed
as needed	Chervil sprigs, fresh	as needed

a   *Smoke-roasting the corn to give the chowder a special, smokey taste.*

b   *A bowl of Corn and Maine Lobster Chowder.*

1. Melt the butter in a soup pot. Sweat the leeks in the butter until tender. Add the skim milk, chicken stock, corn, potatoes, Worcestershire, salt, and sachet. Simmer until the potatoes are tender.

2. Remove and discard the sachet.

3. Combine the ingredients for the liaison. Add it to the soup and return to a simmer to thicken.**

4. Add the garnish to the soup just before serving.

PORTION	KCAL	PROTEIN	FAT	CARB	SODIUM	CHOL
1 portion	120	6 gm	2 gm	18 gm	260 mg	15 mg

*For ingredients and definition see the Cooking Glossary.

** The soup may be properly cooled and stored at this point. Reheat the soup either by bringing it just to a simmer before serving (but do not boil), or by reheating individual portions in a microwave at the highest power setting. Add the garnish after the soup is properly reheated.

FOCUS CHOWDERS

The name of this dish may come from the French term (chaudière) for the pot used to prepare the one-dish meals concocted by the French Canadians. Slaves from African and Caribbean nations brought with them a tradition of simmered soups and stews that used the foods on hand to create dishes of substance and richness out of very little.

Here, a rich, satisfying chowder is prepared from corn which has been lightly smoked to give additional depth to the flavor of the soup. Lobster is used as a garnish. This modified version contains all of the traditional ingredients: broth, onions, potatoes, and seasoning. Once again evaporated skimmed milk is used to replace the heavy cream. And instead of a generous slab of salt pork, a much smaller portion is used to give the familiar flavor we have come to associate with chowders.

CLAM CHOWDER

Yield: 10 portions

40	Clams, fresh, in the shell	40
1¼ quarts	Fish stock	1.25 liters
1 ounce	Bacon, julienne	30 grams
3 ounces	Onions, medium dice	85 grams
3 ounces	Celery, medium dice	85 grams
12 ounces	Idaho potatoes, peeled, medium dice	340 grams
2	Sage leaves, fresh	2
½ teaspoon	Thyme, dried leaves	500 milligrams
1½	Bay leaves	1½
3 drops	Tabasco sauce	3 drops
½ teaspoon	Worcestershire sauce	3 milliliters
9 fluid ounces	Evaporated skimmed milk	270 milliliters
¾ ounce	Arrowroot	20 grams
¾ ounce	Scallions, sliced	20 grams

GARNISH

as needed	Chives, fresh, sliced	as needed
as needed	Parsley, fresh, chopped	as needed

1. Steam the clams in the stock. Remove the clams, chop the meat, and reserve.

2. Strain the steaming liquid through cheesecloth. Reserve.

3. Render the bacon. Add the onions and celery and sauté until translucent.

4. Add the stock, potatoes, sage, thyme, bay leaves, Tabasco, and Worcestershire. Simmer until the potatoes are tender.

5. Combine the evaporated skimmed milk and the arrowroot. Gradually stir this mixture into the soup and continue to simmer for a few minutes, until thickened.

6. Add the scallions. *

7. Add the reserved chopped clams and fresh herbs just before serving.

* The soup may be prepared to this point and then properly cooled and stored. Reheat the soup by bringing it just to a simmer and then add clams and garnish, or alternatively, portion the cold soup into bowls, along with the clams and garnish, and reheat in a microwave at the highest power setting.

PORTION	KCAL	PROTEIN	FAT	CARB	SODIUM	CHOL
1 portion	110	10 gm	2 gm	18 gm	225 mg	25 mg

CRAB AND WILD MUSHROOM CHOWDER

Yield: 10 portions

1 quart	Chicken Stock*	1 liter
1 ounce	Arrowroot	30 grams
12 ounces	Idaho potatoes, small dice	340 grams
5½ fluid ounces	Evaporated skimmed milk	160 milliliters
1 teaspoon	Salt, kosher	5 grams
1 teaspoon	Black pepper, cracked	2 grams
2 teaspoons	Heavy cream	10 milliliters
2 teaspoons	Butter	10 grams
1 tablespoon	Garlic, minced	12 grams
2½ ounces	Onions, small dice	70 grams
1 ounce	Celery, small dice	30 grams
1 ounce	Leek, small dice	30 grams
2 teaspoons	Dry sherry	10 milliliters
1 pound	Assorted wild mushrooms**	450 grams
5 fluid ounces	Mushroom stock**	150 milliliters
10½ ounces	Lump backfin crabmeat	300 grams

1. Dilute the arrowroot in a small amount of cold stock to make a thin paste. Bring the remaining stock to a simmer, add the diluted arrowroot, and simmer until thickened.

2. Add the potatoes to the thickened stock and simmer until they are tender (about 20 to 30 minutes). Away from the heat, add the milk, salt, pepper, and heavy cream.

3. Heat the butter in a separate pot, and add the garlic, onions, celery, and leeks. Sweat until they are tender and translucent. Add the sherry, and the potato mixture.

4. Sweat the mushrooms in the mushroom stock until they are tender. Drain the mushrooms, reserving the stock. Strain the stock into the soup.

5. Place the portioned crabmeat into heated soup cups or plates, top with the mushrooms, and ladle the hot soup over them.

* See the recipe in Chapter 11.

 ** Use whatever mushrooms are available, but try to include a good assortment, such as shiitake, chanterelles, and oyster mushrooms. Slice, quarter, or halve mushrooms as necessary, and remove tough, woody stems, if any. Use the stems to prepare a mushroom stock by simmering them gently in enough water to barely cover.

 To prepare soup in advance, cool it once Step 4 has been completed, reserving the mushrooms and the crabmeat separately. To reheat individual portions in the microwave, place the mushrooms and the soup mixture in a cup and heat on the highest power setting for about 45 seconds. Pour this over the crabmeat, which should be placed in heated bowls.

PORTION	KCAL	PROTEIN	FAT	CARB	SODIUM	CHOL
1 portion	100	8 gm	2 gm	14 gm	245 mg	30 mg

CHOWDER OF CORN AND MAINE LOBSTER

Yield: 10 portions

½ ounce	Butter, unsalted	15 grams
3 ounces	Scallions, split, diced	85 grams
1¼ pints	Skim milk	600 milliliters
1¼ pints	Chicken stock, fortified	600 milliliters
10 ounces	Corn kernels, smoke-roasted	285 grams
8 ounces	Idaho potatoes, peeled, medium dice	225 grams
1 sprig	Thyme, fresh	1 sprig
⅔ teaspoon	Worcestershire sauce	3 milliliters
⅔ teaspoon	Salt	1.5 grams

LIAISON

7 fluid ounces	Evaporated skimmed milk	200 milliliters
½ ounce	Arrowroot	12 grams

GARNISH

4½ ounces	Lobster meat, sliced thin	125 grams
as needed	Chives, fresh, sliced	as needed
as needed	Parsley, fresh, chopped	as needed

1. Melt the butter in a soup pot. Sweat the scallions in the butter until they are tender. Add the milk, stock, corn, potatoes, thyme, Worcestershire, and salt. Simmer until the potatoes are tender.

2. Combine the ingredients for the liaison. Add it to the soup and return to a simmer to thicken.

3. Add the garnish to the soup just before serving.

PORTION	KCAL	PROTEIN	FAT	CARB	SODIUM	CHOL
1 portion	130	9 gm	3 gm	18 gm	275 mg	20 mg

CHILLED GAZPACHO WITH SPICY CRAYFISH

Yield: 10 portions

2 pounds	Plum tomatoes	900 grams
1¾ ounces	Tomato paste	50 grams
3 cloves	Garlic, minced	15 grams
9 ounces	Onions, minced	255 grams
18 ounces	Cucumber, peeled, seeded, diced	500 grams
6 ounces	Red pepper, seeded, diced	150 grams
9 ounces	Fennel, diced	255 grams
1½ fluid ounces	Balsamic vinegar	45 milliliters
1 ounce	Extra-virgin olive oil	30 grams
9 fluid ounces	Chicken stock, fortified	270 milliliters
½ teaspoon	Tabasco sauce	3 milliliters
2 tablespoons	Tarragon, fresh, chopped	6 grams

GARNISH

2½ ounces	Cucumber, peeled, seeded, finely diced	70 grams
2 tablespoons	Fennel tops, chopped	6 grams
10 each	Crayfish tails, cooked, marinated*	10 each

1. Combine all ingredients except the garnish and puree until smooth. Chill the soup overnight.
2. Serve in chilled soup bowls, with garnish.

———

* Marinate cooked peeled crayfish tails in 2 oz./60 milliliters of a balsamic vinaigrette-style dressing.

PORTION	KCAL	PROTEIN	FAT	CARB	SODIUM	CHOL
1 portion	80	4 gm	2 gm	12 gm	220 mg	10 mg

CHILLED GAZPACHO

Yield: 10 portions

1 ounce	Jalapeño pepper, seeded, small dice	30 grams
14 ounces	Plum tomatoes, concassé	400 grams
5 ounces	Green peppers, seeded, small dice	140 grams
2½ ounces	Scallions, split, diced	70 grams
1¾ ounces	Cucumbers, peeled, seeded, small dice	50 grams
1¾ ounces	Celery, small dice	50 grams
3 tablespoons	Basil, fresh, chopped	10 grams
1 tablespoon	Tarragon leaves, fresh, chopped	3 grams
1 quart	Stock (chicken, white beef, or vegetable)	1 liter
¾ fluid ounces	Extra-virgin olive oil	20 milliliters
¾ fluid ounces	Balsamic vinegar	20 milliliters
½ teaspoon	Salt	3 grams
¼ teaspoon	White pepper, ground	.5 grams

| 3 drops | Tabasco | 3 drops |
| 2 teaspoons | Worcestershire sauce | 10 milliliters |

GARNISH

1 ounce	Bread cubes	30 grams
⅓ fluid ounce	Extra-virgin olive oil	10 milliliters
1	Garlic clove, whole	1

1. Combine all ingredients except the garnish and puree until smooth (use a blender, juice extractor, processor, or immersion blender).

2. Chill the soup overnight to allow its flavor to develop.

3. Prepare croutons by sautéing the garlic clove in the oil, then add the bread cubes and sauté until crisp and lightly browned.

4. Serve in chilled soup plates or bowls, garnished with croutons.*

---

* An additional garnish option, shown in the accompanying photograph, is a few slices of smoke-roasted scallops.

PORTION	KCAL	PROTEIN	FAT	CARB	SODIUM	CHOL
1 portion	70	2 gm	2 gm	6 gm	190 mg	5 mg

YELLOW TOMATO GAZPACHO

Yield: 10 portions

1 ounce	Italian hot pepper, seeded, small dice	30 grams
14 ounces	Yellow tomatoes, concassé	400 grams
5 ounces	Green peppers, seeded, small dice	150 grams
3 ounces	Scallions, split, diced	85 grams
5 ounces	Cucumbers, peeled, seeded, small dice	150 grams
⅓ ounce	Basil, fresh, chopped	10 grams
1 tablespoon	Tarragon leaves, fresh, chopped	3 grams
1 quart	Oxtail consommé*	1 liter
1½ fluid ounces	Balsamic vinegar	45 milliliters
½ teaspoon	Salt	3 grams
¼ teaspoon	White pepper, ground	.5 grams
3 drops	Tabasco sauce	3 drops
2 teaspoons	Worcestershire sauce	10 milliliters
1 ounce	Garlic croutons	30 grams

1. Combine all ingredients except the croutons and puree until smooth (use a blender, processor, or immersion blender).

2. Chill the soup overnight to allow its flavor to develop.

3. Serve in chilled soup plates or bowls, garnished with croutons.

---

* For directions to prepare oxtail consommé, see recipe for Oxtail Broth in this chapter.

PORTION	KCAL	PROTEIN	FAT	CARB	SODIUM	CHOL
1 portion	50	2 gm	2 gm	7 gm	185 mg	5 mg

Grilling, Broiling, and Sautéing

The recipes in this chapter employ some of the cooking methods used most often in an à la carte restaurant. They are almost invariably served with a sauce, which more often than not, is the prime source of fat, sodium, and calories. More and more patrons are requesting that sauces be either eliminated or served on the side to try and balance their calorie and fat intake. However, these recipes make use of the many delicious and healthy options provided in the sauce chapter, and introduce a few new ideas as well, intended to make sauces a valuable part of the dish. The choice of sauces is meant to accomplish several things at once: First and foremost, is providing flavor. They may also increase the overall nutritional value of a dish. For example, Mesquite-Grilled Chicken Breast is served with a black bean sauce, and Grilled Mahi Mahi is paired with a warm pineapple salsa to increase the ratio of vitamins, minerals, fiber, and complex carbohydrates.

Grilling and broiling are also excellent methods for the nutritional menu. The typical oil-based marinade is replaced with a quick immersion in an acid and aromatic bath or modified vinaigrette to give some flavor to the meat, poultry, or fish. Compound butters, the traditional companion of grilled entrées, are replaced with Fresh Tomato Salsa (see Chapter 12) or a coulis of red pepper or tomato flavored with ingredients such as horseradish, mustard, jalapeños, or herbs. These exciting recipes are likely to be popular precisely because of the extra flavor, texture, and visual appeal bonus they provide.

FOCUS GRILLED SALMON

Grilled and broiled items are some of the most popular offerings on any menu, probably because of the smokey, lightly charred flavor that foods have when cooked on a grill. The intense heat has an immediate effect, intensifying the food's exterior color and flavor. The interior texture and taste provide a subtle contrast. The satisfaction that comes from eating a perfectly grilled piece of beef or chicken lies primarily in the enjoyment of the play of flavor against flavor, and texture against texture.

Today, the range of items considered appropriate for grilling has practically no limit. Grilled pizzas and breads, vegetables, fruits, and fish are as familiar to many restaurant patrons as the more typical chops, steaks, and chicken.

Determining doneness is a crucial factor in both broiling and grilling. Foods suited to these methods are normally quite tender, which means that they will cook quickly when subjected to the intense heat of a broiler or grill. Therefore, overcooking is of particular concern, since it is the major reason that grilled foods might be dry and lacking flavor. The ability to properly cook foods, whether they have been requested rare, medium, or even well-done, is a skill that comes with practice. A keen eye, a sensitive touch, and the ability to focus one's attention on the job at hand are all very important if foods are to be cooked to be flavorful, moist, and tender.

GRILLED SALMON WITH WARM PINEAPPLE SALSA

Yield: 10 portions

2¼ pounds	Salmon fillets*	1 kilogram
1 teaspoon	Lime juice	5 milliliters
1 tablespoon	Lemon juice	15 milliliters
2 teaspoons	Shallots, minced	10 grams
2 teaspoons	Garlic, minced	8 grams
½ teaspoon	Peppercorns, black, cracked	1 gram

PINEAPPLE SALSA

1¾ ounces	Butter, unsalted	50 grams
1 ounce	Shallots	30 grams
2 teaspoons	Jalapeño pepper, minced	8 grams
¾ ounce	Gingerroot, fresh, minced	20 grams
1¼ pounds	Pineapple, fresh, small dice	600 grams
10 fluid ounces	Orange juice, fresh	300 milliliters
1 tablespoon	Mint, chopped	3 grams
1 tablespoon	Basil, chopped	3 grams
½ teaspoon	Curry powder	1 gram

1. Cut salmon into 3½-ounce/100-gram tranches and sprinkle with the lime and lemon juices, shallots, garlic, and peppercorns. Let marinate briefly.

2. Prepare pineapple salsa while the fish marinates: Heat the butter and add the shallots, jalapeño, and gingerroot. Sauté just until aroma is released. Add the orange juice and allow it to reduce slightly. Add the pineapple, herbs, and curry powder and warm gently. Do not allow the salsa to simmer.

3. Grill the salmon. Serve immediately with the warm salsa.

PORTION	KCAL	PROTEIN	FAT	CARB	SODIUM	CHOL
1 portion	220	20 gm	10 gm	12 gm	80 mg	65 mg

* Tuna, swordfish mahi mahi, and other firm-textured fish are also suitable for this presentation.

GRILLED HERBED SALMON WITH SOUTHWEST WHITE BEAN STEW

Yield: 10 portions

2¼ pounds	Salmon fillet	1 kilogram
2 tablespoons	Lime juice, fresh-squeezed	30 milliliters
2 tablespoons	Parsley leaves, chopped	6 grams
2 tablespoons	Chives, chopped	6 grams
1 tablespoon	Thyme leaves, chopped	3 grams
2 teaspoons	Black peppercorns, cracked	4 grams
1 recipe	Southwest White Bean Stew*	1 recipe

1. Slice the salmon into 3½-ounce/100-gram portions.

2. Pound together the remaining ingredients, except the Southwest White Bean Stew, to form a paste. Rub this mixture on the salmon.

3. Allow the salmon to rest with the herb mixture on it for about 20 minutes.

4. Grill the salmon until nicely browned on both sides and barely cooked through.

5. Heat the bean stew and serve the salmon with it.

* See the recipe in Chapter 18.

If desired, a mixture of julienned jicama and haricots verts tossed with a teaspoon of Lime-Cilantro Vinaigrette—served warm or cold—could be used to accompany this dish. (See the notes to Black Bean Salad in Chapter 13 for the recipe for the vinaigrette.)

PORTION	KCAL	PROTEIN	FAT	CARB	SODIUM	CHOL
1 portion	225	24 gm	7 gm	14 gm	135 mg	55 mg

GRILLED CHICKEN BREASTS WITH SWEET POTATO CAKES

Yield: 10 portions

8 fluid ounces	Apple cider	240 milliliters
1 fluid ounce	Apple cider vinegar	30 milliliters
½ ounce	Shallots, minced	15 grams
1 clove	Garlic, minced	5 grams
5 to 6	Black peppercorns, cracked	5 to 6
2¼ pounds	Chicken breasts, boneless, skinless	1 kilogram
1 recipe	Sweet Potato Cakes*	1 recipe

1. Combine the cider, vinegar, shallots, garlic, and peppercorns in a shallow pan.

2. Add the chicken; turn to coat evenly. Marinate for 1 to 2 hours under refrigeration.

3. Grill the chicken breasts over hot coals for a few minutes on each side, or until cooked through (there should be a slight amount of give when pressed with a fingertip).

4. While the chicken is grilling, bake the cakes in a very hot (450 to 500 degree F/ 230 to 260 degree C) oven until they are golden-brown.*

5. Serve while still very hot.

* The recipe for Sweet Potato Cakes is found in Chapter 16. Prepare the mixture for them as directed in the recipe and shape into cakes that weigh about 1½ ounces/40 grams each. Place the cakes on lightly oiled baking sheets or sizzler platters and serve 2 with each portion.

A suggested sauce to accompany this dish is a double-rich stock, lightly thickened with arrowroot, flavored with Dijon mustard, and finished with evaporated skimmed milk.

PORTION	KCAL	PROTEIN	FAT	CARB	SODIUM	CHOL
1 portion	245	27 gm	3 gm	26 gm	175 mg	70 mg

GRILLED SABLE WITH ARTICHOKES, CAPERS, AND CELERY HEARTS

Yield: 10 portions

2¼ pounds	Sable fillets	1 kilogram
1 teaspoon	Lime juice, fresh	5 grams

VEGETABLE RAGOÛT

1½ pound	Tomato concassé	675 grams
2 ounces	Capers	20 grams
1 clove	Garlic, chopped	1 clove
6 ounces	Artichoke hearts, trimmed, cooked, julienned	200 grams
20 ounces	Fennel, julienned, blanched	400 grams
30 pieces	Potatoes, tournéed, cooked	30 pieces
2½ fluid ounces	Lemon juice, fresh	70 milliliters
2½ fluid ounces	Red wine vinegar	70 milliliters
¾ ounce	Black pepper, freshly ground	20 grams
2½ ounces	Celery heart leaves	70 grams

1. Cut the fish into 3½-ounce/100-gram portions and pound them lightly. Sprinkle with the lime juice and let them marinate briefly.

2. Combine the tomato concassé, capers, and garlic. Let them heat until the garlic loses its harsh aroma. Add the remaining vegetable ragoût ingredients except the celery heart leaves and stew gently until all ingredients are warm and tender.

3. Grill the fish. Remove the vegetable ragoût from the heat and toss in the celery leaves. Pool the ragoût on a heated plate and place the fish on top.

———

A portion of warm pepper relish might be appropriate in place of the ragoût.

Canned artichoke bottoms packed in water can replace fresh artichokes if they are out of season or too expensive.

PORTION	KCAL	PROTEIN	FAT	CARB	SODIUM	CHOL
1 portion	325	30 gm	7 gm	23 gm	270 mg	45 mg

GRILLED SWORDFISH WITH LENTIL RAGOÛT AND HORSERADISH AND APPLE CREAM SAUCE

Yield: 10 portions

2¼ pounds	Swordfish	1 kilogram

MARINADE

¾ fluid ounce	Lime juice	20 milliliters
½ ounce	Shallots, minced	10 grams
3 cloves	Garlic cloves, minced	15 grams
½ teaspoon	Chervil leaves, fresh	1 gram

1 pint	Lentil Ragoût*	480 milliliters
5 fluid ounces	Horseradish and Apple Cream Sauce*	150 milliliters

1. Cut the swordfish into 3.5-ounce/100-gram portions.

2. Combine the lime juice, shallots, garlic, and chervil. Spread evenly on the swordfish steaks and let marinate briefly.

3. Grill the swordfish.

4. Reheat the lentil ragoût and pool it on a heated plate. Place the swordfish on the bed of ragoût.

5. Top with the heated horseradish cream.

This is a good basic grilling recipe for a variety of fish and shellfish. The brief marination very slightly firms the fish and also gives it a hint of flavor.

　　* The recipe for Lentil Ragoût can be found in Chapter 11; the recipe for Horseradish and Apple Cream Sauce is found in Chapter 12.

PORTION	KCAL	PROTEIN	FAT	CARB	SODIUM	CHOL
1 portion	230	26 gm	6 gm	13 gm	225 mg	45 mg

GRILLED SWORDFISH WITH ROASTED PEPPER SALAD

Yield: 10 portions

2¼ pounds	Swordfish, trimmed	1 kilogram
2	Limes, sliced thin	2
1½ ounces	Onions, minced	40 grams
½ fluid ounce	White wine vinegar	15 milliliters
1 teaspoon	Honey	7 grams
¼ teaspoon	White pepper, ground	500 milligrams
1 recipe	Roasted Pepper Salad*	1 recipe

1. Cut the swordfish into steaks that weigh 3½ ounces/100 grams each. Place in a shallow, non-reactive container.

2. Combine the lime, onion, vinegar, honey, and pepper. Pack this mixture evenly around the swordfish. Let the fish marinate for about 30 minutes.

3. Remove the lime slices from the swordfish, and grill them to about medium-rare (carryover cooking should complete cooking). Serve each steak with a portion of the pepper salad.

———

* The recipe for Roasted Pepper Salad can be found in Chapter 13.

Additional suggestions for accompaniments to this dish include grilled scallions or leeks and grill polenta.

PORTION	KCAL	PROTEIN	FAT	CARB	SODIUM	CHOL
1 portion	255	23 gm	12 gm	16 gm	240 mg	40 mg

MESQUITE-GRILLED CHICKEN BREAST

Yield: 10 portions

8 fluid ounces	Apple cider	240 milliliters
1 fluid ounce	Apple-cider vinegar	30 milliliters
½ ounce	Shallots, minced	15 grams
1 clove	Garlic, minced	5 grams
5 to 6	Black peppercorns, cracked	5 to 6
2¼ pounds	Chicken suprêmes, skinless*	1 kilogram

1. Combine the cider, vinegar, shallots, garlic, and peppercorns in a shallow pan.

2. Add the chicken; turn to coat evenly. Marinate for 1 to 2 hours under refrigeration.

3. Heat grill well; add mesquite chips to coals. Grill chicken breasts over hot coals for a few minutes on each side, or until cooked through. (There should be a slight amount of give when pressed with a fingertip.)

4. Serve chicken with appropriate accompaniments.**

---

* A chicken suprême should still have one joint of the wing attached. If desired, the skin may be left on during grilling to protect the flesh from drying, but it should be removed before service.

If desired, this chicken may be basted during cooking with barbecue sauce to coat it with a flavorful glaze.

** Some serving suggestions include slicing the chicken and placing it in a steamed flour tortilla, on a bed of Black Bean Sauce (see the recipe in Chapter 11), or on a bed of fresh greens coated with a vinaigrette. A corn relish or salsa would also make a good accompaniment.

PORTION	KCAL	PROTEIN	FAT	CARB	SODIUM	CHOL
1 portion	170	25 gm	3 gm	12 gm	70 mg	60 mg

INDIAN-STYLE GRILLED BUFFALO

Yield: 10 portions

MARINADE

4 ounces	Yogurt, plain, nonfat	115 grams
2 ounces	Onions, minced	60 grams
¾ ounce	Gingerroot, fresh, minced	20 grams
4 cloves	Garlic, minced	20 grams
1 teaspoon	Cumin seeds, toasted, freshly ground	1 gram
1 teaspoon	Black peppercorns, freshly ground	2 grams
¾ teaspoon	Green cardamom seeds, freshly ground	1 gram
½ teaspoon	Nutmeg, freshly ground	1 gram
2½ pounds	Buffalo round, trimmed, 1-inch cubes	1.15 kilograms
30 ounces	Zucchini, sliced, grilled	850 grams
2½ pounds	Basmati rice, cooked pilaf style	1.15 kilograms
15 ounces	Fresh Mango Chutney*	450 grams

1. Combine all of the ingredients for the marinade.

2. Add the buffalo meat and toss to coat evenly. Marinate under refrigeration for 24 hours.

3. Thread the buffalo on skewers (if using bamboo skewers, be sure to soak them in cold water before using). Grill to the desired doneness.

4. Serve on a bed of basmati rice with grilled zucchini and mango chutney.

---

* See Chapter 12 for the recipe for Fresh Mango Chutney.

PORTION	KCAL	PROTEIN	FAT	CARB	SODIUM	CHOL
1 portion	295	28 gm	7 gm	40 gm	75 mg	55 mg

LAMB CHOPS WITH SHERRY VINEGAR SAUCE

Yield: 10 portions

3 pounds	Lamb chops from the rib	1.3 kilograms
2 tablespoons	Rosemary leaves, whole	6 grams
1 teaspoon	Black peppercorns, cracked	2 grams
14 fluid ounces	Fond de Veau Lié*	400 milliliters
1½ ounces	Brown sugar	45 grams
1¾ fluid ounces	Sherry vinegar	50 milliliters
1 tablespoon	Shallots, minced	15 grams
20 ounces	Lentil Ragoût*	600 grams

1. Trim the lamb chops carefully and french the bones.

2. Rub the chops with rosemary leaves and peppercorns, and let rest with this coating for a few minutes before cooking.

3. Heat the fond de veau lié. Add the sugar, vinegar, and shallots. Simmer until a good consistency is reached. Keep sauce warm.

4. Grill the chops to the desired doneness, marking, if desired, on one side.

5. If necessary, reheat the ragoût. Serve the chops with the ragoût and sauce.

---

* See the recipes in Chapter 11.

PORTION	KCAL	PROTEIN	FAT	CARB	SODIUM	CHOL
1 portion	230	29 gm	13 gm	15 gm	165 mg	85 mg

GRILLED FLANK STEAK WITH ROASTED SHALLOT SAUCE

Yield: 10 portions

2¼ pounds	Flank steak, trimmed	1 kilogram
½ recipe	Marinade for Flank Steak*	½ recipe

SAUCE

1¾ fluid ounces	Pineapple juice, unsweetened	50 milliliters
1 fluid ounce	Lime juice, fresh-squeezed	30 milliliters
½ fluid ounce	White wine vinegar	15 milliliters
1 teaspoon	Black peppercorns, cracked	2 grams
7 ounces	Shallots, roasted, shredded	200 grams
1 pint	Fond de Veau Lié*	480 milliliters
2 tablespoons	Cilantro, chopped	6 grams

1. Combine the flank steak with marinade; marinate for up to 3 hours. Drain well and grill to desired doneness.

2. Let the steak rest while preparing the sauce.

3. Combine the fruit juices, vinegar, and peppercorns. Reduce this mixture by half. Add the shallots and fond de veau lié. Bring the sauce to a simmer and add the cilantro.

4. Slice steak thinly on the bias and serve with the sauce.

———

* See the recipe for Marinade for Flank Steak on the next page and for Fond de Veau Lié in Chapter 11.

STEAK FAJITAS: Serve sliced steak with the sauce and offer Fresh Tomato Salsa (see the recipe in Chapter 12), shredded lettuce, a little shredded cheese, Sour Cream Replacement (also in Chapter 12), chopped scallions and red onions, and Roasted Pepper Salad (see the recipe in Chapter 13).

PORTION	KCAL	PROTEIN	FAT	CARB	SODIUM	CHOL
1 portion	215	25 gm	6 gm	14 gm	125 mg	70 mg

MARINADE FOR FLANK STEAK

Yield: enough for 6 steaks

3 pints	Pineapple juice	1.5 liters
1 pound	Pineapple, fresh, chopped	450 grams
7 ounces	Red onion, thinly sliced	200 grams
2 fluid ounces	Soy sauce, low-sodium	60 milliliters
1 fluid ounce	Red wine vinegar	30 milliliters
1 fluid ounce	Olive oil	30 milliliters
4	Limes, sliced	4
1 bunch	Cilantro, fresh, chopped	1 bunch
1 ounce	Garlic, minced	30 grams
¾ ounce	Jalapeños, minced	20 grams
⅓ ounce	Chili powder	10 grams
5 drops	Tabasco sauce	5 drops

1. Combine all of the ingredients. Use as marinade by adding steak and turning to coat evenly. Marinate minimum of 2 hours up to a maximum of 24 hours.

PORTION	KCAL	PROTEIN	FAT	CARB	SODIUM	CHOL
4 oz	65	1 gm	1 gm	14 gm	105 mg	0 mg

GRILLED QUAIL WRAPPED IN PROSCIUTTO WITH FIGS AND WILD MUSHROOMS

Yield: 10 portions

20 each	Quail, skin removed, split	20 each
5 ounces	Prosciutto, sliced thin	140 grams
3 fluid ounces	Dry sherry	90 milliliters
1 ounce	Shallots, minced (total)	30 grams
3 cloves	Garlic, minced	8 grams
1 teaspoon	Peppercorns, cracked	480 milliliters
1 pint	Fond de veau lié	170 grams
6 ounces	Assorted wild mushrooms, sliced	85 grams
3 ounces	Sundried figs	85 grams

1. Wrap a piece of prosciutto around each halved quail and thread them on skewers. Place them in a shallow pan. Add the sherry, half of the shallots, the garlic, and the peppercorns. Turn to coat them evenly with this marinade. Marinate for about 30 minutes.

2. Grill the quail quickly over hot coals. Brush them lightly with a little of the fond de veau lié when they are removed from the grill. Keep them warm while completing the sauce.

3. Sauté the shallots and wild mushrooms in a hot pan until the mushrooms begin to release some of their moisture. Add the figs and the wine to the mushrooms. Add the remaining fond de veau lié.

4. Serve the grilled quail with the sauce.

———

The grilled quail shown here is accompanied by lightly steamed Hariots Verts (see Chapter 17) and a timbale of creamy polenta. To make creamy polenta follow the recipe in Chapter 17, using 5 ounces/140 grams of cornmeal. Pour the finished creamy polenta into a 2-ounce mold that has been lightly sprayed with vegetable oil. Warm single portions in a microwave or heat larger batches in a steamer or oven.

PORTION	KCAL	PROTEIN	FAT	CARB	SODIUM	CHOL
1 portion	355	43 gm	15 gm	9 gm	240 mg	140 mg

LOIN OF LAMB WITH BLOOD ORANGE SAUCE

Yield: 10 portions

2¼ pounds	Lamb loin, trimmed	1 kilogram
3½ fluid ounces	Vegetable Stock*	100 milliliters
¾ ounce	Arrowroot	20 grams
1¾ fluid ounces	Orange juice concentrate	50 milliliters
2 teaspoons	Black peppercorns, cracked	4 grams
8 fluid ounces	Blood orange juice**	240 milliliters
7 fluid ounces	Orange juice	200 milliliters
5 fluid ounces	Fond de Veau Lié*	150 milliliters
1 tablespoon	Tarragon leaves, chopped	3 grams

1. Cut the lamb loin into 3½-ounce/100-gram portions and reserve.

2. Combine enough of the vegetable stock with ½ ounce/15 grams of the arrowroot to make a thin paste. Heat the remaining stock to a simmer and add the arrowroot. Simmer for a minute or two, until thickened. Add the orange juice concentrate and the cracked pepper to make a glaze. Remove from the heat. Reserve until needed.

3. Combine the orange juices, and use enough to dilute the remaining arrowroot to a thin paste. Bring the juices to a simmer, and add the arrowroot. Add the fond de veau lié and return to a bare simmer. Add the tarragon to finish the blood orange sauce.

4. Dip the portioned lamb into the orange glaze and grill to the desired doneness. Serve the grilled lamb with the blood orange sauce.

---

* See the recipes in Chapter 11.

    ** Blood oranges are available for a limited season, and this recipe is designed to make the most of their flavor and color. It may be prepared using ordinary orange juice, however.

    Serve this dish with steamed green vegetables and Celeriac and Potato Puree (see the recipe in Chapter 17).

PORTION	KCAL	PROTEIN	FAT	CARB	SODIUM	CHOL
1 portion	184	22 gm	6 gm	9 gm	85 mg	65 mg

GRILLED VEGETABLES

Yield: 10 portions

30 ounces	Vegetable, trimmed and sliced as necessary*	850 grams
3 fluid ounces	Vinaigrette-style Dressing**	90 milliliters

1. Toss the vegetable in the vinaigrette to coat it evenly.

2. Cook on a hot grill until the skin (if any) bubbles, and the flesh is soft and properly cooked.

3. Remove from the grill and serve at once.

---

* A variety of vegetables—such as zucchini, eggplant, bell peppers, and mushrooms—are suitable for grilling in this manner. Other vegetables, such as fennel, sweet potatoes and leeks, may require parcooking or blanching prior to grilling.

** The recipe for Vinaigrette-style Dressing is found in Chapter 12.

PORTION	KCAL	PROTEIN	FAT	CARB	SODIUM	CHOL
1 portion	35	1 gm	2 gm	5 gm	20 mg	trace

GRILLED CHICKEN BURRITO WITH TOMATILLO SALSA

Yield: 10 portions

SALSA

8 ounces	Tomatillos, peeled, coarsely chopped	225 grams
4 ounces	Plum tomato concassé	115 grams
4 ounces	Red onions, finely diced	115 grams
½ ounce	Jalapeños, roasted, chopped	15 grams
2 fluid ounces	Lime juice, fresh-squeezed	60 milliliters
¾ ounce	Garlic, minced	20 grams
¾ ounce	Cilantro leaves, chopped	20 grams
1 teaspoon	Oregano leaves, chopped	1 gram
½ teaspoon	Cumin seeds, toasted, ground	1.75 grams
¼ teaspoon	Salt	2 grams
2¼ pounds	Chicken breasts, skinless, boneless	1 kilogram
2 teaspoons	Shallots, minced	10 grams
1 teaspoon	Black peppercorns, cracked	2 grams
10	Flour tortillas	10
5 ounces	Guacamole*	150 grams

1. Combine the tomatillos, concassé, red onions, jalapeños, 1 tablespoon/15 milliliters of lime juice, 1 tablespoon/12 grams of the garlic, ½ ounce/15 grams of cilantro, and all of the oregano, cumin, and salt to make the salsa. Refrigerate until needed.

2. Place the chicken in a shallow container, and add all of the remaining ingredients, except the tortillas. Allow the chicken to marinate for at least 30 minutes before grilling.

3. Grill the chicken on both sides until cooked through; then thinly slice on the bias.

4. Warm the tortillas, spread each one with about ½ ounce/15 grams of guacamole. Roll it into a cone shape. Fill with sliced chicken. Serve with salsa.

* See the recipe in Chapter 12.

    If desired, serve Black Bean Sauce (see the recipe Chapter 11) with this entrée and accompany with a mixture of roasted corn and red peppers or Roasted Pepper Salad (see the recipe in Chapter 13).

PORTION 1 portion	KCAL 235	PROTEIN 28 gm	FAT 3 gm	CARB 23 gm	SODIUM 230 mg	CHOL 60 mg

BROILED SPICY GULF SHRIMP

Yield: 10 portions

1¼ pounds	Shrimp (21–25 count), peeled and de-veined	570 grams
2 teaspoons	Five-spice powder	2 grams
3 drops	Tabasco sauce	3 drops
1 teaspoon	Gingerroot, grated	3 grams
2 cloves	Garlic, finely minced	10 grams
1 tablespoon	Rice vinegar	15 milliliters
½ teaspoon	Prepared fish sauce (nuoc mam)	3 milliliters
¼ teaspoon	Dark sesame oil	2 milliliters

1. Combine the shrimp with the five-spice powder, Tabasco, gingerroot, garlic, vinegar, fish sauce, and sesame oil. Let the shrimp marinate for at least 1 hour.

2. Preheat a grill (charcoal or gas) until very hot. Grill the shrimp for about 2 minutes to cook through.

The portion size may be increased if this dish is to be served as an entrée. It might be presented in several ways. Following is one example:

    Mound a portion of the Marinated Asian Vegetable Salad (Chapter 13) in the center of a plate, and arrange the shrimp and the grilled bread (see Chapter 19) on the plate.

PORTION 1 portion	KCAL 65	PROTEIN 12 gm	FAT 1 gm	CARB 1 gm	SODIUM 95 mg	CHOL 90 mg

BROILED SPANISH MACKEREL WITH TOMATO FONDUE

Yield: 10 portions

2¼ pounds	Spanish mackerel fillets	1 kilogram

TOMATO FONDUE

2 fluid ounces	Olive oil	60 milliliters
2 ounces	Garlic, minced	60 grams
7 ounces	Onion, diced	200 grams
2¼ pounds	Tomato concassé	1 kilogram
10 tablespoons	Herbs, fresh*	15 grams
4 fluid ounces	Tomato juice, fresh	60 milliliters
to taste	Lime juice, fresh	to taste
to taste	Black pepper, freshly ground	to taste

1. Cut the mackerel into 3½-ounce/100-gram portions.

2. Prepare the fondue as follows: Heat the oil and sauté the garlic and onions until they lose their harsh aroma. Add the tomato concassé and cook quickly over high heat, tossing frequently, until most of the free moisture reduces. Add the herbs, tomato and lime juices and black pepper. Reduce very briefly, if necessary.

3. Broil the mackerel, and serve with the tomato fondue pooled around it.

———

* Herbs may be varied according to availability. Some suggestions include basil, tarragon, chives, oregano, cilantro, or marjoram.

This is a good recipe for several kinds of fish, such as bluefish, mahi mahi, tuna, shark, or swordfish. Salmon and trout might also be good prepared this way.

If fresh tomatoes are not especially flavorful, use canned plum tomatoes.

PORTION	KCAL	PROTEIN	FAT	CARB	SODIUM	CHOL
1 portion	244	26 gm	12 gm	8 gm	125 mg	80 mg

SCALLOPS GRATIN WITH WILD MUSHROOMS

Yield: 10 appetizer portions*

18 ounces	Sea scallops, muscle tabs removed	500 grams
1½ fluid ounces	White wine, dry	45 milliliters
2 teaspoons	Shallots, minced	8 grams
10½ fluid ounces	Fish Velouté**	300 milliliters
1 ounce	Pommery mustard	30 grams
¾ ounce	Butter, unsalted	20 grams
3 ounces	Scallions, thinly sliced	85 grams
3 ounces	Tomatoes, peeled, seeded, julienned	85 grams
6 ounces	Shiitake mushrooms, stems removed, sliced	170 grams
2½ ounces	Bread crumbs, fresh	70 grams

1. Portion the scallops on clean plates; cover with plastic wrap. Use the bottom of a spoon to flatten the scallops to an even thickness. Keep refrigerated until needed.

2. Heat the wine, and add the shallots. Sweat until they are translucent, then add the velouté and mustard. Reduce to form a thick sauce.

3. Heat the butter and add the scallions, tomatoes, and mushrooms. Sauté until tender and heated through. Reserve.

4. Coat the scallops with the sauce and top with bread crumbs. Broil until the bread crumbs are lightly browned and the scallops are cooked.

5. If necessary, reheat the sautéed mushroom mixture and serve with the scallops.

---

* Or 5 entrée portions.
    ** See the variation to Velouté-style Sauce in Chapter 11.

PORTION	KCAL	PROTEIN	FAT	CARB	SODIUM	CHOL
1 portion	90	9 gm	2 gm	7 gm	200 mg	25 mg

BROILED RED PERCH WITH LIME-TEQUILA VINAIGRETTE

Yield: 10 portions

2¼ pounds	Red perch fillets, trimmed, bones removed	1 kilogram
10 fluid ounces	Lime-Tequila Vinaigrette*	300 milliliters
7 ounces	Tomato concassé	200 grams
2	Red grapefruits, sectioned	2
2	Yellow grapefruits, sectioned	2
1	Avocado, thinly sliced	1

1. Score the skin of the fillets in a diamond pattern.

2. Place the fish, skin side down, on a sizzler platter and brush with 2 tablespoons/ 30 milliliters of the vinaigrette.

3. Broil the perch, turning once during cooking, until just cooked through (5 to 8 minutes, depending upon the thickness of the individual pieces).

4. Toss the tomatoes, grapefruits, and avocado with the remaining vinaigrette, and serve them with the perch.

* To prepare Lime-Tequila Vinaigrette, follow the directions for Basic Vinaigrette in Chapter 12, replacing the red wine vinegar with a combination of 6 ounces of lime juice, 8 ounces of rice wine vinegar, and 2 ounces of tequila; use peanut or sesame oil. If desired, the tequila may be omitted, and replaced with additional rice wine vinegar. Add chopped cilantro leaves to the vinaigrette.

Other fish, including catfish, golden bass, grouper, or snapper, may be used instead of perch.

The phyllo fan shown in the accompanying photograph is made by folding a sheet of phyllo accordion-style, and then folding it in half to create the fan. The dough may be very lightly sprayed with oil and then dusted with chopped herbs before it is baked in a hot oven until it is crisp and golden-brown.

PORTION	KCAL	PROTEIN	FAT	CARB	SODIUM	CHOL
1 portion	190	21 gm	9 gm	7 gm	130 mg	45 mg

PAN-SEARED SEA SCALLOPS WITH SAFFRON RICE, ASPARAGUS, AND A LIGHT TOMATO-GARLIC SAUCE

Yield: 10 portions

2¼ pounds	Sea scallops, muscle tabs removed	1 kilogram
as needed	Flour	as needed
3½ ounces	Butter, unsalted	100 grams
1 ounce	Garlic, finely minced	30 grams
7 ounces	Tomato concassé, small dice	200 grams
1 pint	Fond de Veau Lié	500 milliliters
2 pounds	Saffron Rice*	900 grams
1 pound	Asparagus, trimmed, blanched	450 grams
3½ ounces	Lemon Glaze**	100 grams

1. Dry scallops as thoroughly as possible. Dust with flour and shake off the excess.

2. Sear the scallops in a seasoned cast-iron skillet or a nonstick pan. Remove and keep them warm.

3. Add the butter and let heat. Add the garlic to the pan and sauté over moderate heat until the aroma becomes sweet.

4. Add the tomato concassé; sauté briefly.

5. Add the jus de veau lié. Stir well to deglaze the pan.

6. Serve the scallops on a bed of the Saffron Rice with the Tomato-Garlic Sauce, and asparagus brushed with Lemon Glaze.

---

* Add ½ teaspoon crushed saffron threads in step 1 of the Basic Rice Pilaf recipe found in Chapter 17.

** Lemon Glaze can be found in Chapter 12.

PORTION	KCAL	PROTEIN	FAT	CARB	SODIUM	CHOL
1 portion	340	27 gm	7 gm	40 gm	185 mg	50 mg

SEARED SALMON WITH FRESH PAPAYA RELISH

Yield: 10 portions

2¼ pounds	Salmon fillet	1 kilogram

RELISH

20 ounces	Papaya, peeled, seeded, small dice	570 grams
3½ ounces	Plum tomato concassé	100 grams
3½ ounces	Bermuda or Vidalia onions, small dice	100 grams
½ ounce	Jalapeños, seeded, minced	15 grams
1¾ fluid ounces	Orange juice, fresh-squeezed	50 milliliters
¾ fluid ounce	Lime juice, fresh-squeezed	20 milliliters
3 tablespoons	Cilantro, chopped	9 grams
2 tablespoons	Mint, chopped	6 grams

1. Cut the salmon into 3½-ounce/100-gram slices and flatten them between parchment or plastic wrap to an even thickness.

2. In a nonstick or well-seasoned cast-iron skillet sauté the salmon to a good color on both sides. Remove from the pan. Place the salmon on a rack and finish cooking in a moderate (350 to 375 degree F/175 to 190 degree C) oven, if necessary.

3. Combine the papaya, tomatoes, onions, jalapeños, and juices, and heat gently in the skillet over low to moderate heat. Once this mixture is warm, add the cilantro and mint.

4. Serve the salmon with the relish.

The salmon could be replaced with fresh tuna, swordfish, mahi mahi, or other firm-textured fish, as well as chicken or pork, if desired. The meat or fish could be grilled instead of sautéed.

PORTION	KCAL	PROTEIN	FAT	CARB	SODIUM	CHOL
1 portion	270	25 gm	7 gm	30 gm	175 mg	55 mg

STIR-FRIED GARDEN VEGETABLES

Yield: 10 portions (entrée) or 20 portions (side dish)

1 pound	Tofu, cut into bite-sized pieces	450 grams
¾ fluid ounce	Soy sauce, reduced-sodium	20 milliliters
½ ounce	Gingerroot, minced	15 grams
3 cloves	Garlic cloves, minced	15 grams
as needed	Flour	as needed
1½ teaspoons	Extra-virgin olive oil	8 milliliters
¼ teaspoon	Sesame oil	2 milliliters
1 ounce	Scallions	30 grams
5 pounds	Vegetables, cut into bite-sized pieces*	2.25 kilograms
2 tablespoons	Sesame seeds	10 grams
8 fluid ounces	Vegetable stock	240 milliliters
3½ fluid ounces	Soy sauce, reduced-sodium	100 milliliters
1 tablespoon	Hot red bean paste	15 grams
½ teaspoon	Five-spice powder	1 gram
30 ounces	Brown rice pilaf, cooked**	850 grams

1. Combine the tofu with the soy sauce and half of the ginger and garlic. Let it marinate briefly.

2. Dust the tofu with flour and shake off any excess.

3. Combine the olive and sesame oils in a wok and heat. Add the tofu and stir-fry.

4. Remove the tofu; add the remaining garlic and ginger and the scallions. Stir-fry until an aroma is released.

5. Add the vegetables in sequence (longest-cooking in first). If necessary, add a small amount of vegetable stock or water to steam the vegetables lightly.

6. When all the vegetables are added and cooked, return the tofu to the stir-fry.

7. Garnish the stir-fry with sesame seeds. Stir together all of the remaining ingredients and add them to the stir-fry as well.

8. To serve, make a bed of pilaf and top with the stir-fry.

* Vegetables should be selected according to the season and their availability.

** Other grains, including barley, quinoa, couscous, and basmati rice may be substituted for brown rice. Or select a noodle, such as soba, Lo mein, or cellophane.

PORTION	KCAL	PROTEIN	FAT	CARB	SODIUM	CHOL
1 portion	213	12 gm	5 gm	36 gm	490 mg	trace

SAUTÉED SOLE WITH PRESERVED MANGO CHUTNEY AND GRILLED BANANAS

Yield: 10 portions

2¼ ounces	Sole fillets, trimmed	1 kilogram
1½ fluid ounces	Skim milk	40 milliliters
1 ounce	Bread crumbs, dry	30 grams
½ teaspoon	Butter, whole, unsalted	3 grams
1 pound	Preserved Mango Chutney*	450 grams
1½ pounds	Bananas, sliced on bias, grilled	700 grams

1. Dip the sole in the skim milk.

2. Place the sole immediately into the bread crumbs and coat evenly. Shake off any excess.

3. Sauté the breaded sole in the butter until just done using ½ teaspoon/3 grams per serving.

4. Serve at once with Mango Chutney and grilled bananas.

* See Chapter 12 for the recipe for Preserved Mango Chutney.

PORTION	KCAL	PROTEIN	FAT	CARB	SODIUM	CHOL
1 portion	200	20 gm	3 gm	26 gm	125 mg	65 mg

CHICKEN SCALLOPINI WITH MUSHROOMS AND CAPERS

Yield: 10 portions

2¼ pounds	Chicken breast, boneless, skinless	1 kilogram
2¾ ounces	Butter, unsalted	50 grams
2¾ ounces	Flour	50 grams
1 pound, 2 ounces	Mushrooms, sliced	500 grams
7 ounces	Capers, drained, rinsed	200 grams
8 fluid ounces	Sherry	240 milliliters
26 fluid ounces	Fond de Veau Lié	800 milliliters
2¼ pounds	Zucchini Noodles*	1 kilogram

1. Cut chicken breasts in half; pound to an even thickness between plastic wrap.

2. Heat the butter. Dust the chicken lightly with the flour, shaking off excess and immediately place in the pan.

3. Sauté the chicken, turning once, until just cooked through. Remove from the pan and keep warm.

4. Add the mushrooms and capers to the pan and sauté briefly. Add the sherry to deglaze.

5,. Add the jus de veau lié and heat the sauce to a boil.

6. Place the chicken on a bed of heated zucchini noodles; pour the sauce over it.

———

* The recipe for Pan-Steamed Zucchini and Yellow Squash Noodles is found in Chapter 17.

PORTION	KCAL	PROTEIN	FAT	CARB	SODIUM	CHOL
1 portion	240	27 gm	9 gm	6 gm	290 mg	75 mg

SAUTÉED MEDALLIONS OF PORK WITH WARM FRUITS

Yield: 10 portions

2¼ pounds	Pork loin, trimmed	1 kilogram
5 ounces	Red Delicious apples, tournéed or large dice	150 grams
4 ounces	Pears, tournéed or large dice	115 grams
1 pint	White wine, semi-dry	480 milliliters
1¾ ounces	Dried cherries	50 grams
3½ ounces	Dried apricots, sulphur-free	100 grams
1 pint	Chicken stock, hot	480 milliliters
1 pint	Pork jus	480 milliliters
1¾ fluid ounces	Brandy, apple-flavored	50 milliliters
1½ pounds	Pumpkin Pasta*	680 grams
1¼ pounds	Haricots Verts with Walnuts*	570 grams

1. Cut the pork into medallions, about 1 ounce/30 grams each. One portion is three medallions.

2. Poach the apples and pears in the white wine until tender. Let them cool in the poaching liquid.

3. Reconstitute the dried fruits in the stock. Strain, and reserve the stock.

4. At service, dry-sauté the pork in a nonstick or properly seasoned sauté pan. Remove from the pan and keep it warm.

5. Deglaze the pan with a small amount of the reserved chicken stock. Add the fruits and heat well. Add the pork jus and the brandy and flame the sauce.

6. Return the pork to the sauté pan to coat lightly with the sauce.

7. Serve the pork on a bed of Pumpkin Pasta with the haricots verts with walnuts. Coat the pork with the sauce and garnish with the fruit.

---

* See Basic Pasta Dough with Variations in Chapter 19. Haricots Verts with Walnuts is found in Chapter 17.

PORTION	KCAL	PROTEIN	FAT	CARB	SODIUM	CHOL
1 portion	380	27 gm	13 gm	39 gm	90 mg	90 mg

SAUTÉED MEDALLIONS OF PORK WITH RED ONION CONFIT AND CIDER-BOURBON SAUCE

Yield: 10 portions

2¼ pounds	Pork loin, trimmed	1 kilogram
14 fluid ounces	Cider-Bourbon Sauce*	400 milliliters
10 ounces	Red Onion Confit, warmed*	300 grams

1. Cut the pork into medallions, about ¼-inch-thick, 1 ounce/30 grams each. Pound the medallions slightly to shape them and even out the thickness.

2. At service, dry-sauté the pork and remove it from the pan.

3. Add the Cider-Bourbon Sauce to the pan to deglaze the fond. Bring the sauce to a simmer and let reduce slightly.

4. Serve the medallions with the sauce (1 fluid ounce/30 milliliters per portion) and the heated Red Onion Confit (1 ounce/30 grams per portion).

———

* The recipe for the Cider Bourbon Sauce is made by adding a small amount of bourbon (about 1 teaspoon/5 milliliters per portion) to the recipe for Cider Sauce found in Chapter 11. The recipe for Red Onion Confit is in Chapter 12.

To serve the entree, return 3 medallions per order to the reduced sauce to glaze them evenly, or pour the sauce over the medallions after they have been arranged on heated plates. Place a 1-ounce/30-gram portion of the confit on each plate.

PORTION	KCAL	PROTEIN	FAT	CARB	SODIUM	CHOL
1 portion	290	21 gm	12 gm	24 gm	70 mg	85 mg

SAUTÉED VEAL WITH RISOTTO AND MARSALA

Yield: 10 portions

2¼ pounds	Veal, top round, cut into 20 medallions	1 kilogram
as needed	Flour	as needed
1¾ ounces	Butter, unsalted	50 grams
9 ounces	Cremini mushrooms, sliced	255 grams
2½ fluid ounces	Marsala	70 milliliters
1 pint	Fond de Veau Lié	480 milliliters
1¾ pounds	Risotto*	800 grams
3½ ounces	Parmesan cheese, grated	100 grams
1 ounce	Lemon zest	30 grams
1¾ pounds	Grilled Japanese eggplant*	800 grams

1. Pound veal slightly to even out thickness. Dust with flour and shake off any excess. Immediately sauté in the heated butter until just cooked through.

2. Remove the veal from the pan and keep it warm.

3. Add the mushrooms to the pan and sauté lightly. Deglaze the pan with the Marsala and let it reduce.

4. Add the fond de veau lié and bring the sauce to a simmer.

5. Finish the risotto by adding a small amount of stock, cook until the liquid is absorbed, stirring constantly. Add the cheese and lemon zest.

6. Fan the grilled eggplant on heated plates and arrange the veal and risotto on the plate. Coat the veal with the sauce.

---

* For the Risotto recipe, see Chapter 17; see Grilled Vegetables recipe in this chapter for the eggplant.

PORTION	KCAL	PROTEIN	FAT	CARB	SODIUM	CHOL
1 portion	363	27 gm	16 gm	27 gm	210 mg	110 mg

SAUTÉED MEDALLIONS OF PORK WITH WARM CABBAGE SALAD

Yield: 10 portions

2¼ pounds	Pork loin, trimmed	1 kilogram

SAUCE

1 pint	Fond de Veau Lié	480 milliliters
2 fluid ounces	Sherry vinegar	60 milliliters
1 ounce	Brown sugar	30 grams

SALAD

1¾ ounces	Bacon, minced	50 grams
3½ ounces	Red onion, small dice	100 grams
2 cloves	Garlic, minced	10 grams
1¾ fluid ounces	Tarragon vinegar	50 milliliters
1 ounce	Sugar, granulated	30 grams
1 teaspoon	Caraway seeds	2 grams
2 pounds	Savoy cabbage, chiffonade	900 grams
1 tablespoon	Parsley, chopped	3 grams

1. Cut the pork into 20 medallions, each approximately 1¾ ounces/50 grams. Pound them lightly to even the thickness and shape. Refrigerate them until needed.

2. Combine the ingredients for the sauce and blend well. Reserve until needed.

3. To make the warm cabbage salad: Render the bacon, add the onion and garlic, and sauté until they are translucent and tender.

4. Add the vinegar, sugar, and caraway seeds; bring to a simmer. Add the cabbage and sweat until it is limp. Add the parsley.

5. At service, dry-sauté the pork medallions (two per order) on both sides until cooked through. Remove from the pan.

6. Add the sauce mixture to the sauté pan and bring to a simmer. Allow it to reduce slightly. Return the pork to the pan to heat through and coat evenly with the sauce.

7. Heat the cabbage salad in the microwave, if necessary.

8. Serve the pork with the warm cabbage salad and the sauce.

PORTION	KCAL	PROTEIN	FAT	CARB	SODIUM	CHOL
1 portion	150	7 gm	5 gm	16 gm	30 mg	10 mg

ROESTI POTATOES WITH CELERIAC

Yield: 10 portions

1 pound	Idaho potatoes, peeled	450 grams
1 pound	Celery root, peeled	450 grams
1 tablespoon	Whole-grain mustard	15 grams
½ teaspoon	Black peppercorns, cracked	1 gram
as needed	Olive oil	as needed

1. Grate the potatoes and celery root and toss together.

2. Mix in the mustard and pepper. Form the potato mixture into 20 equal cakes.

3. Heat enough oil to very lightly film a nonstick or well-seasoned skillet. Sauté the cakes until browned on both sides.

4. Finish the potato cakes in a hot (375 degrees F/190 degrees C) oven.

PORTION	KCAL	PROTEIN	FAT	CARB	SODIUM	CHOL
1 portion	80	2 gm	3 gm	13 gm	70 mg	0 mg

RECIPES

SWISS-STYLE SHREDDED VEAL

Yield: 10 portions

2¼ pounds	Veal, top round, cut into émincé	1 kilogram

SAUCE

1 pint	White wine, dry	480 milliliters
1½ ounces	Shallots, minced	40 grams
10 ounces	Mushrooms, sliced	300 grams
24 fluid ounces	Chicken velouté	720 milliliters
7 fluid ounces	Evaporated skimmed milk	200 milliliters
5 fluid ounces	Glace de viande*	150 milliliters
as needed	Chives, fresh, cut	as needed
1 recipe	Spätzle**	1 recipe

1. Dry the veal as thoroughly as possible; then dry-sauté in well-seasoned cast-iron or nonstick skillet. Remove the veal.

2. Add the wine and shallots to deglaze the pan. Let the wine reduce slightly.

3. Add the mushrooms and cook until they begin to release some moisture.

4. Add the velouté, evaporated milk, and glace de viande. Simmer until the sauce reduces enough to coat the back of a wooden spoon.

5. Return the veal to the sauté pan to reheat briefly. Add the chives to taste.

6. Serve the veal over a bed of heated spätzle.

---

* Directions to prepare glace de viande are found in the note following Fond de Veau Lié (Chapter 11).

** See Chapter 19 for the recipe for Spätzle.

PORTION	KCAL	PROTEIN	FAT	CARB	SODIUM	CHOL
1 portion	309	29 gm	9 gm	26 gm	265 mg	95 mg

TENDERLOIN OF BEEF WITH WILD MUSHROOMS

Yield: 10 portions

2¼ pounds	Beef tenderloin, cut into medallions	1 kilogram

SAUCE

1 pint	Fond de Veau Lié	500 milliliters
1¾ pounds	Wild mushrooms, as available, sliced	800 grams
3½ fluid ounces	Madeira wine	100 milliliters
1 teaspoon	Sage leaves, chopped	1 gram
2 teaspoons	Thyme leaves, chopped	2 grams
½ teaspoon	Caraway seeds	1 gram
½ teaspoon	Black peppercorns, cracked	1 gram
3½ ounces	Leeks, chiffonade, stewed in stock	100 grams

1. Flatten the beef medallions slightly.
2. Dry-sauté them to the desired doneness and remove from the pan.
3. Add the fond de veau lié to deglaze the pan. Add the wild mushrooms and allow them to cook briefly.
4. Add the wine, sage, thyme, caraway, and black pepper. Simmer and check for consistency and flavor.
5. Add the stewed leeks to the sauce.
6. Return the beef medallions to the sauce briefly to reheat and coat.
7. Serve the sauce over the steaks.

PORTION	KCAL	PROTEIN	FAT	CARB	SODIUM	CHOL
1 portion	260	28 gm	13 gm	7 gm	80 mg	90 mg

TENDERLOIN OF BEEF WITH MILD ANCHO CHILI SAUCE
AND POLENTA WITH JALAPEÑO JACK CHEESE

Yield: 10 portions

2¼ pounds	Beef tenderloin, trimmed, portioned	1 kilogram
1 pint	Ancho Chili Sauce*	480 milliliters
2 pounds	Polenta*, prepared, cooled, sliced	900 grams
3½ ounces	Jalapeño Jack cheese, sliced	100 grams
1½ pounds	Zucchini, cut into "leaves", steamed**	680 grams

1. Shape the beef into medallions, using a cheesecloth. At service, dry-sauté to the desired doneness.

2. Remove the beef from the sauté pan; deglaze with the Ancho Chili Sauce. If necessary, thin the sauce slightly with a small amount of stock.

3. Grill the polenta, top with the cheese, and broil until the cheese melts.

4. Place the beef on heated plates, coat lightly with the sauce, and serve with the grilled polenta and zucchini.

---

* See the recipe for Ancho Chili Sauce in Chapter 11. The recipe for polenta is found in Chapter 17.

** To prepare zucchini leaves, cut the skin away in slices, about ⅓ inch thick. Use a paring knife to cut them into leaf shapes. Microwave or pan-steam them until just tender.

PORTION	KCAL	PROTEIN	FAT	CARB	SODIUM	CHOL
1 portion	366	31 gm	17 gm	24 gm	290 mg	80 mg

SAUTÉED VEAL WITH LUMP CRABMEAT AND ASPARAGUS

Yield: 10 portions

SAUCE

4 fluid ounces	Chicken stock	120 milliliters
2 fluid ounces	White wine, dry	60 milliliters
1 fluid ounce	Tarragon vinegar	30 milliliters
1 bunch	Tarragon, fresh	1 bunch
½ ounce	Shallots, minced	15 grams
½ teaspoon	Worcestershire sauce	3 milliliters
1 teaspoon	Black peppercorns, cracked	2 grams
1	Bay leaf	1
20 fluid ounces	Chicken velouté	600 milliliters
6 fluid ounces	Evaporated skimmed milk	180 milliliters
3½ ounces	Glace de viande*	100 milliliters
¾ fluid ounce	Heavy cream	20 milliliters
½ ounce	Arrowroot (dilute in cold liquid)	15 grams
1¾ pounds	Veal loin, cut into 20 medallions	800 grams
as needed	Flour	as needed
1¾ ounces	Butter, unsalted	50 grams
7 ounces	Lump crabmeat, picked	200 grams
1¼ pounds	Asparagus, peeled	570 grams

1. Make a reduction of the chicken stock, wine, vinegar, tarragon, shallots, Worcestershire, pepper, and bay leaf.

2. Add the velouté, evaporated milk, and glace de viande. Bring to a boil.

3. Finish the sauce by adding the diluted arrowroot to thicken, if necessary. Strain. (The portion size is 2 fluid ounces/60 milliliters.)

continued ►

4. At service, dust two medallions per portion in flour, shaking away any excess.

5. Heat the butter (about 1 teaspoon/5 grams per order) in a sauté pan, add the veal, and sauté on both sides until just cooked through.

6. Briefly heat the crabmeat in a microwave. Steam, pan-steam, or microwave the asparagus until al dente. Plate and serve at once.**

---

* Directions to prepare glace de viande are found in the note following Fond de Veau Lié (Chapter 11).

** There are several ways to plate this entrée. One suggestion is to pool the sauce on a plate and arrange the veal on the sauce. The asparagus could be sliced on the bias into ¾-inch lengths and scattered around the veal with the crabmeat piled high on top of the veal.

PORTION	KCAL	PROTEIN	FAT	CARB	SODIUM	CHOL
1 portion	265	25 gm	13 gm	11 gm	270 mg	110 mg

Roasting and Baking

The recipes in this chapter feature a wide variety of foods, all well suited to the special techniques discussed here. One of the major reasons we enjoy roasted foods is their special flavor. The classic "Sunday dinner" of roast chicken is a good example. The nutritional benefit of this dry heat method is that foods can be prepared without adding fats or oils during cooking. Instead, the natural juiciness of the food itself creates a moist, satisfying texture in the finished dish. A variety of special coatings, glazes, and sauces are among the special approaches employed in the recipes in this chapter to further highlight the quality of properly roasted and baked items.

The earliest form of cooking was to place foods over an open fire. This is the same technique as the one we refer to as "spit-roasting." Any food cooked in an oven could properly be referred to as baked. However, there is a generally agreed upon distinction between roasting and baking that is determined by the size of the item being prepared. Roasted foods are generally meats, fish, poultry, and game, which are cooked whole or in large pieces. Baked foods fall into one of three categories: meats, fish, or poultry that have been cut into portion-sized or smaller pieces; fruits and vegetables; items made from batters or doughs.

Smoke-roasting, or pan-smoking as it is also known, allows the chef to cook foods that have the appearance and flavor of traditionally smoked items. The benefit is that the foods need not be treated with salt cures, nitrates, or nitrites. It is vital to stop the smoking process just at the point that the food has developed a golden color and a distinctly smoky taste. Left in a smoke bath for too long, foods can quickly become bitter and acrid.

Apart from an oven and a pan to hold the food being prepared, the most valuable tool is an accurate thermometer. When foods are roasted to the exact moment of doneness, they are certain to be flavorful, juicy, and tender. This usually means taking foods out of the oven when their internal temperature is lower than the desired finished temperature. They will complete cooking; the heat retained in the food will continue to penetrate to the interior. This phenomenon is known as "carryover cooking."

FOCUS   TENDERLOIN OF BEEF WITH BLUE CHEESE AND HERB CRUST

Roasted and baked foods have several qualities that make them ideal for the nutritional kitchen. Foods emerge from the oven, spit-roaster, or smoke-roaster with flavors that cannot be duplicated by any other technique. They also do not have added cooking fats and oils, because these techniques use hot air to cook the foods. Despite the potentially drying effect, these are essentially quite gentle methods, because hot air is less efficient at transferring heat than hot fats, liquids, or even steam.

Traditional roasting often called for coating items with sheets of fatback or with basting liquids consisting mostly of fats such as those rendered from the meat itself. This was done to keep the food's surface from drying out as it roasted. In this recipe, a coating of bread crumbs flavored with herbs, garlic, and a hint of blue cheese is equally effective, without adding significantly to the total fat.

In roasted chicken, the skin bastes the meat as the bird cooks, but it easily can be removed before carving and serving. Placing a few fresh herbs between the skin and the meat gently flavors the chicken as it cooks and gives a subtle but greatly appreciated flavor boost to the naturally delicate taste of the meat.

In classic dishes prepared in a style that the French refer to as "en casserole," foods are surrounded with a moist sauce or cheese-topped custard and cooked to a meltingly smooth texture. Rich potato dishes such as "au gratin," or "Daupinoise" are good examples. They have been modified here by using skim milk thickened with arrowroot and a greatly reduced amount of grated cheese, which gives the suggestion of flavor.

TENDERLOIN OF BEEF WITH BLUE CHEESE AND HERB CRUST

Yield: 10 portions

2¼ pounds	Beef tenderloin, cut in medallions	1 kilogram
4 ounces	White bread, toasted	115 grams
2 ounces	Blue cheese	60 grams
½ ounce	Parsley, chopped	15 grams
½ ounce	Chives, chopped	15 grams
1 pinch	White pepper, freshly ground	1 pinch

SAUCE

1 pint	Fond de Veau Lié	480 milliliters
2 fluid ounces	Madeira wine	60 milliliters

a *Coating the portioned beef tenderloin with the blue cheese and herb mixture.*

1. Shape the medallions, using cheesecloth. Keep chilled until needed.

2. Combine the bread, blue cheese, parsley, chives, and pepper in a processor and process to form a coarse paste.

3. At service, sear the beef on both sides in a dry cast-iron skillet or nonstick pan.

4. Remove the meat and place it on a rack in a roasting pan. Top the medallions with the cheese mixture and roast in a moderate (350 degrees F/175 degrees C) oven to the desired doneness.

5. Deglaze the skillet with the Madeira and let it reduce slightly. Add the fond de veau lié and bring the sauce to a simmer.

6. Pool the sauce on heated plates. Slice the meat in half and arrange on the sauce.

b *Putting the beef in the oven to roast to the desired doneness.*

PORTION	KCAL	PROTEIN	FAT	CARB	SODIUM	CHOL
1 portion	230	25 gm	10 gm	6 gm	240 mg	70 mg

c *The finished dish as it would be presented to your guest.*

ROASTED MONKFISH WITH NIÇOISE OLIVE AND PERNOD SAUCE

Yield: 10 portions

3¼ pounds	Monkfish	1.5 kilograms

MARINADE

⅓ cup	Lime juice	50 milliliters
½ tablespoon	Green peppercorns, rinsed, mashed	5 grams
½ tablespoon	Tarragon, chopped	2 grams
½ tablespoon	Shallots, minced	6 grams

SAUCE

3 ounces	Tomato paste	85 grams
2 fluid ounces	Pernod	60 milliliters
1 pint	Fish Velouté	480 milliliters
¾ ounce	Niçoise olives, pitted	20 grams

1. Trim the monkfish to remove all connective tissue.

2. Combine the lime juice, peppercorns, tarragon, and shallots. Add the monkfish and turn to coat evenly with the marinade. Let it marinate for about 20 minutes.

3. Remove the fish from the marinade and place on a rack on a baking sheet. Sear under a salamander; then roast to an internal temperature of 140 degrees F/60 degrees C.

4. While roasting the fish, prepare the sauce as follows: Sauté the tomato paste until it takes on a rusty color and has a sweet aroma. Deglaze the pan with the Pernod, swirling until the paste is completely dissolved. Add the velouté and the olives.

5. Slice the monkfish into portions of about 4 ounces/115 grams. Serve with the sauce.

PORTION	KCAL	PROTEIN	FAT	CARB	SODIUM	CHOL
1 portion	120	17 gm	2 gm	6 gm	260 mg	40 mg

HERB-BREADED CHICKEN WITH CREAMY MUSTARD GRAVY

Yield: 10 portions

GRAVY

1 pint	Brown poultry stock*	480 milliliters
¾ **ounce**	Arrowroot	20 grams
3½ fluid ounces	Evaporated skimmed milk	100 milliliters
1¾ ounces	Dijon mustard	50 grams
2¼ pounds	Chicken breast, boneless, skinless	1 kilogram
4 ounces	Cornmeal	115 grams
2 ounces	Cornflake crumbs	60 grams
1½ ounces	Mixed, chopped herbs**	40 grams
8 fluid ounces	Buttermilk	240 milliliters

1. Add enough of the stock to the arrowroot to make a thin paste. Bring the remaining stock to a simmer and add the diluted arrowroot. Simmer an additional 1 or 2 minutes, until thickened, and add the milk and mustard. Blend well. Reserve until needed (properly cool and store if made in advance).

2. Trim any visible fat from the chicken. Keep refrigerated until needed.

3. Combine the cornmeal, cornflakes, and half of the herb mixture.

4. Combine the buttermilk with the remaining herbs in a bowl.

5. Dip the chicken breasts into the buttermilk mixture, and then into the seasoned cornmeal/cornflake mixture.

6. Place the breaded chicken on a rack in a roasting pan and bake until cooked through (about 20 minutes in a 375 degree F/190 degree C oven).

7. Reheat the gravy, if necessary, and serve with the chicken.

----

* To make brown poultry stock, prepare chicken stock as directed in the recipe found in Chapter 11, using roasted bones and giblets. Replace the water with 3 parts chicken stock and 1 part brown veal stock for a very rich flavor and body.

** Use a combination of equal parts parsley, tarragon, basil, and chives.

Serve the chicken with corn bread (recipe for Country Corn Bread follows). Additional accompaniments for this dish might be sugar snap peas and morels pan-steamed in chicken or vegetable stock.

PORTION	KCAL	PROTEIN	FAT	CARB	SODIUM	CHOL
1 portion	255	31 gm	3 gm	25 gm	225 mg	75 mg

COUNTRY CORN BREAD

Yield: 18 portions

10½ ounces	Cornmeal, yellow	300 grams
8 ounces	Flour, all-purpose	225 grams
3 tablespoons	Baking powder	36 grams
2 tablespoons	Sugar, granulated	25 grams
1 teaspoon	Salt	5 grams
1 pint	Buttermilk	480 milliliters
3	Eggs, large	3
3 fluid ounces	Egg whites	90 milliliters

1. Combine the dry ingredients. Stir to distribute the baking powder evenly.

2. Blend the buttermilk, eggs, and egg whites in a separate bowl.

3. Add the buttermilk mixture to the cornmeal mixture and stir just until combined. Do not overmix.

4. Spread the batter in a very lightly oiled baking pan or half sheet pan. Bake in a moderate (350 degrees F/175 degrees C) oven (use a convection oven, if available) until a skewer inserted in the center remains clean.

5. Slice as desired.

This batter may be spread on top of stew and used to create a "shepherd's pie" or country-style pot pie.

Any left-over corn bread will tend to go stale very quickly. It can be processed to crumbs in a food processor and used as a coating for meats, fish, or poultry to be baked or broiled, or as part of a stuffing.

PORTION	KCAL	PROTEIN	FAT	CARB	SODIUM	CHOL
1 portion	140	5 gm	1 gm	26 gm	350 mg	40 mg

ROASTED TENDERLOIN OF BEEF WITH
WILD MUSHROOMS AND FRESH ROSEMARY SAUCE

Yield: 10 portions

2¼ pounds	Beef tenderloin, trimmed, tied	1 kilogram
as needed	Black peppercorns, freshly milled	as needed
1 pint	Fond de Veau Lié	480 milliliters
7 ounces	Wild mushrooms, sliced	200 grams
¼ ounce	Shallots, minced, smothered	7 grams
1 clove	Garlic, minced, smothered	5 grams
2 teaspoons	Rosemary leaves, chopped	2 grams

1. Sear the tenderloin on all sides in a dry skillet. Place it on a rack, season liberally with pepper, and roast in a moderate oven (350 degrees F/175 degrees C) to the desired doneness (allow for carryover cooking).

2. Let the tenderloin rest 15 minutes before slicing.

3. Heat the fond de veau lié, and add the mushrooms. Simmer briefly, then add the shallots, garlic, and rosemary. Simmer to develop the flavor.

4. Slice the tenderloin and portion at 3½ ounces/100 grams each. Shingle the beef on heated plates and coat lightly with sauce.

Slicing the tenderloin thinly, to produce as many slices as reasonable while keeping the portion size at around 3½ ounces/100 grams, will help to make the serving appear larger.

A good presentation would be to pool the sauce on heated plates, and add a portion of potatoes. Then lean the slices on the mounded potatoes, fanning them, to give the plate some height. Very lightly drizzle the meat with some additional sauce, if desired.

Good accompaniments to this dish would be Potato Gratin, Potato Puree with Roasted Eggplant and Garlic, or Oven-Roasted Potatoes (all recipes in this chapter), and steamed vegetables such as broccoli, sugar snap peas, or haricots verts.

PORTION	KCAL	PROTEIN	FAT	CARB	SODIUM	CHOL
1 portion	195	23 gm	9 gm	3 gm	65 mg	70 mg

ROASTED SADDLE OF RABBIT WITH WILD MUSHROOMS AND NATURAL JUS

Yield: 10 portions

1½ pounds	Rabbit loin, boneless	680 grams
1 pound	Rabbit leg, lean, small dice, chilled	450 grams
1 ounce	Shallots, minced	30 grams
5 to 6	Black peppercorns, cracked	5 to 6
3 fluid ounces	White wine	90 milliliters
1 pound	Wild mushrooms, diced*	450 grams
2 teaspoons	Chervil leaves, chopped	2 grams
1 teaspoon	Tarragon leaves, chopped	1 gram
1 teaspoon	Basil leaves, minced	1 gram
½ teaspoon	Salt	3 grams
as needed	Caul fat	as needed
1 pint	Brown veal or rabbit stock	480 milliliters

1. Trim the loin well, and reserve until needed.

2. Grind the leg meat into a fine paste in a food processor, and then transfer to a bowl. Refrigerate until needed.

3. Smother the shallots and peppercorns in the white wine until the shallots are tender and the wine has reduced by about half.

4. Add the wild mushrooms and sauté them over moderate to high heat until their released moisture is reduced. Cool this mixture quickly by spreading in a layer on a sheet pan and placing in the refrigerator or freezer until thoroughly chilled.

5. Fold the mushroom mixture into the ground rabbit meat, along with the salt and chopped fresh herbs.

6. Stretch out a piece of caul fat large enough to wrap completely around the loin when it is laid flat. Mound the forcemeat filling down the center of the loin, and use the caul fat to roll up the rabbit in the same manner as for a galantine.

7. Roast the rabbit in a moderate (350 degrees F/175 degrees C) oven until it has an internal temperature of 130 degrees F/55 degrees C. Remove from the oven and allow carryover cooking to bring it up to a final internal temperature of 140 degrees F/60 degrees C.

8. Deglaze the roasting pan with the stock and allow it to reduce slightly to a flavorful jus.

9. Slice the rabbit into portions and serve with the jus.

---

* Trim away any tough stems from the mushrooms before dicing them. The selection of wild mushrooms will usually depend upon the season. If they are unavailable or too expensive, use domestic mushrooms and bolster their flavor by incorporating 1 to 2 ounces/30 to 60 grams of dried wild mushrooms that have been reconstituted in warm stock or wine. Drain the liquid away from the mushrooms and dice them. To provide additional flavor, filter the liquid and then add it to the mushrooms as they cook.

The rabbit loin shown in the chapter introduction photograph is served with a selection of seasonal vegetables and white bean puree. To prepare the white bean puree, use the recipe for Michigan White Bean Soup found in Chapter 14, cooking the beans until they are extremely tender. Puree them to a very fine paste, and use a pastry bag with a plain tip to pipe onto the plate.

PORTION	KCAL	PROTEIN	FAT	CARB	SODIUM	CHOL
1 portion	180	24 gm	7 gm	3 gm	90 mg	70 mg

HONEY-GLAZED DUCK BREAST

Yield: 10 portions

10	Duck breasts, one wing joint attached	10
¼ ounce	Shallots, minced	7 grams
2 cloves	Garlic, minced	10 grams
1 ounce	Tomato paste	30 grams
¾ ounce	Dijon mustard	20 grams
1¾ ounces	Honey	50 grams
1½ fluid ounces	Red wine vinegar	45 milliliters
1 teaspoon	Thyme leaves, chopped	1 gram
¾ teaspoon	Black peppercorns, freshly ground	1.5 grams
20 fluid ounces	Fond de Veau Lié	600 milliliters

1. Remove the skin from the duck breasts, trim away any visible fat, and french the wing bone. Remove the tenderloin and reserve for another use.

2. Sear the duck breast in a nonstick or seasoned cast-iron skillet to get a good color on both sides. Remove and reserve.

3. Add the shallots and garlic to the pan. Sauté briefly until the shallots are translucent.

4. Add the tomato paste and mustard and sauté until the tomato paste has a rusty color and a sweet aroma.

5. Add the honey and vinegar; heat until the honey liquefies. Add the thyme and peppercorns and blend well.

6. Return the duck breasts, along with any juices they may have given off, to the pan and turn to coat evenly with the honey mixture. Remove the ducks to a rack set in a roasting pan and complete the cooking in a moderate (375 degree F/190 degree C) oven until they are medium rare (have reached an internal temperature of 140 degrees F/60 degrees C).

7. Deglaze the skillet with the fond de veau lié. Bring the sauce to a simmer. When the duck has been removed from the oven, deglaze the roasting pan with water—if there are any drippings—and add them to the sauce.

8. Slice the duck breast and serve with the sauce.

The recipe for Fond de Veau Lié can be found in Chapter 11.

HONEY-GLAZED PORK: Substitute pork tenderloins for the duck breast. Use 2¼ pounds/1 kilogram of trimmed pork, and roast to an internal temperature of 150 degrees F/65 degrees C. Slice thinly after the pork has rested about 10 minutes.

This glaze would also complement chicken. If desired, substitute a coarse-grained mustard for the Dijon, and replace the thyme with fresh tarragon. Green peppercorn may be substituted for the black peppercorn. Be sure to rinse away the brine first.

PORTION	KCAL	PROTEIN	FAT	CARB	SODIUM	CHOL
1 portion	230	34 gm	7 gm	5 gm	299 mg	130 mg

DUCK BREAST IN CABBAGE CRÉPINETTE

Yield: 10 portions

10	Duck breast	10

MARINADE

1¾ fluid ounces	Red wine, dry	50 milliliters
1¾ fluid ounces	Chicken stock	50 milliliters
¾ fluid ounces	Balsamic vinegar	20 milliliters
1 teaspoon	Juniper berries, cracked	2 grams
1	Bay leaf	1
1 ounce	Shallots, minced	30 grams
20	Savoy cabbage leaves	20

DUXELLES

3½ ounces	Onions, minced	100 grams
1 clove	Garlic, minced	5 grams
1 pound	Mushrooms, assorted*	450 grams
1 fluid ounce	Madeira	30 milliliters
2 teaspoons	Thyme leaves, chopped	2 grams
1 fluid ounce	Heavy cream, chilled	30 milliliters
2	Egg whites, chilled	2
1 pint	Fond de Veau Lié	480 milliliters

1. Trim the duck breasts well and remove the tenderloins. Pull the tendons out and cut the tenderloins into dice. Refrigerate until needed.

2. Blanch the cabbage leaves in boiling water, drain, and rinse with cool water. Pat dry and keep refrigerated until needed.

3. Combine the red wine, ¾ fluid ounce/20 milliliters of the stock, vinegar, juniper berries, bay leaf, and shallots in a shallow container. Add the duck breasts and turn to coat them evenly. Marinate under refrigeration for about 1 hour.

4. Heat about 1 fluid ounce/30 milliliters of stock in a sauté pan; add the onions and garlic. Cook until they are tender and translucent.

5. Add the mushrooms and sauté until their moisture starts to release into the pan.

6. Add the Madeira and thyme to the mushrooms and continue to cook until a dry duxelles forms. Remove the duxelles from the heat and cool completely.

7. Place the duck meat into the chilled bowl of a food processor and process to a fine paste. Add the egg whites and heavy cream, and mix until blended to make a mousseline farce.

8. Remove the farce to a bowl set over ice. Fold in the duxelles. Keep chilled until needed.

9. Remove the breasts from the marinade and place on a rack in a roasting pan set over hickory chips. Cover the pan tightly and place over direct heat. Pan-smoke the breasts until the smell of smoke is noticeable (about 3 minutes). Remove from the smoke bath and let the breasts rest for 15 minutes.

10. Divide the mousseline and duxelles mixture evenly between the breasts, and place each breast on a single cabbage leaf. Wrap the breast in the cabbage; wrap a second leaf around the breast.

11. Bake the duck in a moderate (350 degree F/175 degree C) oven to an internal temperature of about 130 degrees F/55 degrees C. Serve the duck with heated Fond de Veau Lié.

---

* Mushroom availability varies with the seasons. Choose whatever is currently available. If no fresh wild mushrooms can be found, use domestic mushrooms, and add some additional flavor by adding about 1 ounce/30 grams of dried mushrooms. The dried mushrooms should be reconstituted in warm stock or Madeira before adding them to the duxelles. Add the liquid used to reconstitute the mushrooms to the duxelles as they sauté for the best flavor.

If desired, the breast may be sliced thinly on the bias and fanned on the plate. The fond may be seasoned by adding a small amount of Madeira.

If the duxelles mixture is too loose, it may be bound with a small amount of bread crumbs.

PORTION	KCAL	PROTEIN	FAT	CARB	SODIUM	CHOL
1 portion	250	36 gm	9 gm	4 gm	160 mg	135 mg

ROASTED LOIN OF PORK WITH HONEY AND MUSTARD

Yield: 10 portions

2¼ pounds	Pork loin, trimmed	1 kilogram
6 fluid ounces	Stock (chicken or pork)	180 milliliters
2 cloves	Garlic, minced	10 grams
½ ounce	Shallots, minced	15 grams
1 tablespoon	Thyme leaves	4 grams
1 ounce	Tomato paste	30 grams
2 ounces	Pommery mustard	60 grams
2 teaspoons	Black peppercorns, cracked	4 grams
1 ounce	Honey	30 grams
2 ounces	Red wine vinegar	60 milliliters
1 pint	Fond de Veau Lié	480 milliliters

1. Dry-sear the pork loin on both sides. Remove it from the pan.

2. Add about 2 ounces/60 milliliters of stock to deglaze any reduced fond. Let the stock reduce until nearly dry.

3. Add the garlic and shallots and sweat until they are translucent.

4. Add the thyme leaves, tomato paste, mustard, and pepper to the garlic mixture. Sauté until there is a sweet aroma and the tomato paste takes on a rusty color.

5. Add the honey and vinegar; simmer just until the mixture is blended and thick enough to use as a glaze.

6. Return the pork loin to the pan and roll it to coat evenly with the glaze.

7. Place the glazed pork on a rack in a pan; roast in a moderate (350 degree F/175 degree C) oven until an internal temperature of 150 degrees F/65 degrees C is reached. Remove the pork from the oven and let it rest while the sauce is being completed.

8. Add 2 fluid ounces/60 milliliters of stock to the pan used to prepare the glaze. Bring the stock to a simmer and reduce until it is nearly dry. Add the fond de veau lié; bring to a simmer.

9. Use the remaining stock to deglaze the roasting pan, if there are any drippings in the bottom. Add them to the sauce. Simmer the sauce briefly to reduce until it is thick enough to coat the back of a wooden spoon.

10. Slice the pork into 3½ ounce/100 gram portions and serve with the sauce.

The character of this dish can be changed by making the following substitutions. Use fresh cilantro to replace thyme, Creole mustard for Pommery, maple syrup or molasses for honey. Habañero or other chili-flavored vinegar may be used instead of red wine vinegar. At the last moment scatter a fine dice of jalapeños in the sauce.

PORTION	KCAL	PROTEIN	FAT	CARB	SODIUM	CHOL
1 portion	240	32 gm	8 gm	5 gm	210 mg	135 mg

MEDALLIONS OF PORK STUFFED WITH CHESTNUTS

Yield: 10 portions

FORCEMEAT

3½ ounces	Lean pork trim, chilled, diced	100 grams
1 tablespoon	Egg white, chilled	11 grams
1¾ fluid ounces	Heavy cream, chilled	50 milliliters
7 ounces	Chestnuts, cooked, diced	200 grams
1¾ pounds	Pork loin medallions	800 grams

SAUCE

3½ fluid ounces	Brandy	100 milliliters
14 fluid ounces	Fond de Veau Lié	400 milliliters
3 tablespoons	Brown sugar	40 grams
3 tablespoons	Raisins	40 grams

1. To make the mousseline forcemeat, grind the chilled lean pork trim through a medium die, then place with the egg white in the chilled bowl of a food processor and process to a fine paste.

2. Add the heavy cream in three parts, scraping down the bowl between each addition. Do not allow the mousseline to become warm.

3. Remove the mousseline farce to a bowl set over ice and fold in the chestnuts.

4. Cut pockets in the sides of the pork medallions and pipe an equal portion of the mousseline into each.

5. Sear the medallions in a nonstick skillet or cast-iron pan. Remove them to a rack set in a baking sheet. Bake in a moderate (375 degree F/190 degree C) oven until the mousseline stiffens but is still moist (about 12 to 15 minutes).

6. Prepare the sauce in the skillet used to sear the medallions: add the brandy and heat, then flame to burn the brandy.

7. Add the fond de veau lié, sugar, and raisins. Simmer very gently over low heat until the flavor is properly developed.

8. Serve with the medallions.

To present the medallions, slice each one thinly, and then shingle on heated plates. Pool the sauce around and over the medallions.

A combination wild and long-grain rice pilaf or a portion of pumpkin-flavored pasta (see the variation on the Basic Pasta Dough recipe in Chapter 19) would be good with this dish.

PORTION	KCAL	PROTEIN	FAT	CARB	SODIUM	CHOL
1 portion	220	20 gm	5 gm	55 gm	55 mg	65 mg

PHEASANT BREAST LUXEMBOURG

Yield: 10 portions

5	Pheasant, whole	5

DUXELLES

½ ounce	Butter	15 grams
1 clove	Garlic, minced	5 grams
1 teaspoon	Shallots, minced	5 grams
2½ ounces	Leeks, minced	70 grams
3½ ounces	Chanterelles, diced	100 grams
3 fluid ounces	Madeira wine	90 milliliters
2 teaspoons	Sage leaves, minced	2 grams
½ teaspoon	Salt	3 grams
7 fluid ounces	Heavy cream, chilled	200 milliliters
14 fluid ounces	Fond de faisan lié*	400 milliliters

1. Cut out the backbone and cut away the legs from each pheasant. Trim the first two joints of the wing. Leave the breast attached to the bone and hold in the refrigerator until needed. Trim away 14 ounces/400 grams of lean meat from the legs, and cut into small dice. Keep this meat chilled until needed.

2. Heat the butter in a sauté pan over moderate heat. Add the garlic, shallots, and leeks. Sauté until they are translucent.

3. Add the mushrooms; sauté until they begin to release their moisture.

4. Add half of the Madeira and continue to cook until a dry duxelles forms.

5. Remove the duxelles from the heat and fold in the sage and salt. Let it cool.

6. Grind the lean leg meat through a fine die, and place in the chilled bowl of a food processor. Process to a smooth paste.

7. Make a mousseline farce by adding the chilled heavy cream in three parts, blending after each addition and scraping down the sides of the bowl.

8. Remove the mousseline to a bowl set over ice, and fold in the duxelles.

9. Loosen, but do not remove, the skin from the pheasant breast. Pipe about ¾ ounce/25 grams onto each side of each breast between the skin and the meat. Even the layer of mousseline by smoothing the skin over the breast.

10. Bake the pheasant in a moderate (350 degree F/175 degree C) oven until the juices run clear (about 20 to 24 minutes). Remove the breast meat from the bone, and serve one half per order.

11. While the pheasant is roasting, slowly heat the fond de faisan lié and the remaining Madeira. Adjust the seasoning with some ground pepper, if necessary.

---

* Fond de faisan lié is made by following the recipe for fond de veau lié, substituting pheasant bones for veal. Reserve the bones from fabricating the pheasant to make the fond.

Slice the breast meat on an angle and shingle it on the plate. Pool the Madeira sauce around the breast. Serve with a Rice Pilaf (recipe in Chapter 17) or barley pilaf, or Potato Gratin (recipe in Chapter 16). Other appropriate accompaniments might include Pecan Carrots (recipe in Chapter 17) or steamed asparagus with Lemon Glaze (recipe in Chapter 12).

This recipe could also be prepared using Cornish game hen. To accompany the game hen, modify the sauce by finishing it with 1½ ounces/45 milliliters of dry sherry and 1 tablespoon/15 grams of currant jelly.

PORTION	KCAL	PROTEIN	FAT	CARB	SODIUM	CHOL
1 portion	240	27 gm	11 gm	4 gm	160 mg	30 mg

SALMON BAKED IN PHYLLO

Yield: 10 portions

MOUSSELINE FORCEMEAT

5 ounces	Salmon scraps, diced, chilled	140 grams
2 fluid ounces	Heavy cream, chilled	60 milliliters
1	Egg white, chilled	1
1 teaspoon	Tarragon leaves, chopped	1 gram
1 teaspoon	Basil leaves, chopped	1 gram
¼ teaspoon	Salt	2 grams

DUXELLES

¼ ounce	Butter, unsalted	8 grams
½ ounce	Shallots, minced	15 grams
4 ounces	Mushrooms, button, chopped	115 grams
1½ ounces	Morels, chopped	50 grams

1½ pounds	Salmon fillet, sliced into portions	700 grams
10	Phyllo sheets	10

SAUCE

2 fluid ounces	White wine, dry	60 milliliters
⅛ teaspoon	Saffron threads, crushed	150 milligrams
1 pint	Fish Velouté*	480 milliliters
5 ounces	Tomato concassé, diced	140 grams
1 tablespoon	Chives, fresh, chopped	3 grams

1. To make the mousseline: Puree the salmon in a chilled food processor to a smooth paste. Add the cream, egg white, herbs, and salt. Pulse the machine off and on until the ingredients are just incorporated. Keep chilled until needed.

2. To make the duxelles: Heat the butter. Add the shallots and sauté until they are translucent. Add the mushrooms and cook until the released liquid has cooked away. Remove from the heat, spread in a layer on a sheet pan, and let cool completely.

3. Spread the forcemeat on the salmon and top with the duxelles.

4. Wrap the salmon in the phyllo and bake in a 400 degree F/203 degree C oven for about 12 minutes.

5. To make the sauce: heat the wine and steep the saffron in it. Add it to the velouté and simmer until a deep-golden color is reached. Add the concassé and the chives. Pool the sauce on heated plates and serve the salmon on top.

---

* See the recipe for Velouté-style Sauce in Chapter 11.

PORTION	KCAL	PROTEIN	FAT	CARB	SODIUM	CHOL
1 portion	235	24 gm	8 gm	15 gm	215 mg	60 mg

BREAST OF CHICKEN WITH PEACHES IN ZINFANDEL WINE SAUCE

Yield: 10 portions

5	Chicken breast, whole	5
8 fluid ounces	Apple cider	240 milliliters
1 tablespoon	Shallots, minced	15 grams
1 teaspoon	Garlic, minced	5 grams
¾ fluid ounce	Apple cider vinegar	20 milliliters
9 ounces	Peaches, peeled, sliced	250 grams
1 pint	Fond de Veau Lié	480 milliliters
1¾ fluid ounces	Red Zinfandel	50 milliliters

1. Place the chicken breast (still on the bone) in a shallow container. Combine the cider, shallots, garlic, and vinegar into a marinade. Pour over the breasts and allow chicken to marinate for 30 minutes.

2. Place the breasts on a baking sheet and roast until the juices run clear (about 25 to 30 minutes). Remove from the oven and let them rest for a few minutes.

3. Combine the peaches, fond de veau lié, and Zinfandel. Bring this sauce slowly to a simmer while the chicken is roasting.

4. Remove the breast meat from the bones, and remove and discard the skin. Serve the chicken with the sauce.

———

Barley, rice or bulgur pilaf, or Potato Puree with Roasted Eggplant and Garlic (see recipe in this chapter) would be good accompaniments. Other suggestions include steamed seasonal vegetables, such as green beans, zucchini, broccoli, or sugar snap peas.

PORTION	KCAL	PROTEIN	FAT	CARB	SODIUM	CHOL
1 portion	170	28 gm	2 gm	7 gm	125 mg	70 mg

PAN-SMOKED CHICKEN
WITH APPLES AND GREEN PEPPERCORNS

Yield: 10 portions

2¼ pounds	Chicken breast, skinless, boneless	1 kilogram
24 fluid ounces	Apple cider	720 milliliters
2 fluid ounces	Apple cider vinegar	60 milliliters
1 ounce	Shallots, minced	30 grams
3 cloves	Garlic, minced	15 grams
1 pint	Fond de Veau Lié	480 milliliters
9 ounces	Apples, peeled, sliced	255 grams
1 ounce	Green peppercorns, rinsed, mashed	30 grams

1. Trim the chicken breasts, and place in a shallow container with 8 fluid ounces/250 milliliters of cider, all of the cider vinegar, and half of shallots and garlic. Turn to coat evenly. Let marinate for about 30 minutes.

2. Combine the remaining cider, shallots, and garlic and reduce until syrupy. Add the fond de veau lié, apples, and peppercorns; simmer gently for 5 minutes, then keep warm while cooking the chicken. (If necessary, thin the sauce with a little additional cider.)

3. Remove the chicken from the marinade and place on a rack in a roasting pan over some fine hickory chips. Cover tightly and place over direct heat until the smoke from the chips can be smelled.

4. Pan-smoke the chicken for another 2 to 3 minutes, then remove from the smoke bath. If desired, the chicken can be marked on the grill at this point. Finish cooking the chicken in a 350 degree F/175 degree C oven until the juices run clear. Serve with the sauce.

Slice the chicken breast on an angle and serve on a pool of the sauce. Suitable accompaniments for this dish might be Basic or Orzo Pasta (see recipes in Chapter 19) or Risotto (recipe in Chapter 17). Choose bright seasonal vegetables that will be steamed or lightly "stewed" in stock.

PORTION	KCAL	PROTEIN	FAT	CARB	SODIUM	CHOL
1 portion	175	25 gm	2 gm	14 gm	180 mg	60 mg

PAN-SMOKED CHICKEN BREASTS
WITH ARTICHOKE AND MUSTARD SAUCE

Yield: 10 portions

2¼ pounds	Chicken breasts, boneless, skinless	1 kilogram
2 teaspoons	Vegetable oil	10 milliliters
1 ounce	Shallots, minced	30 grams
5 fluid ounces	Chicken Stock, reduced by half*	150 milliliters
10 fluid ounces	Fond de Veau Lié*	300 milliliters
1 ounce	Dijon mustard	30 grams
2 ounces	Pommery mustard	60 grams
1½ fluid ounces	Balsamic vinegar	45 milliliters
10	Artichoke hearts, blanched, quartered	10
5 ounces	Calamata olives, pitted, halved	140 grams
2 tablespoons	Tarragon leaves, chiffonade	6 grams

1. Trim the chicken breasts and pound them lightly to an even thickness.

2. Place them on a rack in a pan containing some fine wood chips. Cover tightly and place the pan over direct heat until the smoke is easy to smell. Reduce the heat slightly and continue to smoke for another 3 to 4 minutes. Remove the breasts from the pan and finish cooking them on a rack in a moderate (350 degree F/175 degree C) oven.

3. Heat the oil in a second pan and add the shallots. Sauté until they are translucent.

4. Deglaze the sauté pan with the stock. Add the fond de veau lié, mustards, and vinegar. Simmer the sauce until the flavors have developed.

5. Add the remaining ingredients to the sauce. Slice the chicken and serve it with the sauce.

---

* See the recipes in Chapter 11. The stock should be reduced by half before it is measured.

Some good accompaniments to this dish include steamed baby vegetables and polenta cut into triangles, as shown in the accompanying photograph.

PORTION	KCAL	PROTEIN	FAT	CARB	SODIUM	CHOL
1 portion	285	31 gm	4 gm	31 gm	275 mg	65 mg

PAN-SMOKED TURKEY WITH PORT WINE SAUCE

Yield: 10 portions

1 pound 14 ounces	Turkey breast cutlets (10 each)*	850 grams

FILLING

1 tablespoon	Butter	15 grams
1 tablespoon	Shallots, minced	12 grams
1 clove	Garlic, minced	5 grams
2½ ounces	Wild rice, cooked and cooled	70 grams
2½ ounces	Apples, peeled, julienned	70 grams
3½ ounces	Turkey breast meat, ground	100 grams
1 ounce	Heavy cream	30 milliliters
½ teaspoon	Salt	3 grams

SAUCE

9 ounces	Wild mushrooms, sliced	255 grams
1 teaspoon	Sage leaves, chopped	1 gram
1 pint	Fond de Veau Lié	480 milliliters
1¾ fluid ounces	Port wine	50 milliliters

1. Pound the cutlets to an even thickness, and keep chilled while preparing the filling.

2. To make the filling: Heat the butter over moderate heat and add the shallots and garlic; sauté until translucent. Remove them from the heat and cool. Add them to the rice, apples, and ground turkey. Stir until well-blended (ingredients should be kept cool, work over ice if necessary). Add the heavy cream and salt, and stir to blend.

3. Divide the filling evenly between the cutlets, and then roll up so that the filling is completely enclosed.

4. Set the cutlets on a rack in a roasting pan over fine hickory chips. Cover tightly, and set over direct heat until the smoke from the chips can be smelled.

5. Pan-smoke for an additional 2 to 3 minutes over direct heat or in the oven, then remove the turkey cutlets from the smoke bath, and finish baking in a moderate (350 degree F/175 degree C) oven.

6. Heat the mushrooms, sage, fond de veau lié and the port over low heat as the turkey roasts to make a sauce. Serve the turkey with the sauce.

———

* The turkey may be replaced with chicken.

   Slice the rolled cutlets, and shingle them on the plate. Coat the slices with the sauce, and pool some around them. Serve with baked acorn squash and cranberry salsa.

PORTION	KCAL	PROTEIN	FAT	CARB	SODIUM	CHOL
1 portion	180	26 gm	4 gm	6 gm	185 mg	70 mg

LAMB IN A SWEATER

Yield: 10 portions

DUXELLES

1 teaspoon	Olive oil	10 milliliters
1 clove	Garlic, minced	5 grams
1 tablespoon	Shallots, minced	15 grams
12 ounces	Wild mushrooms, diced	350 grams
4 fluid ounces	Madeira wine*	120 milliliters
2¼ pounds	Loin lamb chops, frenched	1 kilogram
10 sheets	Phyllo dough, sheets folded in quarters	10 sheets
14 fluid ounces	Fond de Veau Lié	400 milliliters
to taste	Black pepper, ground	to taste

1. Heat the oil in a sauté pan over moderate heat. Add the garlic and shallots and sauté until they become translucent.

2. Add the mushrooms; sauté until they begin to release their moisture.

3. Add the Madeira, and cook until the mushroom mixture forms a dry duxelles (about 7 or 8 minutes). Remove the duxelles from the heat and cool.

4. Sear the lamb chops in a nonstick skillet or cast-iron pan, remove, and cool. Reserve the pan, if there are any drippings.

5. Divide the duxelles evenly between the lamb chops, and then wrap each chop neatly in a phyllo sheet that has been folded in quarters.

6. Bake the chops in a moderate (350 to 375 degree F/175 to 190 degree C) oven to the desired doneness (about 130 degrees F/55 degrees C internal temperature for medium).

7. Deglaze the pan used to sear the lamb chops with the fond de veau lié and heat to a simmer. Add the Madeira and allow the sauce to simmer slowly while the lamb bakes.

———

To serve, pool the sauce on a heated plate, and slice the lamb parcels in half.

    * The Madeira may be replaced with sherry or a combination of sherry and sherry wine vinegar, if desired.

This recipe could also be used to prepare a suprême of chicken, pheasant, or Cornish game hen.

PORTION	KCAL	PROTEIN	FAT	CARB	SODIUM	CHOL
1 portion	220	220 gm	23 gm	7 gm	13 mg	70 mg

SWEET POTATO CAKES

Yield: 10 portions

12 ounces	Idaho potatoes, peeled, diced	340 grams
12 ounces	Sweet potatoes, peeled, dice	340 grams
4 ounces	Bread crumbs	115 grams
1 ounce	Mayonnaise, prepared	30 grams
3 fluid ounces	Skim milk	90 milliliters
1½ tablespoons	Chives, chopped	5 grams
1½ tablespoons	Dill, chopped	5 grams
¾ teaspoon	Black peppercorns, cracked	750 milligrams
2 tablespoons	Capers, rinsed, chopped	6 grams

1. Boil the Idaho and sweet potatoes separately until tender enough to mash easily.

2. Put them through a ricer while they are still hot. When cool, add the remaining ingredients.

3. Form the mixture into cakes that weigh about 1½ ounces/45 grams each.

4. To finish the cakes, bake them in a hot (475 degree F/245 degree C) oven or cook on a hot, well-seasoned soapstone griddle or cast-iron skillet.

PORTION	KCAL	PROTEIN	FAT	CARB	SODIUM	CHOL
1 portion	115	3 gm	2 gm	23 gm	100 mg	5 mg

FOCUS   ROASTING GARLIC, EGGPLANT, AND PEPPERS

GARLIC   Place whole bulbs, still covered with the papery outer skin, on a bed of coarse salt in a gratin dish or other small baking dish. Roast in a hot oven (the temperature is not critical, 325 to 475 degrees F/165 to 245 degrees C is acceptable) until the skin has turned brown and juices are beginning to escape. Allow the bulbs to cool, then slice away the bottom and squeeze out the flesh. It will have a rich, sweet taste, without the harsh taste of raw garlic.

This puree can be used to flavor a variety of other dishes, as an ingredient in herb purees, or as a coating, between the skin and the flesh, for roasted poultry.

PEPPERS   The method selected to roast peppers will depend upon the quantity being prepared, as well as the particular needs of an individual recipe. The richest flavor is achieved by roasting the peppers directly in an open flame or on a hot grill until the skin is evenly charred. Placing them in a covered container while they cool helps to steam the skin away from the flesh. The yield is slightly less than when peppers are roasted in a very hot oven (450 to 475 degrees F/230 to 245 degrees C) or a convection oven set at 375 degrees F/190 degrees C.

To roast peppers in the oven, cut them in half from stem end to the bottom. Place, cut side down, in the heated oven and roast until the skin appears blistered and dull. It will not become as evenly black as when peppers are charred on a grill or in a flame. Cover the baking sheet with a second inverted sheet to steam the skin loose.

When the peppers are cool enough to handle, peel away the skin, and remove and discard the seeds, stem, and ribs.

a   *Hold the pepper in a gas flame with a kitchen fork.*

b   *Place halved peppers on a lightly oiled sheet and put in oven or under a broiler.*

EGGPLANT   Slice the eggplant in half from stem to blossom end (lengthwise) and score the flesh. Place, cut side down, on a baking sheet lined with parchment paper. It may be helpful to lightly spray the cut portion of the eggplant with some oil.

Roast the eggplant in a hot oven (400 to 425 degrees F/205 to 220 degrees C) until the flesh is very soft. Remove the eggplant and scoop the flesh out. Roasted eggplant can be used as an ingredient in Moutabel (see Chapter 12).

POTATO PUREE WITH ROASTED EGGPLANT AND GARLIC

Yield: 12 portions

1 pound, 9 ounces	Potatoes, baked, pureed	700 grams
12 ounces	Eggplant, roasted, peeled, seeded, pureed	340 grams
¾ ounce	Garlic, roasted, pureed	20 grams
3½ fluid ounces	Skim milk	100 milliliters
2 fluid ounces	Heavy cream	60 milliliters
¾ fluid ounce	Extra-virgin olive oil	20 milliliters
½ teaspoon	Salt	3 grams
to taste	Cayenne pepper	to taste

1. Combine the potato, eggplant, and garlic purees. (This should be done while they are still warm.)

2. Bring the milk, cream, and olive oil to a boil and immediately add them to the combined purees. Add the salt and cayenne pepper.

3. To serve, hold puree warm in a pastry bag, in a bain-marie. Pipe out the mixture as needed.

———

This recipe may be varied by eliminating the eggplant and increasing the amount of potatoes to 2¼ pounds/1 kilogram.

PORTION	KCAL	PROTEIN	FAT	CARB	SODIUM	CHOL
1 portion	120	3 gm	4 gm	19 gm	120 mg	7 mg

PAN-SMOKED SALMON FILLET
WITH TOMATO-HORSERADISH SAUCE

Yield: 10 portions

1 fluid ounce	Lime juice	30 milliliters
2 cloves	Garlic, minced	10 grams
2 teaspoons	Shallots, minced	10 grams
½ teaspoon	Peppercorns, cracked	1 gram
2¼ pounds	Salmon fillets, sliced into portions	1 kilogram
1 pint	Tomato-Horseradish Sauce*	480 milliliters

1. Combine the lime juice, garlic, shallots, and peppercorns in a bowl. Add the salmon slices (3½ ounces/100 grams each), and turn to coat evenly. Let marinate for about 15 minutes.

2. Place the salmon on a rack set over hickory chips in a roasting pan. Cover tightly, and place over direct heat until the smoke from the chips can be smelled.

3. Place the pan in the oven or continue to smoke over direct heat for another 2 to 3 minutes.

4. Remove the salmon, and complete cooking time in a moderate (350 degree F/175 degree C) oven, if necessary.

5. Heat the sauce while the salmon is pan-smoking.

The salmon should be pan-smoked only until it becomes light-golden in color. If it is left in the smoke bath too long, it will take on a disagreeable flavor.

* Pool the Tomato-Horseradish Sauce (see recipe in Chapter 11) on heated plates and place the salmon on top. Some good accompaniments to this dish might be a selection of fresh steamed vegetables, Quinoa Pilaf with Red and Yellow Peppers (see recipe in Chapter 17) or herbed pasta.

PORTION	KCAL	PROTEIN	FAT	CARB	SODIUM	CHOL
1 portion	150	22 gm	5 gm	4 gm	120 mg	55 mg

POTATO GRATIN

Yield: 24 portions

2 quarts	Skim milk	2 liters
4 pounds	Idaho potatoes, peeled, sliced	1.8 kilograms
4 cloves	Garlic, minced	20 grams
1 teaspoon	Salt	5 grams
½ ounce	Arrowroot	15 grams
6 ounces	Gruyère cheese, grated	170 grams
4 ounces	Bread crumbs, fresh, white	115 grams
4 ounces	Parmesan cheese, grated	115 grams

1. Combine the milk, potatoes, garlic, and salt. Bring to a simmer. Simmer until the potatoes are nearly tender.

2. Dilute the arrowroot in a small amount of cold water, milk, or stock. Add to the simmering potato mixture to lightly thicken.

continued ►

3. Remove the potatoes from the heat and stir in the Gruyère cheese. Pour into a 2-inch-deep hotel pan.

4. Combine the bread crumbs and Parmesan. Scatter evenly over the potatoes. Bake in a moderate (350 degree F/175 degree C) oven until browned.

5. Allow the potatoes to set for 10 to 12 minutes before slicing into portions.

PORTION	KCAL	PROTEIN	FAT	CARB	SODIUM	CHOL
1 portion	100	5 gm	2 gm	15 gm	169 mg	10 mg

ROASTED CORN

Yield: 1 pound/450 grams of kernels

3 to 4 ears	Corn in the husk	3 to 4 ears
1 teaspoon	Black peppercorns, cracked	2 grams
2 tablespoons	Fresh herbs*	6 grams

1. Loosen the husk from the corn, but do not pull it away. Sprinkle each ear with some of the pepper and herbs.

2. Pull the husk back up around the corn and tie it in place. Dampen the husks and place on a baking sheet.

3. Roast the corn in a 400 degree F/205 degree C oven until the corn is cooked and tender (about 15 minutes).

4. Remove the corn from the oven, pull away the husk, and cut the kernels from the cob.

———

* A number of herbs make good accompaniments to corn: basil, oregano, cilantro, thyme, chervil, marjoram, tarragon, and chives are all suitable. The leaves may be left whole, or minced if they are very large.

The yield from an ear of corn will vary, depending upon its size. This yield is based on ears that are approximately 5 to 6 inches long.

The next three recipes use roasted corn. Other uses include as an ingredient in cornbread, succotash, soups, or salads.

PORTION	KCAL	PROTEIN	FAT	CARB	SODIUM	CHOL
1 portion	40	2 gm	1 gm	9 gm	8 mg	0 mg

ROASTED CORN AND BLACK BEANS

Yield: 10 portions

1 teaspoon	Olive oil	5 milligrams
2 cloves	Garlic, minced	10 grams
1 teaspoon	Jalapeño pepper, seeded, minced	5 grams
1½ ounces	Red onion, diced	40 grams
1 pound	Corn kernels, roasted	450 grams
1 pound	Black beans, cooked and drained	450 grams
¼ teaspoon	Salt	2 grams
1 tablespoon	Cilantro, chopped	3 grams
1 tablespoon	Lime juice	15 milliliters
1¾ ounces	Tomato concassé, small dice	50 grams

1. Heat the olive oil and add the garlic, pepper, and onions. Sauté until the onions are translucent and start to take on some color.

2. Add the corn, beans, salt, cilantro, tomato, and lime juice. Toss repeatedly over high heat until all of the ingredients are very hot. Serve at once.

If desired, the recipe may be portioned and reheated in the microwave as follows:

Sauté the garlic, pepper, and onions as directed in Step 1. Then, away from the heat, combine all of the remaining ingredients with the sautéed mixture. Weigh out portions at 3½ ounces/100 grams each into microwaveable containers or dishes. Cover loosely with plastic, and reheat on the highest power setting for about 45 seconds. (The time will vary, depending upon the power of the individual machine and number of portions being reheated at once.) Stir to distribute heat evenly, and serve.

PORTION	KCAL	PROTEIN	FAT	CARB	SODIUM	CHOL
1 portion	95	5 gm	1 gm	19 gm	75 mg	0 mg

ROASTED CORN WITH ZUCCHINI

Yield: 10 portions

¼ ounce	Olive oil	7 milliliters
1 tablespoon	Shallot, minced	15 grams
2 cloves	Garlic, minced	10 grams
1 pound	Corn kernels, roasted	450 grams
¾ pound	Red pepper, roasted, peeled, diced	340 grams
8 ounces	Zucchini, seeded, diced	225 grams
¼ teaspoon	Salt	2 grams
1 tablespoon	Basil leaves, chopped	3 grams

1. Heat the olive oil. Add the shallots and garlic and sauté until they are translucent and have a pleasing aroma. Remove from the heat and let the pan cool.

2. Away from the heat, add the corn, red pepper, zucchini, salt, and basil to the shallot/garlic mixture. Toss to combine.

3. Portion the mixture (3 ounces/85 grams per order). Store under refrigeration.

4. At service, microwave portions to order at highest power setting until heated through and tender, or sauté in a small amount of chicken or vegetable stock.

PORTION	KCAL	PROTEIN	FAT	CARB	SODIUM	CHOL
1 portion	60	2 gm	1 gm	13 gm	80 mg	0 mg

MEXICAN CORN SALAD

Yield: 10 portions

22 ounces	Corn kernels, roasted	625 grams
3½ ounces	Red pepper, roasted, small dice	100 grams
3½ ounces	Jicama, julienned	100 grams
3½ ounces	Tomatillo, small dice	100 grams
4 ounces	Tomato concassé, diced	115 grams
½ ounce	Shallots, minced	15 grams
2 teaspoons	Olive oil	10 milliliters
1 teaspoon	Garlic, minced	5 grams
½ teaspoon	Jalapeño, minced	2 grams
½ teaspoon	Cilantro, fresh, chopped	1 gram
⅓ teaspoon	Salt	1 gram

1. Mix all of the ingredients and heat in a microwave or by sautéing lightly (add a little stock or water, if necessary).

2. Serve at once.

PORTION	KCAL	PROTEIN	FAT	CARB	SODIUM	CHOL
1 portion	70	2 gm	2 gm	15 gm	50 mg	0 mg

OVEN-ROASTED POTATOES

Yield: 10 portions

1 pound, 14 ounces	Idaho potatoes, sliced into wedges	**850 grams**
¾ fluid ounce	Olive oil	**20 milliliters**
2 teaspoons	Rosemary, chopped	**2 grams**
3 cloves	Garlic, coarsely chopped	**15 grams**
½ teaspoon	Salt	**3 grams**
¾ teaspoon	Black pepper, butcher grind	**2 grams**

1. Toss the potatoes with the olive oil, rosemary, garlic, salt and pepper.

2. Spread the potatoes in a single layer on a sheet pan lined with parchment paper.

3. Roast the potatoes in a 400 degree F/205 degree C oven until they are tender (about 35 to 40 minutes).

Serve with roasted, grilled entrées.

To make a variation of this dish, replace the Idaho potatoes with sweet potatoes and replace half of the garlic with ginger. Replace the oregano with thyme or cilantro. Add 1 fluid ounce/30 milliliters of fresh lime juice. Reduce cooking time. It may be necessary to lightly cover the dish during the first half of the cooking time.

PORTION	KCAL	PROTEIN	FAT	CARB	SODIUM	CHOL
1 portion	90	2 gm	2 gm	16 gm	100 mg	0 mg

OVEN-ROASTED TOMATOES

Yield: 2 pounds 8 ounces/1 kilogram

2¾ pounds	Plum tomatoes, sliced	1.25 kilograms
2¾ fluid ounces	Extra-virgin olive oil	80 milliliters
1 ounce	Garlic, minced	30 grams
1 ounce	Shallots, minced	30 grams
2 teaspoons	Basil, chopped	2 grams
2 teaspoons	Oregano, chopped	2 grams
1 teaspoon	Thyme, chopped	1 gram
½ teaspoon	Salt	3 grams
1 teaspoon	Black peppercorns, cracked	2 grams

1. Toss together all of the ingredients until the tomato slices are evenly coated.

2. Place the slices on a rack in a sheet or roasting pan.

3. Roast the tomatoes in a convection oven at 275 degrees F/135 degrees C for 1 hour.

4. Let the tomatoes cool. Store under refrigeration.

PORTION	KCAL	PROTEIN	FAT	CARB	SODIUM	CHOL
2 oz	55	1 gm	5 gm	3 gm	70 mg	0 mg

Steaming, Poaching, and Simmering

The moist-heat methods featured in this chapter gently cook foods by surrounding them with steam, a simmering liquid, or a combination of both. The deep, roasted flavors of dry-heat methods are replaced by subtle, delicate tastes that allow foods' pure, sweet flavors to stand out. This does not mean that there is no excitement for the palate when foods are steamed or poached, however.

Chefs usually add aromatic ingredients such as shallots, ginger, fresh herbs, mushrooms, celery, and spices to complement natural tastes, adding a bright counterpoint. The use of flavorful poaching and steaming liquids also increases the overall success of the dish. Moist-heat methods should produce dishes that have a great potential to please, as long as the chef remembers the importance of capturing every last bit of flavor from every ingredient in the dish.

Texture plays an equally important role. Foods should be cooked at the proper heat, and for the correct amount of time, so that they will be plump, moist, and succulent. If a poached chicken or fish has been left in the pot too long, it will dry out just as much as if it had been roasted or grilled too long. Furthermore, most of the flavor will be lost to the cooking liquid, and from there to the escaping steam.

With all of the emphasis given to vegetables throughout this or any book devoted to healthier eating styles, it may be a little discouraging to look through the index and see that there are relatively few recipes for vegetables. Most vegetables can be prepared in quick, healthful ways without requiring any elaborate recipes. In fact, it is the very simplicity of vegetable cookery that often leaves the field a little shortchanged on recipes.

Two of the vegetable cooking techniques most often used in a nutritionally-oriented kitchen are steaming and pan-steaming. Virtually all vegetables can be cooked by one or the other of these techniques with wonderful results.

FOCUS   MOIST HEAT METHODS FOR VEGETABLES

Steaming and pan-steaming minimize the amount of water vegetables come into contact with as they cook. It is important to use enough water, however, so that there will be enough to cook the vegetable to the proper stage of doneness.

The approximate ratio of liquid to vegetable will vary depending upon the density, quantity, and degree of doneness desired.

Steaming broccoli in a tiered steamer. Notice that the florets are arranged in a single layer so that they will cook evenly and quickly.

Sugar snaps are pan-steamed in a very small amount of water. Steam is captured by a lid, cooking the peas to a brilliant green.

New peas are quickly pan-steamed in slightly more water, because a large batch is being prepared.

Cauliflower requires more water than sugar snaps so that the water won't cook away.

ASPARAGUS WITH TOASTED ANCHOVIES, GARLIC, AND LEMON

Yield: 10 portions

1¾ pounds	Asparagus, trimmed	800 grams
4 teaspoons	Olive oil, extra-virgin	20 milliliters
½ teaspoon	Red pepper flakes	3 grams
¾ ounce	Garlic, thinly sliced	20 grams
8	Anchovy fillets, mashed	8
4 tablespoons	Parsley, flat-leaf, chopped	12 grams
3 tablespoons	Lemon juice, fresh-squeezed	45 milliliters
to taste	Black pepper, freshly ground	to taste

1. Trim the woody ends from the asparagus, and lightly peel about half-way up the stalk. Bring about ½-inch of water to a rolling boil in a *sautoir* (a skillet with straight sides). Add the asparagus, cover tightly, and steam for about 3 minutes. Asparagus should be tender, but not soft.

2. Drain the asparagus. If preparing the asparagus in advance, refresh in ice water, drain and wrap well, and refrigerate until needed.

3. Heat the olive oil in a sauté pan; add the red pepper flakes and garlic slices. Sauté over moderate heat until the garlic becomes light gold. Add the anchovies and cook until they appear browned.

4. If necessary, reheat the asparagus by steaming it or dropping it very briefly into some simmering water. Drain well, and add the asparagus to the olive oil mixture. Turn the asparagus gently to coat it evenly.

5. Add the parsley and lemon juice. Before serving, grind some black pepper over the asparagus.

This preparation method may be used with other vegetables, especially cauliflower, broccoli, and green beans.

PORTION	KCAL	PROTEIN	FAT	CARB	SODIUM	CHOL
1 portion	50	4 gm	2 gm	4 gm	114 mg*	4 mg

* Sodium value may be higher

STEAMED SPINACH WITH GARLIC AND PERNOD

Yield: 10 portions

1¾ pounds	Spinach leaves, rinsed and drained	800 grams
1 teaspoon	Butter, unsalted	6 grams
1 teaspoon	Garlic, minced	5 grams
1 teaspoon	Shallots, minced	5 grams
1 teaspoon	Pernod	5 milliliters
½ teaspoon	Black peppercorns, cracked	1 gram
¼ teaspoon	Salt	2 grams

1. Heat the butter and add the garlic and shallots. Sauté until they are translucent.

2. Add the spinach leaves, along with any water still clinging to them. If the leaves are very dry, add a few spoonfuls of water to the pan. Cover tightly and steam until the leaves are barely wilted. Drain away excess water.

3. Drizzle the Pernod over the spinach and add the pepper and salt. Toss and serve while still very hot.

PORTION	KCAL	PROTEIN	FAT	CARB	SODIUM	CHOL
1 portion	25	2 gm	8 gm	3 gm	140 mg	trace

PAN-STEAMED ZUCCHINI AND YELLOW SQUASH NOODLES

Yield: 10 portions

2 pounds	Zucchini	900 grams
2 pounds	Yellow squash	900 grams
2 teaspoons	Butter, unsalted	10 grams
1 tablespoon	Shallots, minced	12 grams
1 teaspoon	Garlic, minced	5 grams
½ teaspoon	Black peppercorns, cracked	1 gram
as needed	Vegetable Stock* or water	as needed
2 tablespoons	Herbs, minced**	6 grams
to taste	Lemon juice, fresh-squeezed	to taste

1. Using a mandoline, cut the zucchini and yellow squash into long thin "noodles," or cut them by hand by cutting the skin away in long, ¼-inch-thick slices, and then into long julienne. Discard the centers.

2. Heat the butter and add the shallots, garlic, and peppercorns. Sweat over moderate heat until the shallots and garlic are translucent.

3. Add the squash noodles to the pan, along with enough stock or water to come to a depth of about ¼ inch. Cover and steam for 2 or 3 minutes, or until noodles are limp. Drain them.***

4. Add the herbs and enough lemon juice to give the vegetables good flavor.

---

* See the recipe in Chapter 11.

** Appropriate herbs include basil, tarragon, chives, cilantro, thyme, or oregano used alone or in combination.

*** The cooking liquid may be saved to use for cooking other vegetables or for preparing stocks.

PORTION	KCAL	PROTEIN	FAT	CARB	SODIUM	CHOL
1 portion	30	2 gm	1 gm	4 gm	4 mg	2 mg

POACHED HALIBUT WITH CELERIAC AND PERNOD

Yield: 10 portions

2¼ pounds	Halibut fillet	1 kilogram
1 ounce	Shallots, minced	30 grams
1 pint	Fish Fumet*	480 milliliters
3 ounces	Tomato paste	85 grams
3 fluid ounces	Pernod	90 milliliters
26 fluid ounces	Velouté-style Sauce*	800 milliliters
3½ ounces	Celeriac, peeled, julienned, steamed	100 grams
as needed	Chives, chopped	as needed

1. Cut the halibut into 10 equal portions.

2. Smother the shallots in a small amount of the fumet, then place the halibut on top of them. Add the remaining fumet, and bring it slowly to a simmer. Cover the pan loosely with parchment paper.

3. Shallow-poach the fish in a slow (300 to 325 degree F/150 to 165 degree C) oven until it is opaque and just cooked through (about 5 to 6 minutes).

4. While the fish is shallow-poaching, sauté the tomato paste until it has a sweet smell, but is not brown. Add the Pernod and swirl until the tomato paste is completely dissolved.

5. Add half of the velouté to the tomato paste, along with the celeriac, and simmer gently until the flavor is developed (about 5 minutes).

6. Remove the fish from the pan and keep warm. Reduce the cooking liquid over high heat by two-thirds. Then add the remaining velouté and reduce once more until the mixture readily coats a spoon.

7. Add the tomato-and-Pernod-flavored velouté, and the chopped chives. Serve with the fish.

---

* The recipes for Velouté-style Sauce and Fish Fumet are in Chapter 11. The velouté should be prepared with a fish stock or fumet.

Serve with Lemon-Dill Rice or Saffron Potatoes (recipes in this chapter). A steamed green vegetable would be an appropriate accompaniment.

PORTION	KCAL	PROTEIN	FAT	CARB	SODIUM	CHOL
1 portion	190	26 gm	3 gm	8 gm	300 mg	40 mg

OCEAN CATFISH IN LOUISIANA SAFFRON BROTH

Yield: 10 portions

SAFFRON CONSOMMÉ

¾ ounce	Olive oil	20 grams
¾ ounce	Garlic, minced	20 grams
7 ounces	Leeks, diced	200 grams
1 teaspoon	Saffron threads, crushed	1 gram
7 ounces	Fennel, diced (reserve feathery tops)	200 grams
7 ounces	Tomato concassé	200 grams
1 piece	Orange rind	1 piece
1	Bay leaf, whole	1
2 teaspoons	Tarragon leaves, whole	2 grams
2 quarts	Fish stock	2 liters
2 quarts	Chicken stock	2 liters
1 pint	White wine	480 milliliters
6	Black peppercorns, cracked	6
1 bunch	Chervil stems	1 bunch
1 recipe	Clarification mix*	1 recipe
1 pint	Fish Fumet**	480 milliliters
2¼ pounds	Ocean catfish	1 kilogram

GARNISH

7 ounces	Leeks, ribbon cut, steamed	200 grams
7 ounces	Fennel, diced, steamed	200 grams
7 ounces	Tomato, julienned	200 grams
10 ounces	Okra, sliced	300 grams
as needed	Chervil leaves	as needed

1. Heat the olive oil; add the garlic and leeks and sauté until they are very aromatic. Add the saffron, fennel, tomato concassé, orange rind, bay leaf, tarragon leaves, fish and chicken stocks, wine, peppercorns, and chervil stems. Bring to a simmer. Simmer for 45 minutes.

2. Strain the broth and allow it to cool. Combine the cooled broth with the clarification mixture to make a consommé. Bring to a simmer. Simmer until broth is perfectly clear (about 1 hour and 15 minutes). Strain carefully and reserve 3 pints/ 1.2 liters of consommé to serve as part of the dish.

3. Scatter an additional handful of chopped leeks and fennel tops in a baking dish, if desired. Arrange the catfish on top. Simmer the fish fumet, add to the dish, cover lightly, and shallow-poach until the fish is cooked (about 8 to 10 minutes). Remove from the oven and keep warm.

4. Heat the garnish vegetables in the fish fumet used to poach the catfish, and place in a shallow soup plate. Top with the fish, and pour hot consommé over all. Sprinkle chervil leaves on each portion.

---

* The clarification mix recipe is found as part of the recipe for Basic Consommé in Chapter 14.

　　** See Chapter 11 for Fish Fumet recipe.

PORTION	KCAL	PROTEIN	FAT	CARB	SODIUM	CHOL
1 portion	220	27 gm	9 gm	7 gm	230 mg	70 mg

HALIBUT "OLYMPIA"

Yield: 10 portions

SAUCE

7 ounces	Leeks, ribbon-cut	200 grams
1 pint	Fish velouté*	480 milliliters
3½ fluid ounces	Heavy cream	100 milliliters
1 teaspoon	Tarragon, chopped	1 gram

MOUSSELINE FORCEMEAT

11 ounces	Halibut trim, chilled	315 grams
1 ounce	Egg whites, chilled	30 grams
½ teaspoon	Salt	3 grams
5 fluid ounces	Heavy cream, chilled	150 milliliters
½ teaspoon	Dill, chopped	500 milligrams
½ teaspoon	Tarragon, chopped	500 milligrams

1½ pounds	Halibut fillet, portioned	680 grams
5 ounces	Salmon fillet, sliced thinly	140 grams
6 fluid ounces	Fish Fumet**	180 milliliters
2 fluid ounces	Dry white wine	60 milliliters

1. Make the sauce as follows: Sweat the leeks in the velouté until they are tender. Add the cream and the tarragon to finish the sauce. Bring to a simmer. Cool the sauce properly and reheat when ready to serve.

2. Prepare the mousseline as follows: Cut the halibut trim into dice. Process the fish and the egg white to a fine paste, scraping down the sides of the bowl for an even consistency. Add the salt and heavy cream; pulse the machine to incorporate the cream until just blended. Fold in the dill and tarragon.

3. Spread the mousseline evenly on the halibut portions and top each portion with a salmon slice. Set the halibut on squares of parchment paper.

4. At service, combine the fish fumet and wine and heat to a simmer. Add the fish, cover lightly with parchment, and shallow-poach until the fish is properly cooked.

5. Remove the fish and keep warm. Add the sauce to the poaching liquid and reduce until the sauce has the consistency of heavy cream. Pool the sauce on the plate and place the salmon on the sauce.

---

* Prepare the fish velouté following the recipe for Velouté-style Sauce found in Chapter 11.

** See the recipe for Fish Fumet in Chapter 11.

PORTION	KCAL	PROTEIN	FAT	CARB	SODIUM	CHOL
1 portion	255	25 gm	13 gm	7 gm	290 mg	75 mg

POACHED SALMON WITH ASPARAGUS AND BASIL SAUCE

Yield: 10 portions

2¼ pounds	Salmon fillet	1 kilogram
1 pound, 5 ounces	Asparagus, peeled, blanched	600 grams
½ fluid ounce	White wine, dry	15 milliliters
½ fluid ounce	Fish Fumet*	15 milliliters
1 tablespoon	Shallots, minced, smothered	12 grams

FOR SERVICE

22 fluid ounces	Basil Sauce**	660 milliliters
5 ounces	Tomato peeled, seeded, julienned	140 grams
as needed	Basil, chiffonade	as needed

1. Slice the salmon fillet thinly on the bias into 1-ounce/30-gram pieces. Wrap a salmon slice around a few spears of asparagus, to make 10 portions with 3 bundles per portion.

2. Combine the white wine, fumet, and shallots in a shallow pan. Add the salmon bundles and cover lightly. Shallow-poach at service until the salmon is just cooked.

3. Remove the salmon bundles, and reduce the poaching liquid until it has syrup-like consistency.

4. Add the Basil Sauce and bring to a simmer. Reduce slightly for a good consistency, if necessary.

5. Finish the sauce with the tomato julienne and basil chiffonade.

6. Place the salmon bundles on heated plates and coat lightly with the sauce.

---

* See the recipe for Fish Fumet in Chapter 11.
** See the recipe for Basil Sauce in Chapter 11.

PORTION	KCAL	PROTEIN	FAT	CARB	SODIUM	CHOL
1 portion	170	25 gm	4 gm	8 gm	195 mg	60 mg

CHILLED POACHED SCALLOPS WITH TARRAGON VINAIGRETTE

Yield: 10 portions

1 pound	Scallops	450 grams
1 pint	White wine, dry	480 milliliters
1 pint	Fish Fumet	480 milliliters
1 tablespoon	Shallots, minced	15 grams
1 teaspoon	Arrowroot, diluted in cold liquid	5 grams
3 fluid ounces	Extra-virgin olive oil	90 milliliters
3 fluid ounces	Tarragon vinegar	90 milliliters
½ teaspoon	Black peppercorns, cracked	1 gram
40 pieces	Asparagus, trimmed, blanched	40 pieces
as needed	Tomato concassé, small dice	as needed

1. Combine the scallops with the wine, stock, and shallots and shallow-poach until the scallops are just cooked through. Remove the scallops, cool, and slice.

2. Strain the cooking liquid from the scallops and measure out 8 fluid ounces/240 milliliters. Bring it to a boil, and add the arrowroot to thicken lightly.

3. Add the olive oil, vinegar, tarragon, and cracked pepper to the thickened poaching liquid to make a vinaigrette.

4. Arrange the asparagus and scallops on the plate. Top with tomato concassé.

5. Drizzle each portion with 2 teaspoons/15 grams of vinaigrette.

————

A combination of seafood—such as shrimp, lean white fish made into paupiettes, oysters, mussels, and clams—may be used in this recipe.

PORTION	KCAL	PROTEIN	FAT	CARB	SODIUM	CHOL
1 portion	175	10 gm	9 gm	11 gm	110 mg	15 mg

POACHED SEA BASS WITH MOUSSELINE AND SUMMER SQUASH

Yield: 10 portions

1 pound, 9 ounces	Sea bass fillet	700 grams
14 ounces	Salmon mousseline*	400 grams
6 ounces	Yellow squash, thinly sliced	170 grams
6 ounces	Zucchini, thinly sliced	170 grams
½ ounce	Shallots, minced	12 grams
3 fluid ounces	Dry white wine	90 milliliters
5 fluid ounces	Fish Fumet**	150 milliliters
12 fluid ounces	Velouté-style Sauce**	360 milliliters
1 bunch	Chives, minced***	1 bunch
½ teaspoon	Salt	3 grams
¼ teaspoon	White pepper, ground	500 milligrams

1. Trim the sea bass and portion it into 2½-ounce/75-gram pieces. Top each piece with 1½ ounces/40 grams of mousseline.

2. Lay the sliced squash, alternating zucchini and yellow squash, to cover each piece.

3. Scatter the shallots in a shallow pan and place the fish on them. Add the wine and fish fumet and bring the liquid to a bare simmer over direct heat.

4. Cover the fish loosely with parchment paper and place in a moderate (325 degree F/165 degree C) oven for another 5 minutes, or until the fish is barely cooked through and the mousseline is set.

5. Remove the fish from the pan and keep warm.

6. Reduce the cooking liquid to about half its original volume. Add the velouté and chives, and bring to a simmer. Add the salt and pepper.

7. Serve the fish with the sauce.

----

* The recipe for Mousseline-style Forcemeat can be found in Chapter 13.

** The recipes for Fish Fumet and Velouté-style Sauce may be found in Chapter 11. Use fish stock to prepare the velouté.

*** The chives may be replaced totally or in part by other herbs, including tarragon, chervil, or parsley.

Saffron potatoes (recipe in this chapter) and steamed seasonal green vegetables make a good accompaniment to this dish.

PORTION	KCAL	PROTEIN	FAT	CARB	SODIUM	CHOL
1 portion	130	20 gm	2 gm	7 gm	245 mg	50 mg

POACHED SALMON AND SOLE WITH CHIVE-CREAM SAUCE

Yield: 10 portions

18 ounces	Salmon fillet	500 grams
18 ounces	Gray sole fillet	500 grams
1 ounce	Shallots, minced	30 grams
3 fluid ounces	White wine	90 milliliters
8 fluid ounces	Fish Fumet*	240 milliliters
1 pint	Chive Sauce*	480 milliliters
1 teaspoon	Butter, unsalted	3 grams
1 clove	Garlic, minced	5 grams
1¾ pounds	Spinach, stemmed	800 grams
1 teaspoon	Pernod	5 milliliters
as needed	Chives, chopped	as needed

1. Cut the fish into strips weighing slightly less than 1 ounce (25 grams) each. Roll them into roulades with one piece each of salmon and sole per roulade. Use a toothpick to hold them secure.

2. Scatter half of the shallots in a baking dish, and place the roulades on top of the shallots. Add the wine and fish fumet. Bring to a simmer. Cover the pan loosely and finish shallow-poaching in a slow (300 to 325 degree F/150 to 165 degree C) oven until just cooked through (about 8 to 10 minutes).

3. Remove the fish from the pan, moisten with a little of the cooking liquid, cover, and keep warm. Reserve about 2 ounces/60 milliliters of the cooking liquid to cook the spinach.

4. Add the Chive Sauce to the cooking liquid, and reduce to a consistency that will coat the back of a spoon.

5. While the sauce reduces, heat the butter in a sauté pan, add the remaining shallots and the garlic, and cook until tender. Add half of the reserved cooking liquid and reduce until nearly dry.

6. Add the spinach and the remaining reserved cooking liquid. Cover the pan and steam until the spinach is wilted.

7. Serve the fish, spinach, and sauce. Make a bed of the spinach and top with two roulades per portion. Make a ribbon of sauce surrounding the spinach. Scatter additional chives on the sauce.

* Recipes for Fish Fumet and Chive Sauce are in Chapter 11.

    A good accompaniment to this dish would be Saffron Potatoes or Rice Pilaf (see this chapter for the recipes).

PORTION	KCAL	PROTEIN	FAT	CARB	SODIUM	CHOL
1 portion	170	23 gm	5 gm	6 gm	230 mg	70 mg

SALMON MOUSSELINE WITH ZUCCHINI TUILES

Yield: 10 portions

1 pound	Salmon fillet, diced, chilled	450 grams
1	Egg white, chilled	1
4 fluid ounces	Heavy cream, chilled	120 milliliters
1 teaspoon	Dill, chopped	1 gram
1 teaspoon	Basil, chopped	1 gram
½ teaspoon	Salt	3 grams
¼ teaspoon	White pepper, ground	500 milligrams
15	Zucchini tuiles, blanched*	15
as needed	Court bouillon**	as needed
10 fluid ounces	Tomato-Basil Coulis	300 milliliters
5 ounces	Wild rice, cooked	140 grams

1. Puree the salmon, egg white, and heavy cream in a food processor to make a smooth forcemeat.

2. Remove from the processor to a bowl set over ice; fold in the herbs, salt, and pepper.

3. Fill zucchini slices with salmon forcemeat and roll up.

4. Shallow-poach the salmon-filled zucchini (1 per order) in a court bouillon; remove from pan and keep warm once the forcemeat has an internal temperature of 140 degrees F/60 degrees C.

continued ►

5. Reduce the poaching liquid by two-thirds and add 1 ounce/30 milliliters of Tomato-Basil Coulis per order. Return the sauce to a simmer.

6. Serve the zucchini tuiles on a bed of the sauce and garnish the plate with a spoonful of the wild rice.

———

* The zucchini tuiles are made as follows: Slice lengthwise into thin slices, and steam until tender. Roll them into a tulip shape and pipe the salmon mousseline into the center of the tulip.

 ** Court bouillon is explained in the Cooking Glossary.

PORTION	KCAL	PROTEIN	FAT	CARB	SODIUM	CHOL
1 portion	190	12 gm	13 gm	8 gm	275 mg	60 mg

SEA BASS IN TOMATO, FENNEL, AND SAFFRON SAUCE

Yield: 10 portions

½ ounce	Olive oil	15 milliliters
1 clove	Garlic, chopped	5 grams
4 ounces	Leeks, ribbon-cut	115 grams
4 ounces	Fennel, medium dice	115 grams
1 ounce	Tomato paste	30 grams
1 quart	Fish Fumet*	1 liter
1 pound	Tomato concassé, diced	450 grams
2 fluid ounces	White wine, dry	60 milliliters
½ fluid ounce	Lemon juice, fresh	15 milliliters
2 teaspoons	Tarragon leaves, chopped	2 grams
½ teaspoon	Saffron threads, crushed	500 milligrams
1	Bay leaf, whole	1
½ teaspoon	Orange zest	.5 gram

½ teaspoon	Salt	3 grams
¼ teaspoon	White pepper, ground	500 milligrams
1¾ pounds	Sea bass, fillet	800 grams
40	Mussels, scrubbed, debearded	40

1. Heat the olive oil and add the garlic. Sauté until it has a pleasant aroma.

2. Add the leeks and fennel. Cover the pot and sweat until the vegetables begin to release their juices.

3. Add the tomato paste and sauté until it begins to take on a rusty color and has a sweet aroma.

4. Add the fumet, tomato concassé, wine, lemon juice, tarragon, saffron, bay leaf, orange zest, salt, and pepper. Simmer until the vegetables are tender (about 30 minutes). (There should be enough saffron to give the broth a deep-golden color.)

5. Add the sea bass to the broth and poach gently until nearly cooked through. Add the mussels and simmer until they are open. Serve in heated soup plates.

---

* The recipe for Fish Fumet is in Chapter 11.

PORTION	KCAL	PROTEIN	FAT	CARB	SODIUM	CHOL
1 portion	130	20 gm	4 gm	4 gm	55 mg	75 mg

POACHED CHICKEN BREAST IN A SPICY BROTH

Yield: 10 portions

2 teaspoons	Olive oil	10 milliliters
1 clove	Garlic, minced	5 grams
2 tablespoons	Tomato paste	20 grams
2 fluid ounces	White wine	60 milliliters
1 quart	Chicken consommé*	1 liter
2 teaspoons	Tarragon leaves, chopped	2 grams
1 teaspoon	Saffron threads	600 milligrams
1 large piece	Orange zest	1 large piece
½ teaspoon	Salt	3 grams
1	Bay leaf, whole	1
3½ ounces	Leeks, ribbon-cut	100 grams
3½ ounces	Fennel, thinly sliced	100 grams
3½ ounces	Okra, diced	100 grams
1 pound	Tomato concassé, diced	450 grams
2¼ pounds	Chicken breast, boneless, skinless	1 kilogram
20	Crayfish	20
½ fluid ounce	Lemon juice	15 milliliters
to taste	White pepper, ground	to taste

1. Heat the olive oil in a soup pot. Add the garlic and sauté over low heat until the aroma is strong. Add the tomato paste and continue to sauté until it has a rusty color and a sweet aroma.

2. Deglaze the pan with the white wine, then add the consommé, tarragon leaves, saffron, orange zest, salt, and bay leaf. Simmer gently for about 15 minutes. Remove and discard the orange zest and bay leaf.

3. Add the leeks, fennel, and okra. Continue to simmer until the vegetables are just tender.

4. Add the tomato concassé and simmer until heated through.

5. Add the chicken breast and poach gently until the chicken is cooked through (about 8 minutes). Add the crayfish for the last 2 or 3 minutes of cooking time. Add the lemon juice and pepper to taste just before serving the dish.

6. Serve the chicken, crayfish, and broth in a heated soup plate.

———

* See the Basic Consommé recipe in Chapter 14.

If desired, flaked red pepper may be added along with the tomato paste (about ½ teaspoon, or more, to suit taste) to give the broth some "heat."

Serve steamed Carolina rice with this dish, and perhaps a crouton made by thinly slicing a whole-wheat baguette, spraying with a thin film of oil, and spreading with a thin layer of pureed roasted garlic and a dusting of grated Parmesan cheese. Brown lightly under a salamander.

PORTION	KCAL	PROTEIN	FAT	CARB	SODIUM	CHOL
1 portion	155	27 gm	3 gm	4 gm	80 mg	65 mg

SUNSHINE BASS WITH A GINGERED NAGE

Yield: 10 portions

COURT BOUILLON (NAGE)

2½ pints	Water	1.2 liters
1¾ pounds	Onions, thinly sliced	800 grams
12 ounces	Carrots, thinly sliced	340 grams
12 ounces	Celery, thinly sliced	340 grams
3½ ounces	Ginger, thinly sliced	100 grams
1 fluid ounce	Apple cider vinegar	30 milliliters
1 fluid ounce	Dry white wine	30 milliliters
½ teaspoon	Salt	3 grams
2½ teaspoons	Black peppercorns, whole	5 grams
2¼ pounds	Sunshine bass fillet	1 kilogram
2½ fluid ounces	Olive oil, extra-virgin	75 milliliters

5 ounces	Shiitake mushrooms, sliced*	140 grams
5 ounces	Red bell pepper, julienned	140 grams
5 ounces	Green onions, sliced on the bias	140 grams
5 ounces	Baby bok choy	140 grams
as needed	Chervil pluches**	as needed

1. Combine water, onions, carrots, celery, ginger, vinegar, wine, and salt; simmer for 20 minutes. Add the peppercorns and simmer for an additional 10 minutes. Strain this court bouillon and discard the vegetables.

2. Spread the oil evenly over the surface of a baking dish (if preparing individual portions, use smaller pans).

3. Add the trimmed bass, cut into 3½ ounce/100 gram portions. Add enough court bouillon to cover the fish by half.

4. Add all of the remaining ingredients except the chervil, bring to a simmer, and then cover lightly with parchment.

5. Finish poaching for an additional 5 to 8 minutes (depending upon the thickness of the fish) in a moderate (325 degree F/165 degree C) oven.

6. Serve the fish and vegetable garnish in the broth, and float the chervil pluches on each portion.

----

* Remove the tough stems from the shiitake and include them in the preparation of the court bouillon (Step 1), if desired.

** A "pluche" is a small cluster of whole chervil leaves, still held intact by a bit of the stem.

Grilled bread (see variation for pizza dough recipe in Chapter 19) would be a good accompaniment to this dish.

PORTION	KCAL	PROTEIN	FAT	CARB	SODIUM	CHOL
1 portion	230	24 gm	3 gm	26 gm	240 mg	70 mg

POACHED BEEF TENDERLOIN

Yield: 10 portions

2¼ pounds	Beef tenderloin	1 kilogram

CONSOMMÉ

1½ gallons	White beef stock	6 liters
2	Short ribs	2
5 ounces	Mirepoix*	150 grams
1	Bay leaf, whole	1
6	Black peppercorns, whole	6
7 ounces	Carrots, tournéed	200 grams
7 ounces	Parsnips, tournéed	200 grams
7 ounces	Potatoes, tournéed	200 grams
1 recipe	Clarification mixture**	1 recipe
7 ounces	Beets, tournéed, cooked until tender	200 grams

CABBAGE BALLS

¾ ounce	Bacon, minced	20 grams
¾ ounce	Garlic, chopped	20 grams
12 ounces	Cabbage, shredded	340 grams
1 fluid ounce	Apple cider vinegar	30 milliliters
1 teaspoon	Caraway seeds	1.75 grams
¼ teaspoon	Salt	2 grams
5 ounces	Cabbage leaves, blanched	140 grams
as needed	Chives, chopped	as needed
as needed	Parsley, chopped	as needed

1. Trim the tenderloin and wrap it tightly in plastic wrap. Reserve all lean trim for the broth.

2. Brown the reserved lean trim and combine it with the stock, short ribs, mirepoix, bay leaf, and peppercorns. Simmer to make a rich broth. Strain and remove all fat.

3. Cook the carrots, parsnips, and potatoes in the broth until tender. Drain and let dry on sheet pans and reserve. Refrigerate until needed for service, if necessary. Reserve the broth.

4. Reduce the broth until it has a strong flavor of beef and vegetables.

5. Combine with a standard clarification mixture to make a double-strength consommé. Reserve.

6. Prepare the cabbage balls: Render the bacon, add the garlic, and sauté until the aroma is sweet. Add the shredded cabbage, vinegar, caraway seed, and salt. Simmer (add stock, if necessary) until the cabbage is very tender.

7. Stuff the blanched cabbage leaves with the shredded cabbage mixture and shape into balls. Reserve.

8. Place the wrapped tenderloin in 170 degree F/75 degree C water to cover. Poach, maintaining temperature, to the desired doneness (about 30 minutes). Unwrap and slice into 3½ ounce/100-gram portions.

9. At service, reheat the vegetables and cabbage balls in the microwave and place them in heated, shallow soup plates. Add hot consommé to the bowl, and top with sliced tenderloin. Add parsley and chives.

---

* Mirepoix is explained in the Cooking Glossary.

** The clarification mixture is found as part of the Basic Consommé recipe in Chapter 14.

PORTION	KCAL	PROTEIN	FAT	CARB	SODIUM	CHOL
1 portion	280	30 gm	11 gm	14 gm	110 mg	75 mg

VEGETABLE TIMBALES

Yield: 20 timbales

½ fluid ounce	Vegetable oil	15 milliliters
3 ounces	Onions, minced	85 grams
3 pounds	Seasonal vegetables (carrots, beets, broccoli, spinach, others), peeled, coarsely chopped	1.3 kilograms
1 pint	Chicken stock, hot	480 milliliters
1	Bouquet garni*	1
8 fluid ounces	Egg whites	240 milliliters
8 fluid ounces	Evaporated skimmed milk	240 milliliters
½ teaspoon	Salt	3 grams
¼ teaspoon	White pepper, ground	500 milligrams

1. Heat the oil; add the onions and sweat until they are tender.

2. Add the chopped vegetables, stock, and bouquet garni. Cover and simmer until the vegetables are tender and most of the stock has reduced away.

3. Remove the bouquet garni.

4. Puree the vegetables until smooth; let them cool slightly.

5. Blend the egg whites, milk, salt, and pepper wtih the vegetables. Taste the mixture and adjust the seasoning, as desired.**

6. Lightly spray 2-ounce timbales with oil and fill them with the vegetable mixture. Cook in a water bath in a 275 degree F/135 degree C oven until set.

7. Unmold the timbales before serving.

---

* Bouquet garni is explained in the Cooking Glossary.

   ** If desired, chopped fresh herbs such as chives, tarragon, thyme, marjoram, parsley, savory, etc., may be added to the mixture. Grated nutmeg, curry powder, additional ground pepper, citrus juices and zests may also be added. The citrus ingredients will "brighten" the flavor.

PORTION	KCAL	PROTEIN	FAT	CARB	SODIUM	CHOL
1 portion	50	3 gm	1 gm	8 gm	110 mg	trace

FOCUS   PREPARING PILAFS

Pilafs of rice appear in a variety of countries where they are known as "pilau," "piliyafi," or "pilaw." The characteristics of a good pilaf are tender kernels of rice (or other grain) that separate easily. Long grain rices are especially preferred for pilafs, because they are less likely to clump together. Short grain rices, more starchy than long grain varieties, are usually reserved for a different cooking style. One of the most delicious rices used for a pilaf is basmati rice. It has an exceptionally long grain, and a delicate aroma when cooked that cannot be matched by any other rice.

Quinoa, barley, kasha, and bulgur wheat can also be prepared by the pilaf method. A number of these grains, with information about how much liquid they require, and approximate cooking times can be found in Table 17-1.

The basic method for a pilaf allows a great deal of latitude for creating variations. The chef can use saffron to give the dish a special color and flavor. Steamed vegetables can be included at the end of the cooking time to offer their special tastes and textures, as well as an inviting splash of color. Fresh herbs, citrus juices, and bits of meat, fish, or poultry can be included, turning this side dish into the main event. Dried fruits, nuts, and sweet spices can give a new twist to a standard preparation.

The quinoa pilaf shown here includes roasted peppers, garlic, sage, shallots, and thyme to create a dish with complex, rich flavors and an unusual texture.

BASIC RICE PILAF WITH VARIATIONS

Yield: 12 portions

26 fluid ounces	Chicken stock, hot	780 milliliters
8 ounces	Onions, chopped	225 grams
½ ounce	Garlic, minced	15 grams
14 ounces	Rice, long grain	400 grams
1 teaspoon	Salt	5 grams
¼ teaspoon	White pepper, ground	500 milligrams
1	Bay leaf, whole	1
1 sprig	Thyme, whole	1 sprig

1. Heat 4 fluid ounces/120 milliliters of stock and add the onion and garlic. Sweat until they are tender and most of the stock has reduced.

2. Add the remaining ingredients and bring the pilaf to a boil.

3. Cover the pan, place in a moderate (350 to 375 degree F/175 to 190 degree C) oven and finish cooking (about 18 minutes). Separate the grains with a fork to prevent clumping. (Grains should separate easily and have a slight bite.)

4. The rice may be served at this point, or cooled as follows: Spread the rice in a thin layer on a sheet pan and let cool. Portion the rice (3 ounces/85 grams per order), cover with plastic wrap, and refrigerate. At service reheat in a microwave at the highest power setting for 30 seconds.

Stock or broth gives the finished pilaf a special flavor, but water can certainly be used.

PORTION	KCAL	PROTEIN	FAT	CARB	SODIUM	CHOL
1 portion	100	3 gm	trace	20 gm	66 mg	trace

TABLE 17-1.

COOKING RATIOS AND TIMES FOR SELECTED GRAINS

TYPE	RATIO OF GRAIN TO LIQUID (CUPS)	APROXIMATE YIELD (CUPS)*	COOKING TIME
Barley, pearled	1:2	4	35 to 45 minutes
Barley groats	1:2½	4	50 minutes to 1 hour
Buckwheat groats (Kasha)	1:1½ to 2	2	12 to 20 minutes
Couscous**	—	1½ to 2	20 to 25 minutes
Hominy, whole***	1:2½	3	2½ to 3 hours
Hominy grits	1:4	3	25 minutes
Millet	1:2	3	30 to 35 minutes
Oat groats	1:2	2	45 minutes to 1 hour
Polenta	1:3 to 3½	3	35 to 45 minutes
Rice, Arborio (risotto)	1:3	3	20 to 30 minutes
Rice, basmati	1:1½	3	25 minutes
Rice, converted	1:1¾	4	25 to 30 minutes
Rice, Long-grain, brown	1:3	4	40 minutes
Rice, Long-grain, white	1:1½ to 1¾	3	18 to 20 minutes
Rice, Short-grain, brown	1:2½	4	35 to 40 minutes
Rice, Short-grain, white	1:1 to 1½	3	20 to 30 minutes
Rice, wild	1:3	4	30 to 45 minutes
Rice, wild, pecan	1:1¾	4	20 minutes
Wheat berries	1:3	2	1 hour
Wheat, bulgur, soaked†	1:4	2	2 hours
Wheat, bulgur, pilaf†	1:2½	2	15 to 20 minutes
Wheat, cracked	1:2	3	20 minutes

  * From 1 cup of uncooked grain.

  ** Grain should be soaked briefly in tepid water and then drained before it is steamed.

*** Grain should be soaked overnight in cold water and then drained before it is cooked.

  † Grain may be cooked by covering it with boiling water and soaking it for 2 hours or cooking it by the pilaf method.

TIMBALES OF DIRTY RICE

Yield: 10 portions

8 ounces	Cranberry beans, fresh	225 grams
14 fluid ounces	Chicken stock	400 milliliters
1¾ ounces	Onions, minced	50 grams
2 cloves	Garlic, minced	10 grams
7 ounces	Converted long-grain rice	200 grams
¾ ounce	Tomato paste	20 grams
1 tablespoon	Habanero vinegar	15 milliliters
2 teaspoons	Roasted jalapeño, minced	10 grams
1 teaspoon	Cumin seeds, toasted, crushed	2 grams
1 teaspoon	Black peppercorns, cracked	2 grams
1 teaspoon	Paprika	2 grams
¼ teaspoon	Cayenne pepper	1 gram
2½ ounces	Cheddar cheese, aged, grated	80 grams
2½ ounces	Corn kernels, roasted	80 grams
10 disks	Green peppers, grilled	10 disks

1. Cook the cranberry beans in boiling water until they are tender. Drain and reserve. Mash with a fork.

2. Combine about 1 ounce/30 milliliters of stock with the onions and garlic, and sweat over medium heat until the onions are tender and translucent.

2. Add the rice and stir to coat.

3. Add the remaining stock, tomato paste, vinegar, jalapeño, cumin, peppercorns, paprika, and cayenne. Stir with a fork to distribute all ingredients evenly.

4. Bring the stock to a simmer, cover the pot, and finish cooking in a moderate (350 degree F/175 degree C) oven. Do not stir once the stock comes to a simmer.

5. Cook the rice until the grains separate easily and are tender to the bite (about 16 to 18 minutes).

6. Use a fork to fold the beans, cheese and corn into the rice and serve topped with a green pepper disk.

7. Pack the molds with about 3 ounces/90 grams of the rice mixture, unmold onto a plate, and top with a green pepper disk.

PORTION	KCAL	PROTEIN	FAT	CARB	SODIUM	CHOL
1 portion	140	6 gm	3 gm	22 gm	70 mg	10 mg

QUINOA PILAF WITH RED AND YELLOW PEPPERS

Yield: 12 portions

1 ounce	Shallots, minced	30 grams
½ ounce	Garlic, minced	15 grams
24 fluid ounces	Chicken stock	720 milliliters
12 ounces	Quinoa	340 grams
½ teaspoon	Salt	3 grams
1	Bay leaf, whole	1
¼ teaspoon	White pepper, ground	500 milligrams
1 sprig	Thyme, whole	1 sprig
7 ounces	Red and yellow peppers, roasted, brunoise	200 grams

1. Sweat the shallots and garlic until tender in about 1 ounce/30 milliliters of the stock.

2. Add the quinoa, remaining stock, salt, bay leaf, pepper, and thyme. Bring the liquid to a boil.

3. Cover the pot tightly and place in a moderate (350 degree F/175 degree C) oven. Cook for about 15 minutes, or until the grain is tender to the bite and very fluffy.

4. Remove and discard the bay leaf and thyme. Fluff the grains with a fork to release the steam.* Using the same fork, gently fold in the peppers. Portion at 3 ounces/ 85 grams per serving.

---

* If the quinoa is not to be served right away, it should be removed from the pot and spread out on a sheet tray to cool. Add the roasted peppers to order as the quinoa is being reheated.

PORTION	KCAL	PROTEIN	FAT	CARB	SODIUM	CHOL
1 portion	106	7 gm	2 gm	20 gm	180 mg	trace

RISOTTO

Yield: 10 portions

1 pint	Stock (chicken, fish, vegetable)	480 milliliters
pinch	Saffron threads, crushed	pinch
¼ fluid ounce	Olive oil	7 milliliters
4 ounces	Onions, small dice	115 grams
10 ounces	Arborio rice	285 grams
8 fluid ounces	White wine, dry	240 milliliters
¼ ounce	Parmesan cheese, grated	8 grams

1. Heat the stock, and add the saffron. Allow the saffron to steep until it has a deep-golden color. Strain the stock and reserve.

2. Heat the olive oil and add the onions. Sweat the onions until they are translucent.

3. Add the rice to the onions. Sauté until the rice is coated evenly with the oil.

4. Add the saffron stock and the wine.

5. Bring the stock to a simmer, cover the pot, and remove it from the heat. When the rice has absorbed the liquid, spread it in an even layer on a sheet pan.

6. Sprinkle the cheese evenly over the top of the rice. Cover loosely and keep this mixture refrigerated until ready to finish.

7. To finish the risotto, place as many portions as are required in a shallow pan with a little additional stock (enough to moisten, no more), and simmer, stirring constantly, until the rice has absorbed all of the liquid and has a creamy texture.

PORTION	KCAL	PROTEIN	FAT	CARB	SODIUM	CHOL
1 portion	125	3 gm	1 gm	24 gm	25 mg	1 mg

WILD AND BROWN RICE PILAF WITH CRANBERRIES

Yield: 10 portions

2 quarts	Chicken stock	960 milliliters
1½ ounces	Onions, minced	40 grams
6 ounces	Brown rice, long grain	170 grams
7 fluid ounces	Apple cider	200 milliliters
6 ounces	Wild rice	170 grams
2 ounces	Dried cranberries, plumped in wine	60 grams
2 ounces	Shallots, roasted, shredded*	60 grams

1. Heat about ½ ounce/15 milliliters of stock in a pot. Add the onions and sweat until they are tender and translucent.

2. Add the brown rice and another 12 fluid ounces/360 milliliters of stock to the pan. Bring the stock to a simmer, cover, and finish cooking by the pilaf method in a moderate (350 degree F/175 degree C) oven for about 40 minutes. Use a fork to separate the grains. They should separate easily, and be tender to the bite.

3. Combine the apple cider, the remaining stock, and the wild rice in a separate pot. Simmer over low to moderate heat until the grains become tender to the bite. They should not burst.

4. Using a fork, stir both rices together. (It may be necessary to drain the wild rice if there is any free liquid visible in the pot.)

5. Drain the cranberries and fold them gently into the rice. Top each portion with the shallots.

---

* To roast shallots, place them, unpeeled, on a bed of coarse salt in a hot (around 375 degree F/190 degree C) oven, until the exterior is very crisp. Allow the shallots to cool, then remove the skin. The flesh should separate easily into shreds.

For a neater presentation, pack the pilaf into a timbale or dariole mold and then unmold onto the plate.

PORTION	KCAL	PROTEIN	FAT	CARB	SODIUM	CHOL
1 portion	25	3 gm	1 gm	24 gm	25 mg	1 mg

BLISS POTATOES WITH MUSTARD

Yield: 10 portions

30 ounces	Bliss potatoes, well-washed	850 grams
as needed	Water	as needed
5 ounces	Chicken stock	150 milliliters
1⅓ fluid ounces	Balsamic vinaigrette	40 milliliters
1⅓ fluid ounces	Extra-virgin olive oil	40 milliliters
¾ ounce	Pommery mustard	20 grams
½ teaspoon	Salt	3 grams
⅓ teaspoon	Black peppercorns, cracked	650 milligrams
⅓ ounce	Arrowroot, diluted in cold water or stock	10 grams

1. Boil or steam the potatoes until they are tender.

2. Cut into ½-inch-thick slices. Reserve.

3. Combine the stock, vinaigrette, olive oil, mustard, salt, and pepper. Bring to a boil.

4. Add the diluted arrowroot to the boiling sauce. Stir until thickened. Remove from the heat, add the potatoes, and gently toss until they are coated.

5. Let the potatoes cool before serving, or serve while still hot.

PORTION	KCAL	PROTEIN	FAT	CARB	SODIUM	CHOL
1 portion	110	2 gm	5 gm	15 gm	150 mg	trace

LEMON-DILL RICE

Yield: 10 portions

14 fluid ounces	Chicken stock	415 milliliters
2 fluid ounces	White wine, dry	60 milliliters
1¾ ounces	Onions, small dice	50 grams
1	Bay leaf, whole	1
1½ fluid ounce	Lemon juice, freshly squeezed	45 milliliters
¾ teaspoon	Lemon zest	2 grams
11 ounces	Rice, long-grain	315 grams
1 tablespoon	Dill, chopped	3 grams

1. Combine the stock, wine, onion, bay leaf, lemon juice, and lemon zest; bring to a boil.

2. Add the rice, and stir once with a fork to separate the grains.

3. Cover the pot and place it in a moderate (350 degree F/175 degree C) oven until the rice has absorbed all of the liquid (about 18 minutes).

4. Remove the cover, fluff the rice with a fork, and fold in the dill.

PORTION	KCAL	PROTEIN	FAT	CARB	SODIUM	CHOL
1 portion	125	3 gm	trace	26 gm	5 mg	trace

CELERIAC AND POTATO PUREE

Yield: 10 portions

10½ ounces	Chef's potatoes, peeled, diced	300 grams
10½ ounces	Celeriac, peeled, diced	300 grams
2 fluid ounces	Skim milk	60 milliliters
2 tablespoons	Heavy cream	30 milliliters
1 tablespoon	Butter, unsalted	15 grams
2 teaspoons	Garlic, roasted*	9 grams
½ teaspoon	Salt	3 grams

1. Boil the potatoes and celeriac separately in water or vegetable stock until very tender. Drain, and place them on a sheet pan in a warm oven to steam dry.

2. Bring the skim milk, cream, and butter to a simmer and keep them warm.

3. Puree the potatoes, celeriac, and roasted garlic through a ricer or food mill while they are still hot.

4. Add the hot milk mixture and salt, and fold together (avoid overmixing).

5. Keep warm to serve.

---

* See Chapter 16 for information on roasting garlic.

    If desired, this mixture may be place in a pastry bag fitted with a plain or star tip and piped out in 2½-ounce/75-gram portions.

PORTION	KCAL	PROTEIN	FAT	CARB	SODIUM	CHOL
1 portion	60	1 gm	2 gm	8 gm	135 mg	10 mg

POLENTA

Yield: 12 portions

1 quart	Chicken stock	**1 liter**
6 ounces	Yellow cornmeal	**170 grams**
2 ounces	Parmesan cheese, grated	**60 grams**
¼ teaspoon	White pepper, ground	**500 milligrams**

1. Combine the stock and cornmeal and bring to a boil. Reduce to a simmer and continue to cook for 30 minutes, stirring constantly.

2. Remove from the heat and stir in the Parmesan and pepper.

3. Brush a sheet pan with water and pour the polenta onto the sheet pan. Allow it to cool and then refrigerate until set.

4. Score the polenta into 3-ounce portions. They may be grilled or reheated in an oven before service.

PORTION	KCAL	PROTEIN	FAT	CARB	SODIUM	CHOL
1 portion	100	5 gm	3 gm	13 gm	150 mg	8 mg

FOCUS BEANS

It wasn't that long ago that about the only place you might find beans on the menu of many restaurants was hiding in the minestrone soup. The proliferation of appetizers, salads, entrees and side dishes based on the humble bean is one of the more fascinating trends in contemporary American cuisine. Now that beans are finally something more than a base for soups or an ingredient in chili stews, patrons and chefs are learning to appreciate them for their special qualities.

Nutrition is their strong suit. Beans and dried peas offer excellent supplies of complex carbohydrates, protein, vitamins, minerals, and fiber, with only modest amounts of fat. They average around 30 to 40 calories in an ounce, after cooking.

Versatility is another point in beans' favor. Apart from their use in delicious soups and stews, legumes are featured in contemporary menus as salsas, sauces, appetizers, side dishes, and salads. They marry well with a number of different spices and herbs. A dish of beans is equally at home with a bouquet of herbs from a typically Mediterranean cuisine and with an Indian curry blend or garam masala.

There is a generous variety of beans available, with more "exotic" offerings being found in stores ranging from specialty shops to supermarkets. Great Northerns and split peas used to make up the bulk of beans available to chefs and consumers alike. Now it is relatively easy to find such interesting examples of dried legumes as the Christmas lima, French green lentils, red lentils, pony beans, flageolets, cranberry beans, and more.

BASIC BEANS

Yield: 10 portions

¾ pound	Beans, sorted, rinsed	340 grams
2 quarts	Stock (vegetable, chicken, veal, beef) or water	2 liters
1	Bouquet garni	1
2 to 3	Garlic cloves, peeled, whole	10 to 15 grams

1. Soak the beans for several hours or overnight in enough cool water to cover them by at least 2 inches*. Drain and rinse them in more cool water.

2. Place the beans in a pot, and add the stock. Bring them to a simmer and add the bouquet garni and garlic.

3. Continue to simmer until the beans are tender enough to mash easily. (There should be no white core in the center of the bean.)** Remove and discard the bouquet garni and garlic.

4. Cool the beans in their cooking liquid for later use, or use in other recipes as desired.

―――――

* The "quick-soak method" may be used if there is not enough time to soak beans overnight. Combine the beans with enough cold water to cover by about 2 inches. Bring the water to a boil, then remove the pot from the heat. Allow the beans to sit in the hot water for about 1 hour. Drain, and continue with the recipe.

** Most beans will cook properly in the amount of liquid indicated in the recipe. Table 17-2 gives *approximate* cooking times. The age of the bean will determine how long the cooking process will take and how much liquid is necessary. Be sure to monitor beans as they cook and add more liquid as needed.

PORTION	KCAL	PROTEIN	FAT	CARB	SODIUM	CHOL
1 portion	130	9 gm	1 gm	34 gm	10 mg	0 mg

TABLE 17-2.
GENERAL GUIDELINES FOR BEAN PREPARATION

NAME	SOAKING TIME (IN HOURS)	LIQUID AMOUNT	COOKING TIME (IN HOURS)
Adzuki beans	4	2 quarts/2 liters	1
Black beans	4	2 quarts/2 liters	1½
Black-eyed peas	N/A	2 quarts/2 liters	¾
Chick-peas	4	2 quarts/2 liters	2–2½
Fava beans	12	2 quarts/2 liters	3
Great Northern	4	2 quarts/2 liters	1
Kidney beans	4	2 quarts/2 liters	1
Lentils	N/A	3 pints/1.4 liters	½
Lima beans	4	2 quarts/2 liters	1–1½
Mung beans	4	2 quarts/2 liters	1
Navy beans	4	2 quarts/2 liters	1½
Peas, split	N/A	3 pints/1.4 liters	½
Peas, whole	4	2 quarts/2 liters	¾
Pink beans	4	2 quarts/2 liters	1
Pinto beans	4	2 quarts/2 liters	1½
Soy beans	12	5 pints/2.3 liters	3–3½

BLACK BEAN CAKES

Yield: 24 portions

1 pound	Black beans, dry	450 grams
2 quarts	Chicken stock	2 liters
1 ounce	Chorizo sausage, crumbled	30 grams
½ ounce	Garlic, minced	15 grams
3½ ounces	Onion, minced	100 grams
1	Jalapeño, seeded, minced	1
¾ teaspoon	Cumin seeds, ground	750 milligrams
¾ teaspoon	Chili powder	750 milligrams
2	Egg whites, lightly beaten	2
¾ fluid ounce	Lime juice, freshly squeezed	20 milliliters
⅓ ounce	Cilantro, fresh, chopped	10 grams
1 teaspoon	Salt	5 grams
as needed	Cornmeal (to dust cakes)	as needed
1¾ ounces	Butter, unsalted	50 grams
1¾ ounces	Yogurt, nonfat, drained	50 grams
1¾ ounces	Sour cream	50 grams
10½ ounces	Fresh Tomato Salsa*	300 grams

1. Rinse and sort the beans. Combine them with enough stock to cover them by about 2 inches and simmer until the beans are tender. The stock should be allowed to reduce until it is almost completely absorbed at the end of the cooking time.

2. Render the chorizo over low heat until a small amount of fat is released.

3. Add the garlic, onion, and jalapeño to the chorizo; sauté until the onions are browned.

4. Add the cumin seeds and chili powder and sauté briefly.

5. Add the sautéed chorizo mixture, egg whites, lime juice, cilantro, and salt to the beans and mix well.

6. Form the beans into cakes and dust them lightly with the cornmeal.

continued ▶

7. Heat the butter and sauté the cakes until a crust forms on both sides.

8. Combine the yogurt and the sour cream. Serve the black bean cakes with the yogurt/sour cream mixture and the salsa.

-----

* The recipe for Fresh Tomato Salsa can be found in Chapter 12.

PORTION	KCAL	PROTEIN	FAT	CARB	SODIUM	CHOL
1 portion	160	10 gm	5 gm	22 gm	190 mg	10 mg

HARICOTS VERTS WITH WALNUTS

Yield: 10 portions

30 ounces	Haricots verts	850 grams
3½ fluid ounces	Water, reserved from blanching	100 milliliters
¾ ounce	Shallots, minced, smothered	20 grams
½ ounce	Walnuts, toasted, chopped	15 grams
2 cloves	Garlic, minced, smothered	10 grams
¼ teaspoon	Salt	2 grams
⅛ teaspoon	White pepper, ground	250 milligrams

1. Blanch the beans until just tender in boiling water. Drain the beans (save 3½ fluid ounces/100 milliliters of cooking liquid), and place in a bowl.

2. Combine the green beans with the blanching water, shallots, walnuts, garlic, salt, and pepper. Toss to coat evenly and serve.

PORTION	KCAL	PROTEIN	FAT	CARB	SODIUM	CHOL
1 portion	40	2 gm	1 gm	7 gm	60 mg	0 mg

SAFFRON POTATOES

Yield: 10 portions

1 quart	Chicken stock	**1 liter**
¼ teaspoon	Saffron threads, crushed	**250 milligrams**
20 pieces	Potatoes, tournéed with one flat side	**20 pieces**
as needed	Herbs, chopped	**as needed**

1. Bring the stock and the saffron to a boil. Steep until golden.

2. Boil the potatoes gently in the saffron-infused stock until tender.

3. Remove the potatoes from the stock. Reheat at service if necessary. Sprinkle with chopped herbs.

PORTION	KCAL	PROTEIN	FAT	CARB	SODIUM	CHOL
1 portion	70	2 gm	trace	15 gm	3 mg	0 mg

PECAN CARROTS

Yield: 10 portions

30 ounces	Carrots, oblique-cut	850 grams
3½ fluid ounces	Water, reserved from blanching	100 milliliters
½ fluid ounce	Honey	15 milliliters
1 tablespoon	Shallots, minced, smothered	12 grams
½ ounce	Pecans toasted, chopped	15 grams
2 teaspoons	Chives, sliced	2 grams
¼ teaspoon	Salt	2 grams
⅛ teaspoon	White pepper, ground	250 milligrams

1. Cook the carrots until just tender in simmering water. Drain the carrots (save 3½ fluid ounces/100 milliliters of cooking liquid), and place in a bowl.

2. Combine the carrots with the blanching water, honey, shallots, pecans, chives, salt, and pepper. Toss to coat evenly and serve.

PORTION	KCAL	PROTEIN	FAT	CARB	SODIUM	CHOL
1 portion	40	2 gm	1 gm	7 gm	60 mg	0 mg

C H A P T E R

18

Stewing and Braising

Among the recipes in this chapter are variations on some familiar, home-style dishes such as Chicken Pot Pie and Chili Stew. More exotic offerings include Braised Cippolini Onions and a renovated rendition of a classic "Newburg" dish.

Stewing and braising are methods that allow the chef to showcase some less tender, more flavorful cuts of meat. The long, slow, gentle cooking also aids the development of a rich, complex sauce. Garnishes can be as varied and colorful as the market and the season will allow.

Variations on basic themes are always a possibility. Chili Stew, for example, might be prepared with game meats such as buffalo or venison, and seasoned with unusual dried and fresh chilies, as in Arizona Buffalo Chili. Traditional recipes for long-simmered braises often rely upon ingredients such as salt pork or fatback to add a special flavor or texture. For nutritional cooking, the best way to approach these ingredients is to determine what role they are expected to play. The smoky flavor and aroma of salt pork can be achieved by very finely mincing and rendering it to infuse the dish with a hint of the flavor. Barding and larding were traditionally done to lean meats to add some moistness to the dish. The sheets of fatback may be replaced by cabbage or romaine leaves, or simply by carefully monitoring the cooking process, never allowing the liquid to come to a boil. Rapid cooking makes meats tough and dry, and dulls their flavors.

Vegetable and legume stews have a great deal of potential. Simply by varying the type of vegetable or bean, or by combining a number of different types, the chef can use the same basic recipe to create some interesting new results. Experimenting with herbs and other flavoring ingredients will further enhance the already impressive versatility of these cooking methods.

FOCUS CHILI STEW

One of the first Tex-Mex dishes to become popular throughout the country was chili. Today, there are countless variations on this basic theme, and hundreds of chili contests. This recipe calls for a beef knuckle, a relatively lean, well-exercised portion of the animal. There are no beans included in this recipe. This is not meant as a definitive answer as to whether or not a true chili contains beans; it's just one of many recipes for this all-time favorite dish.

Instead of sizzling the meat in a lot of oil or lard, the intense "beefy" flavor of this dish is bolstered by using a rich Fond de Veau Lié. The type of chilies selected, as well as the quality of the chili powder, will also have a noticeable impact on the finished product.

As a quick glance through any book devoted to chili will show, there is practically no limit to the ways that this basic formula could be varied. A spicy stew based on lean pork, enhanced with a generous quantity of green chilies is one option. Game meats are also particularly delicious when simmered slowly in the rich chili sauce. The recipe for Arizona Buffalo Chili is one example.

Finding a good source for fresh, dried, and ground chilis is probably the key to a chef's secret formula for great chili stew.

CHILI STEW

Yield: 10 portions

2¼ pounds	Beef knuckle, trimmed, large dice	1 kilogram
4 ounces	Onions, diced	115 grams
1 ounce	Garlic, minced	30 grams
2 tablespoons	Chili powder	14 grams
1 ounce	Tomato paste	30 grams
1 pound, 10 ounces	Plum tomatoes, peeled, seeded, diced	750 grams
1 pint	Chicken stock	480 milliliters
9 fluid ounces	Fond de Veau Lié	275 milliliters
1½ teaspoons	Cayenne pepper, ground	3 grams
½ ounce	Ancho chilis, dried, toasted, chopped	15 grams
10 drops	Tabasco sauce	10 drops
¾ teaspoon	Garlic powder	2 grams
1½ teaspoons	Onion powder	3 grams
½ teaspoon	Salt	3 grams
½ teaspoon	Black peppercorns, cracked	3 grams

1. Dry-sauté the beef on all sides until browned.

2. Add the onions and continue to sauté until they are limp.

3. Add the garlic, sauté until a sweet aroma is apparent.

4. Add the chili powder and the tomato paste. Sauté until the paste begins to turn a rusty color and has a sweet aroma.

5. Add the diced tomato and the chicken stock, and stir well to deglaze the pan. Bring to a simmer.

6. Combine the fond de veau lié with the cayenne, chilies, Tabasco, garlic and onion powders, salt, and pepper. Heat to a simmer.

7. Add the fond de veau lié to the beef mixture. Cover the pot and place in a moderate (350 degree F/175 degree C) oven. Braise slowly until the meat is very tender. Serve.*

* For service, fill a flour tortilla "bowl" with the chili and garnish with Fresh Tomato Salsa (see the recipe in Chapter 12), diced red pepper, sliced green onions, grated Cheddar cheese, cooked rice, a combination of sour cream and drained nonfat yogurt.

To prepare tortilla "bowls," line an ovenproof bowl with a tortilla, and fill with pie weights or dry beans. Bake until crisp and golden in color.

PORTION	KCAL	PROTEIN	FAT	CARB	SODIUM	CHOL
1 portion	280	13 gm	10 gm	37 gm	380 mg	30 mg

ARIZONA BUFFALO CHILI

Yield: 10 portions

2¼ pounds	Buffalo, round, trimmed, 1-inch cubes	1 kilogram
5 ounces	Onions, small dice	140 grams
1½ ounces	Garlic, minced	40 grams
1½ ounces	Tomato paste	40 grams
1 ounce	Chili powder	30 grams
1¾ pounds	Tomato concassé	800 grams
12 fluid ounces	Fond de Veau Lié	360 milliliters
½ ounce	Ancho chilies, finely chopped	15 grams
1 or 2, to taste	Mulata chilies, dried*	1 or 2, to taste
1 or 2, to taste	Chipotle, dried*	1 or 2, to taste
½ teaspoon	Salt	3 grams
½ teaspoon	Black pepper, ground	1 gram
¾ teaspoon	Cayenne pepper, ground	2 grams

GARNISH

10	Flour tortillas	10
10 ounces	Rice pilaf, prepared	285 grams
10 ounces	Fresh Tomato Salsa	285 grams
10 ounces	Bell peppers, roasted, peeled, cut into strips	285 grams
3½ ounces	Scallions, thinly sliced	100 grams
3½ ounces	Cheddar cheese, grated	100 grams
1 ounce	Yogurt, nonfat, drained	30 grams
1 ounce	Sour cream	30 grams

1. Dry-sauté the buffalo on all sides until it is evenly browned.

2. Add the onions and the garlic; continue to cook over medium heat until the onions are translucent.

3. Add the tomato paste and the chili powder and sauté until the tomato paste has taken on a rusty color and a sweet aroma (about 3 to 4 minutes).

4. Add the tomato concassé, fond de veau lié, chilies, salt, pepper, and cayenne. Bring the chili to a simmer. Cover the pot and continue to simmer (on top of the stove or in a 350 degree F/175 degree C oven) until the meat is very tender.

5. Bake the flour tortilla over a mold to shape into a cup (See the note in the Chili Stew recipe in this chapter). Serve with garnish.**

———

* To use mulato and chipotle chiles, toast them on an open flame, or dry sauté in a cast-iron skillet to soften. Cut into strips.

** To serve, place a layer of pilaf in the tortilla cup, fill with chili, and garnish with salsa, peppers, scallions, and cheddar cheese. Combine the drained yogurt and sour cream and place about 1 teaspoon on each portion. Refer to the note following Chili Stew.

PORTION	KCAL	PROTEIN	FAT	CARB	SODIUM	CHOL
1 portion	270	13 gm	9 gm	38 gm	380 mg	20 mg

FOCUS   CHICKEN POT PIE

Pot pies are a typically American dish. According to tradition, a pot pie is nothing more than a rich meat stew, usually chicken, beef, or pork, that includes whatever fresh vegetables are in season. Peas, potatoes, carrots, onions, and celery are the most common selections, but it is easy to add other ingredients. Broccoli, green beans, asparagus, even shredded leafy greens are all appropriate.

To make the stew itself a little lighter, substitute arrowroot diluted in a little stock for a butter-and-flour roux. Not only will this save calories and fats in the dish, it will help to streamline production. Roux-thickened dishes must simmer for 30 to 45 minutes. Arrowroot thickens in less than 5 minutes.

One of the components of a classic pot pie that carries the greatest number of calories and packs away the most fat is the crust. Some choices for the dough in the past might have been puff pastry or brioche dough, both of which include a very high percentage of butter. Even a plain pie dough is loaded with fat. Here, the traditional pie dough, made with 3 parts flour, 2 parts fat (usually shortening, butter or fat) and 1 part water, is replaced with a Plain Ricotta Pastry that reduces the butter content by relying on part-skim ricotta. An alternative would be a top layer of phyllo dough, cut to fit the ramekin, and lightly sprayed with a film of melted butter or oil.

HERB-CRACKER CRUST

Yield: 10 portions

5½ ounces	Flour, all-purpose, sifted	155 grams
1 teaspoon	Sugar	8 grams
½ teaspoon	Salt	3 grams
¼ teaspoon	Baking soda	1 gram
¾ ounce	Butter	20 grams
2 tablespoons	Basil, chopped	6 grams
2 tablespoons	Parsley, chopped	6 grams
1 tablespoon	Tarragon, chopped	3 grams
4½ fluid ounces	Buttermilk, chilled	130 milliliters

1. In a bowl, blend the flour, sugar, salt, and baking soda.

2. Rub the butter into the dry ingredients until a mealy texture is achieved.

3. Add the herbs and buttermilk; mix until a fairly stiff dough is formed. (The dough should not feel sticky.) Add extra flour a little at a time, if necessary.

4. Roll the dough into thin sheets using a pasta machine. Cut to fit the shape of the bowl used to serve the pot pie or stew and place on a baking sheet lined with parchment paper.

5. Bake in a hot (400 degree F/205 degree C) oven (convection, if possible) until golden-brown.

PORTION	KCAL	PROTEIN	FAT	CARB	SODIUM	CHOL
1 serving	65	3 gm	2 gm	14 gm	100 mg	20 mg

CHICKEN POT PIE

Yield: 10 portions

2¼ pounds	Chicken breast, boneless, skinless	1 kilogram
1 quart	Chicken stock	1 liter
12 ounces	Onions, large dice	340 grams
8 ounces	Carrots, large dice	225 grams
8 ounces	Celery, bias-cut	225 grams
12 ounces	Potatoes, peeled, large dice	340 grams
1 ounce	Arrowroot	30 grams
6 fluid ounces	Evaporated skimmed milk	180 milliliters
1 tablespoon	Parsley, chopped	3 grams
2 teaspoons	Tarragon, chopped	2 grams
1 teaspoon	Chervil, chopped	1 gram
½ teaspoon	Salt	3 grams

¼ teaspoon	Pepper	500 milligrams
1¼ pounds	Plain Ricotta Pastry*	570 grams

1. Trim the chicken of any visible fat and cut it into strips or dice.

2. Combine the chicken with the stock and bring the liquid to a gentle simmer. (There should be enough stock to cover the chicken completely. If necessary, add more.) Stew until the chicken is just barely cooked through.

3. Remove and reserve the chicken. Add the onions, carrots, celery, and potatoes to the stock and continue to cook at a gentle simmer until the vegetables are tender.

4. Dilute the arrowroot in a small amount of the milk and add it to the stock and vegetables. Bring the liquid to a full simmer to completely thicken the sauce.

5. Remove the sauce from the heat, and stir in the parsley, tarragon, chervil, salt, and pepper. Return the chicken to the sauce.

6. Portion the chicken mixture into ceramic casseroles.

7. Roll out the ricotta dough and cut it to fit the openings of the dishes. Transfer the dough to the casseroles, pressing and crimping the edges to form a seal.

8. Brush the surface with a little milk or egg wash.**

9. Bake the individual pot pies in a 375 degree F/190 degree C oven until the crust is lightly browned. Serve at once.

---

* The recipe for Plain Ricotta Pastry is found in Chapter 20.

** Prepare an egg wash by beating together 1 egg white with 1 tablespoon of evaporated skimmed milk.

A number of other vegetables could be included in addition to, or in place of, those indicated here. Some suggestions include new peas, corn kernels, diced, roasted peppers, asparagus tips, and diced parsnips or turnips. Peas and corn kernels should be added once the sauce has been thickened and removed from the heat. The final baking of the pie will cook and reheat them sufficiently.

PORTION	KCAL	PROTEIN	FAT	CARB	SODIUM	CHOL
1 portion	220	9 gm	4 gm	35 gm	210 mg	10 mg

CHICKEN AND SHRIMP POT PIE WITH HERB-CRACKER CRUST

Yield: 10 portions

1¼ pounds	Chicken breasts, skinless, boneless	570 grams
1 pound	Shrimp (16–20), peeled, deveined	450 grams
2 quarts	Chicken Stock*	2 liters
4 ounces	Arrowroot	115 grams
1 pound, 5 ounces	Potatoes, medium dice	600 grams
1 ounce	Dijon mustard	30 grams
14 fluid ounces	Evaporated skimmed milk	415 milliliters
1¾ ounces	Butter, unsalted	50 grams
3½ ounces	Onions, small dice	100 grams
3½ ounces	Celery, small dice	100 grams
3½ ounces	Carrots, small dice	100 grams
3½ ounces	Green peppers, small dice	100 grams
¼ ounce	Rosemary, chopped	7 grams
¼ ounce	Thyme leaves, chopped	7 grams
½ teaspoon	Black peppercorns, ground	1 gram
1 fluid ounce	Worcestershire sauce	30 milliliters
½ teaspoon	Tabasco sauce	2 milliliters
1 recipe	Herb-Cracker Crust**	1 recipe

1. Pound the chicken breasts to an even thickness, then portion at 3½ ounces/100 grams per serving. Roll the chicken into roulades and tie them with butcher's twine to secure.

2. Bring the stock to a simmer and add the roulades. Poach them for about 10 minutes, add the shrimp and continue to poach another 5 minutes. Remove and reserve the chicken and shrimp. Skim the surface of the stock.

3. Dilute the arrowroot with a little cold water to make a thin paste. Add the diluted arrowroot to the simmering stock to thicken it to a consistency that will easily coat the back of a wooden spoon.

4. Add the potatoes and simmer until quite tender. Blend the milk with the mustard and add it to make the base for the stew.

5. While the potatoes are simmering, heat the butter in a sauté pan. Add the onions, celery, carrots, and peppers and smother until tender. Add these vegetables and all remaining ingredients (except crust) to the stew and simmer for another 5 minutes.

6. Remove the twine from the roulades and return them to the stew to reheat.

7. Serve the stew with a portion of the Herb-Cracker Crust.

---

* The recipe for Chicken Stock can be found in Chapter 11.

    ** See the recipe in this chapter.

    If desired, grill the chicken and shrimp instead of poaching them.

PORTION	KCAL	PROTEIN	FAT	CARB	SODIUM	CHOL
1 portion	280	27 gm	7 gm	28 gm	305 mg	110 mg

RABBIT AND OYSTER ÉTOUFFÉ

Yield: 10 portions

1 quart	Chicken stock	1 liter
3½ ounces	Onions, minced	100 grams
3½ ounces	Green peppers, minced	100 grams
2 ounces	Celery, diced	60 grams
2 ounces	Scallions, thinly sliced	60 grams
2 ounces	Plum tomato concassé	60 grams
2 cloves	Garlic, minced	10 grams
7 ounces	Flour, all-purpose, browned in oven	200 grams

SEASONING MIX

1 teaspoon	Paprika, hot	2 grams
½ teaspoon	Garlic powder	1 gram
½ teaspoon	Onion powder	1 gram
½ teaspoon	White pepper, ground	500 milligrams
½ teaspoon	Black pepper, ground	500 milligrams
½ teaspoon	Basil leaves, dried	500 milligrams
½ teaspoon	Filé powder	500 milligrams
⅛ teaspoon	Cayenne pepper, ground	250 milligrams

2¼ pounds	Rabbit, disjointed, trimmed	1 kilogram
14 ounces	Oysters, shucked, liquor reserved	400 grams

GARNISH

4 tablespoons	Scallions, green portion, sliced	30 grams
1 pound	Carolina rice, cooked	450 grams

1. Heat approximately 2 ounces of the stock in a pot. Add the onions, peppers, celery, scallions, tomato, and garlic. Cover the pot and sweat until the onions are translucent.

2. Remove the cover and continue to sauté until the onions are browned.

3. Combine the browned flour with the seasoning mix ingredients. Coat the rabbit pieces evenly with the seasoned flour and add them to the vegetable mixture. Cook until the rabbit is evenly browned on all sides.

4. Add the remaining stock, bring to a simmer, and cover the pot.

5. Complete cooking, either on top of the oven or in a moderate (350 degree F/175 degree C) oven, until the rabbit is tender.

6. Remove the rabbit from the sauce and keep it warm.

7. Skim the surface of the sauce; reduce slightly to adjust consistency if necessary.

8. Add the oysters and the rabbit to the sauce and simmer just until the oysters' edges begin to curl.

9. Serve the étouffé topped with sliced scallions on a bed of rice.

PORTION	KCAL	PROTEIN	FAT	CARB	SODIUM	CHOL
1 portion	320	28 gm	8 gm	32 gm	130 mg	80 mg

LOBSTER, SHRIMP, AND SCALLOP NEWBURG

Yield: 10 portions

3	Whole lobster (about 1 pound/450 grams each)	3
2 quarts	Fish Fumet*	2 liters
¾ fluid ounce	Olive oil	20 milliliters
2 fluid ounces	Brandy	60 milliliters
1 ounce	Shallots, minced	30 grams
1 ounce	Tomato paste	30 grams
1¾ ounces	Arrowroot	50 grams
10 fluid ounces	Evaporated skimmed milk	300 milliliters
12 ounces	Shrimp, peeled, de-veined	340 grams
12 ounces	Scallops, muscle tabs removed	340 grams
2 fluid ounces	Sherry, dry	60 milliliters
as needed	Chives, minced	as needed
1 ounce	Butter, unsalted	30 grams
1 pound, 5 ounces	Lemon-Dill Rice**	600 grams

1. Poach the lobsters in the fish fumet for 4 minutes. Remove and pull the meat from the shells. Dice the meat. Reserve the fumet, shells, and 12 ounces/340 grams of lobster meat separately.

2. Chop the lobster shells (and shrimp shells, if available) and sauté in the olive oil.

3. Add the brandy. Flame to cook brandy down.

4. Add the shallots and sauté until they are translucent.

5. Add the tomato paste and sauté until the paste is a rusty color and has a sweet aroma.

6. Add the reserved fish fumet (keep 4 fluid ounces/120 milliliters to deglaze the pan later) and simmer this sauce for about 20 minutes. Strain the sauce, pressing the shells well to release their flavor.

7. Heat reserved fumet in a skillet. Stew the scallops and shrimp until they are barely cooked through. Remove them from the pan.

8. Reduce the fumet slightly. Add the sauce and bring to a simmer. Reduce, if necessary, to achieve the correct consistency.

9. Return the lobster, scallops, and shrimp to the sauce and heat through. Add the sherry, chives and butter to finish.

———

* See the recipe for Fish Fumet in Chapter 11.

   ** See the recipe for Lemon-Dill Rice in Chapter 17. Serve the New-burg with the rice (2 ounces/60 grams per portion).

PORTION	KCAL	PROTEIN	FAT	CARB	SODIUM	CHOL
1 portion	227	23 gm	8 gm	14 gm	300 mg	110 mg

PAELLA VALENCIA

Yield: 10 portions

2 teaspoons	Olive oil	10 milliliters
2 teaspoons	Garlic, minced	10 grams
3½ ounces	Onion, small dice	100 grams
10 ounces	Assorted bell peppers, small dice	300 grams
1½ ounces	Jalapeños, seeded, minced	40 grams
5 ounces	Mushrooms, sliced	140 grams
pinch	Saffron threads, crushed	pinch
18 ounces	Long-grain converted rice	500 grams
2½ pints	Chicken Stock*	1.2 liters
10	Game hen legs, roasted to medium rare	10
20	Clams, scrubbed well	20
20	Mussels, scrubbed and debearded	20
10	Shrimp (16–20 count), peeled, de-veined	10
10 ounces	Petit pois (fresh or frozen)	300 grams

1. Heat the olive oil over medium heat. Add the garlic and onions and sauté until the onions are golden.

2. Add the bell peppers and jalapeños; sauté until they are tender. Add the mushrooms and sauté until they begin to release some of their moisture.

3. Add the saffron and rice; sauté until the grains are coated.

4. Add the stock and bring the liquid to a simmer. Cover and place in a moderate (350 degree F/175 degree C) oven. After 12 minutes, add the game hen legs (remove the skin first), clams, mussels, shrimp, and peas. Replace the cover.

5. Cook the paella for another 6 to 8 minutes, or until the clams and mussels are opened and the shrimp is properly cooked.

6. Portion the paella to include a game hen leg, 2 each of the clams and mussels, a piece of shrimp, and a portion of rice.

* See the recipe in Chapter 11.

Traditionally, paella would be prepared and served directly from a special pan, and it is often made for two or more. The diners serve themselves from the pan.

PORTION	KCAL	PROTEIN	FAT	CARB	SODIUM	CHOL
1 portion	330	40 gm	7 gm	24 gm	400 mg	120 mg

CIOPPINO

Yield: 10 portions

1 fluid ounce	Olive oil	30 milliliters
6 ounces	Onions, finely diced	170 grams
2 bunches	Scallions, diced	2 bunches
2	Green peppers, diced	2
5 ounces	Fennel, diced	140 grams
¾ ounce	Garlic, minced	20 grams
4 pounds	Plum tomatoes concassé	1.8 kilograms
8 ounces	Tomato puree	225 grams
8 fluid ounces	Dry white wine	240 milliliters
1	Bay leaf	1
2 teaspoons	Black peppercorns, crushed	4 grams
20	Cherrystone clams, scrubbed	20
2	Blue crabs, disjointed	2
20	Shrimp (16–20 ct.), peeled, de-veined	20
1¼ pounds	Swordfish, diced	570 grams
3 tablespoons	Basil leaves, chopped	9 grams
10	Garlic-flavored croutons*	10
2 tablespoons	Saffron Aioli**	30 milliliters

1. Heat the oil in a pot. Add the onions, scallions, peppers, and fennel. Sauté until the onions are translucent.

2. Add the garlic and sauté until an aroma is apparent.

3. Add the concassé and puree, wine, and bay leaf. Cover the pot and simmer this mixture slowly for about 45 minutes. If necessary, add a small amount of water.

4. Add the pepper. Remove and discard the bay leaf.

5. Add the clams and crabs; simmer for about 10 minutes.

6. Add the shrimp and swordfish; simmer until they are just cooked through.

7. Add the basil.

8. Serve the cioppino in heated soup plates with a crouton and a scant teaspoon of the aioli.

———

* To make croutons, thinly slice a whole-wheat baguette on the diagonal. Spray each slice very lightly with olive oil, and then scatter with chopped garlic. Toast to a golden-brown under a salamander or broiler.

    ** See the recipe in Chapter 12. If desired, it may be dispensed from a squeeze bottle with a narrow tip, to make a pattern or design on the surface of the stew.

PORTION	KCAL	PROTEIN	FAT	CARB	SODIUM	CHOL
1 portion	215	18 gm	6 gm	18 gm	225 mg	40 mg

BRAISED VEAL ROULADE WITH MUSHROOM SAUSAGE

Yield: 14–16 portions

MUSHROOM SAUSAGE

18 ounces	Veal, or pork, lean, diced	500 grams
6 ounces	Carolina rice, cooked*	170 grams
3½ ounces	Onion, minced	100 grams
2½ fluid ounces	Evaporated skimmed milk	70 milliliters
2	Egg whites	2
1 teaspoon	Onion powder	2 grams
½ teaspoon	Garlic powder	1 gram
½ teaspoon	Pâté spice	1 gram
½ teaspoon	Salt	3 grams
¼ teaspoon	Paprika, hot	1 gram
½ teaspoon	Anise seeds	1 gram
⅛ teaspoon	Cayenne pepper	250 milligrams
7 ounces	Mushrooms, diced**	200 grams
1	Veal breast, boned, trimmed, pounded	1
5 ounces	Onions, coarsely chopped	140 grams
5 ounces	Carrots, coarsely chopped	140 grams
4 ounces	Celery, coarsely chopped	115 grams
2 ounces	Tomato paste	60 grams
1 pint	Brown stock	480 milliliters
1 pint	Fond de Veau Lié	480 milliliters

1. Prepare a forcemeat by grinding the veal through a coarse die. Grind once more, including all of the remaining sausage ingredients, except the mushrooms. Working over an ice bath, fold the mushrooms into the forcemeat. Make a test quenelle to check for flavor and consistency.

2. Divide the forcemeat evenly between the two veal breasts. Roll the breast around the forcemeat, going with the grain. Tie to form roulades.

3. Sear the roulades in a casserole on all sides. Remove them.

4. Add the mirepoix to the casserole and sweat until the onions become limp and slightly golden.

5. Add the tomato paste and sauté until there is a sweet aroma and the paste has a rusty color.

6. Add the brown stock and the fond de veau lié, stir well to release any reduced drippings. Return the roulades to the casserole.

7. Bring the liquid just to a simmer. Cover the casserole and braise in a moderate (350 degree C/175 degree F) oven until the veal is fork-tender.

8. Remove the roulades and let rest briefly. Strain the sauce and degrease it. If necessary, adjust the consistency by reducing the sauce further or thinning it with a small amount of additional stock. Slice the roulade into portions and serve.

---

* The Carolina rice (long-grain rice) should be boiled until it is tender enough to mash easily when pressed with the back of a spoon. A cooking time of about 20 to 24 minutes is usually adequate.

** Use currently available mushrooms, including wild ones. To produce a special flavor when using domestic mushrooms, add 1 ounce/30 grams of reconstituted dried mushrooms.

To serve the roulades, slice them and shingle on heated plates. Coat lightly with the sauce. Serve steamed green beans, glazed carrots, and Spätzle (see the recipe in Chapter 19) with this dish. Other accompaniments might include braised red cabbage, brussels sprouts, and steamed potatoes.

PORTION	KCAL	PROTEIN	FAT	CARB	SODIUM	CHOL
1 portion	240	26 gm	10 gm	9 gm	28 mg	230 mg

LAMB SHANKS BRAISED WITH LENTILS

Yield: 10 portions

10	Lamb shanks, trimmed	10
1 quart	Fond de veau lié*	1 liter
1 pint	White wine, dry	480 milliliters
12 ounces	Lentils, green	340 grams
1	Bouquet garni**	1
8 ounces	Celery, finely diced	225 grams
8 ounces	Carrots, finely diced	225 grams
2 tablespoons	Parsley, chopped	6 grams
1 tablespoon	Thyme, chopped	3 grams
¼ teaspoon	Black pepper, ground	500 milligrams
1 or 2 tablespoons	Orange or lemon juice	15 or 30 milliliters
½ teaspoon	Salt	3 grams

1. Sear the shanks in a dry cast-iron skillet over moderate heat.

2. Add the fond de veau lié, wine, lentils, and bouquet garni; bring the liquid to a simmer.

3. Cover the pot and braise the shanks in a moderate (325 degree F/165 degree C) oven until the lamb and the lentils are both very tender (about 90 minutes).

4. Remove the lamb shanks, degrease the surface of the cooking liquid thoroughly (or, if time allows, cool and refrigerate overnight so that any fat will congeal on the surface where it can be easily lifted away).

5. Add the celery and carrots to the lentils and simmer gently over moderate heat until the vegetables are tender and the sauce has reduced slightly.

6. Adjust the seasoning of the sauce with parsley, thyme, ground pepper, orange or lemon juice, and salt.

7. Serve the lamb shanks (reheated in the sauce, if necessary).

———

* The recipe for Fond de Veau Lié can be found in Chapter 11.
  ** Bouquet garni is explained in the Cooking Glossary.
  In the photograph on the facing page, the lamb shanks are served on a pool of the sauce along with leek ribbons, steamed haricots verts, and a potato and celeriac puree. Steamed or boiled beets have been seasoned to taste with a reduction of orange juice and vinegar.

PORTION	KCAL	PROTEIN	FAT	CARB	SODIUM	CHOL
1 portion	360	40 gm	10 gm	28 gm	230 mg	100 mg

CASSOULET

Yield: 10 portions

2¼ pounds	Onions, thinly sliced	1 kilogram
5 fluid ounces	Red wine	150 milliliters
¾ ounce	Garlic, minced	20 grams
3½ ounces	Tomato paste	100 grams
3¼ pounds	Tomato concassé, smoked*	1.5 kilograms
2 tablespoons	Rosemary leaves, chopped	6 grams
3 tablespoons	Thyme leaves, chopped	9 grams
½ teaspoon	Salt	3 grams
1 pound, 10 ounces	Tomato concassé, fresh	750 grams
10 fluid ounces	Fond de Veau Lié**	300 grams
2 pounds	Navy or Great Northern beans, cooked in stock	900 grams
9 ounces	Duck breast, pan-smoked, seared, julienned	250 grams
1 pound	Turkey sausage, sliced***	450 grams
10 ounces	Pork confit, shredded****	300 grams
1 quart	Chicken Stock**	1 liter
3½ ounces	Bread crumbs seasoned with chopped chives and parsley	100 grams

1. Sauté the onions in a dry pan until browned. Add about 1 ounce/30 milliliters of the wine to help extract sugar and to prevent scorching.

2. Add the garlic, sauté until the aroma is strong, then add the tomato paste. Sauté, stirring constantly, until there is a sweet aroma.

3. Add the rest of the red wine to deglaze the pan and allow it to reduce to a heavy consistency.

4. Add half of the smoked tomato concassé, and the rosemary and thyme. Sauté until any juices released from the tomatoes have reduced.

5. Add the salt, fresh tomato concassé, fond de veau lié, and the cooked beans. Stew gently until the flavors combine and the stew is fairly dry.

6. Sauté the duck, sausage, and pork until warmed. Add the stock and the beans. Heat thoroughly by stewing in the oven or on the stovetop.

7. Stir in the remaining smoked tomato concassé. Top with the bread crumb mixture once the cassoulet has cooked down to a moist, stew-like consistency.

8. Brown the bread crumbs under a salamander or in a very hot (500 degree F/260 degree C) oven.

---

* Smoked tomato concassé is prepared as follows: Make concassé in the normal fashion (peel, seed, and cut flesh of tomatoes into dice). Then, arrange tomatoes on wire mesh screen and place over a thin layer of wood chips in a pan. Cover tightly, and place over direct heat. Heat until the aroma of the smoke is noticeable; then pull the pan off the heat. Allow the tomatoes to smoke for an additional 2 to 3 minutes; then remove the cover.

** See the recipes in Chapter 11.

*** To prepare turkey sausage, grind together 1 pound/450 grams of lean turkey meat with ½ teaspoon/3 grams each of kosher salt and sugar. Add about 4 to 5 cloves of minced garlic, and fennel seed, cinnamon, nutmeg, ground cloves, cayenne, cumin seed, rosemary, thyme, and ground black pepper to taste. Stuff this mixture into sausage casings and twist into 1½-ounce/45-gram links. This may be prepared in bulk and frozen.

**** To prepare pork confit, cut lean pork, trimmed of all visible fat, into large dice. Simmer slowly in stock until the pork is extremely tender.

PORTION	KCAL	PROTEIN	FAT	CARB	SODIUM	CHOL
1 portion	350	34 gm	8 gm	36 gm	285 mg	70 mg

RATATOUILLE

Yield: 20 portions

⅓ fluid ounce	Extra-virgin olive oil	10 milliliters
⅔ ounce	Shallots, minced	18 grams
¾ ounce	Garlic, minced	20 grams
5 ounces	Red onion, medium dice	140 grams
1½ ounces	Tomato paste	40 grams
8 ounces	Zucchini, seeded, medium dice	225 grams
7 ounces	Bell peppers, medium dice	200 grams
7 ounces	Eggplant, peeled, medium dice	200 grams
5 ounces	Yellow squash, seeded, medium dice	140 grams
1 pound	Plum tomatoes, peeled, sliced thickly*	450 grams
1 pint	Stock (chicken or vegetable)	480 milliliters
2 tablespoons	Basil, chopped	6 grams
2 teaspoons	Oregano, chopped	2 grams
½ teaspoon	Salt	3 grams
⅓ teaspoon	Black pepper, ground	700 milligrams

1. Heat the olive oil and add the shallots, garlic, and red onion. Sauté until they are tender and translucent.

2. Add the tomato paste and cook briefly until it has a rusty color and gives off a sweet aroma.

3. Add the zucchini, peppers, eggplant, yellow squash, tomatoes, and stock and stir well.

4. Reduce the heat under the ratatouille and establish a gentle simmer. Stew the vegetables until they are very tender.**

5. Add the basil, oregano, salt, and pepper.

––––––

* To give the ratatouille a richer, deeper flavor, substitute Oven-Roasted Tomatoes for sliced plum tomatoes. The recipe can be found in Chapter 16.

** The ratatouille can be prepared in advance, cooled, and stored. Stop cooking in step 4 when the vegetables are nearly, but not completely tender. Add the seasonings and herbs to the stew just before service. The ratatouille can be reheated in small batches, or by a single portion in a microwave for 45 seconds at the highest power setting. Stir to distribute the heat evenly before serving.

PORTION	KCAL	PROTEIN	FAT	CARB	SODIUM	CHOL
1 portion	50	3 gm	1 gm	9 gm	125 mg	trace

FONDANT POTATOES

Yield: 10 portions

20 pieces	Potatoes, tournéed	20 pieces
1 pint	White stock	480 milliliters
2 fluid ounces	Glace de viande	60 milliliters

1. Place the potatoes in a hotel pan.

2. Add stock, cover, and cook the potatoes in the oven until they are three-quarters done (about ½ hour).

3. Brush the top of the potatoes lightly with the glace de viande; return the potatoes to the oven uncovered and complete cooking time.

PORTION	KCAL	PROTEIN	FAT	CARB	SODIUM	CHOL
1 portion	70	2 gm	trace	15 gm	3 mg	0 mg

THREE BEAN STEW

Yield: 10 portions

8 ounces	Chick peas*	225 grams
8 ounces	Navy or Great Northern beans*	225 grams
8 ounces	Black or kidney beans*	225 grams
½ fluid ounce	Olive oil	15 grams
1 tablespoon	Garlic, minced	15 milliliters
2 teaspoons	Shallots, minced	10 grams
2½ ounces	Celery, small dice	70 grams
2½ ounces	Carrots, small dice	70 grams
4 ounces	Onions, small dice	115 grams
5 ounces	Tomato concassé**	140 grams
2 teaspoons	Curry powder	4 grams
1 teaspoon	Cumin seeds, toasted, ground	2 grams
8 fluid ounces	Vegetable Stock***	240 milliliters

6 fluid ounces	Vegetarian Demi-glace***	180 milliliters
1 teaspoon	Black peppercorns, cracked	2 grams
1 tablespoon	Parsley, minced	3 grams
1 tablespoon	Cilantro, minced	3 grams
1 tablespoon	Mint, minced	3 grams

1. Cook the beans separately until they are just tender to the bite. Drain and reserve.

2. Heat the oil and add the garlic, shallots, celery, carrots, and onions. Sauté until the onions are a light golden color.

3. Add the tomatoes and sauté briefly.

4. Add the curry and cumin and sauté for another 2 minutes.

5. Add the beans, stock, and demi-glace. Bring the liquid to a simmer, cover, and stew over direct heat or in a moderate (350 degree F/175 degree C) oven until all ingredients are extremely tender.

6. If necessary, place the stew over direct heat and cook, uncovered, until the liquid is properly reduced. Add the peppercorns, parsley, cilantro, and mint.

———

* Any selection of beans may be used, as desired. See Chapter 17 for the Basic Bean recipe and cooking times for various beans. Aim for a good variety of colors in the stew for the best appearance in the finished dish.

** Oven-roasted tomatoes may be used to replace the tomato concassé.

*** See the recipes in Chapter 11.

Serve the stew with pieces of cornbread.

VEGETARIAN CURRY   To make the stew into a vegetarian entree, include additional vegetables, such as pumpkin, zucchini, corn, peas, and peppers (for a total of about 4 ounces/120 grams of additional vegetables per portion) and include a 3-ounce/85-gram portion of rice, barley, quinoa, or bulgar.

PORTION	KCAL	PROTEIN	FAT	CARB	SODIUM	CHOL
1 portion	135	8 gm	1 gm	23 gm	5 mg	0 mg

SOUTHWEST WHITE BEAN STEW

Yield: 10 portions

14 ounces	Navy beans, cooked, drained*	400 grams
2 teaspoons	Safflower oil	10 milliliters
4 ounces	Red onions, small dice	115 grams
4 ounces	Assorted bell peppers, small dice	115 grams
2 ounces	Jalapeños, seeded, diced	60 grams
1 ounce	Garlic, minced	30 grams
2 fluid ounces	Sherry wine vinegar	60 milliliters
4 ounces	Tomato concassé	115 grams
2 tablespoons	Cilantro, chopped	6 grams

1. Puree about 2 cups of the cooked beans, and combine with whole beans.

2, Heat the oil and add the onions, bell peppers, jalapeños, and garlic. Sauté until the onions are translucent.

3. Add the bean mixture and sauté, stirring constantly, until the beans are heated through.

4. Add the vinegar and tomatoes; continue to sauté until very hot.

5. Add the cilantro just before serving.

———

* The recipe for Basic Beans may be found in Chapter 17. If desired, this stew may be prepared with other beans.

　　If this stew is prepared in advance, it may be finished through Step 4, cooled, portioned, and properly stored. Then, individual portions may be reheated in the microwave or in a sauté pan. If necessary, add a small amount of stock or water to loosen the stew very slightly, and add the cilantro at the last moment.

PORTION	KCAL	PROTEIN	FAT	CARB	SODIUM	CHOL
1 portion	80	4 gm	1 gm	14 gm	90 mg	0 mg

BRAISED CIPOLLINI ONIONS

Yield: 10 portions

½ tablespoon	Olive oil	8 milliliters
18 ounces	Cippolini onions, trimmed*	500 grams
4 fluid ounces	Red wine vinegar	120 milliliters
12 fluid ounces	Fond de Veau Lié	360 milliliters
to taste	Black pepper, ground	to taste

1. Heat the olive oil over moderate heat. Add the onions and allow them to slowly brown, rolling them in the pan from time to time. Do not allow them to burn.

2. Add the red wine vinegar to deglaze the pan, and then allow the vinegar to reduce by half.

3. Add enough of the fond de veau lié to cover the onions halfway. Bring to a simmer.

4. Cover the pan and braise the onions in a moderate (325 degree F/165 degree C) oven until they are very tender.

5. Remove the onions from the cooking liquid, and allow the liquid to reduce slightly over direct heat. This sauce should coat the back of a spoon easily.

6. Return the onions to the sauce, season to taste with the pepper.

* A cipollini onion is about the same size and shape as a pearl onion, but sweeter. To prepare these onions for cooking, trim away the root and stem ends and remove the papery skin.

This recipe would also work with leeks. To properly trim a leek, cut away the green portion where it starts to branch away from the main stem. Trim off any tough parts of the leaves, and most of the stem end, but leave enough to hold the leek together. Rinse the leeks well to remove all traces of sand. Steam them briefly before browning them in the olive oil.

PORTION	KCAL	PROTEIN	FAT	CARB	SODIUM	CHOL
1 portion	65	3 gm	2 gm	8 gm	155 mg	5 mg

SMOKY BRAISED BLACK-EYED PEAS

Yield: 10 portions

5 ounces	Black-eyed peas	140 grams
1 pint	Chicken stock	480 milliliters
½ slice	Bacon, minced	15 grams
1 ounce	Onion, thinly sliced	30 grams
1 ounce	Tomato concassé, smoked*	30 grams
1	Bay leaf, whole	1
1 sprig	Thyme, whole	1 sprig

1. Simmer the black-eyed peas in stock (enough to generously cover them) until they are nearly tender. Drain, reserving the peas and the cooking liquid separately.

2. Place the minced bacon in a small rondeau and render the fat over low heat.

3. Add the onions and cook slowly until they are a light-golden color.

4. Add the peas and the tomatoes, and enough of the cooking liquid to moisten the mixture. Bring to a simmer.

5. Add the bay leaf and sprig of thyme, cover the pot, and braise in a moderate (350 degree F/175 degree C) oven until the peas are very tender and the liquid has nearly cooked away (about 30 minutes).

6. Remove and discard the bay leaf and thyme.

---

* To prepare smoked tomato concassé, prepare concassé from fresh plum tomatoes. Place the concassé on a fine mesh wire rack. Place fine chips of a hard wood in a roasting pan, cover tightly, and place over direct heat. When smoke is easy to detect, remove the pan from the heat, take off the lid, and quickly place the rack of tomatoes in the pan. Immediately replace the lid. Let the tomatoes smoke for a few minutes. (Do not smoke too long, or the flavor might become harsh.)

PORTION	KCAL	PROTEIN	FAT	CARB	SODIUM	CHOL
1 portion	65	4 gm	1 gm	9 gm	30 mg	5 mg

Pasta and Pizza

Pasta and pizza quickly became the darlings of the healthy generation when their sterling nutritional qualities were discovered. At first, they had appeared as nothing more than starchy, fattening foods to be scrupulously avoided. However, they have definite nutritional qualities, as long as certain ingredients —cheeses, cream- and butter-based sauces, and high-fat meat items such as pepperoni and sausages—are carefully monitored. These ingredients should either be kept to a minimum, or better yet, replaced by fresh vegetables, lean meats and poultry, and aromatics such as mushrooms, hot peppers, and herbs.

Pastas can be used in virtually every menu category. Small portions of filled pastas such as Lobster Cappelletti with Ginger Sauce make appealing appetizers. Cold pasta salads are always popular for either a small-portion starter dish or a luncheon entrée. Main courses can be based on pastas of all shapes, sizes, flavors, and colors. Side dishes of vegetable-flavored pastas break the potato and rice mold.

Pizzas are also tremendously versatile dishes. Pizzas topped with lobster and jalapeños, oven-roasted tomatoes with goat cheese and fresh herbs, or a variety of squashes, eggplant, and mushrooms can be served as small appetizer portions, or made into a whole meal when combined with a salad. As breakfast items they can be topped with fresh and dried fruits for interesting alternatives to muffins, waffles, or pancakes.

FOCUS PASTA RECIPE

Fresh pastas and noodles are no longer considered "exotic" items in this country. Satisfying and relatively easy to prepare, they don't demand any tools other than a fork, a clean work surface, a rolling pin, and a knife. The process can be made even easier if a pasta machine is available.

Pasta dough can be mixed in one of three ways: by hand, in a food processor, or with an electric mixer and a dough hook (for large batches). It is important to keep the dough relatively stiff. If the dough becomes too wet during mixing, a little more flour should be kneaded in. The correct consistency for doughs mixed by either a food processor or in a mixer is a moist, but mealy mixture that does not adhere into a ball until it is pressed together by hand.

A typical pasta formula calls for about one whole egg (large) for every 3 to 4 ounces of flour, and enough water to make a workable dough. To reduce the fat and cholesterol, replace the whole egg with approximately 2 egg whites (from large eggs). The end result is a pasta that rolls well and has a pleasantly firm texture that may require less water, if any. Adding flavoring and coloring ingredients may affect the balance between flour and liquid, so be sure to read carefully the variations following the basic recipe to see what adjustments, if any, may be required.

BASIC PASTA DOUGH WITH VARIATIONS

Yield: 5 pounds/2.25 kilograms

3 pounds, 10 ounces	Semolina flour	1.6 kilograms
10 ounces	Egg whites	285 grams
11 to 12 fluid ounces	Water	330 to 360 milliliters

1. Combine all the ingredients using a dough hook until the mixture is mealy. Add additional water or flour to adjust the consistency, if necessary. (For alternate mixing methods, read the accompanying Focus.)

2. Press the dough into a ball and wrap it tightly in plastic wrap.

3. Let the dough rest for a minimum of 1 hour before rolling and cutting it.*

4. Cook the pasta in boiling water, drain, and serve.**

———

The dough should not form a ball as it is mixed, but it should adhere into one when it is pressed together by hand.

   * To roll out the dough, pass it through the widest setting of a pasta machine, working in small, manageable pieces. Then, fold it in thirds, and repeat three or four more times to knead the dough. Pass

a   *Cutting saffron pasta into fettucini using the cutting attachment for the pasta machine.*

b   *The steps in cutting, filling, and folding capelletti are shown here.*

the dough through successively smaller settings until the desired thickness is reached. It may then be cut into flat pastas such as fettucini or linguini, or into circles or squares and filled to make tortellini, ravioli, or agnolotti.

** To cook fresh (or dried) pasta, bring 1 gallon of water to a rolling boil for each pound of pasta to be cooked (3.75 liters to 450 grams of pasta). Add the pasta to the boiling water and stir gently to separate the strands. Cook just until the pasta is tender to the bite.

If the pasta is being prepared in advance, it should be very slightly undercooked. Then, drain thoroughly, rinse well with cold water, and drain again. Hold under refrigeration. Reheat the pasta by lowering it into simmering water.

Variations

SPINACH PASTA   Add 1¼ pounds/570 grams of pureed raw spinach to the dough, and decrease the water to around 5 ounces.

PUMPKIN, BEET, OR CARROT PASTA   Cook 1¼ pounds/570 grams of pureed pumpkin, beets, or carrots to remove as much of the moisture as possible (without burning). Add the puree to the pasta, and add the water slowly, adding only enough to achieve the correct consistency.

TOMATO PASTA   Cook 8 ounces/225 grams of tomato paste in a sauté pan to remove moisture and intensify the flavor. Reduce the water addition by about 3 ounces, and add the water gradually, stopping when the correct consistency is reached.

FRESH HERB PASTA   Add 3 tablespoons/45 grams of chopped fresh herbs (rinse and dry thoroughly before chopping) to the dough.

SPICE PASTA   Add 2 tablespoons/10 grams of crushed herbs (cumin seeds, peppercorns, etc.) to the dough.

PORTION	KCAL	PROTEIN	FAT	CARB	SODIUM	CHOL
2 oz	150	5 gm	1 gm	31 gm	9 mg	0 mg

SAFFRON PASTA WITH LEMON AND FENNEL

Yield: 5 pounds/2.25 kilograms

10½ fluid ounces	Water, hot	300 milliliters
½ ounce	Saffron threads, crushed	15 grams
3 pounds, 10 ounces	Semolina flour	1.6 kilograms
10½ ounces	Egg whites	300 grams
4	Lemon zest, finely grated (optional)	4
4 ounces	Fennel tops, chopped (optional)*	115 grams

1. Combine the hot water and the saffron to make an infusion. Allow it to cool.

2. Using a dough hook, combine all ingredients except the fennel tops and mix well to form a dough that will hold its shape when pressed together. The dough should not form a ball. If necessary, add more flour or water a little at a time to reach the correct consistency.

3. Wrap the dough and allow it to rest for at least 1 hour.

4. Break off a piece of dough that can be easily rolled through the pasta machine (amount will vary, depending upon the width of the machine's rollers.) Roll the dough out through the machine, working from the largest opening to the smallest.

5. Sprinkle the chopped fennel, if desired, over the sheet of pasta and fold the pasta in half to enclose the fennel. Open the rollers up three settings, and roll the pasta through that setting, then through the two succeeding settings. Cut and shape as desired.

This dough may be used, as desired, to prepare tortellini, ravioli, fettucini, or other flat or filled pastas.

    * If desired, the fennel tops may be replaced by fresh herbs such as parsley, cilantro, mint, or basil.

PORTION	KCAL	PROTEIN	FAT	CARB	SODIUM	CHOL
2 oz	150	5 gm	trace	31 gm	13 mg	0 mg

CHILI PEPPER PASTA

Yield: 5 pounds/2.25 kilograms

1 pound	Dried mild chilies, seeded	450 grams
5 fluid ounces	Hot water	150 milliliters
8 ounces	Egg whites	250 grams
3¼ pounds	Durum semolina flour	1.5 kilograms

1. Combine the chilies with the hot water to soften them.

2. Puree the chilies and the egg whites until smooth.

3. Combine the chili puree with the flour using a dough hook and mix to form a stiff dough.

4. Press the dough into a ball, cover with plastic wrap, and let rest for at least 1 hour.

5. Roll out the dough as needed, depending upon intended use. Cut and shape as desired.

───────

Use a mild-flavored dried chili such as anaheim or poblano. If desired, the chilis may be briefly toasted over an open flame.

PORTION	KCAL	PROTEIN	FAT	CARB	SODIUM	CHOL
2 oz	150	5 gm	trace	31 gm	13 mg	0 mg

JALAPEÑO PASTA

Yield: 4 pounds/1.8 kilograms

5 ounces	Jalapeño peppers, fresh, seeded, chopped	140 grams
8 ounces	Egg whites	225 grams
12 ounces	Durum semolina flour	340 grams
2¼ pounds	Bread flour	1 kilogram

1. Puree the peppers and the egg whites until smooth.

2. Combine the puree with the flours using a dough hook and mix to form a stiff dough.

3. Press the dough into a ball, cover with plastic wrap, and let rest for at least 1 hour.

4. Roll out the dough as needed, depending upon intended use.

The amount of jalapeños may need to be adjusted to taste so that the pasta is not unacceptably hot. Add water or flour as necessary to get the correct consistency.

PORTION	KCAL	PROTEIN	FAT	CARB	SODIUM	CHOL
2 oz	145	5 gm	1 gm	31 gm	14 mg	0 mg

CHORIZO FILLING FOR FILLED PASTAS

Yield: 8 ounces/225 grams

5 ounces	Pork scraps, lean	140 grams
2½ ounces	Rice, well-cooked	70 grams
¼ ounce	Jalapeños, chopped	7 grams
½ ounce	Garlic, chopped	15 grams
2 ounces	Chorizo sausage, chopped	60 grams
⅓ teaspoon	Salt	3 grams
⅓ teaspoon	Cayenne pepper	3 grams
1 teaspoon	Oregano, chopped	1 gram
1 teaspoon	Cider vinegar	5 milliliters
⅓ teaspoon	Chili pepper flakes	3 grams

1. Grind the pork and rice through a medium die twice.

2. Grind the pork and rice mixture a third time, along with all of the remaining ingredients.

3. Chill the filling before using.

PORTION	KCAL	PROTEIN	FAT	CARB	SODIUM	CHOL
1 oz	75	6 gm	5 gm	2 gm	230 mg	20 mg

SHRIMP FILLING FOR FILLED PASTAS

Yield: 1 pound/450 grams

14 ounces	Shrimp, peeled, de-veined	**400 grams**
2 ounces	Ricotta cheese, part-skim	**60 grams**
1 tablespoon	Basil, chopped	**3 grams**
¼ teaspoon	Salt	**2 grams**
⅛ teaspoon	White pepper, ground	**250 milligrams**
½ teaspoon	Lemon or lime juice	**3 milliliters**

1. Grind the shrimp to a fine paste in a food processor. Add the ricotta and pulse the machine on and off a few times until it is just incorporated.

2. Remove the shrimp/ricotta mixture to a bowl, and fold in the basil, salt, and pepper.

3. Add the lemon or lime juice to taste.

4. The filling may be put into fresh ravioli, tortellini, or other filled pastas.

5. Cook the pasta in simmering water or fish fumet until the pasta rises to the surface and is just tender to the bite.

Very large ravioli may be filled with this mixture and then served with grilled red endive, peppers, and whole, grilled shrimp. The dish is served on a bed of Red Pepper Coulis (recipe found in Chapter 11).

PORTION	KCAL	PROTEIN	FAT	CARB	SODIUM	CHOL
1 oz	30	5 gm	1 gm	1 gm	95 mg	35 mg

FOCUS FILLED PASTAS

By cutting and shaping fresh-filled pastas a little differently the chef can create a number of specialties. Cappelletti are shown in the accompanying photograph. The name translates literally as "little hats," and the little pasta "dumplings" do look like the peaked hats worn by bishops and other dignitaries. Peaked agnolotti hail from Emilia-Romagna, while rounded caps are prepared in the Marches and Umbria.

To prepare cappelletti, the dough is cut into squares. A ruler and a pizza cutter make it easy to cut squares of identical proportions. Next, a very small amount of filling is placed in the center. Water is brushed around the edges of the square, and it is folded in half to form a triangle. The edges are pressed firmly to seal the cappelletti tightly. Finally, two points of the triangle are overlapped and pressed together to form a peaked hat. Tortellini are folded and filled in a similar fashion, but instead of squares, the pasta is cut into circles.

Agnolotti are filled pasta squares, usually made with scalloped or ruffled edges. Ravioli may be square, crescent-shaped, or round, with straight or scalloped edges. According to one of the most definitive early writers about Italian cookery, Bartolomeo Scappi, the term "ravioli" originally referred to little dumplings, more similar to gnocchi, while ravioli as we know it today would have been called tortelli. Tortelli are still prepared today; tortelloni is a larger version.

LOBSTER CAPPELLETTI WITH GINGER SAUCE

Yield: 10 portions (appetizer)

FORCEMEAT FILLING

10½ ounces	Lobster meat, raw	300 grams
1	Egg white	1
1 fluid ounce	Heavy cream	30 milliliters
½ ounce	Shallots, minced	15 grams
2 cloves	Garlic, minced	10 grams
1 tablespoon	Chives, minced	3 grams
1 pound	Saffron pasta, rolled into sheets*	450 grams

SAUCE

½ ounce	Shallots, minced	15 grams
½ ounce	Gingerroot, fresh, grated	15 grams

2 fluid ounces	Lime juice, freshly squeezed	60 milliliters
3½ fluid ounces	White wine, dry	100 milliliters
1 pint	Fish velouté	480 milliliters
3½ fluid ounces	Heavy cream	100 milliliters

GARNISH

| 15 pieces | Lobster claws | 15 pieces |
| as needed | Lime zest, blanched | as needed |

1. To prepare the filling: Puree the lobster meat with the egg white in a food processor just until a paste forms. Add the heavy cream and puree until blended. Add the shallots, garlic, and chives; pulse the machine on and off until just incorporated.

2. Cut the saffron pasta into rectangles, fill with the forcemeat mixture, and seal edges with water. Press the edges together, then twist to form into cappelletti.

3. Cook the pasta in boiling water just until tender. Drain and refresh.

4. To prepare the sauce: Combine the shallots, gingerroot, lime juice, and wine; reduce by half. Add the fish velouté and heavy cream and simmer until the flavor and consistency are properly developed.

5. Add the cappelletti to the sauce to reheat. Serve on heated plates or soup bowls garnished with a lobster claw and lime zest.

---

* See the Saffron Pasta recipe in this section.

PORTION	KCAL	PROTEIN	FAT	CARB	SODIUM	CHOL
1 portion	330	18 gm	3 gm	56 gm	215 mg	50 mg

SHRIMP AND HERB RAVIOLI WITH FENNEL SAUCE

Yield: 10 portions (entrée)

RAVIOLI

6 ounces	Shrimp, peeled, de-veined, sliced ½-inch thick	160 grams
1 teaspoon	Pernod	5 milliliters
1 teaspoon	Lemon juice, freshly squeezed	5 milliliters
1½ fluid ounces	Heavy cream	45 milliliters
1 tablespoon	Basil, chiffonade	3 grams
1 tablespoon	Parsley, minced	3 grams
½ teaspoon	Salt	3 grams
⅛ teaspoon	Cayenne pepper, ground	250 milligrams
½ recipe	Basic Pasta Dough, cut into 2-inch circles or squares	½ recipe

SAUCE

8 fluid ounces	Shrimp stock	240 milliliters
4 cloves	Garlic, finely chopped	20 grams
4 ounces	Leeks, medium dice	115 grams
¾ pound	Fennel, medium dice	360 grams
1 teaspoon	Pernod	4 milliliters
1½ fluid ounces	Evaporated skimmed milk	45 milliliters

GARNISH

2 ounces	Carrots, julienned	60 grams
2 ounces	Fennel, julienned	60 grams
2 ounces	Leeks, julienned	60 grams
as needed	Fennel tops, chopped	as needed

1. To prepare the filling: Puree half of the shrimp with the Pernod, lemon juice, and heavy cream until a smooth paste forms. Remove from the processor and, over an ice bath, fold in the basil, parsley, cayenne, salt, and the remaining shrimp.

2. Place a small amount of the filling on a pasta circle, brush the edge with water, top with a second circle, and press the edges well to form ravioli.

3. Cook the ravioli in boiling water until tender and just barely cooked through. Drain and refresh, if necessary.

4. To prepare the sauce: Sweat the garlic in the shrimp stock. Add the leeks and fennel; cook until the vegetables are very tender.

5. Puree the fennel mixture until smooth; strain it through a sieve to remove all fibers.

6. Combine the puree with the Pernod and milk. Return the sauce to a simmer before serving.

7. Combine the sauce with the garnish ingredients. Serve the hot ravioli on a pool of the heated sauce.

PORTION	KCAL	PROTEIN	FAT	CARB	SODIUM	CHOL
1 portion	175	9 gm	2 gm	30 gm	200 mg	30 mg

CHÈVRE CHEESE RAVIOLI

Yield: 10 portions

RAVIOLI

1 teaspoon	Olive oil	5 milliliters
1 tablespoon	Shallots, minced	12 grams
1 clove	Garlic, minced	5 grams
3 ounces	Spinach, blanched, coarsely chopped	85 grams
5 ounces	Chèvre cheese	140 milliliters
5 ounces	Ricotta cheese, part-skim	140 grams
3½ ounces	Egg whites	100 grams
1 ounce	Parmesan cheese, grated	30 grams
4 teaspoons	Basil, chopped	4 grams
1 teaspoon	Oregano, chopped	1 gram
½ recipe	Basic Pasta Dough, cut into 2-inch circles or squares	½ recipe

SAUCE

1 quart	Chicken velouté*	1 liter
2 ounces	Pesto**	60 grams
5 fluid ounces	Heavy cream	150 milliliters
5 ounces	Fresh Tomato Salsa**	140 grams
2¼ pounds	Yellow squash or zucchini, julienned, skin only, blanched	1 kilogram

1. Sauté the shallots and garlic in the olive oil until they are translucent. Remove from the heat.

2. Combine the spinach, chèvre and ricotta cheeses, egg whites, Parmesan, basil, and oregano with the shallots and garlic. Chill this mixture thoroughly.

3. To make the ravioli, place a small amount of filling in the center of one of the pasta circles. Brush the edges with water, top with a second pasta circle, and press the edges to seal. Repeat with the remaining pasta and filling.

4. Prepare the sauce by combining the velouté, pesto, and heavy cream. Heat the sauce to order (3½ fluid ounces/100 milliliters per portion), and place in a heated bowl.

5. Cook the raviolis to order in boiling water until just tender. Drain and place on top of the hot sauce. Serve immediately. Garnish with the salsa and julienned squash.

---

* See the recipe for Velouté-style Sauce in Chapter 11.

   ** See the recipes in Chapter 12 for Pesto and Fresh Tomato Salsa.

PORTION	KCAL	PROTEIN	FAT	CARB	SODIUM	CHOL
1 portion	300	13 gm	11 gm	36 gm	200 mg	30 mg

SPÄTZLE

Yield: 15 portions

5	Egg whites	5
4 fluid ounces	Skim milk, chilled	120 milliliters
9½ ounces	Flour, all-purpose	275 grams
to taste	Nutmeg, ground	to taste
as needed	White beef stock (or water)	as needed
4 teaspoons	Chives, cut	5 grams
¼ teaspoon	Salt	1.25 grams
½ teaspoon	Black pepper, freshly ground	1 gram

1. Cream together the egg whites, milk, flour, and nutmeg. Add more flour as needed to form a batter with approximately the consistency of heavy cream.

2. Drop through a colander, sieve, or spätzle maker into a pot of the simmering beef stock.

3. Cook the spätzle until they rise back to the surface of the stock. Remove with a skimmer and let drain well.

4. Toss with the chives, salt, and pepper. Portion into serving sizes: 3 ounces/85 grams per portion.

5. Sauté the spätzle in a small amount of stock at service.

PORTION 1 portion	KCAL 90	PROTEIN 4 gm	FAT trace	CARB 17 gm	SODIUM 65 mg	CHOL trace

ORZO PASTA

Yield: 10 portions

1½ pints	Chicken stock, simmering	720 milliliters
½ teaspoon	Saffron threads, crushed	500 milligrams
9½ ounces	Orzo pasta (dried)	265 grams
2½ ounces	Mozzarella, whole milk, grated	70 grams
1 fluid ounce	Evaporated skimmed milk	30 milliliters
⅛ teaspoon	Salt	.6 gram

1. Simmer the stock and saffron until the stock has a rich golden color.

2. Add the pasta and cook until it is al dente. Drain the pasta, reserving the stock.

3. Combine the pasta with the grated cheese and the milk. Cook over very low heat until the cheese is melted. Add stock as necessary for a good consistency.

4. To reheat before service, microwave single portions on highest power setting so pasta is very hot, mix, and serve.

PORTION 1 portion	KCAL 140	PROTEIN 6 gm	FAT 3 gm	CARB 20 gm	SODIUM 195 mg	CHOL 35 mg

BASIC PIZZA DOUGH WITH VARIATIONS

Yield: 2 pounds/900 grams

½ fluid ounce	Honey	15 milliliters
12 fluid ounces	Water	360 milliliters
⅓ ounce	Yeast, dry, granulated	10 grams
10 ounces	Bread flour	285 grams
10 ounces	Semolina flour	285 grams
½ teaspoon	Salt	3 grams
as needed	Olive oil	as needed
as needed	Cornmeal	as needed

1. Mix the honey, yeast, one-third of the water, and enough of the bread flour to make a batter of the same consistency as crêpe batter.

2. Cover the batter, place in a warm spot, and let proof about 1 hour, or until a sponge develops. Batter will become frothy and increase in volume.

3. Add the remaining water, bread and semolina flour, and the salt to the sponge and knead with a dough hook or by hand until a smooth elastic dough develops (about

5 minutes). Add additional flour, if necessary. The dough should pull cleanly away from the bowl.

4. Divide the dough into 10 equal pieces, round into balls, and let rise until doubled.

5. Flatten the dough into 7½-inch-wide circles. Place on parchment sheets brushed or sprayed lightly with olive oil and sprinkled with cornmeal; refrigerate until needed.

———

The sponge method is outlined above. To mix the dough using the straight mixing method, follow these steps:

1. Combine the honey, water, and yeast in a mixer bowl. Mix with a dough hook until the yeast is dissolved.

2. Add both flours and the salt. Using the hook, knead the dough until it pulls cleanly from the bowl and has a smooth, elastic texture (about 5 minutes). Shape and store as directed above.

Variations

WHOLE-WHEAT PIZZA DOUGH   Replace one-third of the bread flour with whole-wheat flour and double the amount of yeast.

BUCKWHEAT MANITOBA DOUGH   Replace one-third of the bread flour with buckwheat flour, replace the semolina flour with manitoba flour, and double the amount of yeast.

PITA BREAD   Prepare the basic pizza dough or one of the two variations above. Shape it as for pizza disks and then bake on cornmeal-lined baking sheets in a hot (550 degree F/260 degree C) oven for about 10 to 15 minutes. When the bread is removed from the oven, it will deflate and a "pocket" will form.

GRILLED BREAD   Prepare the basic pizza dough or one of the two variations above. Shape it as for pizza disks and then grill for 3 to 4 minutes on each side over hot coals, or until the bread puffs, blisters, and cooks through.

PORTION	KCAL	PROTEIN	FAT	CARB	SODIUM	CHOL
1 portion	225	6 gm	2 gm	45 gm	155 mg	0 mg

PIZZA WITH TOMATOES AND MOZZARELLA

Yield: 10 pizzas

1 recipe	Basic Pizza Dough	1 recipe
1½ fluid ounces	Extra-virgin olive oil	45 milliliters
1 tablespoon	Basil leaves, chopped	3 grams
1 teaspoon	Oregano leaves, chopped	1 gram
1 ounce	Garlic cloves, minced	30 grams
2¼ pounds	Plum tomatoes, roasted, sliced	1 kilogram
10½ ounces	Mozzarella cheese, part-skim, sliced, frozen	300 grams
10 fluid ounces	Tomato Coulis	300 milliliters
1½ ounces	Parmesan cheese, grated	40 grams
as needed	Basil leaves, chiffonade	as needed
as needed	Black peppercorns, cracked	as needed

1. Bring pizza disks to room temperature and let proof.

2. Mix the olive oil, basil, oregano, and garlic. Spread about 1 teaspoon (6 grams) on each pizza disk.

3. Shingle tomato and mozzarella slices around the outer edge of each disk (about 10 slices of each per pizza), leaving the center empty.

4. Place about 1 fluid ounce/30 milliliters of tomato coulis in the center of each pizza.

5. Sprinkle about 1 teaspoon/4 grams of grated Parmesan on each pizza and add the garnish ingredients to taste.

6. Bake the pizzas in a very hot (550 degree F/260 degree C) oven until the crust is golden and crisp (about 8 to 10 minutes).

PORTION	KCAL	PROTEIN	FAT	CARB	SODIUM	CHOL
1 portion	400	15 gm	16 gm	51 gm	390 mg	15 mg

PIZZA WITH WILD MUSHROOMS AND GOAT CHEESE

Yield: 10 pizzas

1 recipe	Basic Pizza Dough	1 recipe
10 fluid ounces	Tomato Coulis	300 milliliters
9 ounces	Assorted wild mushrooms, sliced	250 grams
7 ounces	Montrachet (goat cheese) with herbs	200 grams
1¾ ounces	Parmesan cheese, grated	50 grams
1¾ ounces	Garlic, coarsely chopped	50 grams
to taste	Black peppercorns, cracked	to taste

1. Bring pizza disks to room temperature and let proof.

2. Spread the tomato coulis in an even layer on the pizza disks and arrange the mushrooms and cheeses on top of the coulis. Scatter the garlic over the pizza. Season with peppercorns to taste.

3. Bake the pizza in a 550 degree F/260 degree C oven for 8 to 10 minutes.

PORTION	KCAL	PROTEIN	FAT	CARB	SODIUM	CHOL
1 portion	340	13 gm	9 gm	50 gm	485 mg	20 mg

ST. ANDREW'S VEGETABLE PIZZA

Yield: 10 pizzas

1 recipe	Basic Pizza Dough	1 recipe
12 ounces	Red peppers, julienned	340 grams
3½ ounces	Red onions, julienned	100 grams
3½ ounces	Leeks, white part, chiffonade	100 grams
1 fluid ounce	Chicken stock	30 milliliters
12 fluid ounces	Tomato Coulis*	360 milliliters
2½ fluid ounces	Vinaigrette-style Dressing*	75 milliliters
7 ounces	Yellow squash, thinly sliced	200 grams
7 ounces	Eggplant, thinly sliced	200 grams
7 ounces	Zucchini, thinly sliced	200 grams
3½ ounces	Shiitake mushrooms, stems removed, sliced	100 grams
3½ ounces	Goat cheese, fresh, crumbled	100 grams
2 ounces	Parmesan cheese, grated	60 grams
1 ounce	Garlic, chopped	30 grams
to taste	Black peppercorns, cracked	to taste

1. Bring pizza disks to room temperature and let proof.

2. Sweat the peppers, onions, and leeks in the chicken stock until tender. Remove them from the heat and cool.

3. Spread about 1 fluid ounce/30 milliliters of tomato coulis on each pizza disk.

4. Combine the vinaigrette with the squash, eggplant, and zucchini slices. Toss to coat. Shingle them around the edge of the disks, leaving the center empty.

5. Place the mushrooms in the center of the pizzas.

6. Scatter the cheeses over the top (about 1 tablespoon/10 grams of goat cheese and 1 teaspoon/5 grams of Parmesan per pizza).

7. Sprinkle the top with 1 teaspoon/3 grams garlic and peppercorns to taste.

8. Bake the pizzas in a very hot (550 degree F/260 degree C) oven until the crust is golden and crisp (about 8 to 10 minutes).

* See Chapters 11 and 12, respectively, for the recipes for Tomato Coulis and Vinaigrette-style Dressing.

PORTION	KCAL	PROTEIN	FAT	CARB	SODIUM	CHOL
1 portion	330	12 gm	7 gm	55 gm	300 mg	10 mg

SHRIMP AND CLAM PIZZA WITH PESTO

Yield: 10 pizzas

1 recipe	Basic Pizza Dough	1 recipe
3½ ounces	Pesto	100 grams
10 ounces	Shrimp, cleaned, de-veined, halved	285 grams
7 ounces	Clams, steamed, coarsely chopped	200 grams
10 ounces	Tomatoes, oven-roasted, sliced	285 grams
6 ounces	Leeks, steamed, thinly sliced	170 grams
1¾ ounces	Parmesan cheese, grated	50 grams
¼ ounce	Basil, chiffonade	7 grams
to taste	Black peppercorns, cracked	to taste

1. Bring the pizza disks to room temperature and let proof.

2. Spread the pizza disks with the pesto (⅓ ounce/10 grams per pizza).

3. Top the pizzas with the shrimp, clams, and tomatoes. (1 ounce/30 grams each of shrimp and tomatoes; ¾ ounce/20 grams each of clams).

4. Arrange the steamed leeks on top of the seafood (½ ounce/15 grams per pizza) and top with grated Parmesan (about 1 teaspoon/5 grams), and basil and peppercorns to taste.

5. Bake the pizzas in a very hot (550 degree F/260 degree C) oven until the crust is golden and crisp (about 8 to 10 minutes).

PORTION	KCAL	PROTEIN	FAT	CARB	SODIUM	CHOL
1 portion	320	17 gm	6 gm	48 gm	340 mg	55 mg

SMOKED MOZZARELLA, PROSCIUTTO, AND ROASTED PEPPER PIZZA

Yield: 10 pizzas

(Foreground) Oven-roasted Tomatoes, Fontina, Prosciutto and Basil. (Background) Smoked Mozzarella, Peppers, Grilled Duck and Oregano.

1 recipe	Basic Pizza Dough	1 recipe
10½ ounces	Smoked mozzarella, sliced thin	300 grams
5 ounces	Prosciutto, trimmed, sliced paper-thin	140 grams
10½ ounces	Peppers (assorted colors) roasted, peeled, cut into strips	300 grams
3½ ounces	Tomatoes, peeled, seeded, cut into strips	100 grams
3½ ounces	Red onions, julienned	100 grams
1 ounce	Jalapeño peppers, finely chopped	30 grams
1 ounce	Garlic, finely chopped	30 grams
3½ fluid ounces	Balsamic vinaigrette*	100 milliliters

1. Bring pizza disks to room temperature and let proof.

2. Lay slices of mozzarella and prosciutto flat on a sheet pan and freeze until ready to assemble the pizzas.

3. Combine all remaining ingredients and toss well.

4. Alternate slices of mozzarella and prosciutto around the outer edge of the disks (1 ounce/30 grams of mozzarella per pizza; ½ ounce/14 grams of prosciutto per pizza).

5. Spread roasted pepper mixture evenly over each disk.

6. Bake the pizza in a very hot (550 degree F/260 degree C) oven until the crust is golden and crisp (about 8 to 10 minutes).

———

* See Chapter 12 for the Vinaigrette-style Dressing recipe. Prepare it using extra-virgin olive oil, balsamic vinegar, and a variety of fresh herbs (chives, cilantro, and oregano is a good combination).

PORTION	KCAL	PROTEIN	FAT	CARB	SODIUM	CHOL
1 portion	405	18 gm	14 gm	53 gm	600 mg	20 mg

BARBECUED CHICKEN PIZZA WITH FRESH TOMATO SALSA

Yield: 10 pizzas

BARBECUE SAUCE

½ ounce	Butter	15 grams
6 ounces	Onion, chopped	175 grams
1 tablespoon	Garlic, minced	15 grams
5 ounces	Tomato paste	140 grams
2 ounces	Chipolte peppers, canned	60 grams
4 fluid ounces	Coffee, brewed	120 milliliters
4 fluid ounces	Worcestershire sauce	120 milliliters
2½ fluid ounces	Apple-cider vinegar	75 milliliters
2½ fluid ounces	Apple cider	75 milliliters
2½ ounces	Brown sugar	70 grams
1 pound, 10 ounces	Chicken breasts, trimmed	750 grams
7 ounces	Monterey Jack cheese, thinly sliced*	200 grams
1 recipe	Basic Pizza Dough	1 recipe
9 ounces	Fresh Tomato Salsa**	255 grams
¾ ounce	Garlic, minced	20 grams

1. Prepare barbecue sauce as follows: Heat the butter and sweat the onions and garlic until they are translucent. Add the remaining ingredients and simmer until the sauce has thickened slightly. It may be used at this point or properly stored under refrigeration.

2. Trim the chicken breasts and cut into pieces of 2½ ounces/70 grams each. Coat the chicken with barbecue sauce and grill to medium rare. (They will complete cooking as the pizza bakes.) Cool and refrigerate until needed.

3. Bring the pizza disks to room temperature and let proof.

4. Arrange the cheese around the outer edge of the disks. Slice the chicken and place on the cheese; sprinkle with garlic. Place salsa in the middle of the pizza.

5. Bake the pizza in a very hot (550 degree F/260 degree C) oven until the crust is golden and crisp (about 8 to 10 minutes).

———

* Lay the slices of Monterey Jack flat on a sheet pan and freeze until ready to assemble pizzas.

** The recipe for Fresh Tomato Salsa is found in Chapter 12.

PORTION	KCAL	PROTEIN	FAT	CARB	SODIUM	CHOL
1 portion	415	29 gm	10 gm	50 gm	280 mg	65 mg

LOBSTER AND JALAPEÑO PIZZA

Yield: 10 pizzas

1 recipe	Basic Pizza Dough	1 recipe
1½ fluid ounces	Extra-virgin olive oil	40 milliliters
10 ounces	Mozzarella, part-skim, sliced thin*	285 grams
1¼ pounds	Lobster meat, blanched, diced	600 grams
10 ounces	Arugula leaves, blanched	285 grams
1½ ounces	Jalapeños, chopped	40 grams
2 ounces	Shallots, thinly sliced	60 grams
2 ounces	Parmesan cheese, grated	60 grams
¾ ounce	Cilantro, coarsely chopped	20 grams

1. Bring pizza disks to room temperature and let proof.

2. Brush or spray the pizza disks with olive oil (1 teaspoon/4 grams per pizza). Layer the sliced cheese around the outer edge of each disk.

3. Top the pizzas with the lobster and arugula, and scatter jalapeños and shallots over the surface.

4. Top the pizzas with Parmesan cheese and cilantro.

5. Bake the pizzas in a very hot (550 degree F/260 degree C) oven until the crust is golden and crisp (about 8 to 10 minutes).

---

* Place the mozzarella in the freezer for 15 or 20 minutes so that it will firm slightly. That will make it easier to slice.

PORTION	KCAL	PROTEIN	FAT	CARB	SODIUM	CHOL
1 portion	425	27 gm	13 gm	47 gm	535 mg	70 mg

CHAPTER

20

Desserts

In the first rush of excitement over nutritional cooking, desserts were most often left out in the cold. Interesting appetizers, side dishes, and entrées grabbed the lion's share of the chef's attention. For several years it seemed that the most imaginative dessert that could be mustered as the meal's finale was either a platter of sliced fresh fruit or a plain poached pear. The problem is that most Western people have come to expect a sweet dessert following their meal. A too-stringent regimen that ignores the importance of dessert often falls flat in the face of the same fresh fruit plate, dinner after dinner.

A platter of fresh, seasonal fruit is not a bad choice; it should be just one of many possibilities. Throughout this chapter, a number of dessert ideas are presented, ranging from a modified version of a Bavarian cream, made with a base of yogurt and ricotta instead of a custard sauce lightened with whipped cream; to a chocolate soufflé made from a base of polenta instead of the traditional "crème pâtissiere"; to a Caramel Sauce that greatly reduces the amount of butter used in the traditional recipe.

In addition to these items, there are a number of special recipes for a variety of doughs and delicate cookies that should enable the chef to create a number of signature desserts featuring local ingredients for strudel fillings, exotic fruit flavors for a rainbow of frozen glaces, and even some traditional favorites such as chocolate mousse.

FOCUS DAIRY BASE

Rich, smooth ice creams, mousses and bavarians are traditionally prepared from a custard base, made by cooking together heavy cream, sugar, vanilla, and egg yolks.

In a nutritional kitchen, such lavish use of high-fat, high-cholesterol, and high-calorie ingredients isn't possible. A combination of nonfat yogurt, low-fat ricotta cheese, maple syrup, and flavorings is an alternative that comes close to the original custard base. Like custard sauce, the base preparation can be flavored and used as a sauce to accompany soufflés. Or, it can be combined with gelatin and beaten egg whites (instead of whipped cream) to produce a Bavarian that is satisfyingly smooth and creamy. Or, it can be lightened with egg whites and flavored to create a wonderful chocolate mousse. It can also be frozen to create a dessert that is incredibly similar to ice cream.

Consider some of the many other ways in which it can be flavored and presented: Adding cooked apples flavored with cinnamon, nutmeg, and brown sugar creates a delicious Apple Pie Glace. Glace quenelles, flavored with berries or tropical fruits, can be sandwiched between Cinnamon Crisps or nestled in cups made from a delicate chocolate cookie batter. A little scoop of a plain or flavored glace can be served along with a slice of warm strudel, glazed pineapple, or grilled bananas.

The dairy base can be flavored in a number of ways. Shown here, clockwise from the top, vanilla, chocolate, strawberry, orange, and blueberry.

DAIRY BASE FOR FROZEN GLACE AND BAVARIANS

Yield: 3¼ pounds/1.6 kilograms

1½ pounds	Ricotta cheese, part-skim	680 grams
1 pound	Yogurt, plain, nonfat	450 grams
12 fluid ounces	Maple syrup	360 milliliters
¾ fluid ounce	Vanilla extract	20 milliliters

1. In a food processor, puree the ricotta cheese until very smooth.
2. Add the remaining ingredients and puree until smooth.
3. The base is ready to be used.

a *A large batch of frozen dairy base is ready to remove from the machine.*

To prepare frozen glace: Add desired flavoring ingredients, and freeze in an ice cream freezer according to directions. Specific recipes follow this one, but some additional suggestions are included here.

BANANA GLACE   Add 1 part (by weight) of pureed ripe bananas to 3 parts of glace base mixture; freeze.

FRESH BERRY GLACE   Add 1 part (by weight) of ripe fresh berries to 3 parts glace. The fruit may be left whole, crushed, sliced, or pureed, as desired.

TROPICAL FRUIT GLACE   Add 1 part (by weight) of ripe pureed tropical fruits such as mango, pineapple, passion fruit, papaya, or a combination of these fruits.

LIQUEUR-FLAVORED GLACE   Add about 1½ fluid ounces/50 milliliters of the desired cordial or liqueur (Amaretto, Kahlua, Grand Marnier, for example) for every 1 pound/450 grams of dairy base.

b *A home-style machine can be used to prepare smaller batches of frozen dairy base with special flavors. Raspberry is shown here.*

PORTION	KCAL	PROTEIN	FAT	CARB	SODIUM	CHOL
2½ oz	90	4 gm	2 gm	14 gm	55 mg	10 mg

CAPPUCCINO GLACE

Yield: 3¼ pounds/1.6 kilograms

8 fluid ounces	Evaporated skimmed milk	240 milliliters
2 ounces	Coffee beans, French-roast	60 grams
1	Cinnamon stick	1
1½ pounds	Ricotta cheese, part-skim	680 grams
8 ounces	Yogurt, plain, nonfat	225 grams
12 ounces	Maple syrup	340 grams
¾ fluid ounce	Vanilla extract	20 milliliters

1. Heat the milk with the coffee beans and cinnamon stick, steep for about 30 minutes. Strain the milk and let it cool.

2. In a food processor, puree the ricotta cheese until very smooth.

3. Add the coffee-flavored milk, yogurt, maple syrup, and vanilla; puree until smooth.

4. Freeze this mixture in an ice cream machine, according to the manufacturer's directions.

PORTION	KCAL	PROTEIN	FAT	CARB	SODIUM	CHOL
1 portion	90	4 gm	2 gm	14 gm	55 mg	10 mg

PUMPKIN GLACE

Yield: 2 pounds/900 grams

1 pound	Pumpkin puree	450 grams
1 pound	Dairy base	450 grams
1 teaspoon	Cinnamon, ground	1 gram
¼ teaspoon	Nutmeg, grated	250 milligrams

1. Combine all of the ingredients in a food processor and blend until smooth.

2. Freeze the pumpkin mixture in an ice cream freezer, according to manufacturer's directions.

PORTION	KCAL	PROTEIN	FAT	CARB	SODIUM	CHOL
1 portion	60	3 gm	1 gm	9 gm	30 mg	4 mg

PEAR SORBET

Yield: 40 portions

9 pounds	Pears, very ripe*	4 kilograms
20 fluid ounces	Reserved poaching liquid*	600 milliliters

1. Quarter the pears; remove the core, stem, and peel; and slice. Combine them with the poaching liquid in a noncorroding pan.**

2. Cover the pan, and bring the liquid to a slow simmer over low heat. Continue to simmer just until the pears are heated through.

3. Puree the pears and the liquid in a food processor or blender until no longer grainy. Strain through a fine sieve, cool, and then freeze in an ice cream machine according to manufacturer's directions.

PORTION	KCAL	PROTEIN	FAT	CARB	SODIUM	CHOL
1 portion	70	trace	trace	18 gm	trace	0 mg

* Any ripe pears, or combination of pears, may be used, including Bartlett, D'Anjou, Comice, or Seckel. Use the poaching liquid reserved from preparing the poached pears in the recipe for A Trio of Pears (found in this chapter).

** Select a pan that is made of stainless steel, enameled cast-iron, or anodized aluminum.

APPLE PIE GLACE

Yield: 2 pounds/900 grams

9 ounces	Granny Smith apples, peeled, cored, sliced	255 grams
2 teaspoons	Butter, unsalted	10 grams
½ ounce	Brown sugar	15 grams
½ teaspoon	Cinnamon, ground	500 milligrams
¼ teaspoon	Nutmeg, grated	250 milligrams
2 fluid ounces	Apple cider	60 milliliters
1¼ pounds	Dairy base	570 grams

1. Combine the apples, butter, brown sugar, cinnamon, and nutmeg. Cook them gently over medium heat until the apples are soft enough to puree easily. Puree the apples.

2. Add the cider to the mixture and chill thoroughly.

3. Combine the dairy base with the chilled apple mixture and freeze in an ice cream machine, according to the manufacturer's directions.

This glace would be good served with Cinnamon Crisps (see the variation on the Almond Tile recipe in this chapter) and Caramel Sauce (also in this chapter).

PORTION	KCAL	PROTEIN	FAT	CARB	SODIUM	CHOL
1 portion	90	3 gm	2 gm	14 gm	40 mg	7 mg

BLUEBERRY GLACE WITH ALMOND TILES AND FRESH FRUIT

Yield: 10 portions

7 ounces	Blueberry puree	200 grams
28 ounces	Dairy base	800 grams
30	Almond Tiles*	30
1 ounce	Blueberries, dried	30 grams
1 pound	Fresh fruit, sliced	450 grams
7 ounces	Raspberry Coulis*	200 grams

1. Combine the blueberry puree and dairy base; freeze in an ice cream freezer, according to the manufacturer's directions.

2. Place an almond tile on the plate, top with a scoop of blueberry glace, then another tile, another scoop of glace, and finally the third tile.

3. Toss together the dried blueberries and fresh fruit.

4. Place a ribbon of the raspberry coulis around the almond tiles and glace. Serve with 1 to 2 ounces/30 to 50 grams of the blueberry and fruit mixture.

---

* The recipe for Almond Tiles is included in this chapter. For the raspberry coulis, see the recipe for Fresh Berry Coulis, also in this chapter.

PORTION	KCAL	PROTEIN	FAT	CARB	SODIUM	CHOL
1 portion	190	8 gm	5 gm	30 gm	100 mg	15 mg

FRUITED BAVARIAN

Yield: 2½ quarts/2.3 liters

2 pounds	Dairy base	900 grams
1 pound	Fruit puree, chilled*	450 grams
3 fluid ounces	Water, cold	90 milliliters
3 fluid ounces	Port wine, white	90 milliliters
2 packages	Gelatin	40 grams
6	Egg whites	6
2 ounces	Sugar, granulated	60 grams

1. Combine the dairy base and the fruit puree in a food processor or blender until smooth.

2. Combine the water and port wine; sprinkle the gelatin on the surface of the water/wine mixture and let it absorb the liquid for a few minutes. Gently heat the gelatin to melt the crystals and stir it into the fruit mixture.

3. Chill the Bavarian base until it mounds when dropped from a spoon. It may be chilled by stirring over an ice bath or by placing it in the refrigerator.

4. Beat the egg whites to soft peaks. While still beating, gradually add the sugar, and continue to beat to form a meringue.

5. Fold the meringue into the flavored Bavarian base. The Bavarian may be used as desired at this point or stored under refrigeration for 2 days.

---

* A variety of fruits may be used for the puree. Fruits such as pineapple, mangoes, or papayas, which have enzymes that would cause the gelatin to break down, must be cooked to inactivate the enzymes before pureeing. Firm fruits, such as apples or pears, will also need to be cooked so they will be soft enough to puree easily.

The Bavarian may be served on its own or used as a filling for tortes prepared from a modified genoise. To present Bavarians, place them in wine glasses, champagne flutes, or hollowed fruits before refrigerating.

PORTION	KCAL	PROTEIN	FAT	CARB	SODIUM	CHOL
1 portion	90	4 gm	1 gm	16 gm	45 mg	2 mg

PEAR BAVARIAN TERRINE

Yield: 2 terrines

3 pounds	Fruited Bavarian*	**1.3 kilograms**
½ recipe	White Sponge Cake*	**½ recipe**

1. Prepare the Bavarian, using cooked pear puree.

2. Slice the baked sponge cake into large dice, and freeze until the pieces are solid.

3. Gently fold together the Bavarian and the frozen cake. Pour into an earthenware terrine mold lined with plastic wrap.

4. Fold the plastic back over the top of the terrine, and refrigerate for several hours or until firm.

5. Unmold the terrine, remove the plastic, and slice.

———

* See the recipes in this chapter.

This terrine could be served with Caramel Sauce, if desired (see the recipe in this chapter).

PORTION	KCAL	PROTEIN	FAT	CARB	SODIUM	CHOL
1 portion	130	4 gm	4 gm	20 gm	60 mg	10 mg

RASPBERRY TORTE

Yield: Two 10-inch tortes

3 pounds	Fruited Bavarian*	1.3 kilograms
10 ounces	White Sponge Cake* (1 layer)	300 grams
4 fluid ounces	Simple syrup	120 milliliters
¾ ounce	Almonds, sliced, toasted	20 grams
1½ ounces	Cake crumbs	40 grams
4 ounces	Heavy cream	115 grams
2 ounces	Raspberries	60 grams

1. Prepare the Bavarian, using fresh or Individually Quick Frozen (IQF) raspberries, and replacing the white port with red port.

2. Slice the sponge cake into four thin layers. Lay one layer in each of two spring-form pans, and brush lightly with the simple syrup.

3. Add one-quarter of the Bavarian filling to each pan, and top with a second layer of cake. Brush with simple syrup.

4. Divide the remaining Bavarian between the two pans. Chill for several hours or overnight. Unmold and press the almonds and cake crumbs on the side of the cake.

5. Whip the heavy cream and pipe onto the cake in small rosettes (twelve per torte, to indicate slicing lines). Garnish with fresh raspberries, and keep the torte refrigerated until ready to serve.

---

* The recipes for Fruited Bavarian and Sponge Cake are in this chapter.

PORTION	KCAL	PROTEIN	FAT	CARB	SODIUM	CHOL
1 portion	120	5 gm	3 gm	19 gm	60 mg	10 mg

CHOCOLATE YOGURT MOUSSE

Yield: 10 portions

1 pound	Yogurt, nonfat	450 grams
2 ounces	Chocolate, dark, sweet	60 grams
7 ounces	Egg whites	200 grams
3½ ounces	Sugar, granulated	100 grams
1½ ounces	Cocoa powder	40 grams

1. Drain the yogurt in a cheesecloth-lined sieve under refrigeration for 24 hours.

2. Bring the yogurt back to room temperature.

3. Melt the chocolate and combine it with the room-temperature yogurt.

4. Combine the egg whites and sugar in a bowl. Heat them gently over barely simmering water to 135 degrees F/57 degrees C. Beat to form a medium-peak Swiss meringue.

5. Sift the cocoa powder twice, then fold it into the chocolate/yogurt mixture. Warm this mixture over simmering water.

6. Fold the meringue into the warmed chocolate/yogurt mixture.

7. Fill ten prepared molds* with the mousse and chill until firmed.

---

* To mold the mousse, use molds made by cutting 3-inch-diameter PVC pipes into 2-inch lengths. Spray the molds lightly with vegetable oil and dust with powdered sugar. Place the molds on an inverted sheet pan that has been coated with plastic.

To serve, unmold the mousse into a chocolate hippen cup, and serve on a pool of apricot sauce or Fresh Berry Coulis (see the recipe in this chapter). If desired, garnish with a rosette of whipped cream, white chocolate curls, and fresh berries.

The mousse may also be piped into champagne glasses, bowls, or other containers, and served directly in the mold. Garnish with an Almond Tile (recipe in this chapter), if desired.

PORTION	KCAL	PROTEIN	FAT	CARB	SODIUM	CHOL
1 portion	170	7 gm	4 gm	31 gm	80 mg	22 mg

HONEY-VANILLA CHEESECAKE

Yield: 12 portions

2 ounces	Walnuts, pieces	60 grams
4 ounces	Graham cracker crumbs	115 grams
3½ fluid ounces	Orange juice, freshly squeezed	100 milliliters
14 ounces	Cottage cheese, 1% fat	400 grams
7 ounces	Ricotta cheese, part-skim	200 grams
8 ounces	Honey	225 grams
4½ ounces	Cream cheese, reduced fat	125 grams
1½ ounces	Yogurt, nonfat, drained*	40 grams
2	Eggs, whole	2
1	Egg white	1
1 ounce	Cornstarch	30 grams
2	Vanilla beans**	2

1. Chop the walnuts finely in a food processor. Add the graham cracker crumbs. Add the orange juice in a thin stream while the machine is running. Stop adding it when the mixture begins to adhere.

2. Press the crumb crust in an even layer over the sides and bottom of a loose-bottomed tart pan. Patch, where necessary, with additional graham cracker crumbs.

3. Puree the cottage and ricotta cheeses in a food processor until smooth. Add the remaining ingredients and blend until very smooth. Transfer to a bowl and finish mixing with an immersion blender for a very fine consistency.

4. Pour the filling mixture over the crust and place in a slow oven preheated to 300 degrees F/150 degrees C. Place a bowl of water below the cheesecake, and turn the oven down to 200 degrees F/95 degrees C. Bake for about 1 hour, or until set. Let the cheesecake cool completely before slicing into portions.

---

* Allow plain, nonfat yogurt to drain for 24 hours in cheesecloth before measuring.

** The vanilla pods should be split in half and then scraped. The beans *only* are added to the cheese mixture. (Or, vanilla extract may be used if vanilla beans are not available.) The scraped pods may be used to flavor granulated sugar, which then may be used in dessert sauces, pastries, and other dishes where a vanilla flavor is desired.

PORTION	KCAL	PROTEIN	FAT	CARB	SODIUM	CHOL
1 portion	180	8 gm	8 gm	20 gm	200 mg	80 mg

CHOCOLATE ANGEL FOOD CAKE

Yield: One 10-inch cake

5 ounces	Cake flour	140 grams
1½ ounces	Cocoa powder, Dutch-process	40 grams
1 teaspoon	Baking powder	4 grams
14 ounces	Egg whites	400 grams
7 ounces	Sugar, powdered	200 grams
1 teaspoon	Cream of tartar	3 grams
1 ounce	Whole butter, melted, cooled	30 grams
2 teaspoons	Vanilla extract	10 milliliters

1. Sift the flour, cocoa, and baking powder together twice, and reserve.

2. Beat the egg whites until they are thick and foamy. Gradually beat in the sugar and cream of tartar, and continue to beat to a medium peak.

3. Fold the sifted dry ingredients into the beaten egg whites gently, to retain as much volume as possible.

4. Add the butter and vanilla and fold them into the batter.

5. Pour the batter into a tube pan or spring-form pan that has been sprayed with vegetable oil coating and lined with parchment.

6. Bake the cake in a moderate (325 degree F/165 degree C) oven until the cake pulls away from the sides of the pan (about 30 minutes). Cool completely before removing the cake from the pan.

This cake should be sliced into sixteen even portions. A variety of toppings and sauces could be served with it, such as a Fresh Berry Coulis (recipe in this chapter), sliced strawberries marinated in Grand Marnier, or a plain or flavored frozen glace.

In the accompanying photograph, the cake has been split horizontally and spread with figs pureed with just enough white grape juice to give a good consistency.

PORTION	KCAL	PROTEIN	FAT	CARB	SODIUM	CHOL
1 slice	90	3 gm	2 gm	17 gm	30 mg	5 mg

POLENTA SOUFFLÉ

Yield: 10 portions

20 fluid ounces	Skim milk	600 milliliters
1 large piece	Orange peel	1 large piece
4 ounces	Sugar, granulated	115 grams
3 ounces	Cornmeal	85 grams
5 fluid ounces	Fruit puree or juice	150 milliliters
1 ounce	Fresh fruit, diced*	30 grams
6	Egg whites	6

1. Bring the milk, with the orange peel, to a simmer. Remove from the heat and allow it to steep for about 30 minutes. Discard the peel.

2. Place the milk in a clean pot, and bring it to a simmer. Add 3½ ounces/100 grams of sugar, and then add the cornmeal in a thin stream, stirring constantly. Stir in the fruit puree and diced fresh fruit.

3. Continue to simmer another 20 minutes, stirring constantly, until the mixture pulls away from the sides of the pot. Remove the Polenta Soufflé base from the pot, and spread in an even layer in a hotel pan. Cover with parchment and allow to cool.

4. When ready to prepare a soufflé, beat the egg whites to a heavy foam and then gradually add the remaining sugar. Continue to beat to a medium peak.

5. Fold the egg whites into the base, and then add to prepared soufflé molds (coat very lightly with butter, dust with sugar), place them in a water bath and bake at 400 degrees F/205 degrees C until they have risen and are golden, but still creamy in the center.

---

* Naturally soft, ripe fruits such as bananas, berries, and peaches are good choices. Other fruits, such as apples and pears, should be cooked before they are pureed. Pureed pumpkin (unsweetened) could also be used.

To make individual soufflés, prepare the base as described above, and then divide it into ten equal portions. Lightly beat the egg whites, then measure out about 1½ ounces/45 grams of egg white for each soufflé, and beat to a medium peak with ½ teaspoon/2.5 grams of sugar.

CHOCOLATE POLENTA SOUFFLÉS Add about 1 ounce/30 grams of cocoa powder along with the cornmeal to the simmering milk. Instead of fruit puree and juice, add 1¾ ounces/50 grams of grated baking chocolate.

Dust the tops lightly with powdered sugar and serve with a sauce made by flavoring the dairy base with an appropriate liqueur or cordial, such as Grand Marnier, Kahlua, dark or spiced rum, etc. Or serve with Cappucino Glace (see the recipe in this chapter).

PORTION	KCAL	PROTEIN	FAT	CARB	SODIUM	CHOL
1 portion	110	5 gm	trace	22 gm	65 mg	1 mg

CARAMEL AND PEAR POLENTA SOUFFLÉ WITH POACHED PEARS

Yield: 10 portions

7 ounces	Sugar, granulated	200 grams
as needed	Water	as needed
5	Pears, ripe, peeled	5
as needed	Pear juice	as needed
1	Cinnamon stick	1
2	Cloves, whole	2
20 fluid ounces	Skim milk	600 milliliters
1 large piece	Orange peel	1 large piece
3 ounces	Cornmeal	85 grams
5 fluid ounces	Pear puree*	150 milliliters
6	Egg whites	6

1. Heat 3 ounces/85 grams of the sugar and water in a pan over moderate heat until it first liquefies, and then becomes a deep golden caramel. Pour the caramel (about 1 teaspoon) into each of the prepared soufflé molds.** (There should be some caramel still sticking to the pan.)

2. Add the pears to the same pan, along with enough water to cover them by half. Add enough pear juice to completely cover; add the cinnamon and cloves. Bring the liquid to a simmer and poach the pears until they are tender. Cool in the poaching liquid.

3. Bring the milk to a simmer with the orange peel in a saucepan. Remove from the heat and allow the milk to steep for about 30 minutes. Discard the orange peel.

4. Place the milk in a clean pot, and bring it to a simmer. Add 3½ ounces/100 grams of sugar; then add the cornmeal in a thin stream, stirring constantly. Stir in the pear puree.

5. Continue to simmer another 20 minutes, stirring constantly, until the mixture pulls away from the sides of the pot. Remove the soufflé base from the pot, and spread in an even layer in a hotel pan. Cover with parchment, and allow it to cool.

6. When ready to prepare a soufflé, beat the egg whites to a heavy foam and then gradually add the remaining sugar. Continue to beat till medium peaks form.

7. Fold the egg whites into the soufflé base, and then add to prepared soufflé molds, place them in a water bath, and bake in a hot (400 degree F/205 degree C) oven until they have risen and are golden, but still creamy in the center.

8. While the soufflés are baking, halve the pears and remove the core. Slice or fan, if desired, and serve with the soufflés.

———

* Cook pears by baking, steaming, or poaching until very soft. Puree until smooth. If desired, poach in pear juice for additional flavor.

** To prepare the soufflé molds, coat them very lightly with butter and dust with granulated sugar.

The soufflé shown at the beginning of this chapter is decorated with a small butterfly made from Almond Tiles batter (the recipe can be found in this chapter) and a drizzle of melted chocolate.

PORTION	KCAL	PROTEIN	FAT	CARB	SODIUM	CHOL
1 portion	200	5 gm	1 gm	45 gm	65 mg	1 mg

STRUDEL DOUGH

Yield: 20 ounces/570 grams

12 ounces	Flour, all-purpose	340 grams
½ fluid ounce	Vegetable oil	15 milliliters
½ teaspoon	Salt	3 grams
1	Egg yolk	1
8 fluid ounces	Water, cold	240 milliliters

1. Using a mixing bowl and dough hook, combine all of the ingredients. Mix at medium speed until the dough forms a smooth ball that is slightly tacky to the touch, but not sticky (about 20 minutes). Allow the dough to rest for about 30 minutes.

2. Over a floured cloth, stretch the dough out until it is very thin.

3. Cut the dough into sheets. Add the desired filling (see, for example, the recipe for Apple Strudel).

PORTION	KCAL	PROTEIN	FAT	CARB	SODIUM	CHOL
12 oz	70	2 gm	1 gm	13 gm	55 mg	51 mg

APPLE STRUDEL

Yield: 2 strudels

1½ ounces	Butter, unsalted	40 grams
3¾ pounds	Granny Smith apples, peeled, cored, and sliced	1.7 kilograms
½ cup	Golden raisins, plumped in warm water	85 grams
½ cup	Brown sugar	100 grams
1 teaspoon	Cinnamon, ground	1 gram
¼ teaspoon	Nutmeg, ground	250 milligrams
12 sheets	Strudel dough, prepared*	12 sheets
1½ ounces	Butter, clarified	40 grams

a *A spray bottle gives greater coverage with a small portion of melted butter.*

b *The filling is mounded along the long side of the dough, and it is carefully rolled to form a strudel.*

c *Shaping a quenelle of frozen dairy base to garnish a serving of Apple Strudel served with Fresh Berry Coulis.*

1. Heat the unsalted butter and sauté the apples, raisins, brown sugar, cinnamon, and nutmeg, in the butter until the apples are very tender. (Alternately, the mixture may be baked in the oven until tender, once the apples have been coated with melted butter.)

2. Cool the apple mixture by spreading it out in a thin layer on a sheet pan and refrigerating.

3. Make a stack of 3 phyllo sheets, then make a second stack of 3 sheets and overlap the second stack by about ¾ of an inch. Mound half of the apple filling along one of the long sides of the dough. Roll up as for a jelly roll, and place the strudel on a parchment-lined sheet pan.

4. Brush or spray the strudel with half of the clarified butter. Score the dough to indicate portions, but do not cut completely through the strudel. (The strudel may be refrigerated overnight or frozen for longer storage at this point.)

5. Repeat Steps 3 and 4 to make the second strudel.

6. Bake the strudel in a hot (450 degree F/205 degree C) oven until the strudel is golden-brown. Slice and serve while still warm.

---

* This recipe may be prepared with fresh strudel dough. Half of the recipe found in this chapter should be enough for two strudels.

To properly handle frozen strudel dough, allow it to defrost under refrigeration for 24 hours. Then, remove the sheets from the package and lay them flat on a lined sheet pan. Cover them with plastic wrap and a clean, lightly dampened towel to prevent them from drying and cracking.

Slice the strudel after baking, and serve with Caramel Sauce (recipe in this chapter), and/or a quenelle of a frozen glace, if desired.

PORTION	KCAL	PROTEIN	FAT	CARB	SODIUM	CHOL
1 portion	200	3 gm	4 gm	40 gm	50 mg	10 mg

FILLING FOR WINTER FRUIT STRUDEL

Yield: filling for two strudels, or 20 portions

3½ ounces	Prunes	100 grams
3½ ounces	Apricots, dried	100 grams
2 ounces	Raisins	60 grams
1 fluid ounce	Brandy	30 milliliters
2¼ pounds	Granny Smith apples, peeled, cored, sliced	1 kilogram
1½ pounds	Pears, peeled, sliced	680 grams
1¾ ounces	Brown sugar	50 grams
1 ounce	Pecans, chopped	30 grams
½ teaspoon	Nutmeg, ground	500 milligrams
1½ teaspoons	Cinnamon, ground	1.5 grams

1. Combine the prunes, apricots, raisins, and brandy. Allow the dried fruit to plump for about 30 minutes.

2. Combine the mixture with the remaining ingredients. Toss until all of the ingredients are evenly blended.

3. Place this mixture on a baking sheet and cover with parchment paper. Bake in a moderate (350 to 375 degree F/175 to 190 degree C) oven until the apples and pears are tender. Remove from the oven and allow to cool.

4. Fill and bake the strudel as explained in the recipe for Apple Strudel in this chapter.

PORTION	KCAL	PROTEIN	FAT	CARB	SODIUM	CHOL
1 portion	100	1 gm	1 gm	24 gm	2 mg	0 mg

TARTE TATIN, ST. ANDREW'S STYLE

Yield: 1 tarte

3 ounces	Sugar, granulated	85 grams
½ ounce	Butter, unsalted	15 grams
2¼ pounds	Granny Smith apples, peeled, cored, sliced	1 kilogram
8 ounces	Sweet Ricotta Pastry*	225 grams

1. In a sauté pan, cook the sugar to a golden caramel.

2. Add the butter and apples. Continue to sauté until the apples are tender and coated with the caramelized sugar. (There should be no excess moisture in the bottom of the pan.) Remove from the heat.

3. Arrange the apple slices in concentric circles in the pan.

4. Roll out the pastry to a 12-inch-diameter circle. Cut vents in the pastry and transfer the dough to the pan. Press it in place.

5. Cook the tarte over high heat just until a caramel aroma rises from the pan. Then finish cooking in a moderate (350 degree F/175 degree C) oven until the crust is golden-brown (about 20 minutes).

6. Loosen the crust from the pan, invert the tarte, and allow it to cool slightly.

7. Cut into portions and serve.**

---

* See the recipe in this chapter.

** Cut the tarte into eight equal portions, or, if desired, the tarte may be sliced into ten equal portions and served with a 2-ounce/60-gram quenelle of plain or flavored frozen dairy base.

This dessert could also be prepared with pears instead of apples.

PORTION	KCAL	PROTEIN	FAT	CARB	SODIUM	CHOL
1 portion	155	2 gm	3 gm	33 gm	100 mg	10 mg

GLAZED PINEAPPLE MADAGASCAR

Yield: 10 portions

18 ounces	Pineapple, peeled, cored	500 grams
2 teaspoons	Green peppercorns, drained, rinsed	10 grams
1½ ounces	Sugar, granulated	40 grams
18 fluid ounces	Orange juice	540 milliliters
2 tablespoons	Honey	40 grams
3½ fluid ounces	Light rum	100 milliliters

1. Slice the pineapple into portions, about 1¾ ounces/50 grams each.

2. Mash the peppercorns and rub them on the surface of the pineapple, then sprinkle all slices evenly with the sugar (about ½ teaspoon/3 grams each) on one side.

3. Combine the orange juice, honey, and rum, and reserve until needed.

4. Heat a sauté pan until it is smoking hot over high heat. Place the pineapple in the pan, sugared side down. Sauté until the sugar is browned and there is a distinct caramel smell.

5. Turn the pineapple and sauté on the second side until browned. Remove the pineapple; add the juice mixture to the pan.

6. Reduce the juice mixture until it has the consistency of maple syrup. Pour this sauce over the pineapple, and serve.

If desired, this dessert could be served with a 1-ounce/30-gram quenelle of plain or flavored frozen dairy base.

PORTION	KCAL	PROTEIN	FAT	CARB	SODIUM	CHOL
1 portion	120	2 gm	trace	21 gm	20 mg	5 mg

CARAMEL SAUCE

Yield: 12 fluid ounces/360 milliliters

3 ounces	Butter, unsalted	85 grams
3½ fluid ounces	Water	100 milliliters
7 ounces	Sugar	200 grams
4 fluid ounces	Evaporated skimmed milk	120 milliliters
2 teaspoons	Arrowroot	6 grams
1 fluid ounce	Rum or other liquor*	30 milliliters

1. Over moderate heat, cook the butter, water, and sugar to a good caramel color. Remove this mixture from the heat.

2. Combine the milk, arrowroot, and rum. Add carefully, away from the heat, to the hot caramel mixture, stirring constantly until dissolved.

3. Return the sauce to the heat and bring it up to a boil, stirring constantly.

4. Remove from heat and cool. The sauce may be used at this point or may be stored under refrigeration for 2 to 3 days.

---

* Dark rum is used for flavor, but rum extract or other cordials and liqueurs—such as Kahlua, brandy, Cognac, or Grand Marnier—could also be used.

If the sauce seems too thick, thin it by adding up to 2 ounces/60 milliliters of additional evaporated skimmed milk.

PORTION	KCAL	PROTEIN	FAT	CARB	SODIUM	CHOL
1 portion	70	1 gm	4 gm	8 gm	25 mg	10 mg

A TRIO OF PEARS

Yield: 10 portions

A Trio of Pears: Poached Pears, Pear Sorbet, and Pear Sauce.

2¼ pounds	Pears, cut into balls of different sizes	1 kilogram
18 fluid ounces	Water	540 milliliters
18 ounces	Sugar, granulated	500 grams
13 fluid ounces	Pear wine	385 milliliters
2	Vanilla beans, split	2
27 fluid ounces	Apple or pear cider	800 milliliters
1	Cinnamon stick	1
to taste	Nutmeg, freshly ground	to taste
18 ounces	Pear Sorbet*	500 grams
1 pint	Pear Sauce*	480 milliliters
30	Oatmeal Cookies*	30
10	Lace Triangles*	10

1. Combine the pears with the water, sugar, wine, and one vanilla bean. Bring to a simmer and poach until the pears are quite tender. Cool in the poaching liquid, then drain, and reserve the liquid. **

2. Combine the cider with the remaining vanilla bean, cinnamon stick, and nutmeg. Bring this to a simmer and keep it warm.

3. Portion the drained pears (3½ ounces/100 grams per portion) and cover with ⅓ cup (80 milliliters) of the warm spiced cider. Serve the pears with Pear Sorbet, Pear Sauce, Oatmeal Cookies, and a Lace Triangle.

---

* The recipes for Pear Sorbet, Pear Sauce, Oatmeal Cookies, and Lace Triangles are in this chapter.

   ** Reserve 1¼ pints/600 milliliters of the poaching liquid to make the pear sorbet.

PORTION	KCAL	PROTEIN	FAT	CARB	SODIUM	CHOL
1 portion	170	1 gm	2 gm	40 gm	7 mg	trace

PEAR SAUCE

Yield: 1 quart/1 liter

2¼ pounds	Bartlett pears	1 kilogram
3½ fluid ounces	Pear wine, dry	100 milliliters
1 ounce	Honey	30 grams
14 fluid ounces	Pear or apple juice	415 milliliters

1. Remove the cores from the pears, but do not peel them. Cut them into cubes.

2. Combine the pears with the wine and honey; simmer slowly over low to moderate heat until the pears are tender and a light tan color.

3. Add ¾ of juice to the pears, then puree through a food mill or ricer.

4. Adjust the consistency of the sauce as needed by adding more apple juice.

PORTION	KCAL	PROTEIN	FAT	CARB	SODIUM	CHOL
1 portion	60	trace	trace	16 gm	0 mg	0 mg

GRILLED BANANAS

Yield: 10 portions

5	Bananas, sliced on bias	5
3 tablespoons	Sugar, granulated	40 grams
10	Almond Tiles	10
15 ounces	Glace, frozen (plain or flavored)	425 grams
10 fluid ounces	Caramel Sauce	300 milliliters

1. Sprinkle the bananas evenly with sugar and grill the bananas over hot coals until marked and heated through.

2. Serve with glace, Almond Tiles and Caramel Sauce.

If desired, a small amount of toasted coconut could be used to coat the glace quenelle.

PORTION	KCAL	PROTEIN	FAT	CARB	SODIUM	CHOL
1 portion	180	4 gm	5 gm	32 gm	80 mg	15 mg

PEARS POACHED IN ZINFANDEL

Yield: 10 portions

10	Bosc pears, peeled, cored, left whole	10
10 fluid ounces	Red Zinfandel	300 milliliters
4 ounces	Currant jelly	115 grams
2 fluid ounces	Orange juice	60 milliliters
½ ounce	Orange zest, grated	15 grams
1	Cinnamon stick	1
2	Cloves, whole	2
½ teaspoon	Ginger, ground	2 grams

1. In a saucepan, combine the pears with the Zinfandel, jelly, and orange juice.

2. Combine the remaining ingredients in a sachet bag and add to the poaching liquid.

3. Place the saucepan over moderate heat and bring slowly to a simmer. Simmer until the pears are tender (about 20 to 30 minutes). Taste the poaching liquid during simmering time, and remove and discard the sachet when the clove and cinnamon flavors are easy to detect.

4. Remove the pears from the poaching liquid and cool.

5. Strain the poaching liquid into a shallow pan and freeze. Scrape the surface to create large grains. Serve this granité with the pears, if desired.

Peaches may also be prepared this way. They should be blanched in boiling water for about 30 seconds to loosen their skins. Cut the peaches in half and remove their pits before poaching. Poaching time should be about 10 minutes for peaches.

PORTION	KCAL	PROTEIN	FAT	CARB	SODIUM	CHOL
1 portion	100	1 gm	1 gm	25 gm	1 mg	0 mg

BAKED FIGS

Yield: 10 portions

10	Medium figs, fresh, stems removed	**10**
1¾ ounces	Almond paste	**50 grams**
10	Phyllo dough sheets	**10**
1 fluid ounce	Butter, clarified	**30 milliliters**

1. Slice an "X" into the top third of each fig.

2. Divide the almond paste in ten equal pieces, roll into balls, and then flatten them by pressing one onto the bottom of each fig.

3. Cut each phyllo sheet into quarters, and spray them lightly with the clarified butter. Stack four pieces of phyllo so that the corners are staggered. Place the fig in the center of the phyllo, and wrap the sheets up around the fruit, making a beggar's purse.

4. Bake the figs in a slow (300 to 325 degree F/150 to 165 degree C) oven until the figs are very soft and the phyllo is golden-brown (about 30 minutes).

Pears and apples could also be prepared in this manner. These fruits should be peeled and cored. The cavity could be filled with a small amount of the Filling for Winter Strudel (see the recipe in this chapter), if desired.

The baked fruits should be dusted with powdered sugar or cocoa powder before serving. If desired, a cordon of Fresh Berry Coulis and a plain or flavored glace (a single 1-ounce/30-gram quenelle) could be served with the baked fruit (Recipes also in this chapter).

PORTION	KCAL	PROTEIN	FAT	CARB	SODIUM	CHOL
1 portion	135	3 gm	4 gm	23 gm	2 mg	7 mg

FRESH BERRY COULIS

Yield: 1¾ pounds/800 grams

1 pound	Raspberries, strawberries, blueberries, fresh or frozen*	450 grams
1 fluid ounce	Kirschwasser	30 milliliters
5 fluid ounces	Honey	150 milliliters
6 fluid ounces	White wine, dry or sweet, as desired	180 milliliters

1. In a blender, puree the berries, Kirschwasser, and about two-thirds of the honey and two-thirds of the wine until smooth.

2. Check the consistency and taste of the coulis. If necessary, add more of the honey to attain the desired sweetness, and more of the wine to reach the desired consistency.

3. Strain the coulis through a fine sieve to remove the seeds. The coulis may be used at this point, stored under refrigeration for 5 to 8 days, or frozen for 2 to 3 months.

---

* Frozen berries should be Individually Quick Frozen (IQF) or low-sugar. This recipe can be increased as desired to use fresh berries, when in season.

The sweetness of fruits may vary dramatically, depending upon such factors as growing conditions, stage of ripeness at harvest time, and handling and storage during shipping. Be sure to taste the sauce and adjust the flavor as necessary.

PORTION	KCAL	PROTEIN	FAT	CARB	SODIUM	CHOL
1 portion	50	trace	trace	10 gm	1 mg	0 mg

LEMON-YOGURT ICING

Yield: 5 ounces/140 grams

4 ounces	Confectioner's sugar, sifted	115 grams
1 tablespoon	Yogurt, plain, nonfat	15 grams
½ teaspoon	Lemon zest, finely grated	3 grams
½ teaspoon	Lemon juice, fresh	3 milliliters

1. Combine all ingredients and blend until smooth. The icing may be used at this point or stored under refrigeration for 4 to 5 days.

2. To use icing, spread in a thin layer on warm muffins and let cool.

PORTION	KCAL	PROTEIN	FAT	CARB	SODIUM	CHOL
1 portion	10	trace	trace	2 gm	trace	trace

CIDER AND RAISIN SAUCE

Yield: 1 pint/480 milliliters

3 ounces	Raisins or dried currants	85 grams
1½ fluid ounces	Bourbon	45 milliliters
1½ pints	Cider, unfiltered	720 milliliters
4 teaspoons	Arrowroot	10 grams

1. Combine the raisins and bourbon, and add enough cider to cover. Allow the raisins to plump for 20 to 30 minutes. Drain, reserving the liquid and the raisins separately.

2. Combine the remaining cider with the liquid from the raisins and, over high heat, reduce to half its original volume. Reduce to a simmer.

3. Dilute the arrowroot in a little additional bourbon and add it to the simmering cider. Add the raisins and heat just until the sauce thickens. Keep warm.

PORTION	KCAL	PROTEIN	FAT	CARB	SODIUM	CHOL
1 portion	35	trace	trace	8 gm	2 mg	0 mg

ALMOND TILES

Yield: about 150 tiles

7 ounces	Bread flour	200 grams
14 ounces	Sugar, powdered	400 grams
21 ounces	Almond paste	600 grams
3 fluid ounces	Milk	90 milliliters
12 ounces	Egg whites, lightly beaten	340 grams

1. Place the flour, sugar, and almond paste in a food processor and process to a fine, granular consistency.

2. Slowly add the milk while the machine is running, and then gradually pour in the egg whites. Blend until smooth.

3. Remove the batter from the food processor and let it rest overnight in the refrigerator before baking.

4. Spread a thin, even layer of dough over the surface of an inverted baking sheet. Bake in a 375-degree F/190-degree C oven until the dough loses its glossy appearance. Remove from the oven and cut into the desired shape, using a knife or pizza cutter. Remove from the pan, cool, and store carefully.

———

This batter may be used to create a variety of delicate cookies. For shells, use a template shaped as desired. Place the template on an inverted baking sheet and spread the batter in a thin, even layer, filling the opening of the template. Remove the template and bake in a 375-degree F/190-degree C oven until the dough begins to dull and the edges look dry. Remove from the oven, lift the cookie away from the baking sheet, and shape into a cup by draping over a rolling pin, inverted cup, or similar object.

CINNAMON CRISPS   Add 1 teaspoon or more, to taste, of ground cinnamon to the batter.

PORTION	KCAL	PROTEIN	FAT	CARB	SODIUM	CHOL
1 each	7	trace	trace	1 gm	trace	trace

CHOCOLATE HIPPENMASSE

Yield: about 10 tiles, but varies according to use

1½ ounces	Sugar, granulated	40 grams
1 ounce	Almond paste	30 grams
½ ounce	Bread flour	15 grams
2 tablespoons	Cocoa powder	10 grams
¼ teaspoon	Cinnamon, ground	500 milligrams
⅛ teaspoon	Salt	500 milligrams
1	Egg white	1
2 teaspoons	Heavy cream	10 milliliters
2 teaspoons	Skim milk	10 milliliters

1. Combine the sugar, almond paste, flour, cocoa powder, cinnamon, and salt in a food processor until the mixture has a grainy consistency.

2. Combine the egg white with the cream and add them to the mixture in the food processor while the machine is still running.

3. Remove the batter and allow it to rest at least 1 hour.

4. Bake the hippenmasse as directed for the Almond Tiles.

PORTION	KCAL	PROTEIN	FAT	CARB	SODIUM	CHOL
1 each	9	trace	trace	1 gm	trace	trace

LACE TRIANGLES

Yield: 288 triangles

1 pound	Sugar, brown	450 grams
10½ ounces	Butter, unsalted	300 grams
10½ ounces	Corn syrup, light	300 grams
12¾ ounces	Flour, all-purpose, sifted	360 grams
6 ounces	Hazelnuts, peeled, toasted, coarsely chopped	170 grams

1. Bring the sugar, butter, and corn syrup to a boil in a pot. Remove from the heat and stir in the flour and hazelnuts.

2. Pour the batter into a baking dish to cool.

3. Roll the dough into 2-ounce/60-gram balls. Flatten them into disks and place on an inverted sheet pan that has been coated with a vegetable oil spray.

4. Bake at 375 degrees F/190 degrees C until the cookies have stopped bubbling completely.

5. Remove from the oven and allow them to cool on the pan until they are set but still flexible.

6. Lift each cookie carefully from the sheet pan, and cut into 6 triangle-shaped pieces. Store between parchment paper in a covered container in a cool, dry place.

PORTION	KCAL	PROTEIN	FAT	CARB	SODIUM	CHOL
1 each	24	trace	1 gm	3 gm	2 mg	2 mg

OATMEAL COOKIES

Yield: 3 dozen

5 ounces	Sugar, brown	140 grams
4 fluid ounces	Honey	120 milliliters
½ ounce	Butter, unsalted	15 grams
1 ounce	Egg whites	30 grams
½ fluid ounce	Evaporated skimmed milk	15 milliliters
1 teaspoon	Vanilla extract	5 milliliters
5 ounces	Oats, quick-cooking	140 grams
4 ounces	Flour, all-purpose	115 grams
3½ ounces	Dried pears, small dice	100 grams

1. Cream together the sugar, honey, and butter until very smooth.

2. Blend the egg whites with the milk and add to the creamed mixture.

3. Stir in the oats and flour, then fold in the pears.

4. Drop by teaspoonfuls onto a lightly greased sheet pan and bake at 350 degrees F/ 175 degrees C for about 10 minutes. Let cool for 10 minutes on the sheet pan, then transfer to racks. Hold, covered, until needed. If necessary, warm gently to soften before serving.

PORTION	KCAL	PROTEIN	FAT	CARB	SODIUM	CHOL
1 each	65	1 gm	1 gm	14 gm	3 mg	1 mg

SWEET RICOTTA PASTRY

Yield: 2¼ pounds/1 kilogram

1 pound	Flour, all-purpose, sifted	450 grams
4½ ounces	Sugar, granulated	125 grams
1¾ ounces	Baking powder	50 grams
⅛ teaspoon	Salt	750 milligrams
8 ounces	Ricotta cheese, part-skim, cold	225 grams
3 fluid ounces	Skim milk, cold	90 milliliters
2	Egg whites, chilled	2
2 ounces	Butter, cold, diced	60 grams
1 tablespoon	Vanilla extract	15 milliliters

1. Place the flour, sugar, baking powder, and salt in the bowl of a food processor; process briefly to distribute baking powder evenly.

2. Add the rest of the ingredients and pulse the machine off and on just until the dough catches. Gather it into a ball, wrap with plastic, and refrigerate until the dough is firm, at least 1 hour.

3. The dough may be rolled out at this point and used to prepare pastries, as desired.

This recipe is used to prepare Tarte Tatin, St. Andrew's Style, which appears in this chapter.

PORTION	KCAL	PROTEIN	FAT	CARB	SODIUM	CHOL
1½ oz	125	4 gm	3 gm	20 gm	190 mg	10 mg

PLAIN RICOTTA PASTRY

Yield: 2 pounds/900 grams

1 pound	Flour, all-purpose, sifted	450 grams
1¾ ounces	Baking powder	50 grams
⅛ teaspoon	Salt	.75 gram
2 fluid ounces	Oil	60 milliliters
8 ounces	Ricotta cheese, part-skim, cold	225 grams
3 fluid ounces	Skim milk, cold	90 milliliters
2	Egg whites, chilled	2

1. Place the flour, baking powder, and salt in the bowl of a food processor; process briefly to distribute baking powder evenly.

2. Add the rest of the ingredients and pulse the machine off and on just until the dough catches. Gather it into a ball, wrap with plastic, and refrigerate until the dough is firm, at least 1 hour.

3. The dough may be rolled out at this point and used to prepare various pastries, as desired.

––––––

This dough is used to prepare Chicken Pot Pie, found in Chapter 18.

PORTION	KCAL	PROTEIN	FAT	CARB	SODIUM	CHOL
1½ oz	115	4 gm	4 gm	15 gm	35 mg	3 mg

SPONGE CAKE

Yield: Two 10-inch cakes

5 ounces	Cake flour	140 grams
2½ ounces	Arrowroot	70 grams
1 pound, 3 ounces	Egg whites	540 grams
9 ounces	Sugar, powdered, sifted	255 grams
1 teaspoon	Cream of tartar	3 grams
1 tablespoon	Vanilla extract	15 milliliters
1 ounce	Butter, unsalted, melted	30 grams

1. Sift the cake flour and arrowroot together three times.

2. Whip the egg whites until they are thick and foamy, but do not hold a peak. Gradually incorporate the sugar and cream of tartar and continue to beat to medium peaks.

3. Fold in the flour and arrowroot and mix gently until blended.

4. Fold in the extract, and butter gently.

5. Pour the batter into a prepared cake pan (spray lightly with vegetable oil, dust with flour, and line with parchment). Bake in a moderate (350 degree F/175 degree C) oven until the sides begin to pull away from the pan.

6. Cool the cake on a rack.

———

CHOCOLATE SPONGE CAKE: replace 1¼ ounces/35 grams of flour with cocoa powder.

   This cake may be used in several desserts, including the Pear Bavarian Terrine and Raspberry Torte recipes in this chapter.

PORTION	KCAL	PROTEIN	FAT	CARB	SODIUM	CHOL
1 slice	90	3 gm	1 gm	18 gm	4 mg	3 mg

Breakfast

Breakfast, as mothers and nutritionists throughout the land keep telling us, is the most important meal of the day. The most up-to-date nutritional guidelines suggest that we eat the majority of our calories earlier in the day. The catch, of course, is that the usual bacon, egg, home fries, and coffee breakfast of the past is too high in calories and laden with fats, sodium, and cholesterol.

There are many other breakfast options, however, that are simple, fast, and good sources of well-balanced nutrition. Cold cereals are fine, as long as they are low in sugar and fat. Served with fresh fruit and skim milk, they provide quality carbohydrates and a variety of vitamins and minerals.

Many of the recipes in this chapter are modifications of some traditional breakfast items that have good taste and texture. Rather than eliminate whole eggs, butter, and oil, these recipes use them in greatly reduced amounts. For example, instead of adding butter to a pancake recipe to get a rich, cake-like texture, cake flour and fruit purees are used for tenderness and moisture. Egg whites provide additional lightness.

French toast, a perennial favorite, is prepared with far fewer egg yolks, and served with delicious toppings, such as the Winter Fruit Compote, that make the lack of melting butter less noticeable. In Four-Grain Waffles, delicious, nutty grains boost the flavor and offer nutritional bonuses.

FOCUS   FOUR-GRAIN WAFFLES

Waffle and pancake batters typically include flour, milk, eggs, sugar, baking soda, and oil or melted butter. Flour provides the overall structure. The milk holds all of the ingredients in a homogenous batter. Eggs act as both tenderizer (due to the presence of fats in the yolk) and strengthener (because of the proteins in the white); in addition, they provide color and flavor. Sugar gives the finished waffles or cakes a delicate texture and a wonderful golden color; and it also makes them taste sweet and feel moist. Baking soda gives them a pleasing, fluffy texture. Finally, the oil or butter allows the batter to take on a discernible crust on the outside and a tender, melting texture on the inside. The more oil used, the crisper the finished product will be.

Manipulating all of these components to retain the desirable qualities of the finished dish without using too much of any high-fat or high-calorie ingredient requires some care. It is not possible to eliminate the oil, but it can be greatly reduced. In this formula, about one-third of the amount called for in a traditional recipe is used. Sugar is similarly cut back. Whole eggs are replaced by one whole egg and two egg whites.

Cornmeal, whole-wheat flour, and rolled oats give this recipe intriguing tastes, a crisp texture, and additional nutrients. Other breakfast items have been similarly modified to increase overall nutritional value.

FOUR-GRAIN WAFFLES

Yield: 8 portions (Two 6-inch-square waffles each)

12 fluid ounces	Buttermilk, nonfat	360 milliliters
1	Whole egg	1
2	Egg whites	2
2 fluid ounces	Vegetable oil	60 milliliters
4 ounces	Flour, all-purpose	115 grams
3 ounces	Flour, whole-wheat	85 grams
¼ cup	Cornmeal	40 grams
2½ ounces	Rolled oats	70 grams
1 tablespoon	Baking powder	12 grams
1 ounce	Sugar, granulated	30 grams

A properly cooked, golden waffle.

1. Combine the buttermilk, whole egg, egg whites, and oil. Stir until evenly blended.

2. Combine the flours, cornmeal, rolled oats, baking powder, and sugar. Stir to distribute all ingredients evenly.

3. Mix the liquid and dry mixtures together; stir just until evenly moistened. Do not overmix.

4. Preheat a waffle iron. Spray lightly with vegetable oil, if the iron does not have a nonstick coating.

5. Ladle the batter onto the waffle iron, close, and cook until the waffles are golden-brown and release easily from the surface (about 2 to 3 minutes).

———

The same suggestions for toppings, sauces, and accompaniments found with the Pumpkin Pancake recipe can be used for waffles.

PORTION	KCAL	PROTEIN	FAT	CARB	SODIUM	CHOL
1 portion	244	8 gm	9 gm	34 gm	220 mg	30 mg

PUMPKIN OR BANANA PANCAKES

Yield: 18 medium pancakes

4½ ounces	Oat bran	130 grams
5 ounces	Flour, all-purpose, sifted	140 grams
1 tablespoon	Baking soda	10 grams
½ ounce	Sugar, granulated	15 grams
8 ounces	Yogurt, nonfat, plain	225 grams
4½ ounces	Bananas, peeled, mashed, or pumpkin flesh, steamed, mashed	138 grams
1 fluid ounce	Vegetable oil	30 milliliters
1 teaspoon	Vanilla extract	5 milliliters
4¾ ounces	Egg whites	135 grams

1. Stir together all dry ingredients to mix evenly.

2. Blend yogurt, fruit, vanilla, and half of the oil with the dry ingredients just until moistened.

3. Beat the egg whites to medium peak and fold them into the batter.

4. Use the remaining oil to lubricate the griddle, if necessary.* Drop the batter by 2-ounce ladlefuls onto a heated griddle and cook on the first side until the bubbles burst on the upper surface. Turn the pancakes and continue to cook until the second side is golden-brown. Serve at once.

---

* Soapstone or cast-iron griddles may benefit from a very light coating of vegetable oil at the start of cooking time. Use a brush to apply a thin film, and then rub away any excess with a wiping cloth. Nonstick griddles or pans will not require additional oil.

Serve with sliced, fresh, seasonal fruits and plain or flavored nonfat yogurt. Other suggested toppings include a Warm Fruit Compote, Maple and Apple Butter Syrup (recipes in this chapter), and Cider and Raisin Sauce (see recipe in Chapter 20).

The pancakes may also be served with apple butter thinned with a little maple syrup.

PORTION	KCAL	PROTEIN	FAT	CARB	SODIUM	CHOL
1 each	65	3 gm	2 gm	10 gm	60 mg	trace

SAUSAGE-STUFFED FRENCH TOAST WITH WINTER FRUIT COMPOTE

Yield: 8 portions

1 pound	Pullman loaf	450 grams
1 pound	Breakfast sausage*	450 grams
3	Whole eggs	3
12 ounces	Egg whites	340 grams
5 fluid ounces	Skim milk	150 milliliters
½ teaspoon	Cinnamon, ground	1 gram
as needed	Oil or butter	as needed
12 fluid ounces	Winter Fruit Compote*	360 milliliters

1. Slice the Pullman loaf into eight equal pieces. Cut a pocket by slicing through one side of each piece.

2. Cook the sausage until completely done, drain on absorbent toweling, and then fill each slice of bread with about 2 ounces/60 grams of sausage. Press tightly to seal.

3. Combine the whole eggs, egg whites, skim milk, and cinnamon.

4. Preheat a griddle or nonstick skillet over medium heat. If necessary, spray a thin film of oil or clarified butter into the pan (not necessary if using a nonstick skillet).

5. Dip the French toast into the egg and milk mixture and immediately cook in preheated pan until golden on both sides (about 1½ minutes on the first side, 1 minute on the second).

6. Slice the toast on the diagonal and serve on a pool of warm Winter Fruit Compote.

———

* The recipes for Breakfast Sausage Patties and Winter Fruit Compote are found in this chapter.

In the photograph on the facing page, the dried fruits have been arranged in the center of the plate, and the sauce has been garnished with julienned apples. Dust with additional ground cinnamon or powdered sugar, if desired.

FRENCH TOAST STUFFED WITH FRUIT Use the filling mixture for either the Apple Strudel or the Winter Fruit Strudel (recipes in Chapter 20) to replace the cooked sausage.

PORTION	KCAL	PROTEIN	FAT	CARB	SODIUM	CHOL
1 portion	347	21 gm	6 gm	50 gm	150 mg	100 mg

BREAKFAST SAUSAGE PATTIES

Yield: Approximately 5 pounds/2.27 kilograms

4 ounces	Onions, minced	115 grams
1 quart	Chicken stock	1 liter
8 ounces	Carolina rice, uncooked	225 grams
3 pounds	Pork loin, lean, trimmed, cubed	1.36 kilograms
1 teaspoon	Salt	5 grams
1 tablespoon	Poultry seasoning	7 grams
½ tablespoon	Ginger, ground	4 grams
½ tablespoon	Chili pepper flakes	4 grams
2 fluid ounces	Corn syrup	60 milliliters

1. Sweat the onions in 2 fluid ounces/60 milliliters of stock until tender. Add the rice and an additional 22 fluid ounces/660 milliliters of stock. Cook, using the pilaf method, until dry.

2. Spread the rice on a sheet pan to cool. Refrigerate until thoroughly chilled.

3. Combine the pork with the salt, poultry seasoning, ginger, and chili pepper flakes. Toss to coat evenly and let marinate while rice chills.

4. Combine the meat and the rice and grind through coarse die into a bowl set in an ice bath. Working over ice and using a wooden spoon, slowly stir in the corn syrup and the remaining cold stock.

5. Make a test patty and bake or dry-sauté. Check the patty for seasoning and consistency. Make any necessary adjustments.

6. Portion forcemeat into 1½-ounce/40-gram patties. Dry-sauté at service.

PORTION	KCAL	PROTEIN	FAT	CARB	SODIUM	CHOL
1 patty	70	5 gm	3 gm	4 gm	50 mg	20 mg

a *The crepe is being prepared in a nonstick pan to reduce the amount of oil necessary to prevent it from sticking and tearing.*

b *A variety of fillings can be used. An apple filling is shown here, and instead of rolling the crepe, it is folded into quarters.*

BASIC CRÊPE BATTER

Yield: About 30 crêpes

8 fluid ounces	Skim milk, chilled	240 milliliters
8 fluid ounces	Cold water	240 milliliters
6 ounces	Flour, all-purpose	170 grams
4	Egg whites	4
1 tablespoon	Vegetable oil	15 milliliters

1. Place all ingredients in the bowl of a food processor and combine until smooth.

2. Strain the batter through a sieve, and then let rest for about 15 minutes.

3. Spray a nonstick pan very lightly with oil, and heat it over medium heat. Ladle the batter into the pan and cook on the first side until the edges start to look dry.

4. Turn the crêpe once and cook briefly on the second side. Remove from the pan, and continue until all of the crêpes are cooked.

Crêpes may be filled with sweet or savory fillings. Sweet fillings such as those for either the Apple or Winter Fruit Strudels (see chapter 20) would be good choices. Some suggestions for savory fillings include a combination of steamed fresh vegetables combined with reduced fat pot, farmer, or goat cheese, flavored with fresh herbs; Ratatouille (see Chapter 18); cooked beans seasoned with cilantro, topped with Fresh Tomato Salsa (see Chapter 12); or scrambled eggs (made with 2 egg whites for every whole egg) topped with any of the tomato sauces in Chapter 11.

PORTION	KCAL	PROTEIN	FAT	CARB	SODIUM	CHOL
1 each	30	1 gm	1 gm	5 gm	10 mg	trace

OAT BRAN AND DRIED FRUIT MUFFINS

Yield: 16 muffins (1.5 ounces each)

5½ ounces	Dried fruit, assorted, coarsely chopped	150 grams
4 ounces	Oat bran	115 grams
3 ounces	Rolled oats	85 grams
2½ ounces	Flour, all-purpose	70 grams
1½ ounces	Brown sugar	40 grams
¾ ounce	Baking powder	20 grams
1 teaspoon	Cinnamon, ground	2 grams
5 ounces	Banana, ripe, mashed	140 grams
2 teaspoons	Orange zest	6 grams
2 fluid ounces	Orange juice, fresh	60 milliliters
1 fluid ounce	Vegetable oil	30 milliliters
2	Egg whites	2
8 fluid ounces	Skim milk	240 milliliters

1. Combine the dried fruit, all the dry ingredients, and the banana in the bowl of a food processor. Process just until evenly mixed. Remove to a mixing bowl and make a well in the center of this mixture.

2. Combine the remaining ingredients and pour them into the well in the dry ingredients. Mix until just combined.

3. Drop the batter into paper-lined muffin tins (1½ ounces/50 grams per muffin).

4. Bake at 400 degrees F/205 degrees C until the surface springs back when lightly pressed (about 20 minutes).

5. Remove muffins from the tins and let cool.

PORTION	KCAL	PROTEIN	FAT	CARB	SODIUM	CHOL
1 each	110	3 gm	2 gm	19 gm	165 mg	trace

SPICED GRAHAM MUFFINS

Yield: 12 muffins (1½ ounces/50 grams each)

3½ ounces	Raisins	100 grams
4 fluid ounces	Water, warm	120 milliliters
4 ounces	Flour, all-purpose	115 grams
3½ ounces	Flour, whole-wheat (graham)	100 grams
2 teaspoons	Baking powder	8 grams
1 teaspoon	Cinnamon, ground	2 grams
¼ teaspoon	Cloves, ground	500 milligrams
1	Egg, whole	1
2 ounces	Yogurt, plain, nonfat	60 grams
1 fluid ounce	Vegetable oil	30 milliliters
2 ounces	Sugar, granulated	60 grams

1. Plump the raisins in the warm water for about 20 minutes. Drain, reserving the raisins and the soaking liquid separately.

2. Sift together the flours, baking powder, cinnamon, and cloves.

3. Beat together the egg, yogurt, oil, sugar, and cooking liquid from the raisins.

4. Combine the dry and wet ingredients, mixing just until moistened. (Some lumps in the batter are desirable; do not overwork the batter.)

5. Stir in the reserved raisins. Drop 1½ ounces/50 grams of batter per muffin into paper-lined muffin tins.

6. Bake the muffins at 375 degrees F/190 degrees C for 14 to 15 minutes.

If desired, these muffins may be glazed with Lemon-Yogurt Icing (recipe is found in Chapter 20).

PORTION	KCAL	PROTEIN	FAT	CARB	SODIUM	CHOL
1 each	120	3 gm	3 gm	22 gm	80 mg	20 mg

GRANOLA

Yield: 2¼ pounds/1 kilogram

Granola is shown here as part of a parfait that includes nonfat yogurt and fresh fruit for an attractive breakfast dish.

2½ ounces	Sesame seeds	70 grams
2½ ounces	Almonds, slivered	70 grams
2 ounces	Sunflower seeds	60 grams
4 ounces	Cashews, unroasted	115 grams
3 ounces	Shredded coconut, unsweetened	85 grams
10½ ounces	Rolled oats, old-fashioned	300 grams
4 ounces	Honey	115 grams
3 ounces	Currants, dried	85 grams

1. Toast the sesame seeds in a dry skillet until browned. Remove them.

2. Add the almonds to the skillet and toast until they are a pale golden color. Add the sunflower seeds and continue to toast until the almonds have a deep golden color.

3. Add the cashews, coconut, and oats to the skillet. Continue to toast, stirring frequently, until lightly browned.

4. Add the sesame seeds back to the skillet, along with the honey. Heat for about 5 minutes, or until the honey has coated all of the ingredients.

5. Remove the pan from the heat, and stir in the currants. Spread the mixture in an even layer on a sheet pan.

6. Bake the granola in a moderate (350 degree F/175 degree C) oven until the mixture has a rich golden-brown color (about 10 to 15 minutes).

7. Line a sheet pan with several layers of absorbent toweling. Turn the granola out onto this pan; cover with additional toweling. Place the pan on a cooling rack and allow it to cool completely.

8. Break the granola into small chunks. Store in sterilized jars with tight-fitting lids. Hold in dry storage until needed.

———

This granola formula contains nuts and seeds, items that are high in fat calories, which is also true of the grated coconut or coconut oil, found in many commercially prepared granolas. It is important to carefully measure the amount of granola being served in order to avoid offering a dish that is unacceptably high in calories and total fat. Granola is often used as a topping, because the recommended serving of 1½ ounces/40 grams would be barely enough to cover the bottom of a cereal bowl.

PORTION	KCAL	PROTEIN	FAT	CARB	SODIUM	CHOL
1½ oz	170	5 gm	9 gm	20 gm	10 mg	0 mg

WINTER FRUIT COMPOTE

Yield: 1 pint/480 milliliters

4 ounces	Dried fruits*	115 grams
¼ teaspoon	Port wine, white	500 milligrams
1 pint	Cider, unpasteurized, unfiltered	480 milliliters
2 teaspoons	Arrowroot	5 grams
2 teaspoons	Cinnamon, ground	4 grams
1 teaspoon	Nutmeg, ground	2 grams

1. Combine the dried fruits with the wine and allow them to plump for several minutes. Drain the fruit and reserve the fruit and the wine separately.

2. Bring the cider to a boil. Dilute the arrowroot with a little of the reserved port, and add it to the cider. (Add enough to thicken the cider to the same approximate consistency as maple syrup.)

3. Add the dried fruit and spices to the sauce, simmer for an additional minute, and remove from the heat. The sauce should be kept warm for service.

———

* A variety of dried fruits, singly or in combination, may be used in this recipe: kiln-dried cherries, blueberries, currants, cranberries, apricots, dates, figs, raisins, or prunes.

If desired, a garnish of peeled and cored Granny Smith apples, cut into julienne, may be added. Use about 1 ounce/30 grams per order, and add it just before service. The apples should "wilt" slightly, but they should not become extremely soft.

PORTION	KCAL	PROTEIN	FAT	CARB	SODIUM	CHOL
1½ oz	60	trace	trace	15 gm	5 mg	0 mg

WARM FRUIT COMPOTE

Yield: 1 pint/480 milliliters

8 ounces	Mixed seasonal fruits, sliced	225 grams
4 ounces	Fresh Berry Coulis*	120 milliliters
4 fluid ounces	Peach or apricot nectar	120 milliliters
2 tablespoons	Orange zest	20 grams

1. Combine all of the ingredients. Heat gently over low heat just until warmed. Do not boil.

2. Serve immediately or keep warm during service.

Fresh berries, peaches, nectarines, apricots, bananas, mangoes, papayas, pineapples, and cherries would all be appropriate in this compote. Let the season act as the guide, and select very ripe fruits so that they will sweeten the sauce. If the sauce is too sweet, the taste should be adjusted with a few drops of lemon, lime, or orange juice.

    * See Chapter 20 for this recipe.

PORTION	KCAL	PROTEIN	FAT	CARB	SODIUM	CHOL
1½ oz	80	1 gm	trace	15 gm	5 mg	0 mg

MAPLE AND APPLE BUTTER SYRUP

Yield: 1 pint/480 milliliters

6 fluid ounces	Apple butter, prepared	180 milliliters
4 fluid ounces	Cider, fresh, unfiltered	120 milliliters
6 fluid ounces	Maple syrup	180 milliliters

1. Combine the apple butter and cider and heat gently to a simmer.
2. Add the maple syrup and return once more to a simmer. The syrup may be used at this point.

PORTION	KCAL	PROTEIN	FAT	CARB	SODIUM	CHOL
1 oz	55	trace	trace	13 gm	5 mg	0 mg

STEEL-CUT OATS WITH CINNAMON AND DRIED FRUITS

Yield: 10 portions

5 pints	Water or skim milk	2.3 liters
10 ounces	Steel-cut oats	300 grams
½ teaspoon	Salt	5 grams
5 ounces	Dried fruits*	140 grams
1 teaspoon	Cinnamon, ground	2 grams
1 ounce	Honey	30 grams

1. Bring the water or milk to a boil. Gradually add the oats in a thin stream, stirring constantly, as for polenta.

2. Reduce the heat to a simmer, and continue simmering the oatmeal, stirring frequently, for about 15 to 20 minutes.

3. Add the salt, dried fruits (pitted and diced if necessary), and cinnamon and simmer for an additional 10 minutes. The oatmeal will be quite thick at this point.

4. Serve in heated bowls and drizzle about ¾ of a teaspoon of honey over each portion.

————

* A variety of dried fruits, singly or in combination, may be used in this recipe: kiln-dried cherries, blueberries, currants, cranberries, apricots, dates, figs, raisins, and prunes.

Many people like to pour additional milk around their oatmeal. Fresh, cold skim milk should be offered along with this hot cereal.

PORTION	KCAL	PROTEIN	FAT	CARB	SODIUM	CHOL
1 portion	240	13 gm	2 gm	44 gm	220 mg	5 mg

CHAPTER

22

Presentation and Service of Beverages

The service of all beverages, whether they contain alcohol or not, deserves the same attention to quality as any food item. If a restaurant has full bar service, then it should purchase the best quality liquors at a reasonable price to fill the "well" used to prepare standard drinks. Equally important is having a well-stocked bar with a number of "call" brands.

All cocktails should be measured properly each time that they are prepared. This is important for several reasons: controlling inventory, providing consistent quality, eliminating profit loss through inaccuracy in pouring, and serving alcohol responsibly. This last factor cannot be ignored by any operation that serves alcohol, even if only wine and beer are offered.

The human body is capable of handling a certain level of alcohol without suffering adverse effects, but this ability can be easily affected. A person who is tired, is taking certain medications, has not eaten recently, or is under emotional stress may well find that a drink "hits a little harder" than usual. One's size, weight, and general well-being all play a role in determining how much and how well he or she will be able to hold his or her liquor. The person serving alcohol needs to keep track of the behavior of guests who are drinking alcoholic beverages, and to stop serving them *before* they have slurred speech, obviously slowed reaction time, and a total loss of inhibitions. The ability to determine who has had enough, and when, is a finely honed skill, which requires enormous knowledge of the human character and boundless tact.

The recipes for nonalcoholic beverages in this chapter are intended to help develop a repertoire of drinks that can be made available to all patrons. The special emphasis on enticing flavors, colors, and textures makes a "virgin" cocktail a more appealing and appropriate alternative.

FOCUS   Mineral Waters and Fruit Juices

There are over 700 distinct brands of bottled water sold in the United States. The annual consumption currently stands at a total of 1.6 billion quarts, more or less. There is a difference between mineral waters, natural spring water, and plain bottled water.

Imported mineral waters such as Evian, Pellegrino, or Perrier are under the supervision of the country in which they are bottled. They must be bottled at the source, in a pure state. Each country's health department requires that specific standards be adhered to—standards that do not necessarily extend to the United States.

In this country, federal regulations do not require that the water be bottled at the source, nor do they even require that the source be listed on the label. The only requirement is that if the term "natural spring water" appears, the water must be a mineral water that arrives above the ground without being pumped and nothing can have been added to it. Bottled water with no special designation on the label may simply be tap water that has been purified.

This does not mean that there are no quality domestic mineral waters, however. In fact, many of the most well-known waters in this country have been bottled according to the same exacting standards used by Evian, Perrier, or Pellegrino. Most of the famous bottled brands are drawn from springs that have been flowing for thousands of years in this country and throughout the world. They are usually from carefully protected sources with long-established reputations for consistency and purity.

Many famous mineral waters were reputed to have special curative powers. Spas grew up around these water sources, to provide for the comfort and well-being of those who came to "take the waters." Today, as we continue to learn about how the body maintains a good balance, the value of fresh, pure water is recognized to be as important a part of any health regime as exercise, lack of undue stress, and of course, a good diet.

BITTERS AND SPARKLING MINERAL WATER

Yield: 1 portion

| 2 to 3 teaspoons | Bitters | 3 to 5 milliliters |
| 5 fluid ounces | Sparkling mineral water, chilled | 150 milliliters |

1. Pour the bitters into a chilled stemmed wine glass containing several ice cubes.
2. Top with the mineral water and serve.

PORTION	KCAL	PROTEIN	FAT	CARB	SODIUM	CHOL
1 portion	12	0 gm	0 gm	3 gm	1 mg	0 mg

BITTERS AND ORANGE JUICE

Yield: 1 portion

2 to 3 teaspoons	Bitters	3 to 5 milliliters
5 fluid ounces	Orange juice, fresh-squeezed, chilled	150 milliliters
1	Orange slice, thin	1

1. Pour the bitters into a chilled stemmed wine glass containing several ice cubes.
2. Top with the orange juice, garnish with a slice of orange, and serve.

PORTION	KCAL	PROTEIN	FAT	CARB	SODIUM	CHOL
1 portion	70	1 gm	trace	16 gm	1 mg	0 mg

MANDARIN FRAPPE

Yield: 1 portion

1	Lime, whole	1
1	Mandarin orange	1
as needed	Crushed ice	as needed
1	Lime twist	1

1. Fill a cocktail shaker cup with crushed ice. Squeeze the lime and the orange, and add the juices to the cup. Stir to chill completely.

2. Fill a tall glass with additional crushed ice. Strain the juices over the ice in the glass.

3. Rub lime twist around the rim of the glass, and garnish with it.

PORTION	KCAL	PROTEIN	FAT	CARB	SODIUM	CHOL
1 portion	80	2 gm	1 gm	22 gm	1 mg	0 mg

PASSION FRUIT COCKTAIL

Yield: 1 portion

1	Passion fruit, whole	1
5 fluid ounces	Orange juice, fresh-squeezed	150 milliliters
1	Orange slice	1
1	Cherry	1
as needed	Crushed ice	as needed

1. Cut the passion fruit in half and scoop out the pulp.

2. Press the pulp through a nylon sieve to separate the seeds.

3. Pour the orange juice through the sieve, pressing the passion fruit seeds to extract their flavor.

4. Fill a tall cocktail glass with crushed ice, and pour passion fruit and orange juice over ice.

5. Garnish the drink with an orange slice and a cherry.

PORTION	KCAL	PROTEIN	FAT	CARB	SODIUM	CHOL
1 portion	90	1 gm	trace	22 gm	5 mg	0 mg

CANTALOUPE COCKTAIL

Yield: 6 portions

20 ounces	Cantaloupe, flesh only, diced	570 grams
1 pint	Orange juice, fresh-squeezed	480 milliliters
1½ fluid ounces	Lime juice, fresh-squeezed	45 milliliters
8 to 10	Ice cubes	8 to 10
¼ teaspoon	Vanilla extract	1 gram
6	Lime slices, wafer-thin	6

1. In a blender, combine all ingredients except the lime slices. Blend until very smooth and frothy.

2. Serve in frosted old-fashioned glasses and garnish with lime slices.

PORTION	KCAL	PROTEIN	FAT	CARB	SODIUM	CHOL
1 portion	70	1 gm	trace	17 gm	15 mg	0 mg

THE AMERICAN COCKTAIL

Yield: 1 portion

6 to 8	Grapes, green seedless	6 to 8
1 fluid ounce	Lime juice	30 milliliters
4 fluid ounces	Grape juice, white	120 milliliters
as needed	Crushed ice	as needed

1. Place the grapes in a chilled champagne flute.

2. Fill a cocktail shaker cup with crushed ice and add the lime and grape juices. Stir to chill completely.

3. Strain the juice over the grapes and serve immediately.

PORTION	KCAL	PROTEIN	FAT	CARB	SODIUM	CHOL
1 portion	95	1 gm	trace	25 gm	5 mg	0 mg

SEABREEZE

Yield: 1 portion

3 fluid ounces	Grapefruit juice, fresh-squeezed, chilled	90 milliliters
2 fluid ounces	Cranberry juice, chilled	60 milliliters
1	Grapefruit piece	1

1. Combine the juices in a chilled stemmed wine glass.

2. Garnish with grapefruit slice and serve.

PORTION	KCAL	PROTEIN	FAT	CARB	SODIUM	CHOL
1 portion	70	trace	trace	12 gm	5 mg	0 mg

JUICY FLING

Yield: 1 portion

3 fluid ounces	Orange juice, fresh-squeezed	90 milliliters
1 fluid ounce	Grapefruit juice, fresh-squeezed	30 milliliters
1 fluid ounce	Pineapple juice, unsweetened	30 milliliters
2 ounces	Raspberries, fresh or IQF, some reserved for garnish	60 grams

1. Combine all the ingredients in a blender. Blend until smooth and frothy.
2. Pour the drink into a tall cocktail glass filled with ice cubes.
3. Garnish with additional raspberries.

PORTION	KCAL	PROTEIN	FAT	CARB	SODIUM	CHOL
1 portion	115	1 gm	1 gm	24 gm	5 mg	0 mg

MADRAS

Yield: 1 portion

3 fluid ounces	Orange juice, fresh-squeezed, chilled	90 milliliters
2 fluid ounces	Cranberry juice, chilled	60 milliliters
1	Orange slice	1

1. Combine the juices in a chilled stemmed wine glass.
2. Garnish with orange slice and serve.

PORTION	KCAL	PROTEIN	FAT	CARB	SODIUM	CHOL
1 portion	75	1 gm	trace	19 gm	5 mg	0 mg

LEMONADE

Yield: 1 quart/1 liter

6 fluid ounces	Lemon juice, fresh-squeezed	**180 milliliters**
2 ounces	Sugar, super-fine	**60 grams**
2 fluid ounces	Water, hot	**60 milliliters**
24 fluid ounces	Water, cold	**720 milliliters**
1	Lemon, thinly sliced	**1**
1	Lime, thinly sliced	**1**

1. Combine the lemon juice with the sugar and hot water; stir until the sugar is completely dissolved.

2. Add the cold water and sliced lemons and limes; chill until ready to serve.

3. Serve over ice. Garnish with lemon and lime slices.

PORTION	KCAL	PROTEIN	FAT	CARB	SODIUM	CHOL
1 portion	45	trace	trace	12 gm	trace	0 mg

FROZEN CAPPUCCINO

Yield: 1 portion

3 ounces	Coffee, frozen in cubes	85 grams
2 fluid ounces	Evaporated skimmed milk	60 milliliters
2 teaspoons	Sugar	10 grams
2 teaspoons	Coffee-flavored syrup	10 milliliters
to taste	Cinnamon (optional)	to taste

Combine all ingredients in a blender and mix until very smooth and frothy.

If desired, powdered instant espresso and plain ice cubes may be used. About 3 ounces of plain cubes and a heaping tablespoon of the espresso powder are needed.

PORTION	KCAL	PROTEIN	FAT	CARB	SODIUM	CHOL
1 portion	100	4 gm	trace	20 gm	75 mg	2 mg

GAZPACHO COCKTAIL

Yield: about 10 portions

46 fluid ounces	Tomato juice	1.3 liters
4 ounces	Cucumber, peeled, seeded, grated	115 grams
1½ ounces	Scallions, minced	40 grams
2½ fluid ounces	Lemon juice	75 milliliters
1½ fluid ounces	Worcestershire sauce	45 milliliters
dash	Tabasco sauce	dash
to taste	Garlic powder	to taste
to taste	Black pepper, freshly ground	to taste
10	Parsley sprigs	10

1. Combine all of the ingredients, except the parsley, in a pitcher and stir well.

2. Refrigerate for at least 1 hour.

3. To serve, pour about 5 ounces/150 milliliters into a glass filled with ice cubes. Garnish with parsley.

PORTION	KCAL	PROTEIN	FAT	CARB	SODIUM	CHOL
1 portion	30	1 gm	trace	7 gm	50 mg	0 mg

TROPICAL FRUIT SMOOTHIE

Yield: 1 portion

6 fluid ounces	Pineapple juice, unsweetened, chilled	180 milliliters
6	Strawberries, rinsed, hulled	6
½	Banana, sliced	½

1. In a blender, combine the pineapple juice, five of the strawberries, and the banana. Blend until smooth and thick.

2. Pour the smoothie into a large footed cocktail glass and garnish with the reserved strawberry.

PORTION	KCAL	PROTEIN	FAT	CARB	SODIUM	CHOL
1 portion	190	2 gm	1 gm	46 gm	5 mg	0 mg

HOT MULLED CIDER

Yield: 10 portions

3 pints	Cider, fresh, unpasteurized	1.4 liters
1	Cinnamon stick	1
3 to 4	Cloves, whole	3 to 4
3 to 4	Allspice berries	3 to 4
from 1 orange	Orange peel	from 1 orange
10	Orange slices, thin	10

1. Combine the cider, cinnamon, cloves, allspice berries, and orange peel in a saucepan and heat to a simmer.

2. Simmer until the flavor of the spices and orange peel are infused into the cider.

3. Keep cider warm; serve in heated mugs or glasses, garnished with a slice of orange.

PORTION	KCAL	PROTEIN	FAT	CARB	SODIUM	CHOL
1 portion	60	trace	trace	14 gm	10 mg	0 mg

HOT COCOA

Yield: 10 servings

5 ounces	Cocoa powder	85 grams
7 ounces	Sugar, granulated	200 grams
1 teaspoon	Cinnamon, ground	1 gram
20 fluid ounces	Evaporated skimmed milk	600 milliliters
2½ pints	Skim milk	1.2 liters

1. Combine cocoa powder, sugar, and cinnamon; stir well to remove all lumps.

2. Gradually add the evaporated skimmed milk to form a syrup. Heat to a boil. This mixture may now be used to complete the cocoa, or may be cooled and stored for later use.

3. To finish the cocoa, add milk and bring almost to a boil, whipping to create a foam.

PORTION	KCAL	PROTEIN	FAT	CARB	SODIUM	CHOL
1 portion	100	6 gm	1 gm	20 gm	80 mg	5 mg

Appendix

TABLE A-1.

VITAMINS AND MINERALS

VITAMINS RDA FOR ADULTS	SOURCES	FUNCTION	DEFICIENCY/ EXCESS	STABILITY
Thiamine (B₁) RDA: Men 1.4 mg Women 1.0 mg	Pork, liver, legumes, fresh green vegetables	Carbohydrate metabolism, maintaining healthy nerves, normal appetite	Def.: beri-beri	Destroyed by heat and water
Riboflavin (B₂) RDA: Men 1.7 mg Women 1.5 mg	Milk, liver, lean meats, eggs, leafy vegetables	Breakdown of fatty acids for energy, release of energy from food	Def.: rare, except in alcohol abusers	Destroyed by U.V. rays and fluorescent lights, stable in heat and acid
Niacin Men 18 mg Women 14 mg	Liver, lean meats, wheat germ, leafy green vegetables	Carbohydrate metabolism	Def.: pellegra excess: liver damage, skin rashes, peptic ulcer	
Vitamin B₆ Pyridoxine RDA: 2 to 2.2 mg	Meat, liver, whole grain cereals, vegetables	Aids in synthesis of nonessential amino acids, fat and carbohydrate metabolism	Def.: convulsions, anemia, depression, nausea	Stable to heat, light, oxidation
Vitamin B₁₂ RDA: 3 μg	Liver, meats, milk, eggs (only animal foods)	Growth, blood formation, amino acid synthesis	Def.: pernicious anemia	Stable during normal cooking
Folacin (most common vitamin deficiency) RDA: 400 μg	Green leafy vegetables, liver, milk, eggs	Blood formation, amino acid metabolism	Def.: megaloblastic anemia, diarrhea	Unstable to heat and oxidation
Ascorbic Acid (vitamin C) RDA: 60 mg	Citrus fruits, strawberries, cantaloupe, broccoli, cabbage	Production and maintenance of collagen (base for all connective tissue), healing, resistance	Def.: Scurvy (smoking cigarettes seems to interfere with use of vitamin C)	Unstable; destroyed by oxygen, water
Vitamin A (retinol) RDA: 1000 R. E.	Liver, carrots, sweet potatoes, green leafy vegetables, egg yolk, milk fat	Building of body cells, bone growth, healthy tooth structure, normal vision in dim light	Def.: night blindness Excess: joint pain, nausea, rashes	Fairly stable in light and heat, easily destroyed by air and ultraviolet light
Vitamin D RDA: unknown	Animal fat, fortified milk, sunlight	Bone development (promotes the absorption of calcium and phosphorus)	Def.: rickets Excess: hypercalcemia	Stable to heat, aging, and storage
Vitamin E (tocopherols) RDA: 10 I.U.	Leafy vegetables, egg yolk, legumes, vegetable oils, peanuts	Protects cell structure, antioxidant	Def.: blood disorder (rare) Excess: least toxic	Destroyed by rancidity
Vitamin K RDA: unknown	Cabbage, leafy vegetables, liver, vegetable oils	Essential for clotting of blood	Def.: lack of prothrombin (important in blood clotting) Excess: jaundice	Destroyed by strong acids, alkalis, and oxidizing agents

continued ►

MINERALS RDA FOR ADULTS	SOURCES	FUNCTION	DEFICIENCY/ EXCESS	STABILITY
Calcium RDA: 800 mg	Milk, dairy products, canned salmon w/bones	Bone and tooth formation, coagulation of blood, regulates muscle contraction	Def.: osteoporosis	N/A
Phosphorus RDA: 800 mg	Milk, poultry, fish, meats, cheese, nuts, cereals, legumes	Energy exchange, buffer system	Def.: unknown	N/A
Sodium	Common salt, some canned foods, salt-cured meats, pickles	Regulates electrolyte and water balance (extracellular fluid)	Excess: linked to hypertension	N/A
Potassium	Meats, cereals, vegetables, legumes, fruits	Regulates electrolyte and water balance (intracellular fluid), muscle contractions		N/A
Iron RDA: Men 10 mg Women 18 mg	Liver, meat, whole or enriched grains, green vegetables	Essential for hemoglobin production, constituent of tissue cells, transporting oxygen	Def.: anemia	N/A
Iodine RDA: 150 μg	Iodized salt, seafoods	Necessary for the formation of thyroxine (a hormone of the thyroid gland)	Def.: goiter	N/A

Other minerals: Magnesium, chloride, sulfur, zinc, copper, manganese, chromium, fluorine, molybdenum, selenium, cobalt.

TABLE A-2.
WEIGHTS AND MEASURES EQUIVALENCIES

Dash	less than ⅛ teaspoon	2 pints	1 quart (approximately 1 liter)
3 teaspoons	1 tablespoon (½ fluid ounce)	4 quarts	1 gallon
2 tablespoons	⅛ cup (1 fluid ounce)	8 quarts	1 peck
4 tablespoons	¼ cup (2 fluid ounces)	4 pecks	1 bushel
5⅓ tablespoons	⅓ cup (2⅔ fluid ounces)	1 gram	0.035 ounces
8 tablespoons	½ cup (4 fluid ounces)	1 ounce	28.35 grams
10⅔ tablespoons	⅔ cup (5⅓ fluid ounces)	16 ounces	1 pound (453.59 grams)
12 tablespoons	¾ cup (6 fluid ounces)	1 kilogram	2.21 pounds
14 tablespoons	⅞ cup (7 fluid ounces)	1 fifth bottle	25.6 ounces (approximately 1½ pints)
16 tablespoons	1 cup		
1 gill	½ cup	1 measuring cup	8 ounces
1 cup	8 fluid ounces	1 coffee cup	Usually 6 ounces
2 cups	1 pint		

MEASURES OF COMMONLY USED FOODS

Arrowroot
1 tablespoon = 3 grams

Baking powder/soda
1 teaspoon = 4 grams
2 tablespoons = 1 ounce = 30 grams

Bread crumbs, fresh
4 slices = 2 cups crumbs, loosely packed
2 cups crumbs = 2 to 2½ ounces = 60 to 70 grams

Bananas, medium, peeled
1 each = 4 ounces = 115 grams
1 each = ⅓ cup, mashed

Brown sugar
1 cup = slightly less than 8 ounces

Capers
1 tablespoon = ¼ ounce = 7 grams

Carrots
2 medium = 7 ounces = 200 grams
2 medium = 1 cup, grated, loosely packed

Cheddar cheese, grated
1 cup = 2½ ounces = 70 grams

Citrus zest
1 teaspoon = 5 grams
2 tablespoons = ¾ ounce = 20 grams

Cream of tartar
1 teaspoon = 3 grams
1 tablespoon = ⅓ ounce = 9 grams

Confectioners sugar
1 cup = 4 ounces = 115 grams

Eggs, large
5 each = 1 cup = 8 ounces = 225 grams

Egg whites, large
9 each = 1 cup = 8 ounces = 225 grams

Egg yolks, large
10 each = 1 cup = 8 ounces = 225 grams

Flour, all-purpose, unsifted
1 cup = 4 ounces = 115 grams

Flour, bread, unsifted
1 cup = 4½ ounces = 130 grams

Flour, cake or pastry, sifted
1 cup = 3⅓ ounces = 95 grams

Flour, whole wheat, unsifted
1 cup = 4¼ ounces = 125 grams

Garlic
1 clove = 1 teaspoon minced = 4 to 5 grams

Granulated gelatin
1 teaspoon = 3 grams
¼ cup = 1 ounce = 30 grams

Granulated sugar
1 cup = 7 ounces = 200 grams
1 tablespoon = ½ ounce = 15 grams

Herbs, dried and fresh
1 teaspoon = 1 gram
1 tablespoon = 3 grams

Herbs and spices, powdered (including blends such as curry)
1 teaspoon = 2 grams
1 tablespoon = 7 grams

Honey
1 teaspoon = 7 grams
2 tablespoons = ¾ ounce = 20 grams

Lettuce, trimmed, chopped or torn
1 cup = 2 to 2¾ ounces = 60 to 75 grams

Mustard, prepared
1 tablespoon = ½ ounce = 15 grams
1 cup = 8 ounces = 225 grams

Nuts, coarsely chopped
1 cup = 5 ounces = 140 grams

Nuts, finely chopped (loosely packed)
1 cup = 4 ounces = 115 grams

Pears and apples (small to medium, peeled and cored)
3 each = 1 pound = 450 grams
3 each = 3 cups sliced
3 each = 2 cups (plus), puréed

Peppercorns, ground or cracked
1 teaspoon = 2 grams
1 tablespoon = 7 grams

Raisins
½ cup = 3 ounces = 85 grams

Rice, converted
2½ cups = 1 pound = 450 grams

Rice, long-grain
1 cup = 5½ ounces = 150 grams

Saffron threads, crushed
½ teaspoon = 500 milligrams
1 tablespoon = 1¾ grams

Salt (table)
¼ teaspoon = 2 grams
½ teaspoon = 3 grams
1 teaspoon = 5 grams
1 tablespoon = ½ ounce = 15 grams

Seeds (sesame, poppy, cumin, fennel, dill)
1 teaspoon = 2 grams
1 tablespoon = 6 grams

Spices, ground
1 teaspoon = 2 grams
1 tablespoon = ¼ ounce = 7 grams

Yeast, envelope
1 each = ¼ ounce = 7 grams

Suggested Sources for Nutrition Information

HANDBOOKS, ETC.

Bowes and Church's Food Values of Portions Commonly Used (15th edition), revised by Jean A. T. Pennington, Ph.D., R.D., HarperCollins, New York, 1989

Composition of Foods, Agriculture Handbook No. 8–1, 8–4, 8–5, 8–6, 8–9, 8–10, 8–11, 8–12, 8–13, 8–15, 8–16, 8–17, 8–20. Prepared by the United States Department of Agriculture, Science and Education Administration

Handbook of the Nutritional Value of Foods in Common Units, prepared by Catherine F. Adams for the United States Department of Agriculture, New York: Dover Publications, Inc. 1986

Nutrient Values of Muscle Foods, National Live Stock and Meat Board, Chicago, Illinois, 1988

SOFTWARE

You may wish to consult foodservice and consumer periodicals and magazines for annual previews of software packages.

CBORD Diet Analyzer Supplied by CBORD Group, Suite 300, First Bank Building, The Commons, Ithaca, New York, 14850

Diet Simple Plus, Version 2.0 Supplied by N-Squared Computing, 3040 Commercial St. SE, Suite 240, Salem, OR 97302. Phone: (503) 364-9118

Diet Self-Study, Academy Version Supplied by Whole Grain Software, 1427 Bancroft Way, Berkeley, CA 94702. Phone: (415) 848-5903

COMPANIES THAT PROVIDE COMPUTER NUTRIENT ANALYSIS SERVICE

Computrition, 21049 Devonshire Street, Chatsworth, California, 91311. (818) 341-9739 or (800) 222-4488

Data Control Information Service, 347 Seneca Road, Hornel, New York, 14843. (607) 324-5510

DDA Software, P.O. Box 26, Hamburg, New Jersey, 07419. (201) 764-6677

ESHA Research, P.O. Box 13028, Salem, Oregon, 97309. (503) 585-6242

Health Development, Inc., 1165 West Third Avenue, Columbus, Ohio, 43212. (800) 222-4630 or (614) 294-2688 (for Ohio residents)

Health Management Systems, 1409 Willow Street, Suite 200, Minneapolis, Minnesota, 55403. (612) 874-9444

Nutriquest Capital Systems Group, Inc., 1803 Research Boulevard, Suite 600, Rockville, Maryland, 20850. (301) 762-1200

Nutrition Counseling Service, 2444 39th Place, NW, Washington, D.C., 20007. (202) 338-7328

Practocare, 10951 Sorennto Valley Road, San Diego, California, 92121. (800) 421-9073 or (800) 421-9074 (for California residents)

GENERAL NUTRITION INFORMATION

Nutrition Concepts and Controversies, Fifth Edition, by Eva M. Nunnelley Hamilton, M.S., Eleanor N. Whitney, Ph.D., R.D., and Frances S. Sizer, M. S., West Publishing Company, 1991

Jane Brody's Nutrition Book by Jane E. Brody, W. W. Norton & Co., revised edition 1987.

Personal Nutrition, 2nd Edition, Marie A. Boyle and Gail Zyla, West Publishing, 1992

The Tufts University Guide to Total Nutrition, Harper & Row, 1991

The Mount Sinai School of Medicine Complete Book of Nutrition, edited by Victor Herbert, M.D., F.A.C.P. and Genell J. Subak-Sharpe, M.S., St. Martin's Press, 1990

Eat for Life, edited by Catherine E. Woteki, Ph.D., R.D. and Paul R. Thomas, Ed.D., R.D., National Academy Press, 1992

COOKBOOKS

The books included in this list are those which offer specific recipes and strategies to prepare dishes that are based on sound nutritional principles: lower overall calorie count, reduced quantities of fat, cholesterol, and sodium, and increased amounts of vitamin-, mineral-, and fiber-rich foods. There are several other books that can provide inspiration as well as additional recipes which meet individual nutritional guidelines. Books that feature specific ethnic cuisines or that focus on vegetarian cooking styles are often good places to start.

Controlling Your Fat Tooth, Joseph C. Piscatella, Workman Publishing, New York 1991

Choices for a Healthy Heart, Joseph C. Piscatella, Workman Publishing, New York, 1987

American Heart Association Cookbook, Fifth Edition, The American Heart Association, Random House, Inc., 1991

The Art of Low-Calorie Cooking, Sally Schneider, Stewart, Tabori & Chang, New York, 1990

Jane Brody's Good Food Book, Jane A. Brody, Bantam Books, 1985

Jane Brody's Good Food Gourmet, Jane A. Brody, W. W. Norton and Co., New York, 1990

New Spa Food, Edward J. Safdie, Clarkson N. Potter, Inc., New York, 1990

Eat Right, Eat Well—The Italian Way, Edward Giobbi and Richard Wolff, M.D., Alfred A. Knopf, Inc., New York, 1985

MAGAZINES AND NEWSLETTERS

MAGAZINES

Eating Well Magazine
Weight Watchers
Cooking Light
Prevention Magazine

NEWSLETTERS

Environmental Nutrition, 2112 Broadway, New York, NY 10023

University of California at Berkeley Wellness Letter, published by Health Letter Associates, PO Box 420148, Palm Coast, FL 32142

Mayo Clinic Nutrition Letter, Rochester, MN 55905

Nutrition Action Healthletter, by the Center for Science in the Public Interest, Suite 300, 1875 Connecticut Ave, N.W., Washington, D.C. 20009-5728

Tufts University Diet & Nutrition Letter, 53 Park Place, New York, NY 10007

Cooking Glossary

Allumette A very fine julienne, known as the matchstick cut.

Baguette A loaf of bread shaped into a long cylinder.

Battonet A stick-shaped vegetable cut in which pieces measure about ¼ to ⅓ inch square and 1 to 2 inches long.

Blanch To cook a food very briefly in order to remove strong odors, set the color, improve the texture, set the shape of an item, shorten final preparation time, or make skins easier to remove.

Bouquet garni A bunch of herbs, aromatics, and spices tied together inside celery stalks or leek leaves. The standard ingredients are parsley stems, a sprig of fresh thyme, celery or leeks, garlic, and peppercorns.

Brunoise/small dice A neat cut in which pieces are quite regular, about ¼ inch on each side.

Carryover cooking The cooking action of residual heat that remains in foods after they have been removed from the heat source.

Chiffonade To cut into fine shreds.

Clarification A mixture of ingredients, typically containing ground meats or fish, egg whites, mirepoix, and aromatic ingredients used to prepare a consommé.

Concassé See TOMATO CONCASSÉ

Confit A preserve made by cooking the main ingredients (meat or vegetable) in a flavorful substance (typically, pork, goose and duck fat, but replaced with ingredients such as honey or an extremely rich stock) until tender enough to spread easily.

Cordon A ribbon of sauce ladled so that it surrounds the main item.

Coulis A sauce (savory or sweet) made by puréeing the main ingredient to achieve a texture that ranges from very smooth to slightly coarse.

Court bouillon "Short broth" in French. A vegetable-based broth that includes ingredients such as onions, thinly sliced carrots, celery, leeks, fresh herbs, spices, wine or vinegar, used to poach or steam foods.

Debeard To remove the shaggy inedible fibers from a mussel. These fibers are used to anchor the mussel to its mooring.

Demiglace "Half-glace" in French. A highly-concentrated, flavorful sauce made by reducing a brown sauce (fond or jus de veau) with brown stock to half its original volume.

Deglaze To release the reduced drippings in a roasting or sauté pan by adding a liquid and stirring over heat.

Disjointed   Cut into pieces by cutting through the joints. Rabbits, chickens, crabs, and lobsters are often referred to as being "disjointed."

Duxelles   A preparation made by sautéing a mixture of minced shallots, finely chopped mushrooms, white wine, and herbs in butter or oil until all liquids have been reduced. Duxelles is used as stuffing or as an ingredient in other preparations such as sauces or forcemeats.

Émincé   A meat cut in which lean meat is sliced into thin, regular strips.

Fermière   A disk-shaped vegetable cut into pieces that are sliced so that they retain their natural shape.

Fine brunoise/fine dice   A neat cut in which pieces are quite regular, about $\frac{1}{16}$ inch on each side.

Fond de veau (lié)   A base sauce made by simmering browned veal bones, mirepoix, and a bouquet garni or sachet d'épices in brown veal stock. When thickened with a starch such as arrowroot, it is known as fond de veau lié.

Forcemeat   Meat which has been so finely ground that it achieves a soft, paste-like consistency. The grinding action forces together lean meat with binders such as fat, cream, eggs, and/or starch-based ingredients such as rice.

Fortified wine   A wine to which a certain amount of alcohol and sugar has been added to increase the overall alcohol content. Marsala, Madeira, ports, and sherries are all examples.

Fumet   A stock made by allowing the major flavoring ingredient to cook with aromatics before the liquid is added to extract the greatest flavor in the shortest cooking time. Typically used for fish, shellfish, and vegetables.

Galantine   A forcemeat-based specialty in which a forcemeat is placed in a casing and poached. Traditional galantines were rolled in the skins of the birds from which they were prepared; nutritional cooking frequently wraps the forcemeat in plastic wrap.

Glace de viande   A meat-based stock which has been reduced to the point at which the texture becomes viscous and syrupy.

Julienne   A stick-shaped vegetable cut in which pieces measure about $\frac{1}{8}$ inch square and 1 to 2 inches long.

Large dice   A neat cut in which pieces are quite regular, about $\frac{1}{2}$ to $\frac{3}{4}$ inch on each side.

Lozenge   A diamond-shaped vegetable cut in which pieces are about $\frac{1}{3}$ to $\frac{1}{2}$ inch on each side and $\frac{1}{4}$ inch thick.

Mark on a grill   To turn a food that is being grilled (without flipping it over), turn it 90 degrees after it has been on the grill for several seconds to create a cross-hatch mark that is associated with grilled foods.

Medallions   A cut of meat, usually from the loin or tenderloin, shaped so that it has a neat, round shape and a uniform thickness.

Medium dice   A neat cut in which pieces are quite regular, about $\frac{1}{3}$ inch on each side.

Mince   To chop into fine, fairly regular pieces.

Mirepoix   A combination of vegetables used to give flavor to various stocks, sauces, gravies, as well as poached, simmered, braised, and stewed dishes. The standard ratio is two parts onions, one part carrot, one part celery.

Mousseline   A forcemeat with very fine texture.

Nage   A court bouillon or lightly flavored broth.

Noisette   A cut of meat, similar in shape to a medallion, but usually with smaller dimensions than a medallion.

Parisienne   A cut prepared using a small melon baller, also known as a "parisienne" scoop.

Paysanne   A neat cut in which pieces are $\frac{1}{2}$ inch square and about $\frac{1}{8}$ inch thick.

Pluches   Herb leaves which are whole, left intact by a small bit of stem.

Purée   To chop an item extremely finely.

Quenelles   Small football-shaped dumplings traditionally shaped by molding a mixture with two spoons.

Raft   The solid mass that forms in a consommé when a clarification mixture has cooked long enough.

Ragoût   A stew.

Reduce To cook a liquid long enough to lose its original volume, concentrating the flavor, color, and body of the original item.

Remouillage A second stock made from bones which have already been used to prepare a stock. This "second wetting" is frequently used either to prepare glace de viande or as the liquid to prepare subsequent batches of stock.

Ribbon cut A neat, regular cut in which foods are cut into extremely thin strips.

Rough chop To cut foods into fairly regular pieces. The dimensions can vary according to the overall cooking time required; the longer the cooking time, the larger the piece.

Roulade A rolled item. Meats which are filled, rolled, and tied into cylinders are referred to as roulades, as are sponge cakes which are filled and rolled.

Roux A traditional thickener made by cooking together flour and butter. (Oil or other fats may be used to replace butter).

Sachet d'épices A cheesecloth parcel of herbs and spices (usually dried) used to infuse a simmered or poached dish with a special flavor. A standard sachet usually includes parsley stems, dried thyme leaves, bay leaves, and cracked peppercorns. Other ingredients may be added as desired.

Smoking point The temperature at which fats start to break down when heated.

Smother To cook something over gentle heat in enough liquid or fat to barely cover it, until it begins to release its own essence.

Steep/infuse To allow a highly aromatic, flavorful, or colorful ingredient to sit in warm or hot liquids until the essential flavors and colors (essence) of the ingredient are extracted.

Stock A basic element in a kitchen's mise en place made by simmering flavorful ingredients in water to extract flavor and color.

Supreme The breast of a bird (domestic or game) in which bones have been removed, with the exception of one portion of the wing bone. That section is scraped free of all meat and sinew, and is referred to as "frenched."

Sweat To cook a food (especially aromatic vegetables) over low heat in a small amount of a flavorful liquid or stock with cover on the pot until it releases its own juices.

Terrine A forcemeat-based loaf, traditionally baked in an earthenware dish.

Timbale A small mold, usually taller than wide, used to prepare custards or other dishes; also used to refer to dishes prepared in these molds.

Tomato concassé Peeled, seeded tomatoes which have been chopped, julienned, or cut into dice.

Tourné A barrel-shaped vegetable cut.

Tuiles/tiles Thin, wafer-like cookies (or foods cut to resemble these cookies). Tuiles and tiles are frequently "shaped" while still pliable by pressing them into molds or draping them over rolling pins or dowels.

Velouté A sauce made by thickening stock. Traditionally made by simmering stocks with roux; in nutritional cooking roux is replaced by arrowroot.

Vinaigrette A cold sauce made by forming an emulsion of oil and vinegar in a specific ratio. Traditional vinaigrette calls for 3 parts oil and 1 part vinegar; in nutritional cooking, the majority of the oil is replaced with a thickened stock.

White mirepoix A mirepoix in which the carrots are either omitted or replaced by parsnips. Frequently leeks are used to replace some of the onions as well.

Nutrition Glossary

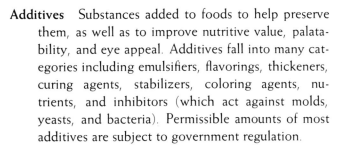

Additives Substances added to foods to help preserve them, as well as to improve nutritive value, palatability, and eye appeal. Additives fall into many categories including emulsifiers, flavorings, thickeners, curing agents, stabilizers, coloring agents, nutrients, and inhibitors (which act against molds, yeasts, and bacteria). Permissible amounts of most additives are subject to government regulation.

Amino acid A compound composed of hydrogen, carbon, oxygen, and nitrogen, the amino acid is the building block of all proteins. There are 20 to 22 amino acids used to produce all of the proteins found in the human body: 8 must be supplied in the diet (9 for infants and small children). See also *essential amino acids*.

Antioxidants Substances that retard the breakdown of tissues in the presence of oxygen. May be added to foods during processing, or may be naturally-occurring. As an example, many fats, especially vegetable oils, contain Vitamin E, which acts to protect the oils from becoming rancid for a limited period of time.

Appetite A learned or habitual response to a variety of stimuli that encourages a person to eat. The cues which encourage appetite may be internal (onset of real hunger, drop in blood sugar) or external (sights and smells of appealing foods).

Arteriosclerosis A condition in which fibrous tissue and fatty deposits build up on the artery walls, causing thickening and loss of elasticity. This is one of the risk factors associated with the development of cardiovascular diseases.

Atherosclerosis A type of arteriosclerosis in which fatty deposits have caused the walls of arteries to dramatically thicken, constricting the passageway so that the blood supply to the heart and brain is reduced to the point that there is danger of coronary heart disease or stroke.

Basal metabolism The amount of energy, expressed in calories, required by the body at rest to carry on all the necessary involuntary functions to sustain life (breathing, digestion, heart beat, etc.)

Blood pressure A measurement of the pressure exerted by blood flowing through arteries. Expressed in both systolic and diastolic pressure, which represent the pressure as the heart pumps, and as it relaxes, respectively.

Calorie (Kilocalorie, Kcal, or Calorie) The amount of heat necessary to raise the temperature of a kilogram (liter) of water 1 degree Centigrade. It is a measure of the energy supplied in foods.

Carbohydrate The term is derived from "carbo" (carbon) and "hydrate" (water) reflecting the components of all carbohydrates: carbon, oxygen, and hydrogen. It is the source of energy preferred by the body. Carbohydrates include simple carbohydrates (also known as simple sugars) and complex carbohydrates (referred to as starch or fiber). Simple carbohydrates are generally formed from one or two sugars (referred to as mono- or di-saccharide), which may be naturally-occurring (those found in fruits or milk), or refined (added sugars, including honey, table sugar, molasses, and corn syrup).

Cholesterol A fatty acid, belonging to a group known as the sterols, a category of lipid (the general term for fats of all types). Essential to hormone production, creation of cell membranes, acts as protection for nerve fibers, responsible for production of Vitamin D on the skin's surface in the presence of sunlight. See also *dietary cholesterol* and *serum (blood) cholesterol.*

Complementary proteins A combination of foods, each of which supplies varying amounts of different amino acids so that the amino acids lacking or in insufficient supply in one food are complemented by those found in the second food.

Complete proteins A food source that provides all of the essential amino acids in the correct ratio so that they can be used in the body for protein synthesis.

Complex carbohydrates Long chains composed of many sugars, referred to as polysaccharides. One of the forms of complex carbohydrates is starch, which is the plant's storage system that holds energy to support future growth. The other is fiber, the structural component of plants. These carbohydrates may be found in foods as they naturally occur (whole grains or whole-grain meals and flours) or they may be refined during the processes of polishing and bleaching.

Denaturation A change in the structure of a protein brought about by applying heat, an acid, a base, or by agitation (whipping, stirring, beating).

Dietary cholesterol The cholesterol found in the foods included as part of the diet. Only found in land and sea animals. Egg yolks, most organ meats, and some shellfish are especially high in dietary cholesterol. Some individuals experience a sensitivity to dietary cholesterol.

Energy nutrients The substances found in foods that can be broken down in the body, and used for energy, as well as for the growth, repair and replacement of tissues. These nutrients include carbohydrates, protein, and fat.

Enrichment Addition of lost nutrients to a processed food. These nutrients are naturally present in whole foods, but are lost during processing or refining. Some or all of the lost nutrients may be replaced.

Essential amino acid One of the amino acids that the body requires but cannot produce itself. There are 8 amino acids required by adults. Small children and infants require an additional amino acid. All of the essential amino acids must be supplied, in the correct ratios, in order for the body to produce the proteins necessary for health.

Essential nutrients Compounds needed by the body which must be supplied through the diet. Includes water, vitamins, minerals, carbohydrates, proteins, and fats. Although fiber does not supply the body with nutrients, since it cannot be digested, it is another essential component of a healthy diet.

Fat One of the essential nutrients. Fat supplies the body with essential fatty acids, as well as being the most concentrated source of energy. Fats are solid (or plastic) at room temperature; oils are liquid.

Fatty acid The basic chemical unit of fats; composed of carbon, hydrogen, and oxygen.

Fermentation The effect produced by compounds that act on various substances to transform them or metabolize them in the absence of oxygen. For example, sugar is fermented by enzymes in yeast to form carbon dioxide and alcohol during bread baking.

Fiber The portion of plant foods composed of complex carbohydrates. Soluble fiber is the pectin and gums found in whole grains, fruits, and vegetables; insoluble fiber is lignin and hemicellulose found in whole grains, fruits, and vegetables. Fiber cannot be digested by humans.

Fortification The addition of nutrients, typically vitamins and minerals, that were not originally present in the food. Examples include the addition of iodine to salt, calcium to flour, and Vitamins A or D to skim milk.

Gluten The protein found in flours, especially wheat flour, that is capable of forming the elastic strands that enable yeast-leavened breads to rise by stretching enough to trap the gases released during fermentation.

Glycogen The form in which the body stores carbohydrate in the liver and in muscle tissue to be available for use when glucose stores are depleted.

Gram A gram (abbreviated as GM) is the weight of one cubic centimeter (or milliliter) of water under specifically defined conditions of temperature and pressure.

Healthy Body Weight (abbreviated as HBW) A weight determined by using any of a number of calculations that is considered "best" for an individual. Usually this weight is based on a number of factors measured by health care providers or fitness experts, including percentage of body fat in relation to lean muscle mass, activity level, age, gender, and overall health and fitness conditions. The weight calculated in this way may be above or below the "ideal" body weight values given in standard insurance charts or "reasonable" body weight calculated by using a standard formula based on height, frame size, and activity level.

High-Density Lipoprotein (HDL) Clusters of lipids associated with protein particles capable of transporting fats through the bloodstream. HDL has a higher protein content than other lipoprotein in relation to its fat content. HDL is sometimes referred to as the "good cholesterol." Its function appears to be the return of cholesterol from storage areas to the liver so that it can be dismantled and eliminated from the body. See also Low-Density Lipoprotein (LDL).

Homogenization A mechanical process that forces mixtures of fats and other liquids through a fine mesh to make fat globules smaller and of approximately the same size so that they will disperse evenly and will not separate out of the mixture and rise to the top.

Hydrogenation The process of forcing hydrogen to bond at open sites in a mono- or polyunsaturated oil to produce a product that is more solid at room temperature. Shortenings and margarines are examples of hydrogenated fats. Once hydrogenated, a fat becomes more saturated than it was originally, though it may still be considered predominantly unsaturated.

Hypertension The term used to indicate chronic elevated blood pressure. This condition is often associated with atherosclerosis, obesity, inactivity, and diets high in sodium and fats.

Incomplete protein A protein found in plant foods that is either entirely lacking one or more of the essential amino acids, or has a supply that is small enough that it cannot be used by the body to promote the growth, repair, or replacement of body tissue. The deficiency can be compensated for by eating a variety of foods throughout the day that will supply adequate amounts of all of the essential amino acids.

Lipids The name given to a family of substances that includes triglycerides (known as fats and oils), phospholipids (lecithin is an example), and sterols (the most familiar is cholesterol). These compounds are essential to the body, and are found throughout the food supply as well as being produced by the body. Those produced in the body are usually known as "blood" or "serum" cholesterol or triglycerides.

Low-density Lipoprotein (LDL) Clusters of lipids associated with protein particles capable of transporting fats through the bloodstream. LDL has a lower protein content than high-density lipoprotein in relation to its fat content. LDL is usually associated with an increased risk of heart disease. Its function is the transport of cholesterol from the liver to other body cells.

Macro mineral (major mineral) An essential mineral nutrient that is found in the human body in amounts greater than five grams.

Metabolism The total of all chemical reactions that occur in living cells. These reactions convert food into an energy source that the body can use.

Mineral An organic compound that is an essential component of the diet. Provides no energy, and is therefore referred to as a non-caloric nutrient.

Monounsaturated fat A fat or oil that is composed of fatty acids that have one point that is not bonded with hydrogen. Oils which have a high proportion of monounsaturated fats tend to be flavorful; examples include oils found in or produced from avocados, olives, and most nuts.

Nutrients Compounds required by the body in order to maintain life. The six classes of nutrients (known as the *essential nutrients*) include carbohydrates, fat, protein, vitamins, minerals, and water.

Pasteurize To preserve and/or sanitize foods by heating them at a sufficient temperature for a specified length of time in order to destroy certain microorganisms and to arrest fermentation. The exact temperature and length of time required varies from food to food. Milk and certain fruit juices are routinely pasteurized.

Polyunsaturated fat A chain of fatty acids in which two or more points are not filled with a hydrogen atom. Oils composed predominantly of polyunsaturated fats are often of plant origin, liquid at room temperature, with a neutral flavor. They are found in, or refined from, corn, sunflower, safflower, and cottonseed.

Protein A compound formed by carbon, hydrogen, oxygen, and nitrogen when arranged into strands of amino acids. One of the six categories of essential nutrients. Found in a variety of food sources, including meats, milk and dairy products, eggs, grains, vegetables, and legumes.

Protein-sparing The condition whereby carbohydrates and fat supply sufficient stores of energy so that protein is able to perform other vital functions: growth, maintenance, and repair of tissue.

Recommended Dietary Allowances (RDA) Suggested levels of a variety of nutrients prepared by the Food and Nutrition Board (FNB) of the National Academy of Sciences/National Research Council (NAS/NRC). Separate recommendations are made for different sets of healthy people, grouped by age and gender. Recommendations for energy (calories) are expressed as a range, while those for protein, vitamins A, D, E, thiamin, riboflavin, niacin, B6, B12, folacin, calcium phosphorus, magnesium, iron, zinc, and iodine are all expressed as single figures. Ranges noted as "Estimated safe and adequate intakes" are provided for Vitamin K, biotin, pantothenic acid, copper, manganese, fluoride, chromium, selenium, molybdenum, sodium, potassium, and chloride. All recommendations include a substantial margin of safety and are not to be considered *minimum* requirements for *healthy* individuals.

Satiety The feeling of fullness or satisfaction after eating. Fat is capable of providing a more lasting sense of fullness, since it is digested last, and more slowly, than other nutrients.

Saturated fat A chain of fatty acids in which all available sites for hydrogen bonds are full. Fats that are composed predominantly of saturated fats tend to be highly flavored; spreadable or solid at room temperature; and of animal origin. The "tropical oils" including coconut, palm, and palm kernel oils are exceptions to both of the preceding general statements. Saturated fats are associated with an increase in serum cholesterol levels.

Serum cholesterol Cholesterol found in the bloodstream. May also be referred to as "blood cholesterol." Carried by lipoproteins, this cholesterol is generally produced in the body from the triglycerides provided by a diet high in saturated fats.

Simple carbohydrates Also known as sugars, which may be single (monosaccharides) or double (disaccharides). These sugars are either "naturally-occurring" (e.g., fructose found in fruit) or "refined sugars" (e.g., sucrose found in table sugar).

Trace mineral (micro mineral) An essential mineral nutrient found in the body in amounts less than five grams.

Vegetarian An individual who has adopted a specific diet (or lifestyle) that reduces or eliminates all sources of animal products. *Vegans* eat no foods derived in any way from animals (some even exclude honey); *lacto-ovo vegetarians* include eggs and dairy products in their diet. Other people refer to themselves as "vegetarians" but will occasionally eat fish or poultry, preferring to exclude only red meats.

Vitamin An organic compound considered an essential nutrient. Vitamins provide no energy, and are referred to as non-caloric nutrients. They may be water-soluble or fat-soluble.

Water One of the six essential nutrients. Vital to the proper function of the body. Provides no calories, and is sometimes referred to as the "forgotten nutrient."

Index

Sugar(s), 120
  added, 38–40, 42–43
    sweetening without, 48–49
    moderating use of, 2–3
Sugar substitutes, 40
Summer squash, poached sea bass with
    mousseline and, 414
Summer-style lentil soup, 296
Sunshine bass with a gingered nage, 422
Sweeteners. *See* Sugar(s)
Sweet potato(es)
  cakes, 389
    grilled chicken breasts with, 324
  soup, 301
Sweet ricotta pastry, 551
Swiss-style shredded veal, 354
Swordfish
  in cioppino, 466
  grilled
    with lentil ragoût and horseradish
      and apple cream sauce, 327
    with roasted pepper salad, 328
Syrups, 120
  maple and apple butter, 570

Tabbouleh, smoked chicken with, and
    tomato-herb sauce, 250
Tandoori marinade, 230
Tapenade, 227
Tarragon vinaigrette, chilled poached
    scallops with, 413
Tarte tatin, St. Andrew's style, 537
Tenderloin of beef with blue cheese and
    herb crust, 362
Tenderloin of beef with mild ancho chili
    sauce and polenta with jalapeño
    jack cheese, 356
Tenderloin of beef with wild
    mushrooms, 355
Tequila-lime vinaigrette, broiled red
    perch with, 342
Terrine
  Mediterranean seafood, 239
  pear bavarian, 522
  rabbit, 242
  roasted pepper and eggplant, 243
  St. Andrew's garden, 240
  venison, seared, 244
Three bean stew, 476
Timbales
  of dirty rice, 430
  vegetable, 426
Tomatillo salsa, grilled chicken burrito
    with, 338
Tomato(es)
  coulis, 198
  fondue, broiled Spanish mackerel
    with, 340
  gazpacho
    granité, 267
    yellow, 318
  oven-roasted, 399
  pasta, 487

pizza with mozzarella and, 504
salad, carpaccio of beef with fresh
    artichokes and, 254
salsa
  fresh, 225
  fresh, barbecued chicken pizza
    with, 510
sauce
  coulis, 198
  with fennel and saffron, sea bass in,
    418
  garlic-, light, pan-seared sea
    scallops with saffron rice,
    asparagus, and a, 344
  herb-, smoked chicken with
    tabbouleh and, 250
  horseradish-, 201
  horseradish-, pan-smoked salmon
    fillet with, 392
  with jalapeños and balsamic
    vinegar, 202
soup
  basil-, 287
  gazpacho, yellow, 318
  pan-smoked bisque, 305
vinaigrette, 217
Torte, raspberry, 523
Tortellini, sage, turkey broth with
    mushrooms and, 273
Tortilla soup, 286
Trio of pears, a, 540
Tropical fruit glace, 516
Tropical fruit smoothie, 585
Tropical oils, 28
Tuna, carpaccio of, with shiitake salad,
    256
Turkey
  broth with mushrooms and sage
    tortellini, 273
  ground, 96, 99
  pan-smoked, with port wine sauce,
    386

Valley Central schools, 166
Vanilla-honey cheesecake, 526
Variety meats, 99
Veal
  roulade, braised, with mushroom
    sausage, 468
  sautéed
    with lump crabmeat and asparagus,
      357
    with risotto and Marsala, 351
  Swiss-style shredded, 354
Vegetable(s), 105–9. *See also specific*
    vegetables
  garden, stir-fried, 346
  grilled, 337
  lemon glaze for, 224
  moist-heat cooking methods for,
    403
  pizza, St. Andrew's, 506
  preparation of, 108–9

purchasing, 107–8
salad, Asian, marinated, 265
stock, 190
timbales, 426
Vegetarian demi-glace, 184
Vegetarianism, 56
Velouté-style sauce, 193
Venison terrine, seared, 244
Vermont, Creative Cuisine program in,
    162
Vinaigrette
  asparagus with crabmeat and, 247
  beet, seared scallops with, 262
  five-mustard, 214
  lime-tequila, broiled red perch with,
    342
  orange-basil, asparagus salad with,
    251
  port wine, 216
  ratatouille, 213
  -style dressing, 211
  tarragon, chilled poached scallops
    with, 413
  tomato, 217
Vinegar, 123
  balsamic, tomato sauce with jalapeños
    and, 202
  sherry, sauce, lamb chops with, 331
Vitamin A, 75
Vitamin and mineral supplements,
    73
Vitamin B-12, 74
Vitamin C, 74
Vitamin D, 75
Vitamin E, 75
Vitamin K, 75
Vitamins, 72–80
  fat-soluble, 74–75
  grain products enriched with, 76
  ordering and purchasing foods and,
    78
  preparation and cooking of food and,
    79–80
  storing and handling foods and, 78–
    79
  water-soluble, 74

Waffles, four-grain, 557–58
Walnut(s)
  haricots verts with, 444
  salad of oak leaf lettuce with blue
    cheese, pears, and, 260
Warm fruit compote, 569
Water
  bottled, 83
    offering a wide selection of,
      3–4
  mineral
    about, 575
    sparkling, and bitters, 576
  as nutrient, 84
Watercress and potato soup,
    299